THE STORY OF

FOOTBALL

REVISED EDITION

DAVE ANDERSON

Foreword by **Troy Aikman**

A BEECH TREE PAPERBACK BOOK
New York

Permission for photographs is gratefully acknowledged: page 3—The Dallas Cowboys; pages 11, 70—Corbis-Bettmann; page 13—Underwood & Underwood/Corbis-Bettmann; pages 15, 23, 26, 30, 32, 34, 36, 40, 41, 44, 45, 46, 53, 57, 64, 67, 71, 79, 81, 87, 89, 95, 102, 106, 110, 115, 117, 120, 132, 135, 138, 140, 142, 144, 145, 147, 149, 152—UPI/Corbis-Bettmann; page 18—The Bettmann Archive; page 19—AP/Wide World Photos; page 24—The University of Notre Dame; pages 28, 38, 56, 124—NFL Photos; pages 33, 48, 60, 69, 98, 105, 134—UPI/Bettmann; page 50—The Indianapolis Colts; pages 59, 61, 100—UPI/Bettmann Newsphotos; pages 72, 75, 86, 92, 93—Reuters/Corbis-Bettmann; page 84—Reuters/Bettmann; pages 94, 118, 121, 128—ALLSPORT USA; page 112—The New Orleans Saints

Inquiries should be addressed to
William Morrow and Company, Inc.
1350 Avenue of the Americas
New York, NY 10019

Printed in the United States of America.

The Library of Congress has cataloged the Morrow Junior Books edition of
The Story of Football as follows:
Anderson, Dave.
The story of football/Dave Anderson.
p. cm.
Includes index.
Summary: Traces the history of this American sport from the first college game at Rutgers in 1869 to the present.
ISBN 0-688-14314-8
1. Football—United States—History—Juvenile literature. [1. Football—History.] I. Title.
GV950.A53 1997   796.332'0973—DC20
96-46539   CIP AC

10 9 8 7 6 5 4 3 2 1
First Beech Tree Edition, 1997.
ISBN 0-688-14315-6

AS A QUARTERBACK FOR THE DALLAS COWBOYS, I'VE always tried to learn as much as possible about what I do—how to read the defense, how to find my receivers, how to throw accurate passes, how to escape from the opposing team's pass-rush. Even though I've been fortunate enough to be on three Super Bowl championship teams, I'm still trying to learn.

If you enjoy football, you probably think that you already know plenty about the game, but *The Story of Football* will teach you even more.

In addition to learning how football began in the United States more than a century ago and how it developed into the spectacle it is now, Dave Anderson introduces you to all the famous players, coaches, and teams, as well as to football's fundamentals—rushing, passing, pass-receiving, kicking, blocking, and defense. There's even a chapter on coaching.

But what appeals to me about this book is that it projects a sense of the action of the game. From the time when I played at Henryetta (Oklahoma) High School to UCLA to the Cowboys, I've always enjoyed the action—the real reason people like to play football and people like to watch it.

The Story of Football also explains why teamwork is so important. If your players on the field don't play together, you won't have a winning team. Whenever the Cowboys win, my name is usually in the newspaper headlines and my passes are on the television highlights. But without my teammates, I never would have accomplished what I have.

All the action and teamwork are here in The Story of Football, a book for everyone who enjoys the game. I'm sure you'll learn something about football. I know I did.

Contents

part One

"ALL FOOTBALL COMES FROM STAGG"

LAMAR HUNT COULDN'T BELIEVE IT. HIS DAUGHTER Sharon had just bounced a small red, white, and blue ball over the roof of their home into their backyard.

"What's that?" he asked.

"A super ball. That's its real name, Daddy, super ball."

"It sure bounces super."

Hunt, the owner of the Kansas City Chiefs, didn't realize it at the time, but that high-bouncing hard-rubber ball would inspire the name of football's most important game. After the 1966 merger agreement between the National Football League (NFL) and the American Football League (AFL), a championship game was scheduled for the two titleholders.

"In our discussions, we kept referring to it as the 'final game' or the 'championship game' or whatever, but it was awkward," Hunt has recalled. "One day I happened to say, 'When we get to the super bowl...' and everyone knew what I was talking about. The term must have come from that 'super ball' my daughter had."

In time the NFL adopted Super Bowl as the official name for its championship game.

Now, year after year, Super Bowl games are listed by Roman numerals, as if ordained for history. More than a hundred thousand spectators have filled a huge stadium for this championship game of the National Football League; more than a hundred million people have watched it on television. In college football the New Year's Day bowl games entertain America on TV for nearly twelve continuous hours. High school games unite small towns and neighborhoods of big cities. And in their own backyards little boys grow up throwing a football, pretending to be the latest popular quarterback.

This is the spectacle of the game as we know it today. But in the beginning, as with all our sports, football's roots were small, its appeal was limited, its appearance almost ancient.

On November 6, 1869, half a century before the NFL was organized in 1920, at New Brunswick, New Jersey, teams from Rutgers and Princeton played what historians consider to be the first college football game. The rules ordered "no throwing or running with the round inflated ball," but it could be batted or dribbled. More of a soccer game than a football game, it attracted about one hundred spectators, along with the twenty-five players on each team, to a grassy field where a Rutgers gymnasium would stand one hundred years later.

To identify themselves, the Rutgers players, along with about fifty students, wore scarlet-colored scarves wrapped turban-style around their heads, and because of this, Rutgers teams in all sports now are known as the Scarlet Knights.

"To appreciate this first game to the full, you must know something of its background," one of the original Rutgers players, John W. Herbert, wrote. "The two colleges were, and still are, of course, about twenty miles apart. The rivalry between them was intense. For years each had striven for possession of an old Revolutionary cannon, making night forays and lugging it back and forth time and again. Not long before the first football game, the canny Princetonians had settled this competition in their own favor by ignominiously sinking the gun in several feet of concrete."

After issuing the challenge for the first football game, Rutgers won 6–4, with the points scored one at a time on kicks that went over the goal line, not through uprights. In a rematch a week later Princeton won, 8–0. Originally a third game had been scheduled, but the faculties of both institutions ordered it canceled. The games, the administrations agreed, had been interfering with the players' studies. After

only two games college football was faced with its first accusation of athletic "overemphasis"—a problem that would evolve along with the sport itself.

When Princeton played Cornell in 1903, helmets were not mandatory.

The following year Columbia organized a football team that played both Rutgers and Princeton using the soccer-type rules of the time.

The Rules Transition

Although there were no college games recorded during the 1871 season, Yale played its first game the next year, defeating Columbia, 30–0. And in 1874 the transition from soccer to football began. Harvard, which had organized a team the previous fall but had not been able to schedule an opponent, invited McGill University of Montreal, Canada, to send its football team to Cambridge, Massachusetts, for a May 15 game. But when the McGill team warmed up, its players were running with the ball.

"What game are you playing?" the Harvard captain asked.

"Rugby," the McGill captain said. "Rugby is our game."

"Our game is soccer—kicking the ball," the Harvard captain said. "Our rules don't allow us to run with the ball. But you are our guests. We will play under your rules."

"No," the McGill captain said, "we will play one game under your rules, one game under our rules."

Although the game played under rugby rules ended in a 0–0 tie, Harvard's players clearly preferred those rules. The next year, on November 13, 1875, the Harvard team traveled to New Haven, Connecticut, to play Yale for the first time. Again the rules created some confusion until Yale, always a proper host, agreed to play a game more like rugby than soccer. Yale lost 4–0, but football, as we know it now, had really begun.

The next year Yale, having adopted the rugby style, won, 1–0, with a freshman named Walter Camp, who would later compete on six Yale football teams under that era's casual eligibility rules. Camp later became a Yale coach and the most famous All-America team selector. For several decades the highest honor in college football was to be chosen for Walter Camp's All-America team.

Harvard would not defeat Yale again until 1890, by which time the first American football rules had been devised—downs, yards to gain, tackling below the waist, blocking, 4 points for a touchdown (not 6 points, as it is now). Also that year Harvard was serious enough about football to institute spring practice. Three years later the Harvard Crimson wore slippery leather uniforms instead of cloth.

During those years, "The Game," as the Harvard-Yale rivalry is known now in the East, was played at a neutral site—Springfield, Massachusetts. Special trains would arrive from Boston and New Haven, and organized cheering would explode from the standing-room-only crowds. One of the earliest mascots, the first real Yale bulldog, Handsome Dan, waddled onto the sidelines at Springfield in the first game there.

Yale, Harvard, and Princeton—still known as the Big Three—dominated college football along with the University of Pennsylvania in those early years. But as the twentieth century began, this new American game also was being played at colleges across the land.

Stagg Shapes the Game

The first important American coach was Amos Alonzo Stagg, who devoted himself to football after having been an All-America end in 1889. Stagg was a Yale divinity student, but instead of becoming a minister, he began coaching in 1890 at Springfield (Massachusetts) College, then moved in 1892 to the University of Chicago, where he would remain through the 1932 season. Although he was forced into mandatory retirement there at age seventy, he was still eager to coach. Stagg was hired the next year by the University of the Pacific in Stockton, California. He happened to travel to his new job on a train that President Herbert Hoover was on.

"When that train got there," one of his sons recalled later, "there were hundreds of people at the station. He assumed that they were there to see the president, but they were there to greet him."

By then Stagg was revered as a coach who had shaped the game of football as we know it now. He is credited by some historians with having pioneered the forward pass, the T-formation, the single and double flanker, the huddle, the shift, the man-in-motion, the quick kick, the short kickoff, and the short punt formation. On a field goal, he used a placekick rather than a dropkick. He invented uniform numbers, the tackling dummy, the blocking sled, padded goalposts, and, to the agony of players everywhere, wind sprints.

Amos Alonzo Stagg, the first important American football coach

"All football," the famous Notre Dame coach Knute Rockne would later say, "comes from Stagg."

Stagg died in 1965 at the age of one hundred and two, but he had established the college record of 314 victories that Paul (Bear) Bryant surpassed as the University of Alabama coach and that Eddie Robinson surpassed as the Grambling coach. Stagg won 244 games at Chicago, 60 at Pacific, and 10 at Springfield.

Other coaches, notably Glenn (Pop) Warner, for whom America's most popular boys' football league is named, also influenced the game.

Praised by Stagg as "one of football's excellent creators," Warner invented the single wing and the double wing formation, along with such plays as the reverse, the naked reverse, the crouching start, the rolling block, the unbalanced line, the screen pass, and the hidden-ball play. He also devised the spiral punt, the numbering of plays, and fiber padding, which evolved into today's sturdy plastic helmets and other protective equipment. Beginning in 1895 at Georgia, Warner went on to coach at Cornell, the Carlisle Indian School, the University of Pittsburgh, Stanford, and Temple.

Warner's teams won 313 games, one fewer than Stagg's total, with a philosophy that concentrated on serious practice.

"You play the way you practice," he once said. "Practice the right way, and you will react the right way in a game."

Inspired by Stagg's championship teams at Chicago, Michigan put together one of the most powerful teams around the turn of the century. Its 1901 team had an 11-0 record, outscoring its opponents, 550–0, and winning the first Rose Bowl game at Pasadena, California, on New Year's Day 1902, with a 49–0 rout of Stanford.

"In 1901," the Michigan coach, Fielding (Hurry Up) Yost, later said, "we used spinners, reverses, double reverses, laterals, split backs—everything that is in the modern game except the forward pass."

Yost got his "Hurry Up" nickname from the quickness he

demanded of his team in running the next play. As soon as one play ended, the Michigan quarterback, Boss Weeks, would be calling signals while the opposing tacklers were dragging themselves to their feet and returning to the line of scrimmage.

Heisman and the First Pro

Another important coach was John Heisman, who spread the gospel of football throughout the nation, starting before the turn of the century and on into the 1920s.

Heisman, for whom the trophy now honoring the nation's outstanding college player is named, moved all over the country—Oberlin, Akron, Clemson, University of Pennsylvania, Washington and Jefferson, Rice, and Georgia Tech. In his later years he was the athletic director at the Downtown Athletic Club in New York City, the club that sponsors the Heisman Trophy balloting.

Meanwhile the game's rules were changing almost year to year, as administrators and coaches sought to develop a balance between offensive and defensive football as well as protection from injuries.

John Heisman (right), the coach for whom the Heisman Trophy is named, chats with an assistant in 1922.

In the process the first pro football player appeared. William (Pudge) Heffelfinger had been an All-America guard at Yale in 1889, 1890, and 1891. The following year he was playing for the Chicago Athletic Association when he was offered five hundred dollars by the Allegheny Athletic Association team to appear at Pittsburgh in a November 12 game against the rival Pittsburgh Athletic Club. Midway in the first half, Heffelfinger recovered a fumble and ran 25 yards for the game's only touchdown in the 4–0 victory.

"Game performance bonus," the Allegheny team's financial statement read, "to W. Heffelfinger for playing: (cash) $500."

With that payment, professional football had begun. Football itself had outgrown its infancy. It was ready for its adolescence and, eventually, for maturity.

JIM THORPE AND KNUTE ROCKNE

ON A DUSTY DIRT FIELD IN CANTON, OHIO, IN 1915, THE Canton Bulldogs with Jim Thorpe were playing the rival Massillon Tigers with Knute Rockne. The two most famous players of that era, Thorpe was a bruising running back and Rockne was a determined defensive end when he wasn't catching passes. On one play Rockne broke through to tackle Thorpe for no gain. Not long after that, Rockne again tackled Thorpe for no gain. But the next time Thorpe carried the ball, he slammed past Rockne for several yards. On his way back to the huddle, Thorpe spoke to Rockne. Two versions of that encounter have drifted down.

According to one version, Thorpe is supposed to have said, "That was just a warning, Rock. People came here and paid to see Jim run. You better let Jim run."

As told by Rockne himself, the other version is: "Jim never actually said it that way. It was more like, 'I'm glad you're slowing down, Rock. Now the people who're paying to see me run can get their money's worth.'"

Whatever was said that day, Jim Thorpe and Knute Rockne created the headlines that popularized football long before television was invented.

Rockne, a Norwegian immigrant who grew up in Chicago, was the Notre Dame end whose pass catching led to the adoption of the forward pass as a strategic weapon. Rockne remained at Notre Dame as one of college football's most famous coaches until his death in 1931 in a plane crash.

Thorpe, an American Indian from the Sac and Fox tribe in

Oklahoma, was a running back at the Carlisle (Pennsylvania) Institute, a vocational school operated by the federal government for Indian students.

"The Greatest Athlete"

Thorpe was more than a football player. He is considered to have been one of the world's outstanding all-around athletes. At the 1912 Olympics in Stockholm, he won gold medals in both the decathlon and pentathlon.

Jim Thorpe was told, "You, sir, are the greatest athlete in the world."

The decathlon consists of ten events, then spread over three days instead of the current two days: the 100-meter dash, long jump, shot put, high jump, 400-meter run, discus, 110-meter hurdles, pole vault, javelin, and 1,500-meter run. The pentathlon, which has been replaced in the Olympics by the modern pentathlon, originally had these five events: 200-meter dash, 1,500-meter run, long jump, discus, and javelin. As he stood on the victory stand, Thorpe was presented his two gold medals by King Gustaf V of Sweden.

"You, sir," the king said, "are the greatest athlete in the world."

In the United States, tacklers who had tried to stop Jim Thorpe and athletes who had tried to run and jump against him agreed with King Gustaf V's assessment. James Francis Thorpe and his twin brother, Charles, were born on May 28, 1888, in a cabin on the

Sac and Fox reservation near Bellemont in the Oklahoma Territory, as it was known before statehood. James also had an Indian name given him by his mother that morning as she noticed the sun on the path to her cabin.

"Wa-tho-huk," she called him, meaning, "Bright Path."

As a youngster, Jim attended the Haskell Institute in Oklahoma, where he first competed in football, baseball, and track-and-field. When he was sixteen, he arrived at Carlisle, where Pop Warner was the football coach. Thorpe played football there in 1907 and 1908, then rejoined the team for the 1911 season. Despite its small enrollment—it was more of a vocational school than a college—Carlisle played some of the nation's best college teams. On November 11, 1911, the Indians were in Cambridge to oppose Harvard, perhaps the best team of that era. From 1908 through 1916, the Crimson had a 71-7-5 record under Coach Percy Haughton, including 33 consecutive victories.

Jim Thorpe displays one of football's forgotten arts— the dropkick.

Harvard took a 6–0 lead, but by the end of the first half Carlisle was ahead on Thorpe's three field goals of 23, 43, and 37 yards. In those years teams used the dropkick, not the place-kick of today, where the ball is spotted by a ball holder. In the dropkick the kicker stood alone, as a punter does. When the ball was snapped to him, he dropped it with one end pointing to the ground so that the ball would bounce straight up. As it bounced up, he kicked it.

In the second half Harvard rallied for a 15–9 lead, but then Thorpe took over. Carrying the ball on nine consecutive plays, he slammed across the goal line for a touchdown and dropkicked the extra point, creating a 15–15 tie; touchdowns were worth 5 points then. In the final minutes Carlisle moved to the Crimson's 43-yard line. On fourth down, standing at the 50-yard line, Thorpe lined up for a field-goal attempt. His dropkick sailed between the uprights. Carlisle won, 18–15, with Thorpe having scored all his team's points. Harvard would not lose another game until 1915, and in his locker room Haughton marveled at Thorpe's performance.

"Watching him turn the ends, slash off tackle, kick, and tackle," the Harvard coach said, "I realized that there was the theoretical super player in flesh and blood."

The next year Thorpe won his Olympic gold medals, which later were taken away from him when it was disclosed in 1913 that he had received about sixty dollars a month to play semipro baseball in North Carolina in 1908 and 1909, a common practice among collegians of that era. He had played under his real name instead of adopting a fictitious name, as most other players did. Rule 26 of the Olympic charter forbade an athlete from competing in the Games if he or she had been paid to play a sport—even if it was different from his or her Olympic sport.

"I was not very wise in the ways of the world," Thorpe wrote in a letter of apology to the Amateur Athletic Union, "and did not realize this was wrong."

Thorpe died in 1953, still bitter over having his Olympic medals taken away. "I won them, didn't I?" he said in 1948. "Why don't they give them back to me? They're no good to anyone else, are they?" Finally, in 1981, after decades of campaigning by Thorpe's family, the International Olympic Committee restored Thorpe's amateur status and agreed to replace his medals and trophies.

During the 1984 Olympic Games in Los Angeles, his medals and trophies were on display, a reminder of what he had accomplished in 1912.

After the 1912 Olympics, Thorpe returned to Carlisle and resumed playing football. With his field goals and extra points, he accounted for 198 points that season, including 25 touchdowns. The next year he joined baseball's New York Giants as an outfielder. Never a regular, he was later traded to the Cincinnati Reds, back to the Giants, and then to the Boston Braves. He had his best season in 1919, batting .327.

During the years Thorpe was playing major league baseball in the summer, he also played football in the fall for the Canton (Ohio) Bulldogs, one of the early professional teams.

In 1915 Thorpe kicked field goals of 45 and 18 yards in a 6–0 victory for the Bulldogs over the rival Massillon (Ohio) Tigers—described in the *Cleveland Plain Dealer* as "the two greatest aggregations of ex–college football stars ever gathered on professional teams in Ohio." It was the same game in which Thorpe opposed Knute Rockne, who occasionally played for the Tigers while he was an assistant coach at Notre Dame.

That was one of Rockne's last games as a player. After having been Jesse Harper's assistant coach for four seasons, he took command as Notre Dame's coach in 1918—only five years after he had helped put Notre Dame on the football map and the forward pass into football vocabulary in a startling upset of Army.

Knute (pronounced Nōōt) Kenneth Rockne was born on March 4, 1888, in Voss, Norway, where his father, Lars, manufactured carriages. The carriages were so beautiful that one earned a prize at the Great Liverpool Fair in England. When his father read about the Chicago World's Fair in 1891, he built another carriage, hoping to win a prize there, too. When that carriage won the grand prize in Chicago, his father decided to remain in that growing midwestern city. He wrote to his wife, Martha, and asked her to come to Chicago with their three children.

Knute was five years old when he saw the Statue of Liberty from the deck of a boat steaming up New York Bay. Later, as a Chicago schoolboy, Rockne washed windows and delivered packages for pocket money. But his heart was in sports, primarily track-and-field—so much so that his father suggested that college was beyond him, that he should drop out of high school and get a job. He worked in the Chicago post office while he trained at the Illinois Athletic Club as a half-miler and pole vaulter. But he wanted to pursue his ambition to be a college athlete. He applied to Notre Dame, then a small college, which allowed him to take an entrance exam even though he did not have a high school diploma. He passed. As a freshman, Rockne was twenty-two years old, but older college students were not unusual in those years.

By chance Rockne's roommate was Charles (Gus) Dorais, of Chippewa Falls, Wisconsin, where he had been a high school football star. Three years later their names would be carved into football history.

The First Forward Pass

Rockne had not played much football as a Chicago schoolboy. But at Notre Dame he quickly developed into a dependable end, although he was only 5-9 and 155 pounds, somewhat small even then. As the team's captain-elect in 1913, he was about to leave the campus for his summer vacation when Coach Jesse Harper mentioned that a game had been scheduled with Army at West Point, New York, on November 1, the first time that Notre Dame would play one of the established eastern teams. Rockne and Dorais later visited Harper in his office.

"Can we take a couple of footballs with us?" Rockne asked. "We've got summer jobs together at a resort on Lake Erie, and we want to do some special practicing."

Harper tossed them two footballs. But what even the coach didn't realize at the time was that Rockne and Dorais were hoping to take advantage of some new rules governing the forward pass. First allowed in 1906, the forward pass had been used by some teams, although not extensively. But in their private workouts during off-hours from their jobs as waiters, Dorais polished his skill at throwing a football with a perfect spiral (even though it was a much fatter, rounder ball than the type used today) and Rockne learned to catch a pass in full stride.

"Mobility and change of pace," Rockne kept telling Dorais, "They're not going to know where we're going or when we get there."

On returning to the Notre Dame campus, they put on a display of passing and catching that convinced Harper of its usefulness. Wisely the coach did not use much passing in three one-sided victories—87–0 over Ohio Northern, 20–7 over North Dakota, and 62–0 over Alma, a small Michigan school. Harper was saving the surprise for Army, which was stunned in a 35–13 upset.

Army had led at halftime, 14–13, but then Dorais and Rockne took over. In the second half, Dorais completed 10 of 13 passes, with Rockne catching 7. For the game Dorais completed 14 of 17 for 243 yards.

On the sports pages of the *New York Times* the next day, a headline read: NOTRE DAME OPEN PLAY AMAZES ARMY. The story praised the "most sensational football ever seen in the East," a tribute to what Rockne and Dorais had devised. The introduction of the forward pass as an offensive weapon would be only the beginning of Rockne's contributions to football. As the Notre Dame coach for thirteen seasons through 1930, he would produce a record of 105 victories against only 12 losses and 5 ties for a remarkable .897 percentage. He would have five unbeaten seasons (1919, 1920, 1924, 1929, and 1930). He

As an end at Notre Dame, Knute Rockne was only 5-9 and 155 pounds.

would have two teams recognized as national champions (1924 and 1930).

The 1924 team would inspire one of football's most famous nicknames—the Four Horsemen.

Notre Dame defeated Army, 12–7, at the Polo Grounds in New York City that year, shortly after the release of the motion picture *The Four Horsemen of the Apocalypse*, starring Rudolf Valentino, one of Hollywood's most popular stars. In the press box after the game, Grantland Rice, then one of America's leading sportswriters and a columnist for the *New York Tribune*, began typing.

"Outlined against a blue-gray October sky," he wrote, "the Four Horsemen rode again. In dramatic lore they were known as Famine, Pestilence, Destruction, and Death. These are only aliases. Their real names are Stuhldreher, Miller, Crowley, and Layden...."

When the team assembled for practice on Monday in South Bend, four horses and a photographer were waiting. George Strickler, later a sports columnist for the *Chicago Tribune* and then Notre Dame's sports information director, posed Harry Stuhldreher, Don Miller, Jim

The Four Horsemen: Miller, Layden, Crowley, Stuhldreher

Crowley, and Elmer Layden on horseback, each wearing his helmet and holding a football. That photo established the Four Horsemen as the most celebrated backfield in football history, then or now.

The Gipper

Four years later Rockne's 1928 team would justify one of football's most famous phrases: "Win one for the Gipper."

George Gipp had been a gifted halfback in 1920, a triple threat as a runner, passer, and punter. On defense he was a sure tackler. He also had a sense of self-confidence that Rockne quickly understood.

"I learned very early," Rockne once said, "to place full confidence in his self-confidence."

For all of Gipp's self-confidence, he was somewhat of a loner. He wasn't interested in publicity. He seldom granted interviews or posed for photos. For that 1920 season Gipp not only was named by Walter Camp to the All-America team, but he also was selected as the nation's outstanding college player. Had there been a Heisman Trophy that year, Gipp probably would have won it. But when Notre Dame completed its season with a 25–0 victory over Michigan State, he was in the college infirmary at South Bend with a life-threatening infection. Antibiotic drugs had not yet been developed. Gipp's condition quickly worsened. Soon he had pneumonia.

"Someday in a tough game," he told Rockne, a daily visitor to his bedside, "ask the players to win one for the Gipper."

In 1928, before a game with Army at Yankee Stadium, the coach walked to the center of the locker room to address his team. His players had been in grammar school when Gipp had died, but each knew of his fame. Rockne told them about what Gipp had said on his deathbed.

"I've never used that request until now," Rockne said. "But this is the time."

Notre Dame won that game, 12–6, on a touchdown pass from Butch Niemiec to Johnny O'Brien in the closing minutes. The legend

A rare photo of the legendary Notre Dame halfback George Gipp

of George Gipp would drift through the decades to come. In the motion picture *Rockne*, the role of the halfback was played by Ronald Reagan, who later became the President of the United States; Rockne was portrayed by Pat O'Brien.

On March 31, 1931, at the peak of his fame, the forty-three-year-old Notre Dame coach was aboard Transcontinental Western Flight 955 out of Kansas City, bound for Los Angeles, where he was to sign a motion picture contract. Suddenly in the skies over the Kansas farmland, the plane sputtered, then crashed. Knute was dead. But what he accomplished at Notre Dame, both as a player and as a coach, helped guide football into its present role in American society.

GEORGE HALAS AND THE T-FORMATION

ONE DAY DURING CALVIN COOLIDGE'S ADMINISTRATION, an Illinois senator introduced George Halas and Red Grange to the president.

"These gentlemen," the senator explained, "are with the Chicago Bears."

"How interesting," the president said, "I've always enjoyed animal acts."

At the time not everybody, certainly not President Coolidge, was aware of pro football. But more than any other two people in the evolution of the game, George Halas and Red Grange taught America that when a football player left college, his career was merely beginning. One of pro football's Hall of Fame coaches, Weeb Ewbank, often joked that "hindsight is twenty-twenty," meaning that it's easy to look back and be correct. In a look back at National Football League history, it's easy to realize that 1933 was its turning point.

Until then the NFL had been a hodgepodge. In its maiden season, 1921, teams represented six cities that have had franchises for decades (Chicago, Green Bay, Cleveland, Cincinnati, Detroit, and Buffalo) as well as several smaller cities—Canton, Akron, Dayton, Columbus, Rock Island, and Rochester.

Most games were played on dirt fields with small rickety wooden grandstands. A few thousand people, sometimes only a few hundred, attended. In its early years the NFL not only was without many spectators but was also without a balanced schedule or a championship game. In 1926, for example, the NFL had twenty-two teams, with the Frankford (Pennsylvania) Yellowjackets having a 14-1-1 record

In the 1933 NFL championship game, end Bill Hewitt laterals to end Bill Karr.

for first place while the Hammond (Indiana) Pros and the Louisville (Kentucky) Colonels shared last place, each with a 0-4 record.

Year by year after that, the NFL slowly dwindled, until it sank to only eight teams in 1932. But for the 1933 season the NFL was split into Eastern and Western divisions, each with five teams. When the winners of the two divisions met in the first NFL championship game, the Bears defeated the New York Giants, 23–21, on a razzle-dazzle last-second 32-yard touchdown—a fake smash into the line by fullback Bronko Nagurski, who stopped and threw a pass to end Bill Hewitt, who then lateraled to end Bill Karr for the touchdown.

Competitively that first NFL championship game was the equivalent of today's Super Bowl game. But financially the players' share reflected the Depression that had so many Americans out of work. The bonus check for each member of the Bears was $210.23.

Red Grange received one of those checks. The halfback was in his next-to-last season with the Bears by then, but in 1925 he had become pro football's first national attraction. As an All-American at Illinois, he was known as "the Galloping Ghost," a single-wing tailback best remembered for his performance against Michigan in the 1924 dedication of the Illinois stadium. He returned the opening kickoff 95 yards for a touchdown, returned a punt 67 yards for a touchdown, then scored on runs of 54 yards and 44 yards—all in the game's first twelve minutes.

Grange later scored on a 13-yard run and threw a 20-yard touchdown pass. Before the game ended in a 39–14 victory, he had run for 212 yards in 15 carries, completed 6 passes for 64 yards, scored 5 touchdowns, and passed for another.

But the Michigan student newspaper minimized Grange's performance, declaring, "All Grange can do is run." That prompted Bob Zuppke, the Illinois coach, to compare Grange to a famous opera singer of that era, saying, "And all Galli-Curci can do is sing." Immediately after Grange's senior season, he joined the Bears for a barnstorming tour arranged by C. C. (Cash and Carry) Pyle, a fast-talking promoter. Grange earned a quick one hundred thousand dollars, a stupendous sum at the time. But his decision had been opposed even by Zuppke, who typified the disdain that college coaches had for pro football then.

"Football," the Illinois coach told him, "just isn't a game to be played for money."

"You get paid for coaching, Zup," Grange retorted. "Why is it wrong for me to get paid for playing?"

Grange was paid handsomely. But he earned every cent, as did his Bear teammates. Beginning with the first sellout crowd ever for a pro football game, thirty-six thousand at Wrigley Field on Thanksgiving Day 1925, through January 31, 1926, Grange and the Bears played nineteen games before a total of nearly four hundred thousand spectators in seventeen cities as they crisscrossed the country. At the Polo

The Galloping Ghost, Red Grange

Grounds in New York, he attracted at least sixty-five thousand, plus uncounted thousands who scaled the bleacher walls. At the Los Angeles Coliseum he drew more than seventy-five thousand.

"No one," a weary Grange said afterward, "will ever attempt anything like this again."

No one ever has. But with that tour Grange established himself in the era known as the Roaring Twenties as the football player. He was to football then what Babe Ruth was to baseball, Jack Dempsey to boxing, Bobby Jones to golf, Bill Tilden to tennis. But the NFL wasn't yet strong enough to absorb him. Grange and Pyle demanded one-third ownership in the Bears, but Halas and his partner, Dutch Sternaman, refused.

Seeking their own stage, Grange and Pyle formed the American Football League for the 1926 season. Grange was the co-owner and halfback of the New York Yankees in this new league. When the AFL folded after one season, the Yankees, whose team name was inspired by the success of Babe Ruth's baseball Yankees, joined the NFL for the 1927 season. Grange missed most of that season because of a damaged knee, the most prevalent injury in football—then or now. This is especially true for a running back, whose legs are hit when he is tackled. To prevent this injury, some players now wear light metal-and-rubber knee braces that absorb the shock of contact. Red Grange never had the opportunity to wear a protective knee brace, but in 1929 he rejoined the Bears, his disagreement with Halas forgotten.

Halas, who died in 1983 at age eighty-eight, was one of the founders of the NFL on September 17, 1920, at a meeting in Canton, Ohio.

Men from twelve midwestern cities gathered that day in Ralph Hay's showroom for the Hupmobile, a popular automobile at the time. Halas was there representing the Decatur (Illinois) Staleys, who would move to Chicago in 1921 and one year later be named the Bears.

"We only had two chairs at that meeting," Halas often recalled. "Everybody else sat on the runningboards or the fenders."

In the beginning Halas was a rare triple threat—owner, coach, and captain (as right end on offense and defense). By the time he stopped coaching at age seventy-three, his record (including playoff games) over four separate ten-year tenures was 325-151-31 (.673) and the Bears had won eight NFL titles. Only the Green Bay Packers had won more: eleven. But the tough, crusty man known as the Papa Bear always argued that his team also should have been declared the 1924 champion despite the Cleveland Bulldogs' better record. In those years, before there was a championship game between the two division winners, the NFL title was awarded at a league meeting.

"I left the meeting to go to the washroom," Halas said. "And when I got back, they had voted the championship to Cleveland."

The Bears' Wing in Canton

Halas had the personality of the pioneer he was. At the Pro Football Hall of Fame in Canton, Ohio, he once stared at a photo in which he was shown arguing with a referee.

"I don't know what I was talking about," he said, "but I'm sure I was right."

George Halas, the Papa Bear

He usually was right. He was sixty-eight when he coached the Bears to the NFL title in 1963, defeating the Giants at Wrigley Field, 14–10.

"There isn't room," he said the next day, "for many of these things in one lifetime."

In his lifetime the Papa Bear had more room than most people. In addition to his championship teams, he virtually created a private wing for the Bears at the Pro Football Hall of Fame shrine. In addition to Halas himself, twenty-two members were established Bear players during their careers, more than that of any other team—Doug Atkins, George Blanda, Dick Butkus, George Connor, Mike Ditka, Paddy Driscoll, Danny Fortmann, Bill George, Red Grange, Ed Healey, Bill Hewitt, Stan Jones, Sid Luckman, Link Lyman, George McAfee, George Musso, Bronko Nagurski, Walter Payton, Gale Sayers, Joe Stydahar, George Trafton, and Bulldog Turner.

"Nagurski," the Papa Bear once said of his fullback of the thirties, "what a man!"

Nagurski, at 6-2 and 225 pounds, had joined the Bears from the University of Minnesota, where he actually had been chosen for two positions on one 1929 All-America team—fullback and tackle. In those years All-America teams consisted of only eleven positions, since a player had to perform on both offense and defense. Nagurski's strength was legendary. His Minnesota coach, Fats Spears, often joked that he found Bronko plowing a field near his hometown of International Falls, Minnesota.

"I stopped to ask directions," Spears would say, "but instead of pointing with his hand, Bronko pointed with the plow."

Nagurski enjoyed going along with that gag. Soon after he joined the Bears, some older players teased him about his strength. One player asked him how he got so strong.

"Plowing fields," he said.

"That's nothing," one of the Bears said. "Most of us have plowed a field at one time or another."

"Without a horse?" Bronko said.

The Cracked Bricks

But on the football field nobody joked about Nagurski's strength. In a game at Wrigley Field, he smashed through several tacklers on a 35-yard touchdown run and careered into the end zone. Unable to stop in time, he crashed into the brick wall beyond. Old-timers insist that the ivy on that wall covers a crack that Nagurski put in the bricks.

"I don't know if I cracked the wall," he said years later. "I have a feeling it was cracked before. But I did hit it pretty hard."

His famous teammate Red Grange often insisted that he was fortunate to have played with Nagurski rather than against him.

"I had to try to tackle Bronk in scrimmages occasionally," Grange once recalled, "and there was something strange about tackling him. When you hit him, it was almost like getting an electric shock."

Bronko Nagurski was named to the 1929 All-America team at two positions.

Opposing players knew the feeling. On a road trip the train carrying the Pittsburgh team had to slam to a sudden stop, spilling the players out of their seats. One of the Steelers shook his head.

"We've hit Nagurski," he joked.

For eight seasons Nagurski terrorized NFL tacklers as the Bears' fullback before he joined the wrestling circuit. But in 1943, with the NFL's manpower depleted by World War II, he rejoined the Bears at age thirty-five after a lapse of six years. Used at tackle for most of the season, he returned to fullback for the Bears' last two games. In wrapping up the Western Division title against the rival Chicago Cardinals, he gained 81 yards in 15 carries. In the NFL title game, he scored the touchdown that provided the Bears with a lead they never relinquished.

"Bronko wasn't a spectacular breakaway runner," Halas once said, "but for football purists he was a picture runner. He had perfect form for a fullback. He ran so low to the ground that his back was almost parallel to it. And at the moment of contact with a tackler, he dipped

Bronko Nagurski of the Bears crashes through two Giants in the 1934 NFL title game.

his shoulder and brought it up with terrific impact, like an uppercut. It made no difference how much momentum the tackler had or how much he weighed. Bronko's countersmash with his shoulder bounced the tackler off him like rain hitting a tin roof."

Bronko Nagurski had been the symbol of the Bears' power as a running team. Then, in 1934, the NFL changed the shape of the ball slightly. Longer and narrower, it made passing easier. And in 1939 a rookie quarterback named Sid Luckman joined the Bears and soon turned it into the NFL's most feared passing team.

At the time, the modern T-formation was considered to be a radical offense. Clark Shaughnessy, the Stanford coach, designed it with the backs in the form of a T—the quarterback crouched behind the center, the fullback lined up directly behind the quarterback, the two halfbacks on each side of the fullback. Shaughnessy had developed it at the University of Chicago as Amos Alonzo Stagg's successor. But at Stanford, which had won only one game in 1939, he used the T-formation to turn the 1940 team into the Rose Bowl champion with a 10-0 record. His stars were left-handed quarterback Frankie Albert, halfbacks Hugh Gallarneau and Pete Kmetovic, and fullback Norm Standlee.

"A lesser coach," Albert said, "would have been afraid to try something so radical. We were skeptical, but he sold us on it."

Some of the Bear players probably were skeptical, too. But with Luckman at quarterback the Bears dazzled the NFL with the T-formation that turned the single-wing offense into a dinosaur.

"Luckman could do it all," Halas once said. "Pass, run, kick, defend, and think."

While at Columbia University, the 6-0, 200-pound Luckman had known only the single-wing offense, which was geared to the tailback running or passing on almost every play. When he reported to the Bears, he suddenly had to learn the new and complicated T-formation. Halas assigned one of his assistant coaches, Luke Johnsos, to tutor the rookie passer. In his first year Luckman was the backup quarterback.

Halas wanted it that way. The Bears' playbook had 350 plays, many with several variations. Halas knew that Luckman needed time to memorize and master all those plays.

The 73–0 Game

By the 1940 season Luckman was in command. So were the Bears, who won the Western Division title with an 8-3 record, qualifying for the NFL championship game against the Redskins in Washington that would provide the most famous score in NFL history.

When the Bears arrived in the nation's capital, they read in the Washington newspaper that some of the Redskins had called them "crybabies," a reference to the Redskins' 7–3 victory over the Bears earlier that season. In the locker room before the game, George Halas didn't give a pep talk. He didn't even raise his voice. He simply held up the newspapers and pointed to the red-crayon circles around the Redskin quotes.

"Gentlemen," the coach said, "we're not crybabies. Go out and play the football you can."

With a roar, the Bears burst onto the field. Moments later, on their first play from scrimmage, they had a touchdown—a 68-yard run around left end by fullback Bill Osmanski behind perfect blocking.

One of the NFL's best passers, Sid Luckman, could also run.

The next time the Bears got the ball, an 80-yard march ended with Luckman sneaking across the goal line. Not long after that, Joe Maniaci dashed 42 yards for another touchdown. By halftime the Bears led 28–0, and they rolled to a crushing 73–0 victory. The score established that the Bears were a special team, that Sid Luckman was a special quarterback, and that the T-formation was a special offense.

The Bears won the NFL title again in 1941, 1943, and 1946—all with Luckman as quarterback.

But to some of his teammates, Luckman's finest moment occurred when the Bears, as the 1943 champions, were playing the College All-Stars at the start of the 1944 exhibition season. When the All-Stars jumped to a 14–0 lead, Luckman began growling in the huddle.

"Where did you men get those uniforms—steal them?" he snapped. "Those uniforms are not supposed to be disgraced."

Responding to the challenge, the Bears won, 24–21. In their locker room later, center Bulldog Turner and guard George Musso, each of whom would be inducted later into the Pro Football Hall of Fame, looked over at their quarterback.

"Sid, you're the greatest," Turner said. "You picked all of us up by our cleats and made us win this game."

"Nobody else could have done it," Musso said. "I've seen you do some great things, but this was the greatest."

In those years, the Washington Redskins also had a special passer— Slingin' Sammy Baugh, a whipcord Texan with an arm like a lariat. When he took off his burgundy-and-gold Redskin jersey for the last time after sixteen seasons, he held sixteen NFL passing records and three NFL punting records. Out of Texas Christian University, he had been special from the day he reported to the Redskins' training camp as a rookie. Coach Ray Flaherty was diagramming the team's pass plays on a blackboard.

"On this one," Flaherty said, "I want you to hit the receiver in the eye."

When his career ended, Sammy Baugh held 16 NFL passing records.

Baugh looked up at his new coach. "One question," he said. "Which eye?"

When the Redskins were demolished by the Bears in that 1940 NFL championship game, Sammy Baugh didn't have any excuses. Many of the Redskin rooters in Griffith Stadium that day believed it might have been a different game if end Charley Malone had not missed a touchdown pass when the Bears had an early 7–0 lead. Malone lost Baugh's pass in the sun, the ball hitting him in the chest and falling to the ground.

"Suppose Malone had caught that ball," Baugh was asked later, "would that have changed the game?"

"It might have," Baugh said, forcing a smile for the reporters. "It might have made it 73–7."

Two years later Baugh and the Redskins would upset the Bears in the NFL championship game, 14–6. But over a span of fourteen seasons starting in 1933, the Bears won five NFL championships and eight Western Division titles—far more than any other team of that era.

By then, nobody confused George Halas or the Bears with an animal act.

THE BLACK KNIGHTS AND JOHNNY U

IN THE YEARS AFTER WORLD WAR II, THE ARMY TEAM WAS known as the "Black Knights of the Hudson"—"Black Knights" because they wore black jerseys with gold numbers and gold helmets, "of the Hudson" because they represented the United States Military Academy, which is situated on the craggy cliffs of West Point above the Hudson River.

Of all those Black Knights, two remain on a pedestal today—fullback Felix (Doc) Blanchard and halfback Glenn Davis. Their nicknames were "Mister Inside" and "Mister Outside." Blanchard won the Heisman Trophy as the nation's outstanding college player in 1945; Davis won it the next year. During their three seasons together, they scored a total of 89 touchdowns (51 by Davis, 38 by Blanchard). In that time Army never lost a game, winning 27 and tying 1 (a memorable 0–0 struggle with Notre Dame in 1946).

"Blanchard and Davis were the best one-two punch, in my belief," their coach, Colonel Earl (Red) Blaik, later wrote, "that college football ever saw."

Other college teams have had a single player who arguably was better than either Blanchard or Davis, but few college teams have ever had two players at their level at the same time. In the history of the Heisman Trophy, first awarded in 1935, they were the only two running backs from the same college to win it in consecutive years. Decades later their time at Army is still remembered as the Blanchard-Davis era.

Blanchard was not only husky and strong at 6-1 and 208 pounds, but he was also fast. He could toss the 16-pound shot put 52 feet

**"Mr. Inside,"
fullback Felix
(Doc) Blanchard,
on his way to a
touchdown in the
1945 Army-Navy
game**

and run the 100-yard dash in 10 seconds flat. In addition to his battering-ram style as a fullback, he was an agile pass catcher, a devastating blocker, and a bruising linebacker on defense. He also could punt and kick off. He was a complete player.

"Blanchard is as good as Nagurski," said Steve Owen, then the New York Giants' coach, "only he has more finesse."

"Blanchard," said Herman Hickman, then Army's offensive line coach, "is the only man who runs his own interference."

As a blocker Blanchard also ran interference for Davis, a swift breakaway threat who one season averaged a remarkable 11.7 yards each time he carried the ball. He also was a good passer and a good pass receiver. As a defensive back he was a sure tackler. Much of his talent was geared to sheer speed. He ran the 100-yard dash in less than 10 seconds.

"Glenn Davis was emphatically the fastest halfback I ever knew," Colonel Blaik once said. "He was not so much a dodger and side-stepper as a blazing runner who had a fourth and even a fifth gear in reserve, could change direction at top speed and fly away from tacklers as if jet-propelled."

Whenever Colonel Blaik reminisced about Davis, the coach enjoyed remembering a 20–13 victory over Michigan when the Army quarterback, Arnold Tucker, was unable to lift his right arm because of an injury. Lacking his best passer, the Cadets' coach designed a game plan in which Davis would do the passing, often on option plays.

"He completed 7 out of 8 for 168 yards, accounting for our first touchdown and setting up the third," Colonel Blaik said. "He also

**"Mr. Outside,"
halfback Glenn
Davis, on the
move in 1946
against Penn**

ran through guard for 59 yards and our second touchdown."

Davis was somewhat small at 5-9, but he was a sturdy 170 pounds. He would go on to play for the Los Angeles Rams, helping them win the 1951 NFL title after serving as an Army lieutenant. Blanchard never played in the NFL, preferring to stay in the Army Air Force as a pilot. While based in England in 1959, he survived a crash landing. He had stayed with his jet fighter rather than parachute and let it fall into a London residential area.

But in Army history Blanchard is remembered best for his exploits as a football player.

"For a big man," Colonel Blaik once recalled, "he was the quickest starter I ever saw. In the open he ran with the niftiness as well as the speed of a great halfback. Twice in Navy games, I saw him run through a head-on tackle without breaking stride and race on to a touchdown."

One time, though, Blanchard did not run through a tackle. It was during the Army-Notre Dame rivalry.

During the first two years of the Blanchard-Davis era, Army often was accused of dominating other college teams that had lost some of their best players to military service during World War II. But by 1946 the colleges had regained many of those players. Notre Dame in particular was a powerhouse again after 59–0 and 48–0 losses to Army the previous two years. Their rivalry resumed at Yankee Stadium.

"When two great teams meet," Frank Leahy, the Notre Dame coach, said later, "defense tends to dominate."

Their famous 0–0 tie was preserved by defense, if not by one tackle. From the Army 42-yard line, Blanchard thundered around right end and appeared on his way to a touchdown. But from across the field, Johnny Lujack, who is best remembered as the Notre Dame quarterback but was also a defensive back, angled toward the big fullback. With a low tackle Lujack tumbled Blanchard at the Notre Dame 36-yard line.

Army would go on to remain undefeated in 32 consecutive games before losing to Columbia, 21–20, in 1947, an upset sparked by end Bill Swiacki's spectacular catches. But the Blanchard-Lujack collision will always be considered the most memorable moment of that time, the moment that symbolized the transition from the Blanchard-Davis era to the Frank Leahy era.

A Notre Dame tackle during Knute Rockne's reign, Leahy returned there in 1941 as the new head coach. Including two earlier seasons at Boston College, Leahy's career record at the time of his 1953 retirement due to illness was 107-13-9. He had six unbeaten Notre Dame teams, including four recognized as national champions. Each of those four championship teams had a Heisman Trophy winner— quarterback Angelo Bertelli in 1943 (using T-formation plays borrowed from the Chicago Bears), quarterback Johnny Lujack in 1947, end Leon Hart in 1949, and halfback Johnny Lattner in 1953. Usually a pessimist, Leahy spoke with a scholarly vocabulary that mesmerized his players.

"At times a defeat is an asset," he once said. "It may have countless other effects that will outweigh the disadvantages concomitant with defeat."

Even so, Leahy's teams were seldom defeated. During his devotion to Notre Dame's tradition, he once was approached by Mickey McBride, the co-owner of the Cleveland franchise in the All-America Football Conference that planned to start operations in 1946 as the NFL's rival. McBride wanted to hire Leahy as the Cleveland coach, but Leahy declined.

"If you think I am a worthy coach," he told McBride, "then you will be pleased by Paul Brown—we are one and the same in our philosophies toward the game."

Paul Brown's Dynasty

In a sense Paul Brown was the product of another tradition—the continuing popularity of the game in Massillon, Ohio—first during pro football's early years and later with the Massillon High School team,

Paul Brown, whose namesake team dominated the league

which Brown coached to an 80-8-2 record over nine seasons. He moved on to Ohio State and, during World War II, to the Great Lakes Naval Station team, which was based near Chicago and had some of the nation's best college players. He was still there when Leahy recommended him as the coach of the Cleveland team in the AAFC.

Not only was Brown hired, but the team also was named after him—the Cleveland Browns.

Brown was such a good coach, he created a monster of a team that was so efficient it destroyed the element of competition in the AAFC and, following the 1949 season, the league itself. In four seasons the Browns won four championships while accumulating a regular-season record of 47-4-3. Before the 1950 season the NFL absorbed three AAFC teams—the Browns, the San Francisco 49ers, and the Baltimore Colts. But the NFL establishment snickered at the thought that the Browns might be as good as the best NFL teams, especially the 1949 champion Philadelphia Eagles.

"To me," said Earle (Greasy) Neale, the coach of the Eagles, "the Browns are a basketball team. All they can do is throw."

True, the Browns had dominated the AAFC with Otto Graham throwing passes to his ends, Dante Lavelli and Mac Speedie, and to Dub Jones, a halfback who often lined up far to the right as one of the first flankerbacks. But the Browns did more than throw. With the 238-pound Marion Motley at fullback, they ran. And if their offense sputtered, they salvaged field goals with Lou (The Toe) Groza as their placekicker. They also had a dependable defensive unit, with Bill Willis at middle guard.

Quietly, around the same time that Jackie Robinson was breaking in as the first black player in major league baseball, Paul Brown had helped to integrate pro football with Motley and Willis in 1946.

Marion Motley, one of the first black NFL players, slams past a tackler.

During the early years of pro football, several black players had been on the small-town teams of the period. Fritz Pollard, an All-America running back at Brown University, not only played on some of those early teams but also coached. Paul Robeson, an All-America end at Rutgers, played at Akron and Milwaukee before deciding to concentrate on a singing career. But in the growth of the NFL, black players had mostly been ignored until the Los Angeles Rams signed Kenny Washington and Woody Strode in 1946.

George Taliaferro, a running back from Indiana selected by the Bears in 1949, was the first black college player chosen in the NFL draft. But he decided to sign with the Los Angeles Dons of the AAFC.

By then Motley and Willis were recognized as two of the Browns' best players. Perhaps with the idea of deflating the Browns in their NFL debut in 1950, the NFL scheduled them to open the season in

Otto Graham

Philadelphia against the defending champion Eagles, but the plan backfired. The Browns won, 35–10, as Graham threw 3 touchdown passes and scored another touchdown himself. He completed 21 of 38 passes for 346 yards as the Browns accumulated 487 yards of total offense. After the game, Pete Pihos, an Eagle pass receiver on two NFL championship teams, was asked by his wife what had happened.

"Honey," he said, "we met a team from the big league."

Paul Brown had molded a team that would win the NFL's Eastern Division title every season from 1950 through 1955 as well as three NFL championships in that span. More than that, Brown would popularize the organizational approach not only to pro football but also to college football.

Many of the techniques that are accepted procedure now were unknown until Brown introduced them—year-round coaching staffs, notebooks and classrooms, film scouting, grading players from film study, lodging the team at a hotel the night before home games, specific pass patterns, face bars on helmets, switching offensive players to defense to take advantage of the free-substitution rule, which created offensive and defensive teams, and using messenger guards to bring in the next play from the sideline. He also exercised complete control over the Browns' organization.

"Complete control," he once said. "There is no other way for a team to operate and be a winner."

That complete control was eroded after Art Modell, a New York advertising executive, purchased the Browns in 1961. Following the 1962 season, Paul Brown was out, only to surface six years later as part-owner and coach of the Cincinnati Bengals, a team that eventually qualified for Super Bowl XVI as the 1981 American Conference champions, with Forrest Gregg as coach. (In 1996 Modell would desert Cleveland, taking his team to Baltimore—which had been vacated in 1984 by the Colts' move to Indianapolis.)

Weeb Ewbank's Colts

Meanwhile, one of Paul Brown's disciples, Wilbur (Weeb) Ewbank, developed the Baltimore Colts into a two-time NFL champion, the 23–17 winner of what is often called "the greatest game ever played"—the 1958 NFL championship game with the New York Giants that required the first sudden-death overtime in NFL history.

After having been Paul Brown's offensive line coach, Ewbank took command of the Colts in 1954 with a five-year plan. According to his timetable, the Colts would be a title contender in 1958. As it turned out, they won the NFL championship that year. But in addition to Ewbank's coaching and the talent of many skilled players, the Colts had discovered a Hall of Fame quarterback, Johnny Unitas, for the price of what in 1956 was an eighty-five-cent long-distance phone call from Baltimore to Pittsburgh.

Unitas had had an inconspicuous career as a college quarterback at the University of Louisville. Then he had been released as a

Johnny Unitas, from six dollars a game to two NFL titles with the Baltimore Colts

rookie by the Pittsburgh Steelers during training camp in 1955. He returned to the city of Pittsburgh, where he had grown up. He got a construction job working on a pile driver and played semipro football with the Bloomfield Rams of the Greater Pittsburgh League for six dollars a game.

"We played Wednesdays and Saturday nights," he once recalled. "We sort of made up the plays as we went along. I'd tell the receivers what patterns to run, and I'd pass to the one who looked most open. Each team only had about three or four good players, and they could do pretty much what they wanted against the rest. At the same time you might have a 140-pound blocker trying to hold off a 225-pound lineman crashing in on you, so you had to take punishment. I was hardened enough to escape injury. We won the league championship, which was more satisfying than the six dollars a game I was getting. It was football, and I was able to keep in practice."

Unitas was hoping that the Browns, who had corresponded with him, might invite them to their 1956 training camp.

"No need for you this season," Paul Brown had told Unitas in a telegram after the Steelers had cut him. "Suggest you come to camp next summer for tryout. Contact me in the spring."

But one day in February 1956, Don Kellett, the Colts' general manager, phoned Unitas at his Pittsburgh home.

"We'd like to get a look at you," Kellett said. "We have a tryout camp in May. Why don't you come down and work out?"

Unitas made the Colts as a second-stringer. In their fourth game that season, with the Colts leading the Bears, 21–20, their starting quarterback, George Shaw, suffered a serious knee injury. Unitas was inserted. But his inexperience was obvious. He fumbled three times and had another pass intercepted as the Colts lost, 58–27. Another coach might have been impatient with the rookie, but Ewbank consoled him.

"Don't worry about it," the coach said. "You're my quarterback again next week."

By the end of that 1956 season, Johnny U, as he came to be known, had established himself. By the end of the 1957 season, he was voted the second-team All-Pro quarterback behind Y. A. Tittle of the San Francisco 49ers, a ten-year veteran. By the end of the 1958 season, he was looked upon as the NFL's best quarterback, especially after his performance in the championship game that season— the one he put into sudden-death overtime.

In the dusk at Yankee Stadium, the scoreboard clock blinked 1:56—one minute and fifty-six seconds to play. Not much time. Perhaps not enough time for the Colts, who were losing, 17–14.

After having forced the Giants to punt, the Colts had the ball on their own 14-yard line. But they had to get close enough to kick a tying field goal in order to force sudden-death overtime. As the Colt offense trotted onto the field, Unitas hunched into the huddle.

"Unless the clock is stopped," he said, "we won't have time for any more huddles. Stay alert. I'll call the plays at the line of scrimmage."

Unitas threw a pass to halfback Lenny Moore for an 11-yard gain; then he completed another pass to wide receiver Raymond Berry, a 25-yard gain to midfield. Quickly he hit Berry again at the Giants' 35-yard line, then found him at the 13-yard line. With the clock flashing the final seconds, Steve Myhra, the Colts' placekicker, hurried onto the field. Quickly he booted a 20-yard field goal with seven seconds remaining, to tie the score at 17–17.

In overtime the Giants won the toss and elected to receive the kickoff. But the Colt defense forced a punt.

Starting at their own 20, the Colts marched deep into Giant territory. On a second down at the 8-yard line, Unitas called a daring play—a sideline pass to tight end Jim Mutscheller that, had a Giant intercepted, might have backfired into a Giant touchdown. Instead

Alan Ameche scoring the sudden-death touchdown in the 1958 NFL championship game

the cool crew-cut quarterback hit Mutscheller at the 1-yard line. On third down, fullback Alan Ameche blasted into the end zone. The Colts had won, 23–17.

"That pass to Mutscheller," Unitas was asked later, "weren't you risking an interception?"

"When you know what you're doing," Unitas answered, smiling, "you don't get intercepted."

In completing 26 of 40 passes for 349 yards and 1 touchdown, Johnny U had put himself into NFL history. The following season he again led the Colts to the NFL title over the Giants in the championship game. He also set one of the NFL's most revered individual records—passing for at least 1 touchdown in 47 consecutive games, football's version of Joe DiMaggio's 56-game hitting streak in baseball. But even in losing those two championship games, the Giants, who had won the NFL title in 1956, were responsible for lifting pro football to the equal of major league baseball in the hearts of many American sports followers.

In those years the Giants had several storied players—Frank Gifford and Alex Webster at running back, Charlie Conerly at quarterback, Kyle Rote at wide receiver, Andy Robustelli at defensive end, Sam Huff at middle linebacker, Jim Patton at safety, and Pat Summerall as their placekicker.

Jim Lee Howell, a tall friendly man who had once been a Giant end, was the head coach of those teams. In his quiet way Howell preferred to give credit for the team's success to two of his assistant coaches who would soon be much more famous. Vince Lombardi was in charge of the offense, Tom Landry in charge of the defense. Both would leave the Giants for the opportunity to be a head coach—Lombardi, in 1959, to go with the Green Bay Packers; Landry, in 1960, going with the Dallas Cowboys, an expansion team.

The NFL had come of age. But its success had inspired the creation of a new rival, the American Football League, which eventually would make the NFL itself bigger and better.

VINCE LOMBARDI AND JOE NAMATH

IN THE YEARS WHEN VINCE LOMBARDI WAS DRIVING THE Green Bay Packers to five NFL championships in seven seasons (including victories in the first two Super Bowl games), he quickly was described as a legend. But whenever the Packers' coach heard or read that, he shook his head.

"I'm not a legend," he said once. "You have to be Halas to be a legend. George Halas is seventy-four years old, and he's done something for the game. I'm not a legend."

Lombardi is a legend now. He's also a yardstick by which all current coaches are measured, especially Packer coaches. Bart Starr, his Hall of Fame quarterback, took over as the Packer coach in 1975 but in nine seasons had only moderate success. Starr was followed in 1984 by another Lombardi disciple, Forrest Gregg, a Hall of Fame offensive tackle and, later, by Mike Holmeren, the coach of the Super Bowl XXXI champions. Each had the same burden—to turn the Packers into champions again, as Lombardi had. Lombardi arrived at Green Bay in 1959, after the Packers had won only one game the previous season. Gregg had been on that team, mostly as a substitute.

"I almost quit at the end of that 1958 season," Gregg later acknowledged. "I was not about to stick around if this new guy kept the old system. But the first day of training camp, Vince Lombardi sold me on his system."

That first day one of the Packers' pass receivers did not run a pattern precisely. He was twenty yards downfield when Lombardi began shouting at him. And the coach continued to shout until the player had returned to the huddle for the next play. Watching the scene,

Gregg realized that under Lombardi none of the Packers would be able to get by with a halfhearted effort, as that pass receiver so often had the previous season.

"The year before," Gregg recalled, "nothing had ever been said to that player by any coach, no matter how much he loafed. That sold me on Lombardi; this was the kind of coach I wanted."

Lombardi was the kind of coach all the Packers wanted, at least when they look back now on their glory years with one of the most dominant teams in NFL history. Perhaps the finest tribute to what Lombardi accomplished for those Packers is that ten of them are in the Pro Football Hall of Fame—Starr, Gregg, running backs Jim Taylor and Paul Hornung, center Jim Ringo, middle linebacker Ray Nitschke, defensive end Willie Davis, defensive tackle Henry Jordan, cornerback Herb Adderley, and safety Willie Wood.

Quite significantly, six of those Hall of Famers (Starr, Gregg, Taylor, Hornung, Ringo, and Nitschke) were on the Packers before Lombardi arrived. But under his coaching they fulfilled their potential, if not exceeded it, while contributing to five championship teams: 1961, 1962, 1965, 1966, and 1967.

Vince Lombardi rides the Packers' 1961 title.

Through the years the Packers have won more NFL titles, twelve, than any other team. But until Lombardi arrived, the Packers had not won a title since 1944; as one of the NFL's original "town teams," they had won the championship in 1936 and 1939, and had been awarded the title in 1929, 1930, and 1931. During that era their coach was Earl (Curly) Lambeau, one of the franchise's founders on August 11, 1919, at a meeting in the *Green Bay Press-Gazette*'s dingy editorial room. At the time Lambeau, who would be the team's coach through 1949, was also working for the Indian Packing Company, which he persuaded to pay for the team's uniforms. Hence the Packers' name, even though that firm soon went out of business.

In their first season the Packers had a 10-1 record against teams from other Wisconsin and Michigan towns. By 1921 the Packers joined the NFL for its first season, losing to the Chicago Bears, 20–0, in the start of what would be the NFL's most enduring rivalry.

Within a decade the Packers were awarded their first of three consecutive NFL titles with such Hall of Fame players as halfback Johnny McNally (also known as Johnny Blood), quarterback Arnie Herber, tackle Cal Hubbard, and guard Mike Michalske. But the club, which had survived financial troubles in 1922, nearly folded when a spectator won a five-thousand-dollar court verdict after falling out of the stands. Green Bay businessmen saved the franchise for end Don Hutson, who had been an All-America end at Alabama, to lead it to NFL championships in 1936, 1939, and 1944.

But by 1958 the Packers had dwindled into one of the NFL's worst teams. They were searching for a man to take command not only of the team but also of the organization.

At the time Lombardi was the New York Giants' offensive coach. In college he had been a guard at Fordham, one of the "Seven Blocks of Granite" built in 1937 by Frank Leahy, then an assistant coach there. The other linemen were Leo Paquin, Ed Franco, Nat Pierce, Alex Wojciechowicz (later a Hall of Fame center and linebacker for the Philadelphia Eagles), Al Barbartsky, and Johnny Druze.

Lombardi's coaching career began at St. Cecilia's High School in Englewood, New Jersey, where he won six state titles. He then joined Colonel Red Blaik's staff at Army before being hired by the Giants in 1954.

After five years as a Giant assistant under Jim Lee Howell, the then forty-five-year-old Lombardi enjoyed the challenge of trying to turn the Packers into a contender, if not preserving a franchise that might be moved to another city if the team did not succeed quickly. In his first game, the Packers upset the rival Bears, 9–6. When the season ended, the Packers had a respectable 7-5 record, the first time they had finished above .500 since 1947. Most of the players were holdovers from the previous season, when the Packers had a 1-10-1 record, the worst in the NFL. The difference obviously was Lombardi's coaching.

"I demand a commitment to excellence and to victory," Lombardi once said, "and that is what life is all about."

Although his Packer players didn't always appreciate Lombardi's "commitment to excellence" during their punishing practice sessions, they cherished the victories that his repetition of practice plays created. To their coach, once a Latin teacher at St. Cecilia's, coaching was teaching. And in teaching, repetition is necessary until the students absorb the lesson. Lombardi applied that teaching philosophy to football.

"Do it again," he would say after a play in practice. "Do it again until we get it right."

Of all the plays that the Packers did, again and again, the "sweep" was Lombardi's favorite. In the sweep the two guards, Jerry Kramer and Fuzzy Thurston, pulled out of the line and led the blocking around end for halfback Paul Hornung, who also was following another blocker, fullback Jim Taylor.

That sweep had been in coaches' playbooks for decades. But as the Packers rolled to one championship after another, it became known as the Green Bay Sweep, the trademark of Lombardi's teams.

Jim Taylor gallops behind Jerry Kramer (64) and Fuzzy Thurston (63), following a handoff from quarterback Bart Starr (15).

Hornung, called "Golden Boy" because of his blond curly hair, had been the 1956 Heisman Trophy winner as a Notre Dame quarterback. With the Packers he started out as a quarterback. But when Lombardi arrived in Green Bay, he switched Hornung to halfback and depended on Starr at quarterback.

The NFL-AFL Merger

Following the Packers' NFL championship in 1965, the NFL agreed to an eventual total merger with the American Football League. In the process, Super Bowl I was created—the first meeting of the NFL and AFL champions.

The AFL had begun play as a rival league in 1960 in eight cities— New York, Boston, Buffalo, Dallas, Houston, Denver, Oakland, and Los Angeles—but within three years, two teams had been trans-

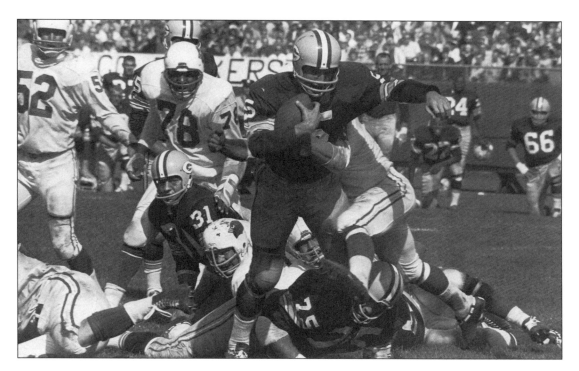

planted. The Chargers went from Los Angeles to San Diego; the Dallas Texans moved to Kansas City and were renamed the Chiefs. Then, in 1966, the Miami Dolphins were organized; in 1968 the Cincinnati Bengals would be added. The AFL teams also were competing with the NFL teams for the best college talent.

As the salaries and bonuses soared higher and higher, club owners in both leagues agreed to merge the teams into one NFL, which would begin with the 1970 season. But until then, they would play the Super Bowl and work together on a common draft of college players.

The first Super Bowl was played on January 15, 1967, as the finale of the 1966 season. As NFL champions again, the Packers opposed the Kansas City Chiefs, who had won the AFL title, at the Los Angeles Coliseum. In the days prior to that long-awaited confrontation,

Lombardi was obviously much more tense than he had been for any other game as the Packers' coach.

"You're not only representing the Green Bay Packers," he told his players, "but the entire National Football League."

After struggling to a 14–10 lead at halftime, the Packers exploded for a 35–10 victory. Starr completed 16 of 23 passes for 260 yards. Max McGee, a longtime Packer wide receiver, came off the bench to replace Boyd Dowler, injured early in the game. McGee, who had caught only 3 passes all season, grabbed 7 for 138 yards and 2 touchdowns. Early in the second half, safety Willie Wood intercepted one of Len Dawson's passes to set up the Packer touchdown that broke the game open.

During the postgame interview Lombardi was asked to compare the Chiefs with other NFL teams.

"The Chiefs are a good team," he finally blurted, "but they don't compare with the top teams in the NFL. Dallas is a better team. Four or five NFL teams could have beaten the Chiefs...."

But later Lombardi was disturbed that he had been that blunt about the Chiefs in comparing them with NFL teams. "I wish I could get my words back," he said. "It was the wrong thing to say, the wrong thing. I came off as an ungracious winner."

The next year the Packers won Super Bowl II, 33–14, over the Oakland Raiders. It would be Lombardi's last game as their coach. Two weeks earlier the Packers had won what is now known as the National Football Conference title for the third consecutive year. In the final seconds of a game played in thirteen-degree-below-zero weather at Lambeau Field in Green Bay, the Packers had edged the Cowboys, 21–17, in the final seconds when Starr barged into the end zone from the 1-yard line behind Jerry Kramer's block.

During the Packers' last time-out Lombardi had chosen to go for the touchdown and victory rather than try for a point-blank field goal that would have forced sudden-death overtime.

"If you can't run the ball in there in a moment of crisis like that,"

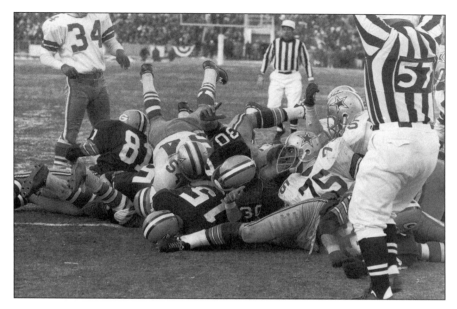

Bart Starr (15) puts the Packers into Super Bowl II behind Jerry Kramer's block in the final seconds of the 1967 NFL championship game.

Lombardi said, "you don't deserve to win. These decisions don't come from the mind, they come from the gut."

His decision to leave the sideline and concentrate on his role as the Packers' general manager came from the gut, too. But shortly after the 1968 season ended, with the Packers having slipped under coach Phil Bengtson to a 6-7-1 record, Lombardi moved to Washington as the Redskins' part-owner, executive vice president, and coach.

"I miss the fire on Sunday," he explained.

By that Lombardi meant that he had missed the thrill of the game that a coach has. In his first season with the Redskins, he lifted them to a 7-5-2 record. But in the months that followed, he was stricken with cancer. Unable even to attend training camp, he died on September 3, 1970, shortly before the season was to open. But to the end he never changed.

"Once when I visited him, my hair had gotten pretty long," Hornung later recalled. "He called me near the bed and he said, 'Hey, get a haircut.'"

The $427,000 Contract

By then a shaggy-haired quarterback, Joe Namath of the New York Jets, had taken over the Super Bowl stage. The Jets, originally known as the Titans, were one of the AFL's charter franchises in 1960. But with an underfinanced owner, Harry Wismer, the Titans struggled. Before the 1963 season the club was purchased by a group headed by Sonny Werblin, a show business impresario. Werblin hired Weeb Ewbank as coach, the team's name was changed to the Jets, and they moved into the brand-new Shea Stadium in 1964. Then Werblin really created headlines.

Jets quarterback Joe Namath established the AFL's credibility.

Outbidding the St. Louis Cardinals of the NFL, the Jets signed Namath, who grew up in Beaver Falls, Pennsylvania, and had been a quarterback at Alabama, to a $427,000 contract. That was a dazzling amount of money at the time, especially for a rookie who needed a knee operation.

Not that Namath considered himself to be a risk. When he arrived in New York for the operation, he attended an informal get-together that Werblin had arranged with several New York sportswriters. Just stop by, Werblin told them, meet the $427,000 quarterback, and maybe ask him a question. One sportswriter did.

"Joe," he said, "suppose you don't make it—what happens to the money?"

Namath stared straight at the sportswriter and replied firmly, "I'll make it."

Namath made it. In his third season, 1967, he was the first passer in pro football history to throw for more than 4,000 yards. To be exact, his total was 4,007 yards. At the time skeptics thought that Namath was merely a product of the AFL, that he really wasn't good enough to make it big in the NFL, but Vince Lombardi was not among the skeptics.

"Joe Namath," said Lombardi early in 1968, "is an almost perfect passer."

When the Jets qualified for Super Bowl III against the Baltimore Colts, skeptics still doubted Namath's skill. But he didn't doubt it. In the days before that game, he insisted that the upstart AFL had more good quarterbacks than the NFL establishment did.

"We've got better quarterbacks in our league," he said. "John Hadl [San Diego Chargers], Daryle Lamonica [Oakland Raiders], myself, and Bob Griese [Miami Dolphins]."

Namath also put down Earl Morrall, who had been the Colts' quarterback in the absence of the injured Johnny Unitas, thereby annoying Colts' coach Don Shula and his entire squad. On the Thursday night before Super Bowl III, while accepting a Miami Touchdown Club award as pro football's outstanding player that season, Namath made a short

Joe Namath was called "an almost perfect passer" by Vince Lombardi.

speech. In it he talked about the upcoming Super Bowl.

"We're going to win Sunday," he said. "I'll guarantee you."

In the game on Sunday, he made good his guarantee. The Jets won, 16–7, astonishing not only the Colts but also the entire NFL establishment.

"We showed a lot of people they were wrong," Namath said in the locker room. "Beautiful."

The next year the Kansas City Chiefs stunned the Minnesota Vikings, 23–7, in Super Bowl IV. Suddenly the AFL and the NFL were tied two apiece in the four Super Bowl games as they awaited the 1970 season. The twenty-six teams would then be realigned into two thirteen-team conferences, the NFC and the AFC, each with three divisions. The merger was complete. In the process Joe Namath had emerged as one of the most controversial players in football history, and Vince Lombardi had emerged as a legend.

THE SUPER BOWL AND JOE MONTANA

FOR ALL THE MILLIONS OF DOLLARS THAT MANY OF THEM make, athletes in every sport yearn for the ring that symbolizes a championship. "My career won't be complete," each will say, "unless I get the ring."

The ring is usually huge, with clusters of diamonds. But money can't buy one. Only a championship can. More than any other sports event, the Super Bowl created the obsession with winning the ring. And as the twenty-first century approaches, the ring symbolizes the Super Bowl's maturity into the most spectacular one-day annual event in sports, dwarfing a World Series or NBA Finals game.

Super Bowl Sunday is virtually a national holiday. Highways, department stores, and theaters are empty, but pizza parlors are swamped with take-out orders for house parties. More than 138 million people, a record for any type of television program, watched at least a portion of Super Bowl XXX on January 28, 1996. Six other Super Bowl games are among the ten most-watched programs in television history.

The Super Bowl championship team—such as the Green Bay Packers with Brett Favre and Reggie White, the San Francisco 49ers with Joe Montana, and the Dallas Cowboys with Troy Aikman and Emmitt Smith—reigns as America's team. Its popularity even has college football, which has resisted a championship playoff for years, organizing a confrontation between the No. 1 and No. 2 ranked teams in a postseason bowl game.

College football, after all, is still where the NFL gets its players. Teams and athletes representing Nebraska, Miami, Penn State, Florida

State, Notre Dame, and Florida kept winning mythical national titles as well as the Heisman Trophy and All-America honors, but many other players emerged from small colleges, such as Grambling, whose coach, Eddie Robinson, surpassed Paul (Bear) Bryant's record of 323 victories.

"Game Plan for Your Life"

Once a small black college known as Louisiana Negro Normal and Industrial Institute, dedicated to farming, Grambling is now a sprawling university, but it's perhaps best known for Robinson's development of more than two hundred players for the NFL, notably Hall of Famers Willie Davis, Willie Brown, and Buck Buchanan, along with Doug Williams, the Washington Redskins' quarterback in their Super Bowl XXII triumph. With a record of 405-157-15 prior to his farewell 1997 season, Robinson is remembered for more than football.

"Eddie had a game plan for your life," said Paul (Tank) Younger, once a Rams' fullback, "not just for a Saturday."

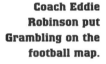

Coach Eddie Robinson put Grambling on the football map.

In his early years as the Grambling coach, Robinson mowed the grass on the football field, sewed torn uniforms, taped his players' ankles, and drilled the band that played at halftime. As the school grew, so did his staff and his facilities. But at six-thirty every morning he would go to the athletic dormitory and wake his players with a cowbell. Even those who didn't have early classes had to get up.

"This will give you extra time to tutor a teammate who needs it," he explained. "The smarter you are, the better example you make."

Robinson, who had majored in English literature at Leland College, a small Baptist school in Baker, Louisiana, often quoted Kipling, Longfellow, and Tennyson to his players. His aura transcended racial resentment. In 1985, shortly before his record 324th victory, a white man from Alabama arrived at his Grambling office.

"I loved Bear Bryant," the stranger said, "but if somebody has to break his record, I'm glad it's you. Because you're a real gentleman, sir."

Around that time, for the second time in a decade, a new pro league had challenged the NFL by competing for some of its players. The World Football League had tried in 1974 and failed. The United States Football League folded in 1986, but the birth of both leagues had been inspired by the NFL's success, particularly the growth of the Super Bowl into America's biggest sports spectacle, an achievement sparked primarily by six teams.

Those six teams won twenty-three of the first thirty-one Super Bowl games—five each by the 49ers and the Cowboys, four by the Pittsburgh Steelers, and three each by the Green Bay Packers, the Washington Redskins, and the Raiders of Oakland and Los Angeles.

The success of Super Bowl teams prompted a familiar question—are the players of today better than the players of the past? The usual answer is that today's players are bigger, stronger, and faster. Through the years the improvement in coaching techniques also has created a smarter player. But for all that, it is difficult to compare players or teams of different eras. Any player or any team can only truly be judged against its current competition and the standards of the time.

But to be considered among the best of any era, a player or a team must perform at a winning level consistently over a period of time.

The Steelers' Four Rings

For those reasons the Steelers of the seventies, with their four Super Bowl championships in six years, deserve to be rated among the best teams in football history.

The success of the Steelers had begun with the toss of a coin. In the NFL draft of college players each year, the first choice goes to the team that had the worst record the previous season. According to most NFL scouts in 1970, the first choice was obvious. It would be Terry Bradshaw, a husky quarterback out of a small college, Louisiana Tech, who resembled a blond Li'l Abner, the comic book character. But during the 1969 season, both the Steelers and the Bears had the worst record: 1 victory, 13 defeats. To determine the first choice in the draft, Commissioner Pete Rozelle tossed a coin.

The Steelers won the toss.

As a rookie Bradshaw struggled, as did the Steelers, a team that had struggled throughout its history. Of all the NFL owners, Art Rooney of the Steelers was perhaps the most beloved—also the most beleaguered. After the 1968 season he knew it was time to change coaches again. He hired Chuck Noll, once a guard for Paul Brown in Cleveland, at the time an assistant coach under Don Shula with the Colts.

In their first season under Noll, the Steelers had that 1-13 record. But in retrospect it enabled the Steelers to obtain the passer who would turn their franchise around.

By the 1972 season Bradshaw had not yet completely established himself as the Steeler quarterback, but he was on his way. He also was joined by Franco Harris, a rookie fullback from Penn State who would gallop through opposing defensive units for more than a decade. Harris's most memorable moment occurred as a rookie after he, Bradshaw, and defensive tackle Mean Joe Greene had helped put the Steelers in the NFL playoffs for the first time in their history.

In the opening playoff game against the Oakland Raiders at Three Rivers Stadium, the Steelers were losing, 7–6, with only twenty seconds remaining. On fourth down at their own 40-yard line, Bradshaw threw a desperation pass toward halfback John (Frenchy) Fuqua, who went up for the ball with Jack Tatum, a Raider safety. The ball rebounded to Harris, who caught it at his shoe tops and ran untouched into the end zone. Touchdown, and the Steelers won, 13–7.

Franco Harris runs toward his "immaculate reception" of Terry Bradshaw's pass deflected by the collision of Steeler halfback John (Frenchy) Fuqua and Raider safety Jack Tatum.

At the time the NFL rule was that a pass could not ricochet from one offensive player to another offensive player. But the officials ruled that the ball had rebounded off Tatum, not Fuqua.

Harris's catch was dubbed the "immaculate reception." It put the Steelers into the AFC championship game, which they lost to the Miami Dolphins. But two seasons later, on January 12, 1975, the Steelers won their first NFL title for Art Rooney, conquering the Minnesota Vikings,

16–6, in Super Bowl IX. They repeated the next year, 21–17, over the Dallas Cowboys as wide receiver Lynn Swann made several acrobatic catches, including one for a 64-yard touchdown.

Bradshaw, Harris, Swann, and their Steel Curtain defense also won Super Bowl XIII, 35–31, over the Cowboys and Super Bowl XIV, 31–19, over the Los Angeles Rams.

Roger Staubach and Tom Landry

Of the six teams that have dominated the Super Bowl, the Cowboys are the only one to have won it five times over a quarter of a century —with their teams of 1971, 1977, 1992, 1993, and 1995. Those early champions prompted the franchise to call itself "America's team," a phrase disputed by several NFL rivals. But for all the debate, the early Cowboys indeed were a popular team with a popular quarterback. Roger Staubach had joined the Cowboys after four years in the Navy, some of it in Vietnam as a supply officer. As a junior at the Naval Academy, he had won the Heisman Trophy in 1963. Eight seasons later he led the Cowboys to a 24–3 victory over the Dolphins in Super Bowl VI, completing 12 of 19 passes for 119 yards and 2 touchdowns. The next day he was awarded the keys to a new car by *Sport* magazine as the game's most valuable player. In his acceptance speech he displayed his sense of humor as well as his spiritual outlook.

"I enjoy my Christian ideals," he said. "I believe there's something greater than what we're here for."

Asked if there were zone defenses "up there," he laughed and replied, "From what I understand, every pass is a touchdown up there." Reminded that if you were a defensive back, every pass wouldn't be a touchdown, he smiled.

"Up there," he said, "they don't have any defensive backs."

Six years later, in Super Bowl XII after the 1977 season, Staubach guided the Cowboys to a 27–10 triumph over the Denver Broncos. Ironically the Broncos' quarterback, Craig Morton, had been

Roger Staubach of the Cowboys scrambles away from 49er tacklers in the 1971 NFC championship game.

Staubach's predecessor before Coach Tom Landry decided to go with the former naval officer with the quick arm, the quick feet, and the quick brain. As the Cowboys' coach since the team began operating in the 1960 season, Landry occasionally had been hounded by having to choose between two capable quarterbacks—Don Meredith and Morton in the late sixties, Morton and Staubach in the early seventies.

On the sideline in his snap-brim hat, Landry projected a sense of calm leadership that reflected his complete absorption in the game until his unceremonious dismissal early in 1989 by the Cowboys' new owner, Jerry Jones.

"Leadership," said Landry, "is a matter of having people look at you and gain confidence, seeing how you react. If you're in control, they're in control. It's not that I'm unemotional or computerized. But as a coach I seldom see a play as others do. If it's a pass play, I'm trying to read the opposing team's pass defense. I usually don't even see

Tom Landry's leadership philosophy: "Having people look at you and gain confidence"

the ball in the air. If it's a running play, I'm looking at the point of attack where the key block is. I have to know whether a play broke down because of our blocking or because the other team changed its defense. If you were to see me as a cheerleader, that would mean I was only watching instead of thinking."

His players treated Landry with fond respect, knowing that a mistake would provoke the coach's famous stare, whether in practice or a game.

"One time I messed up an assignment," safety Cliff Harris once confessed. "I could feel his eyes on me like a ray gun from fifty yards away."

Of all Landry's running backs, Tony Dorsett developed into the most dependable as well as the most gifted. But as a rookie who had won the Heisman Trophy at Pitt, he did not open the 1977 season as a starter. Realizing that Dorsett was annoyed, Landry called him aside and explained that a Cowboy rookie had to know the team's complex offensive system completely before being trusted as a starter, especially as a pass receiver.

"I realize that, coach," Dorsett said, "but I can catch 'em on Sunday."

"First," the coach said softly, "you've got to catch 'em in practice."

Landry did what no other coach has done—win the Super Bowl six years apart with two virtually different teams. Other coaches whose teams won the Super Bowl more than once have done it mostly with the same players. The distinction of winning the Super Bowl to complete a perfect season is held by only one coach. Under the firm gaze of Don Shula, the Miami Dolphins swept through the 1972 season with a 17-0 record, finishing with a 14—7 victory over the

Washington Redskins in Super Bowl VII. The next year the Dolphins repeated in Super Bowl VIII, 24–7, over the Vikings.

Don Shula's 347 Victories

In assessing the NFL coaches of the modern era, John Madden, himself the coach of the Super Bowl XI champion Oakland Raiders and later a television analyst, chose Shula as the best.

"Shula has won with different teams in different cities," Madden said. "He won in Baltimore with Johnny Unitas at quarterback, and he won there with Earl Morrall at quarterback when Unitas was hurt. Then he took over a team in Miami that had Larry Csonka and Bob Griese and he won the Super Bowl twice. Then he developed a completely different team in 1982 that lost, 27–17, to the Washington Redskins in Super Bowl XVII with David Woodley at quarterback. Then he inserted Dan Marino at quarterback the next year."

Csonka, the Nagurski-like fullback of the Dolphins' two Super Bowl champions, remembered Shula's arrival at Miami in 1970 when a labor dispute delayed the opening of the NFL training camps.

"When we finally got to camp," Csonka said, "Shula told us, 'We've got to make up for lost time. We're going to have four workouts a day.' We had two in the morning at eight and eleven, another in the after-

Tony Dorsett of the Cowboys was a Heisman Trophy winner at Pitt.

noon at two, another at seven at night until the sun went down. Sometimes we even kept practicing in the dark until he was happy. No other team in pro football ever had four workouts a day before or since."

In one of those workouts, Csonka was lined up as a dummy blocker for Griese in a passing drill.

Suddenly the big fullback heard Shula shouting at him from forty yards away. "Csonka," the coach was yelling, "what are you doing?"

At first Csonka had no idea why the coach was shouting at him. But in another moment he knew.

"You lined up a step too wide," Shula yelled. "If a linebacker had been coming, you'd have been too far out to block him."

The day Don Shula broke George Halas's record for NFL victories

Thinking back to that moment, Csonka once said, "Right then I knew I'd better concentrate every second." That's the type of concentration Shula demanded, the type that produced that perfect season.

In addition to Csonka and Griese, the 1972 Dolphin team alternated Jim Kiick and Eugene (Mercury) Morris at halfback, had Paul Warfield at wide receiver, and had what was nicknamed its "No Name" defensive unit, even though it had two All-Pro performers: middle linebacker Nick Buoniconti and safety Dick Anderson. But even when the unbeaten Dolphins were preparing for the Super Bowl game, Shula didn't let them lose their concentration.

"All those games we've won," he told his players, "they won't mean anything if we lose this game."

The Dolphins won and were champions again the next year. Don Shula had established himself as one of the NFL's best coaches. O. A. (Bum) Phillips, then the coach of the Houston Oilers, put Shula's skill in its proper perspective.

"Shula can take his'n and beat your'n," Phillips said in his Texas twang, "or he can take your'n and beat his'n."

When Shula retired as the Dolphins' coach after the 1995 season, his 347 victories (including 19 in the postseason) had established a NFL record, surpassing George Halas's 324 with the Bears.

"How 'Bout Them Cowboys?"

Shula's successor with the Dolphins was Jimmy Johnson, who had coached the Cowboys in their Super Bowl XXVII and XXVIII victories over the Buffalo Bills. Johnson, who had also coached the University of Miami to two national college championships, had joined the Cowboys in 1989, when Jerry Jones, his former University of Arkansas teammate and roommate, purchased the Dallas franchise.

In Johnson's first season the Cowboys had a dismal 1-15 record, but he quietly was building a winner.

He drafted quarterback Troy Aikman, the No. 1 choice for that 1989 season, and in 1990 he selected running back Emmitt Smith. He also swung a deal to obtain defensive end Charles Haley from the 49ers. By the 1992 season Johnson, wisely using draft choices acquired from the Vikings in a trade for running back Herschel Walker, had the Cowboys ready to roll to consecutive Super Bowl titles.

"How 'bout them Cowboys?" Johnson liked to shout.

After a personality clash with Jones early in 1994, Johnson departed. Jones quickly hired Barry Switzer, once the University of Oklahoma coach. Johnson worked for two years as a studio television analyst for the Fox network, which had outbid CBS for the National Conference games with a record $1.58 billion over four years—more proof of pro football's popularity, which had blossomed during Pete Rozelle's reign as commissioner.

When Shula decided to stop coaching the Dolphins, Johnson took over, returning to the Miami area two weeks before the Cowboys won Super Bowl XXX, their first with Switzer as coach and their fifth overall, matching the 49ers' total.

By then pro football was learning to live with two new developments in its structure: free agents and a salary cap. Once a player's contract was up, he was free to move from one team to another, and a team's total player payroll was not allowed to exceed a certain ceiling—$41.6 million, for example, in 1996. It also was learning to live with restless owners, who were moving teams to other markets—the Rams to St. Louis from Anaheim, the Browns (renamed the Ravens) to Baltimore from Cleveland, the Oilers to Nashville from Houston, and the three-time Super Bowl champion Raiders back to Oakland from Los Angeles, where they had resided after a federal jury had granted a move from Oakland in 1982 without NFL approval.

Jerry Jones, the Cowboys' owner, had circumvented the salary cap in 1995 by paying large signing bonuses, which for salary cap terms were prorated over the length of the contract, notably a $13 million bonus to cornerback Deion Sanders in a seven-year, $35 million deal.

Sanders helped the Cowboys win Super Bowl XXX, 27–17, over the Pittsburgh Steelers, just as he had helped the 49ers win their fifth Super Bowl the year before. In the 49ers' 49–26 rout of the Chargers, quarterback Steve Young threw a record six touchdown passes, including three to wide receiver Jerry Rice.

Young, who had been playing in the shadow left by Joe Montana, maintained the 49er reign that developed after Bill Walsh arrived as coach in 1979.

As the 49ers won their first four Super Bowls, Montana was chosen as the game's most valuable player three times. After defeating the Cincinnati Bengals, 26–21, at the Pontiac (Michigan) Silverdome in Super Bowl XVI, the 49ers returned three years later and dominated the Dolphins, 38–16, at Palo Alto, California. Over the next three seasons the Chicago Bears and the New York Giants earned Super Bowl rings for the first time, and the Redskins for the third time.

But then Montana guided the 49ers to two more titles. His 10-yard touchdown pass to John Taylor in the waning seconds at Joe Robbie Stadium in Miami created a 20–16 comeback victory over the Bengals in Super Bowl XXIII, and his five touchdown passes riddled the Denver Broncos, 55–10, in Super Bowl XXIV.

Bill Walsh's Sculptures

With his success and flair for the dramatic, Montana was touted as arguably the best quarterback in history, while the 49er coach in three of those triumphs, Bill Walsh, earned his niche among the best coaches.

The slim, silver-haired Walsh was known as a sculptor of quarterbacks. In a decade as an assistant coach with the Bengals and Chargers, he developed Ken Anderson and Dan Fouts; in his two years as head coach at Stanford University, he polished both Guy Benjamin and Steve Dils into the nation's leading college passers; when he took command of the 49ers in 1978, his offense enabled Steve DeBerg to complete 347 passes, a NFL record since surpassed by Warren Moon, Drew Bledsoe, and Dan Marino. Halfway through the 1980 seasons Walsh decided that Montana was his new quarterback.

"Joe is the quarterback of the future," Walsh said the next year. "He's got a fine arm and he's got the quickness of feet that Joe Namath had."

Montana fulfilled Walsh's prophecy. But just as he was credited by Walsh for having the intelligence and the athletic ability that enabled him to accomplish what he did, the former Notre Dame quarterback credited the 49er coach with having brought out the best in him.

"If something goes wrong," Montana once said, "the coach

Joe Montana

tells me right there on the sideline what I should've done. I don't always agree, but when I see the films, I realize he was right. He's always right."

The best coaches usually are. After Walsh left the 49ers for the television booth, one of his assistants, George Seifert, took over as head coach and charted the record 55–10 rout of the Broncos for the 49ers' fourth Super Bowl ring. But just when the 49ers were dreaming of a third consecutive title, the Giants stunned them, 15–13, in the National Conference championship game on Matt Bahr's 42-yard field goal as time expired. The Giants prevailed, 20–19, in Super Bowl XXV when a 47-yard field-goal attempt by Scott Norwood of the Buffalo Bills drifted wide as time expired. With two Super Bowl rings in five seasons, Bill Parcells was considered the best coach in the long history of that flagship franchise before he suddenly resigned in 1991. But his legacy lingers.

"Give 'em a good design," Parcells liked to say, meaning the game plan, "and get 'em to play hard."

It sounds simple, but that philosophy also has been true of Bill Walsh and Don Shula, just as it was true of Amos Alonzo Stagg and Knute Rockne so many years ago. As football approaches the twenty-first century, it indeed has changed from 1869, when Rutgers and Princeton played that first game. But in the sense that the best teams were those with the best coaches and the best players, football has hardly changed at all.

On their way to the Pro Football Hall of Fame were some of the best players, notably wide receiver Jerry Rice, running backs Emmitt Smith and Barry Sanders, quarterbacks Troy Aikman and Steve Young, defensive ends Reggie White and Bruce Smith, and defensive back Rod Woodson, in addition to Joe Montana and Lawrence Taylor.

"The players," said television analyst John Madden, "make the game."

part **TWO**

"EIGHT YARDS MIGHT NOT SEEM LIKE MUCH"

TO UNDERSTAND WHAT IT'S LIKE TO BE A RUNNING BACK, listen to Larry Csonka, who has explained it as well as anyone ever has.

"To gain 8 yards might not seem like much," he once said, "until you put eleven defensive players in those 8 yards."

Big Zonk, as he was known, was the 240-pound fullback on the 1972 Miami Dolphins who won Super Bowl VII to complete a perfect 17-0 record. But at any level of football competition, 8 yards on a running play represents a sub-

In nine seasons, Jim Brown rushed an average of 104 yards per game.

stantial gain. For all the emphasis today on passing, running (or rushing, as the statisticians prefer to describe it) is considered by many coaches to be even more important to a team's offense.

In order for a passing attack to succeed, a team usually must "establish," as coaches like to say, its running game. Without an effective running game, it's easier for an opposing team to gear its defense to stop the pass.

Even though Walter Payton has surpassed Jim Brown's career total of 12,312 rushing yards in NFL regular-season competition, the onetime Cleveland Browns'

fullback remains the standard by whom all ballcarriers are measured. Although Brown stopped playing in 1965 after only nine seasons so he could pursue a career as a motion picture actor, he set three of the most significant NFL records—126 touchdowns, a 5.22-yard average per rush, and a 104.3-yard average per game. Most running backs never have a 100-yard game, but Jim Brown *averaged* more than 100 yards per game throughout his career. He also *averaged* more than 5 yards per carry.

With a 6-2, 228-pound physique that tapered to a thirty-two-inch waist, Brown blended power and speed as no other running back ever has. When a yard or two was needed for a first down, he would blast through the middle of the line. If he suddenly had some room beyond the line of scrimmage, he would take off for a long gain, often outrunning some defensive backs. From the time he joined the Browns out of Syracuse University in 1957, he was the backbone of the Brown's offense for nine seasons—so much so that the Cleveland coach, Paul Brown, occasionally was criticized for using him too much.

"But when you have a cannon," the coach said, "you shoot it."

Despite his heavy-duty role, Jim Brown never missed a game because of injury. If anything, he seemed to inflict more punishment on tacklers than he received.

"All you can do," Sam Huff, the Giants' middle linebacker, once said, "is grab him, hold on, and wait for help."

"God's Halfback"

That same feeling has been shared by tacklers trying to stop Walter Payton, the Chicago Bears' running back. Over his thirteen seasons, Payton rushed for a record 16,726 yards, a tribute not only to his development of his gifts as a runner but also to his dedication to conditioning his body. In the off-season, he worked out as much as six or seven hours a day to keep himself strong, especially his legs.

"When I don't work out, I get bored, restless, and lazy," he said.

"I lose my edge, and that's one thing I can't afford to lose."

Payton's continual workouts hardened his 5-11, 202-pound physique into what appeared to be a statue of what the perfectly proportioned athlete should look like. Fred O'Connor, a Bears' assistant coach, once described Payton's physique.

"God must've taken a chisel," O'Connor said, "and decided, 'I'm going to make a halfback.'"

During his career at Jackson (Mississippi) State, a predominantly black school, Payton scored 464 points. In addition to his 65 touchdowns, he kicked 5 field goals and 59 extra points. He rushed for 3,563 yards, caught 27 passes for another 474 yards, completed 14 of 19 passes for 4 touchdowns, averaged 43 yards on kickoff returns, and punted for a 39-yard average. For all that, he received little national publicity, and as a senior finished a distant twelfth in the Heisman Trophy voting. But the NFL scouts knew all about him. He was signed by the Bears and began playing for them in the 1975 season.

"When I came into the NFL, on a scale of one to ten, I was only a five," Payton said during the 1981 season. "Now, maybe because of experience and all that, maybe I've become an eight."

Payton was underestimating himself. Like most running backs, he knew he couldn't do much without good blocking. But once sprung beyond the line of scrimmage, he had the speed and the strength to dazzle defensive backs. In a tough 10–7 victory over the Vikings

Walter Payton of the Bears broke Jim Brown's career rushing record.

in 1977, he piled up 275 yards for an NFL single-game record.

"They opened the holes," Payton said of his blockers after that game, "and I just ran."

In a sense that's true. The best running backs operate mostly on instinct. In taking a handoff or a pitchout from the quarterback, a running back peers out from under his helmet to see if his blockers are creating a hole in the line for him according to the design of the play—the point of attack, as coaches call it. If that hole is there, he will run through it, then look to see where the linebackers and defensive backs are. By now the running back is no longer thinking. Instead he is reacting to what's in front of him—darting one way, dodging another.

No Time to Think

"You don't have time to think things out when you're running, you just do it," Franco Harris has said. "If you stop to think, it's usually too late to do anything."

Harris rushed for 12,120 regular-season yards. But counting post-season competition, the fullback on the Steelers' four Super Bowl championship teams had 13,676 yards. In his nineteen playoff, championship, and Super Bowl games, he rushed for a total of 1,556 yards. If a yard is a yard is a yard, in the postseason as well as the regular season, Harris was responsible for 16,700 yards in what is known as all-purpose yardage, including 2,791 as a pass receiver and 233 early in his career on kickoff returns.

Harris grew up in Mount Holly, New Jersey, not far from Fort Dix, where his father was stationed as an Army sergeant. His father had met his mother during World War II in Italy, where she lived. Because of his mother's Italian ancestry, Harris inspired Pittsburgh fans to organize "Franco's Italian Army" during his rookie season in 1972. He endured as one of the Steelers' most popular players for more than a decade.

As a runner, Harris, a first-round draft choice out of Penn State, had a tiptoe style, unusual for a fullback. Instead of slamming at the line, as most fullbacks do, the 6-2, 225-pound Harris often changed direction. Sometimes he seemed to run sideways until he found room to run. That style helped him score 100 regular-season touchdowns.

Harris's style is added proof that the best running backs are born, not made.

"With a runner," says John Robinson, the former Rams' coach, "you can really hurt him when you begin to coach him where to run. To be a good runner, he's got to be able to do things you can't coach. That's why a good running back can play well as a rookie in the NFL right away; he doesn't have to learn that much like a quarterback does. With a good running back, all he really has to do is carry the ball. His instincts do the rest."

When Eric Dickerson joined the Rams in 1983 out of Southern Methodist, he blended his instincts with Robinson's offense for 1,808 rushing yards, a record for an NFL rookie. Tall, fast, and strong at 6-3 and 220 pounds, he lifted the Rams into the playoffs the next year with 2,105 yards, breaking the record of 2,003, set by O. J. Simpson with the Buffalo Bills in 1973. Over his career Dickerson rushed for 13,259 yards, second to Payton on the all-time list.

Determination at 5-9 and 5-8

But two shorter running backs, Emmitt Smith and Barry Sanders, have shown that determination can be as important as instinct. Smith is 5-9 and 209 pounds, Sanders 5-8 and 203 pounds.

Smith was an All-America at Florida, but the Cowboys got him with the seventeenth choice in the first round of the 1990 draft.

"There were all these people saying, 'He's too slow,' or 'He's too small,'" said Jimmy Johnson, the Cowboys' coach then. "All I know is, every time I saw a film of him, he was running 50, 60, 70, 80 yards for a touchdown. That looked pretty good to me."

In helping the Cowboys win three Super Bowl titles in his first six seasons, Smith led the NFL in rushing four times while joining Jim Brown as the only running backs with six consecutive seasons with at least 10 touchdowns at the start of their careers. And in 1996 he completed his degree in therapeutic recreation at the University of Florida.

"We had a deal," his mother, Mary, said. "When Emmitt left college at the end of his junior year to join the Cowboys, we agreed that he wasn't going to buy a house until he went back and completed college. It's like I always told him, 'How can you go around telling kids to stay in school if you didn't stay yourself?' You have to do what you preach."

Emmitt Smith escapes from a Buffalo Bill defender during Super Bowl XXVIII.

That determination to get his college degree reflected his determination as a running back.

"Emmitt has great vision and balance and intelligence and all of those things," said Nate Newton, the Cowboys' 330-pound guard. "But most of all, Emmitt has great will."

That will was apparent in the 1993 season finale against the Giants in a game for the NFC East title.

The winner would earn a bye in the first week of the playoffs; the loser would be a wild-card team. Late in the first half Smith suffered a separation of his right shoulder, one of football's most painful injuries. Most players would not have returned to the game. He played not only the entire second half but also into overtime, when he positioned the field goal that decided the 16–13 victory.

"Run behind me and pick me up," he told Newton before the second half began. "I don't want to lay on the ground."

For the game, Smith rushed for 168 yards and caught 10 passes for 61 yards, including an overall 72 yards after the injury.

"I never felt pain like that before," he said later. "I can't describe it to you. You have to be in my shoes or see the expression on my face to know what it's like."

Barry Sanders, having been voted the Heisman Trophy in 1988 while at Oklahoma State, joined the Detroit Lions with more headlines and more tributes.

Barry Switzer, then the Oklahoma coach, raved that Sanders was "so quick, he could fly through a keyhole." As a Lions' rookie he flew through tacklers, rushing for 1,470 yards, but disdained an opportunity to lead the NFL. In the final minutes of the season finale Coach Wayne Fontes told him, "You're 10 yards away from leading the league in rushing. Do you want to go in?"

"Coach," said Sanders, "let's just win it and go home."

The Lions won it, 31–24, as Sanders finished second to Christian Okoye's 1,480 yards for the Chiefs. He simply wasn't interested in an individual honor.

Barry Sanders fends off a Redskin tackler.

"When everyone is out for statistics, you know, individual fulfillment, that's when trouble starts," he said. "I don't ever want to fall victim to that."

He hasn't, but tacklers throughout the NFL have fallen victim to his ability to change direction.

"He's like a little sports car," said Trace Armstrong, a Dolphins' defensive end. "He can stop on a dime, then go from zero to sixty in seconds. His being short actually adds to his package because he's more difficult to find in the piles and more difficult to draw a bead on."

Kids Who Enjoy the Chase

In earlier years, several other running backs put together Hall of Fame yardage—John Riggins, Tony Dorsett, Earl Campbell, and Larry Csonka.

At his best, Csonka was a battering-ram fullback who enjoyed crashing into linemen and linebackers. He accumulated 8,081 yards, mostly with the Dolphins; his yardage with the Memphis Southmen of the World Football League is not counted by NFL statisticians. But just as Big Zonk defined running with his theory that "8 yards might not seem like much until you put eleven defensive players in those 8 yards," he also defined what it takes for someone to be a running back at heart, to have the makings of a running back.

"Running backs have to be big and strong," he once said, "but they also have to enjoy the chase, like kids do. If you were a kid who loved to have people chase you, you've got the beginnings of a running back. If you were scared of being chased, there's no way you could become one. It's an inner something that can't be changed. Show me a kid who's ten years old, and I'll tell you right away if he can be a running back. That doesn't mean he will be one, but I'll know if he's got the soul of a running back."

For a running back, whether he is in the NFL or is a youngster, the threat of a knee injury always lurks on the next play.

"Every running back," Csonka said, "is aware that he's running on ice. He never knows where the thin ice is, where the big injury is waiting for him. But inside himself a running back really believes that he can't be injured. He knows that he's going to have injuries, but

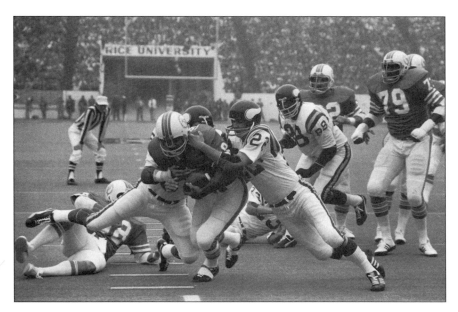

Larry Csonka slams through Viking tacklers in Super Bowl VIII.

never one that will really cripple him, never one that will finish him.

"As a kid I never thought about getting hurt. I ran through herds of cows. I ran through creeks. And if I fell down, I came up running. I never laid there moaning that I was hurt. When the other kids wouldn't run into the briar patch because they didn't want to get all scratched up, I never thought of being scratched up as being hurt."

Being hurt, according to Larry Csonka's philosophy, is the knee injury that shortened the career of halfback Gale Sayers.

As a Bears' rookie out of the University of Kansas in 1965, the 6-0, 200-pound Sayers was an instant All-Pro selection. During a 61–20 triumph over the 49ers that year, he scored 6 touchdowns for the Bears, tying the NFL record set by Ernie Nevers of the Chicago Cardinals in 1929 and equaled by Dub Jones of the Browns in 1951. Among his touchdowns that day, one was a 50-yard run from scrimmage, another was an 80-yard pass play, and a third was an 85-yard punt return.

During a 1968 game Sayers was tackled by Kermit Alexander, a 49er cornerback. His knee, which required surgery, was never the same after that. Although he would be named All-Pro in each of his first five seasons, the 1971 season was his last.

At his best Sayers was among football's most instinctive running backs. Avoiding tacklers, he seemed to slide sideways, then burst ahead at full speed. Watching films of his runs, teammates and opponents shook their heads in disbelief at the running back that George Halas called "the best he had ever seen." And as the Papa Bear, one of the NFL's founders, Halas had seen them all, from Jim Thorpe and Red Grange to Jim Brown and Walter Payton.

The King's Dark Alley

Other old-timers insist that Hugh McElhenny, somewhat forgotten in recent years, was the best, especially during his peak seasons with the 49ers, beginning in 1952.

Out of the University of Washington, this 6-1, 198-pound halfback was virtually a tightrope walker with a football. His balance was remarkable as he weaved his way through tacklers, so many of whom he left grasping the air instead of him. As a rookie, he averaged 7 yards a carry while rushing for 684 yards. After one of McElhenny's long runs, the 49er quarterback, Frankie Albert, shook his head.

"He's the king," Albert said, "the king of the runners."

From then on, the King was McElhenny's nickname. He accumulated 11,375 all-purpose yards as a runner, receiver, punt returner, and kickoff returner, including 5,281 rushing yards. Another teammate, quarterback Y. A. Tittle, labeled him "the finest running back I ever saw; there never was an open-field runner like him." Quite a career for someone who as a youngster had been confined to bed for five months and on crutches for another seven months because of an accident in which he had severed tendons of one foot on a broken milk bottle. In reflecting on his ability, he once described what it was like for him to be a running back.

"It's like walking down a dark alley," McElhenny said. "And then you see at the end of the alley a glimpse of light from the cross street. That's the goal line. You're desperately trying to get to the cross street, but on the way, even though the alley is so dark you can't see a thing,

Hugh McElhenny, "The King," seems to be floating past a Browns tackler.

you sense a telegraph pole to your right and you shy away from it. A few steps farther, you know there's a doorway with a man in it, even though you can't see him. You just feel it, so you turn away from that, too. Haven't you had that experience? I have. And then you're glad to reach that cross street with the bright lights—the goal line."

McElhenny teamed in the 49er backfield with Joe Perry, a fullback who blasted for 9,723 yards. Teams seldom have two running backs of that quality. But the Packers of the Vince Lombardi era did—Jim Taylor at fullback and Paul Hornung at halfback.

Taylor, at 6-0 and 215 pounds, was a terror who enjoyed crashing into tacklers rather than avoiding them. One day when Lombardi asked why he didn't try to sidestep a tackler, Taylor replied, "You've got to sting 'em, coach. If you give a guy a little blast, maybe next time he won't be so eager. You've got to make 'em respect you. You've got to punish them before they punish you. You've got to give more than you take." Taylor did, accumulating 8,597 career yards. Hornung, 6-3 and 210, a Heisman Trophy winner at Notre Dame, had only 3,711 rushing yards for the Packers, but he scored 62 touchdowns.

"Inside the 20-yard line, Hornung is one of the greatest I have ever seen," Lombardi once said. "He smells the goal line."

For a running back there is no higher compliment. For a running back the goal line is why he's out there carrying the ball.

THREE SECONDS TO THROW

THREE SECONDS. SAY THEM SLOWLY. ONE...TWO...THREE. That's the amount of time that a passer usually has from the moment he takes the snap from the center, hurries back a few yards, searches for a receiver, and throws the football. Occasionally he might have a second or two more. Sometimes he might have even less than three seconds. But in timing a pass play, most coaches believe that a quarterback has no more than three seconds to throw the ball.

Any longer than that, a passer usually has been either tackled or forced to scramble, which means eluding tacklers while hoping to find an open receiver.

Three seconds. That's all. In a game passing is not like playing catch in the backyard. In a game passing is not only throwing the football to a receiver in less than three seconds but completing it for a gain. To do that on the NFL level, a quarterback must have several talents—a strong and accurate arm, quick footwork, intelligence in reading a defense, good vision in finding an open receiver, toughness in standing in there against the pass rush, and leadership in the clutch of a close game.

Of all those talents, however, the most important is a strong, accurate arm. Without it a player can't be a passer. That doesn't mean he can't be a good football player at another position. But if he is going to be a passer, he must have a strong, accurate arm.

Even in the NFL some passers have stronger arms than others, but accuracy is equally important. Troy Aikman, who led the Dallas Cowboys to three Super Bowl championships in four seasons, throws passes that resemble laser beams. Husky at 6-4 and 228 pounds, he

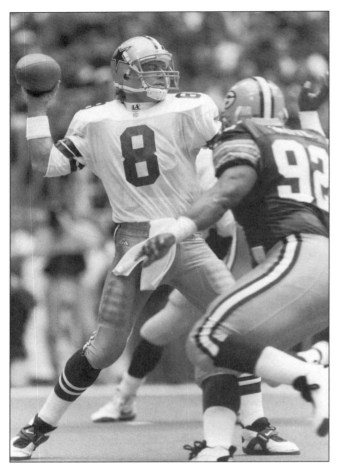

Troy Aikman, about to let loose another laser-beam pass for the Cowboys

has been described by Phil Simms, the NBC television analyst who was the Giants quarterback for fifteen seasons, as "the most accurate" passer.

"When you put strength and accuracy together," Simms said, "Troy is the best in the game."

Another attribute of a good passer is toughness—not only the mental toughness to perform despite the pressure to win that is always on a quarterback but also the physical toughness to absorb the pounding of the pass rushers.

"Troy is maybe the toughest quarterback," a Cowboy teammate, cornerback Everson Walls, once said. "What pretty much sums up Troy was the eleven beatings he took his rookie year. How he kept the same demeanor the whole time."

Aikman, who joined the Cowboys in 1989 as the No. 1 draft choice out of UCLA, grew up on a 172-acre ranch with cattle, pigs, and chickens in Henryetta, Oklahoma, a town of about six thousand people, but he's not a real cowboy.

"Not me," he joked. "I can't even ride a horse."

But he can throw a football. And in his quiet way he likes to sit at his computer and chat with people all over the world. "It puts us on the same level," he said. "It's nice having a normal conversation with somebody without them knowing who I am."

"Making Something Happen"

More and more, because of their importance to their teams, quarterbacks become celebrities who must struggle to maintain their privacy. But Packers quarterback Brett Favre is the Wisconsin spokesman for the National Punt, Pass, and Kick competition for youngsters.

"I grew up in that competition," Favre said, "so it was a natural thing for me to do. We bring in all the kids to compete at halftime at one of our games each season, and I always go to talk to them before the game."

Out of Kiln, Mississippi, Favre went to Southern Mississippi and was drafted by the Atlanta Falcons in the first round in 1991, but he stood on the sideline during his rookie season. Traded to the Packers in 1992, he quickly developed into one of the NFL's best passers and its most valuable player in 1995 and again in 1996, as the Packers went on to win Super Bowl XXXI.

Brett Favre of the Packers dances away from three Cowboy pass-rushers.

"The ability to improvise is the most important thing," Favre said. "You can practice something all week, but when you get into a game, it rarely goes exactly like you practiced it. I've been able to make plays. I think that's my knack. Making something happen when nothing is there."

Steve Young, the left-handed quarterback who succeeded Joe Montana with the 49ers, occasionally made something happen as a runner, especially squirming for long yardage in leading the 49ers to their fifth Super Bowl title.

"There is a benchmark of championships here that is nowhere else," he said. "I just want to keep that tradition going. That's the real test for me."

When confronted by that real test, in Super Bowl XXIX against the San Diego Chargers, he threw a record 6 touchdown passes, including 3 to Jerry Rice, the first a 44-yarder only one minute and twenty-four seconds into the game.

"I never threw 6 touchdown passes in a game in my life," he said later. "Then I throw 6 in the Super Bowl. Unbelievable."

49er quarterback Steve Young follows through.

Reading Defenses

Young had done what a quarterback is expected to do: produce points and win games, as Terry Bradshaw did in leading the Pittsburgh Steelers to four Super Bowl championships. But not even Bradshaw was an instantly productive quarterback.

As a rookie he threw his short passes too hard. He had to learn how to throw a pass with what coaches call "touch," meaning lofting the ball just beyond the reach of a linebacker or floating it out to a running back on a screen play.

Bradshaw also had to learn how to read defenses, especially the zone defenses that are designed to confuse a quarterback. In a man-to-man defense, for example, a cornerback is assigned to cover a wide receiver anywhere in the field. But in a zone defense, a cornerback may cover a wide receiver for only a few strides; once the wide receiver leaves the cornerback's zone and enters another zone, another defensive back will cover him. In trying to look for a receiver in the mass of players between them, a quarterback also has to realize what type of zone defense the opposing team is using.

For a quarterback to do that quickly, almost instinctively, he needs experience. Bradshaw wasn't completely comfortable in reading defenses until his fifth season, 1974, when the Steelers went on to win their first Super Bowl title.

"In a game against the New England Patriots late that season,"

Terry Bradshaw was the Steeler quarterback on four Super Bowl championship teams.

center Ray Mansfield once said, "Terry suddenly was in complete charge. He knew it and we knew it. That was the game when Terry really came of age, and so did our entire team."

Without a productive quarterback a team might win a few games. But it will never win a divisional championship, much less a Super Bowl game. One of the NFL's most productive quarterbacks was Otto Graham, who led the Cleveland Browns to three NFL titles and four All-America Football Conference championships as well as ten consecutive divisional titles from 1946 through 1955.

"For me, the key to reading defenses was reading the linebackers," Graham always said. "The linebackers are going to blitz or they're not."

Graham didn't have as strong an arm as some passers, but his arm was strong enough. And he was an exceptional athlete. While at Northwestern University he was chosen as an All-American in basketball as well as football. He later played pro basketball briefly.

"What helped me more than anything else in adjusting to the T-formation was the fact that I was a good basketball player," he said. "The mechanics of quarterbacking are the same as in basketball. The footwork and the pivoting are identical."

As a quarterback, Graham mastered the art of the pass to a wide receiver near the sideline.

"The secret is to have the receiver come back," he said. "You tell a guy to make a ninety-degree cut toward the sideline, but with his momentum he's actually still going downfield. By making the receiver cut back, he has the defender beaten by two steps. The defender is also blocked off by the receiver's body. I threw the ball in relation to where the defensive back was, not where the receiver was."

Forty years after Graham stopped playing, he still held the NFL career record for the highest average gain as a passer, 8.63 yards. In his ten seasons with the Browns, he threw for 23,584 yards and 174 touchdowns. He also endeared himself to coach Paul Brown because he seldom threw costly interceptions.

All coaches dislike having their passer intercepted because it turns over the ball to the opposing team. Occasionally an interception is run back for a touchdown. In his heyday as a coach, Brown complained about interceptions more than most coaches. If a passer repeatedly was intercepted, Brown didn't keep him long. Once, after trading a new quarterback, Brown had a simple explanation.

"That young man," he said, "did not understand how I feel about interceptions."

The Dreaded Interception

Brown apparently passed on his philosophy to Weeb Ewbank, once his offensive line coach with the Browns and later the head coach of the Baltimore Colts and the New York Jets. During Joe Namath's early years with the Jets, he had games where he was intercepted much too often, at least in Ewbank's judgment.

"Suppose," the coach was asked, "Namath keeps throwing all these interceptions?"

"In that case," Ewbank said quickly, "we'll just have to get rid of him."

The Jets didn't get rid of Namath, of course. He learned to throw fewer interceptions. When the Jets won Super Bowl III in a 16–7 upset of the Baltimore Colts, he completed 17 of 28 passes for 206 yards with no interceptions. But even the best passers have days when interceptions occur. In a 1970 game against the Chicago Bears, the Colts won, 21–20, even though Johnny Unitas threw five interceptions. When asked about the interceptions after that game, Unitas shrugged.

"They happen," he said.

Interceptions sometimes happen by accident—when a pass bounces off a receiver or a defensive player downfield, or when a pass is batted into the air by a defensive player even before it crosses the line of scrimmage. In fairness, an interception of that type is usually not the passer's fault. But in the statistics it is charged as an interception. To be a good passer, however, a quarterback should not be overly concerned with throwing interceptions. If he worries too much about being intercepted, he will not take the chances that a good passer should take. Ideally he should be careful in throwing a pass but not too careful; he must take a risk occasionally but not often.

Interceptions happen more often to passers who prefer to throw the ball far downfield, as Namath and Unitas did, rather than toss short, safer passes.

In a 1972 game between the Jets and the Colts, Namath and Unitas accumulated 822 yards. While throwing for 6 touchdowns in a 44–34 victory, Namath produced 496 yards with only 15 completions in 28 attempts. In the final quarter he collaborated with wide receiver Rich Caster for a 79-yard touchdown. But Unitas's second touchdown pass narrowed the Jets' lead to 37–34 and inspired Namath.

Before his knees were damaged, Joe Namath sometimes resembled a ballet dancer when he passed.

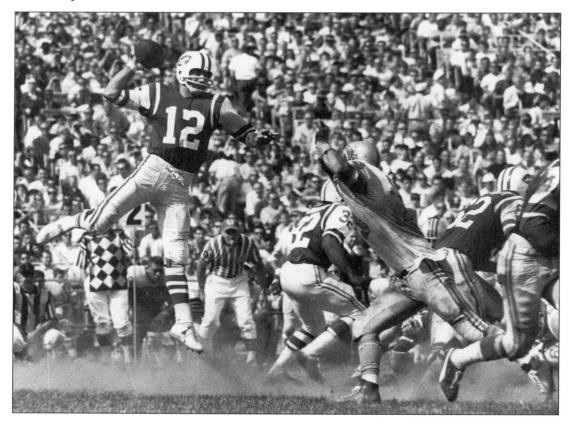

"Waiting for the kickoff," Namath later explained, "I was thinking about another long pass to Caster on the first play, but I wasn't sure if I should risk it, only 3 points ahead. But then I said to myself, 'If you ain't confident, you don't belong here,' so I decided to score again quick."

On first down Namath threw a pass that Caster caught behind the Colt defense for an 80-yard touchdown, clinching the game. Namath's total of 496 yards in that game remains among the highest in NFL history. The record of 554 yards was set by Norm Van Brocklin of the Los Angeles Rams in a 1951 game against the New York Yanks, a franchise that later moved to Dallas, where it was renamed the Texans, and that eventually emerged as the Baltimore Colts, now the Indianapolis Colts.

Then as now, NFL quarterbacks were coached to pass from what coaches called "the pocket," meaning the pocket formed behind the offensive lineman who were blocking the opposing defensive players rushing the passer. Otto Graham and Norm Van Brocklin were two of the best "pocket" passers. So were Johnny Unitas and Joe Namath later on. But by then another type of passer had emerged— "the scrambler."

The Escape Artists

In his eighteen seasons with the Minnesota Vikings and the New York Giants, Fran Tarkenton completed 3,686 passes for 47,003 yards and 342 touchdowns. His success created a new breed of quarterbacks who scrambled almost by design. In the coaches' language, they were "roll-out" passers, who moved toward the sideline before passing rather than drop straight back into the "pocket" of blockers.

As coaches gradually accepted the concept of scrambling, Roger Staubach of the Dallas Cowboys emerged as an escape artist who either darted away from pass rushers before throwing or scooted upfield for rushing yardage.

Slender and quick on his feet, Staubach was at his best in the last

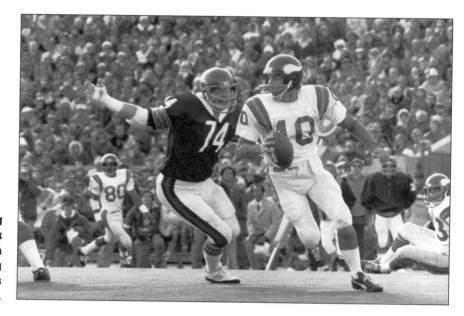

Viking quarterback Fran Tarkenton scrambles away from a Bears tackler.

few minutes of a close game with the outcome at stake. Against the Redskins he once ran 29 yards for the winning touchdown in the final minutes. In a 1972 playoff game against the 49ers, he fired two touchdown passes in the last two minutes for a stunning 30–28 victory. Although the Cowboys' coach, Tom Landry, would have preferred that Staubach not scramble, he didn't object.

"Roger does what he must do," Landry once said, "and he does it well. We have no play where Roger is supposed to run. He runs enough."

In one sense Staubach apparently ran too much. During what would be his final season in 1979, he suffered five concussions in collisions with tacklers. Those concussions contributed to his decision a few months later to end his career. The threat of injury was one reason coaches don't like their quarterbacks to scramble; it exposes them as an unprotected target for tacklers.

Looking to his own future, Staubach wisely called the right play: Don't risk serious injury.

Staubach was always smart. Equally important for a quarterback, he also was a leader. Even though Landry called all the Cowboy plays from the sideline, Staubach had the privilege of changing the play to one he thought might be better. Often he did that when he walked up behind the center and checked the opposing team's defense. In barking signals he would call out words and numbers for the new play he wanted. Changing a play that way is known as using an "audible," something all quarterbacks do.

"Roger can always change the play," Landry often joked, "as long as his play works."

Staubach's play usually did work. One reason for that was the way he barked his "audible," boldly and confidently. As the leader of the offensive unit, a quarterback must make his teammates believe in him as a play caller and as a passer. In some cases that belief begins in the huddle. One of the best quarterbacks in the huddle was Bobby Layne, who led the Detroit Lions to three NFL titles. In the 1953 championship game, the Lions were losing, 16–10, to the Cleveland Browns with about four minutes remaining. With the ball on their own 20-yard line following the kickoff, the Lions leaned into the huddle.

"Just block a little bit," Layne told his teammates, "and ol' Bobby will pass you right to the championship."

He did just that, connecting with wide receiver Jim Doran for a 33-yard touchdown and a 17–16 victory. But every so often a quarterback has to know when to listen to his teammates. During the 1962 season in a game against Washington, the Giants were at the Redskins' 5-yard line. Y. A. Tittle, the Giants' quarterback, already had thrown 6 touchdown passes. One more and he would tie the NFL record shared by Sid Luckman and Adrian Burk. But in the huddle he called for a running play.

"No, no," said Alex Webster, the Giants' fullback. "Throw a pass."

"I don't want to show 'em up," Tittle said, referring to the Redskins. "We'll run the ball."

"If you don't call a pass," said Frank Gifford, the Giants' halfback, "we're all going to walk off the field."

Tittle surrendered. He threw a pass to tight end Joe Walton for a touchdown, scoring a 49–34 victory.

"You only get a chance like that," Gifford said later, "once in a lifetime."

Dan Marino's Records

Tittle also shared with George Blanda the NFL record for touchdown passes in one season, 36, until Dan Marino shattered it in 1984. In only his second year as the Miami Dolphins' quarterback, Marino threw 48 touchdown passes while establishing two other season records with 362 completions and 5,084 passing yards. He later set the career records for completions, passing yardage, and touchdown passes.

"We've never had to tell Dan," said his coach, Don Shula, "that he's too young to do this, or that he's not ready to do that."

Dan Marino whipping a pass for the Dolphins

Before his third start as a rookie out of the University of Pittsburgh, the tall, husky quarterback was sitting with Shula in Baltimore in the Dolphin locker room. As a hard rain fell outside, Shula pointed to a few plays listed on the game plan.

"We won't use those plays now," the coach said.

"How come?" the rookie quarterback asked.

"It's raining too hard," the coach replied.

"That doesn't make any difference," Marino said.

It didn't. Through the continuous rain, Marino completed 11 of 18 passes for 157 yards and two touchdowns in a 21–7 victory. Shula had a quarterback who would impress some of football's most famous passers.

"For throwing the ball," Joe Namath said, "Marino is the best I've ever seen."

As important as a passer is to every team, a quarterback is dependent on the other members of that team. If a quarterback is surrounded by good players, he has the opportunity to do well. If he's surrounded by lesser players, he won't have much of an opportunity to do well. But by the nature of his being the passer, a quarterback's importance is often out of focus.

Invariably a quarterback will get too much credit when his team wins, too much blame when it loses.

But that's the glory and the price of being a passer, no matter what the level of competition may be.

"LOOK THE BALL INTO YOUR HANDS"

IT ISN'T OFTEN THAT A MODERN-DAY FOOTBALL PLAYER IS unanimously considered the best ever at his position. There's always a debate about somebody else who was better. But wide receiver Jerry Rice is that rarity. There's no debate. He planned it that way.

"When I hang my shoes up," he once said, "I would like to hold every record possible."

After twelve seasons with the San Francisco 49ers he already did. At the end of the 1996 schedule not only did he hold the NFL career record for touchdowns by any player with 165, but his 1,050 receptions for 16,377 yards were also first on the all-time lists. And he had done it with more style than show.

"I might spike one now and then," he said, meaning the ball, "but you'll never see me rub it in."

Except once. In a game against the Eagles early in his career, a defensive back had taunted him.

"He had talked so much noise to me, we'd gotten into it," Rice recalled. "I scored and turned around and spiked the ball in his face, but that was the last time I did that. I thought about it and I said to myself, 'Well, Jerry, you achieved what you wanted, you didn't have to do that.'"

For all of Rice's speed and strength at 6 feet and 196 pounds, his devotion to conditioning reflects a work ethic that he developed when he helped his father, a bricklayer, build houses in Starkville, Mississippi. Their home was not far from Mississippi Valley State, where he once caught 24 passes in a game.

"I can get the job done," he says, "but I don't see myself as a natural. I'm shy. The pressure is every second. I have to perform."

Jerry Rice has performed as no other pass receiver ever has in pro football, where the rules are continually shaped to help the passing game that spectators cherish.

Just as a football team needs a good passer, it also needs good pass receivers. No matter how accurate a pass is, if it's not caught, it's simply another incompletion.

Jerry Rice's specialty: running with the ball after the catch

More than anything else, a receiver needs good hands to hold a pass. If he isn't able to hold a pass, he should look for another position. But other talents are necessary. To be effective, a receiver needs the speed to get downfield past the defensive backs. He needs the moves, or the fakes, to fool defensive backs into believing he is going in one direction when he knows he will actually go in another direction. He needs the strength and courage to fight for the ball "in a crowd," as coaches say, meaning in a tangle with one or perhaps two defensive backs. He needs the ability to escape for extra yardage instead of being tackled immediately. And he needs to work with his passer in developing their timing—the precise moment when he is in the clear and the ball is on its way.

Once upon a time pass receivers were known simply as ends; later they were known as flankers, split ends, and tight ends. Now they are known as wide receivers and tight ends.

The First Flankers

Shortly after World War II some teams began using three pass receivers rather than two. The third was technically a halfback, but he lined up so far to the right or left that he was considered to be "flanked" near the sideline—hence the name flankerback or simply flanker (now called a wide receiver). Two of the first flankers were Elroy (Crazy Legs) Hirsch of the Los Angeles Rams and Dub Jones of the Cleveland Browns.

Lynn Swann leaping for a Steeler touchdown against the Rams in Super Bowl XIV

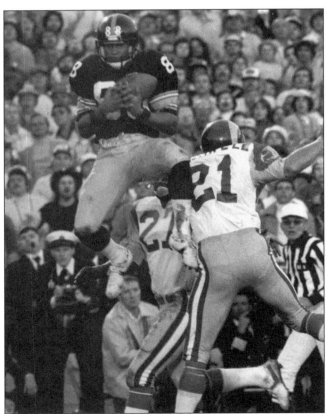

Hirsch and Jones had been running backs in college and during their first few pro seasons. But in order to take full advantage of his speed as a receiver, each was used as a flanker.

With the gradual increase in emphasis on passing, the receiver on the other side of the field from the flanker eventually was "split" out so far from the tackle that he became known as the split end. After a few years the NFL decided not to differentiate between them anymore. From then on, each was simply a wide receiver. According to the latest offensive philosophy, some teams use as many as four wide receivers (plus the tight end), sometimes leaving only one running back lined up behind the quarterback.

Although speed was always a factor in choosing pass receivers, many coaches' desire for speed and more speed occurred following the success of Bob Hayes, an Olympic sprint gold medalist, with the Dallas Cowboys.

At the 1964 Summer Olympics in Tokyo, Hayes won the 100-meter dash and ran the anchor leg for the victorious United States team in the 4 x 100-meter relay. The following year he joined the Cowboys, after having been an outstanding college football player at Florida A&M. Through the years some world-class sprinters, such as Buddy Young, had succeeded in the NFL, but others had not—notably Ray Norton.

The difference was that Hayes, like Young, had been a football player who also was a sprinter.

"Bob Hayes was a football player who became an Olympic champion," explained Jake Gaither, his college coach, "not an Olympic champion who tried to be a football player."

But even with his football background, Hayes had difficulty adjusting to NFL collisions.

"I can't get past the linebacker. He grabs me every time," Hayes once told a Cowboy assistant coach during his rookie season. "He won't let me get past him."

"You've got to learn to get past him," the coach said.

"I can't do it," Hayes said. "He gets me every time."

"You'll learn how to do it," the coach said, "or you'll be on your way home."

Hayes learned. So did other football players who happened to be sprinters. And because they learned, they increased the strategic importance of the wide receiver.

The wide receivers line up wide, usually one to the right and one to the left; sometimes they both line up on the same side (either right or left) with the inside man in what is called the slot. When teams use three wide receivers, two usually line up either to the right or to the left. The tight end usually lines up next to the right tackle, occasionally next to the left tackle. Some teams use a double tight end formation, either with one next to each tackle or with the two tight ends side by side.

On running plays the tight end is used to block. For that reason a tight end is usually bigger and stronger than a wide receiver, but not as fast.

The Tight Ends

Mike Ditka was one of the first tight ends. When he was drafted from the University of Pittsburgh by the Bears, the team he would later coach, he was thought of primarily as a linebacker. But the Bears' coach then, George Halas, preferred to utilize his ability to catch the ball, along with his ability to block. Other early tight ends in the evolution of the position were Ron Kramer of the Packers, John Mackey of the Colts, and Pete Retzlaff of the Eagles. In more recent years Kellen Winslow of the San Diego Chargers added a new dimension—height and speed. Winslow is 6-5 and weighs 242 pounds.

"When you think about Winslow, you think about Superman," said Don Shula, the Dolphin coach. "He climbs the highest buildings."

Mark Bavaro played tight end as if he could lift the highest buildings. During a 1986 game he caught a pass from Giant quarterback Phil Simms and bulled his way to another 15 yards, shedding half a dozen 49er tacklers as if they were puppies. He helped the Giants win two Super Bowl titles before finishing his career with the Browns and the Eagles. But whenever he was reminded of his highlight play in San Francisco, he shrugged.

"Bad tackling," he would say.

Since the passer must know where a receiver will be, a receiver never runs just anywhere he wants to go. Instead he runs what coaches call a pass pattern or a pass route. Each pattern is designed for a receiver to run a certain way to a certain area on the field. On a 5-yard square-out pattern, for example, a wide receiver would run exactly 5 yards straight downfield, then cut at a ninety-degree angle to the sideline. On a post pattern, a wide receiver or a tight end would run downfield, then angle toward the goalposts.

When a team needs a first down, a receiver tries to make sure that he is downfield far enough so that a completed pass would provide a first down, not leave his team short of it.

One of the masters of the first-down completion was Fred Biletnikoff, a Raider teammate of wide receiver Cliff Branch for several seasons. Not as fast as Branch, he used deception to fool the cornerback assigned to cover him. He also used dedication, staying to practice long after the Raiders' team workout was over. He would find someone, perhaps one of the backup quarterbacks or sometimes an equipment manager, to throw extra passes. For half an hour, occasionally longer, Biletnikoff would practice his patterns and practice the apparently simple process of catching a pass.

With a defensive back all over him, however, it's not always simple for a receiver to catch a pass.

To assure concentration by a receiver, coaches use a familiar phrase as a constant reminder—"look the ball into your hands"—meaning that a receiver should keep his eyes on the ball until he has grasped it firmly and pulled it into his body. But to be where the passer believes he will be, a receiver must run his pattern as precisely as possible. On most patterns a passer will lead his receiver, meaning he will throw the ball to where the receiver will be when the ball gets there. That helps a receiver keep his body between the defensive back covering him and the ball.

Precision in Patterns

Don Hutson, who still holds six NFL pass-receiving records, is believed to have been the first to understand the advantage of running precise patterns.

Tall at 6-1 but slender at 178 pounds, Hutson joined the Green Bay Packers in 1935 from the University of Alabama, where he had

Hall of Famer Don Hutson practices "looking the ball" into his hands.

been an All-America selection on his senior team, a Rose Bowl winner. In that last year before the NFL draft of college talent began, Hutson signed with the Packers because they had a respected passer in Arnie Herber at a time when many other NFL teams were using offenses built around running backs. In later years Cecil Isbell succeeded Herber as the Packers' quarterback. In eleven seasons Hutson led the league in scoring five times, in pass receiving eight times, in pass-receiving yardage seven times, and in pass-receiving touchdowns nine times.

Several years later, during the Vince Lombardi era in Green Bay, some Packers got tired of hearing old-timers brag about how good Hutson had been. One day they decided to look at some old films, which quickly convinced them of Hutson's skill.

"He's even better than the old-timers told us he was," said Jess Whittenton, then a Packer cornerback. "He had moves that some of the receivers around now haven't even thought of yet. Hutson was great."

Perhaps the most unusual praise of Hutson's style came when Willie Mays, the Hall of Fame baseball player, attributed his skill at catching long fly balls near the outfield fence to Hutson.

"I saw Hutson in the movies once," Mays said. "I saw how he

caught the ball and stopped real fast. I told myself that if he could do that with a football, I could do it with a baseball. I went out and ran hard at the fence and stopped. I kept doing it until I could do it well. He'd catch the ball and twist away from a guy going to tackle him. I caught a baseball and twisted away from the fence."

Don Hutson raised the stature of the pass receiver, thereby raising the stature of the passing game as a strategic weapon.

"I LINED UP AT A FORTY-FIVE-DEGREE ANGLE"

SOME OF THE DETROIT LIONS WERE SNICKERING. WITH two seconds remaining on the clock, Tom Dempsey was lining up to kick a field goal from the 37-yard line, *his* New Orleans Saints' 37-yard line—a distance of 63 yards from the goalposts, which in 1970 were on the goal line, not at the back of the end zone, as they are now. Nobody in the NFL had ever kicked a field goal that far.

Tom Dempsey kicks a record 63-yard field goal.

"There was a big boom, a really loud thud," Dempsey's holder, Joe Scarpati, said later.

Quickly the ball sailed up, up, and over the crossbar as time expired. The Saints had won, 19–17, on an unlikely field goal by an unlikely kicker with half a right foot and a withered right arm. His kicking shoe resembled a hammer—which some NFL opponents considered illegal.

"I didn't have a regular shoe," Dempsey said, "because I didn't have a regular foot."

In the NFL he was a kicker, but at 6-1 and 265 pounds, he had been a regular football player at Palomar (California) Junior College, a defensive end whose father had taught him to ignore his disability.

"Whenever my dad heard me say, 'I can't,'" Dempsey remembered, "he'd say, 'There's no such thing as can't. You can do anything you want to do. You just have to do it differently.'"

More than a quarter of a century later people realize just how differently.

Tom Dempsey was among the last of the straight-ahead kickers, in contrast with today's soccer-style kickers, many of them imported from Europe, who at first inspired laughs when they began appearing in the NFL during the 1960s.

"Our kicker," Alex Karras, a defensive tackler for the Lions, often joked then, "would come on the field yelling, 'I am going to kick a touchdown.'"

Nobody laughs anymore. Every NFL team has a soccer-style placekicker now. So do most college and high school teams. Soccer-style kickers are a reminder that the "foot" is still in football. When the sport began more than a century ago, the ball was meant to be kicked, not thrown. Hence the name of the game.

On many teams the kicker is smaller and shorter than the other players. It isn't necessary for a kicker to be as tall or as heavy as most of his teammates. Many of the NFL placekickers are under 6 feet and weigh about 175 pounds. Placekicking and punting are positions that require mostly leg strength, concentration, and poise.

For all the emphasis on passing and running today, placekicking and punting still represent an important part of football.

Coaches speak of their "special teams." But that is merely another name for their kicking teams—the field-goal/extra-point unit, the kickoff unit, the punting unit. To thwart those units, an opponent also has a unit that tries to block the field goal or the extra point as well as a kickoff-return unit and a punt-return unit.

Each team usually has two specialists. The placekicker tries to make field goals (worth 3 points) and the point after touchdown (worth 1 point). He also kicks off. The punter tries to boot the ball deep into the other team's territory, usually on fourth down.

Of the two, the placekicker is in the headlines more often, for better or for worse. Sometimes he will kick a field goal or an extra point that creates the margin of victory in a game. Sometimes he will miss a field goal or an extra point that is the difference in a loss. Hero or goat—that is his glory and his burden.

Lou Groza's Square Toe

Although soccer-style placekickers are numerous now, the importance of a field-goal kicker was established by Lou (The Toe) Groza of the Cleveland Browns. He was a conventional kicker, meaning that he stood squarely to the goalposts and swung one foot straight ahead, kicking the ball with the square toe of his football shoe.

In contrast, a soccer-style kicker stands at a forty-five-degree angle to where his holder will spot the ball, then strides and swings one leg from the side, kicking it with the side of his foot.

Until Groza came along, most placekickers did not try field goals from beyond the 40-yard line. In 1946, when the Browns were playing in the All-America Football Conference, he was a substitute offensive lineman as well as a kicker. That season coach Paul Brown noticed that as soon as the Browns' offense neared midfield, Groza would start unlimbering his right leg on the sidelines. One day Brown turned to him.

"Do you think you can kick one this long?" the coach asked.

"I think I can," Groza said. "I'd sure like to try one."

That season Groza kicked a 49-yard field goal and a 50-yard field goal, as well as another 50-yard field goal in Miami against a howling tropical wind. With their powerful placekicker, the

Lou Groza shrank the field in half as the Browns' field-goal kicker.

Browns had shrunk the field in half. To get a quick 3 points on a field goal, they had only to move their offense into Groza's range.

In his NFL career, Groza kicked 234 field goals, not counting those made during the playoffs—including the 16-yarder that won the 1950 championship game, 28–27, over the Rams. He also developed into an All-NFL offensive tackle.

During that era some placekickers also played another position, as Groza did. George Blanda, a quarterback with the Bears before moving on to the Houston Oilers and the Oakland Raiders, kicked until he was forty-eight years old. Blanda established the NFL record for scoring. He accumulated 2,002 total points as he kicked 335 field goals and 943 extra points, and, as a quarterback, scored 9 touchdowns.

Pete Gogolak's Legacy

In 1964 the Buffalo Bills signed the first soccer-style placekicker, Pete Gogolak, a rookie out of Cornell University who had been kicking that way for six years. As a junior at the Ogdensburg (New York) Free Academy, not far from the St. Lawrence River, he was a tight end on the football team. The day before their first game, Coach Bill Plimpton asked for volunteers to be the placekicker. Gogolak raised his hand. So did two teammates.

"The other two kicked straight ahead," Gogolak said; "then I lined up at a forty-five-degree angle."

Gogolak had learned to kick a soccer ball in Hungary before his family immigrated to the United States after the Soviet suppression of the revolution there.

"The coach yelled, 'Hey, Gogo, we do it different over here,' and the holder, a quarterback named Steve Munn, looked at me as if he thought I was going to kick him instead of the ball," Gogolak once recalled with a laugh. "But I asked the coach to let me try it my way. When the ball was snapped, I got off a 50-yard-kick, but the ball never got higher than three feet off the ground.

"Everybody was yelling, 'Send this guy back to Europe!' but I knew I had something. I didn't kick that year, but I went out on my own and kicked off a tee. The next year I tried three field goals and made two. I kicked off, mostly. The first time the returners were on the 25-yard-line, and I kicked the ball over their heads into the end zone.

"My father sent some of my game films to Syracuse, but the coach then, Ben Schwartzwalder, wasn't interested. My father contacted Cornell, and the freshman coach called back, and that's where I went. But even after I'd kicked well at Cornell, there was almost total unacceptance of the soccer style. None of the NFL teams drafted me that year."

The Bills, then in the AFL, drafted him in the twelfth round after a tryout.

"I had to go up there and kick in the snow for them," Gogolak said. "My first game, an exhibition against the Jets in Tampa, I kicked a 57-yard field goal, the longest one I ever kicked. That year, 1964, we won the AFL title."

Pete Gogolak, the first of pro football's soccer-style kickers

Before the 1966 season Gogolak signed with the New York Giants, hastening the NFL-AFL merger.

"That same year my brother Charley joined the Redskins, the next year Jan Stenerud joined the Chiefs, and after that American kids started kicking a football soccer-style, even if they didn't have a European background. Kicking also attracted American kids who were soccer players."

Stenerud came to America from Norway as a skier for Montana State before he joined the college football team as a kicker. With a record 373 field goals with the Chiefs, Packers, and Vikings, he was the first pure kicker to be elected to the Pro Football Hall of Fame.

Oddly enough, Nick Lowery, who succeeded Stenerud with the Chiefs in 1979, surpassed Stenerud's total during the 1996 season with the Jets, a team that had cut him twice shortly after his graduation from Dartmouth. Seven other teams, including the Redskins and Colts twice each, also had released Lowery before he stuck with the Chiefs.

"These were great experiences," Lowery said of his early rejections. "I'd never change them for the world because they made me stronger and made me better. I think in life it doesn't matter where you are but where you've come from and what you've overcome."

Nick Lowery adds to his record field-goal total.

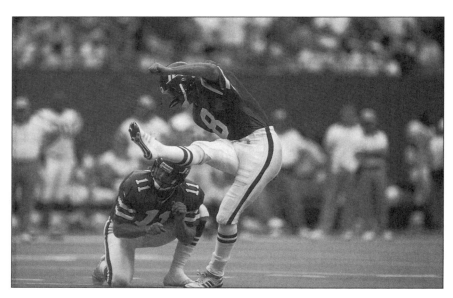

The Last-Minute Pressure

The son of a U.S. Foreign Service official, Lowery was born in Munich, Germany, where he learned to kick a soccer ball. Two of the NFL's most accurate kickers also learned to kick in other countries— Morten Andersen in Denmark and Gary Anderson in South Africa— before moving to the United States and learning to thrive on the last-minute pressure that accompanies their role.

"Pressure works for me," said Morten Andersen, who moved to the Falcons from the Saints as a free agent in 1995. "I love the challenge of having three seconds to go and being two points behind. I love it because it brings out the best in me."

"I have a simple philosophy," said Gary Anderson, who moved to the Eagles from the Steelers as a free agent in 1995. "I take one kick at a time. When I'm on the field I just focus on the kick. Accuracy is the truest measure of a kicker."

For a placekicker, the snap from the center to the ball holder must be consistently accurate. Most centers study the spiral of their snap, so that the laces on the football will be facing away from the ball holder when he catches it and spots it, holding it gently with a fore-finger atop one end. If a kicker were to kick the side where the laces are, it might affect the accuracy of the kick.

For a punter it's a two-man operation—the punter and his center, also know as a long snapper. On a punt, the punter stands 15 yards behind the line of scrimmage. He needs that distance because he needs more time. He must catch the snap cleanly, step forward, and then follow through, usually with his kicking leg finishing high above his head.

Although a good average for a punter is anything over 40 yards, the record punt in the NFL is 98 yards, set by Steve O'Neal of the Jets in 1969 at Denver.

Through the years the record career punting average has endured at 45.10 yards, set by Sammy Baugh, more famous as the Redskins' passer. His average of 51.40 in 1940 is the one-season record. The

Ray Guy of the Raiders once punted the ball high into the Louisiana Superdome's gondola.

most respected punter in recent years has been Ray Guy of the Raiders, with a career average of nearly 43 yards. His most memorable punt occurred in the 1976 Pro Bowl at the Louisiana Superdome. A television-screen gondola hung ninety feet above the field.

"Is it all right," Guy asked John Madden, the AFC coach, "if I try to hit the gondola?"

Madden agreed. On his next punt Guy boomed the ball up, up and into the gondola. Whistles blew. He was ordered to punt again. But more than anything else, Ray Guy, out of Southern Mississippi, proved how important a kicker can be. In the 1973 draft the Raiders had selected him on the first round.

"GREAT OFFENSIVE LINEMEN ARE SMART"

FOR ALL THE HIGHLIGHTS AND HEADLINES FEATURING quarterbacks and running backs, few would exist without the blocking that protects a passer throwing to a pass receiver or a ballcarrier hurrying through the line. And that protection keeps getting bigger and bigger.

When the Dallas Cowboys won Super Bowl XXX, the listed weights of their five offensive linemen added up to 1,620 pounds, an average of 324: left tackle Mark Tuinei, 314; left guard Nate Newton, 323; center Derek Kennard, 333; right guard Larry Allen, 326; and right tackle Erik Williams, 324.

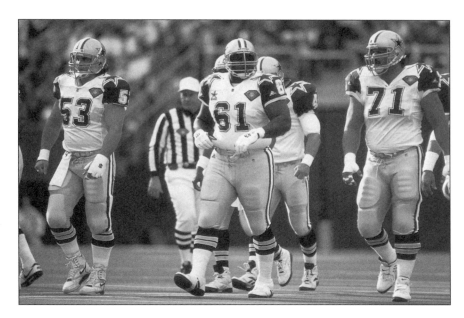

Nate Newton (61) and Mark Tuinei (71) anchored the Cowboys' offensive line.

"But what people don't realize is that we're in shape," Newton said. "In the fourth quarter we've still got our stamina."

In football, blocking is one of the most important skills and also one of the least appreciated. Good blocking provides time for a quarterback to stand there against the pass rush and find his receiver and it provides the holes that a running back needs to get past opponents trying to tackle him.

"You can design the best offensive plays in football," says John Madden, once the Oakland Raiders' coach, "but if your blockers don't do their job, those plays are worthless."

For that reason, Madden believes, as do many other football coaches, that in assembling a team the most important single group of players are offensive linemen. Without a good offensive line, a passer doesn't have time to operate with his receivers. Without a good offensive line, a running back is usually tackled before he can go anywhere.

If a team is having a bad season on offense, the fault often can be traced to the offensive line. If a quarterback, for example, is often sacked, which means he's tackled for a loss of yardage before he can pass, his line isn't protecting him. If a running back isn't getting much room to run, his line isn't opening many holes for him.

Turning that theory around, if a team is playing well on offense, it's usually because the offensive line is blocking well.

In today's football the offensive line consists, from left to right, of a tackle, a guard, a center who snaps the ball, a guard, and a tackle. On a running play a tight end is also considered a lineman because he is blocking; some teams use two tight ends. (On a pass play a tight end is usually a receiver.) But on a pass play usually one running back, often the fullback, remains to block for the quarterback in case an opposing linebacker rushes.

By the nature of their role, offensive linemen usually toil without attention, usually without a nickname. Every so often, however, an offensive line becomes popular enough to be dubbed with a nickname. One of the few offensive lines ever to emerge as slightly famous was the "Electric Company," who blocked for O. J. (The Juice) Simpson of the Buffalo Bills in 1973, when he set an NFL one-season rushing record of 2,003 yards.

"They called us the 'Electric Company,'" guard Reggie McKenzie said, "because we turned on the Juice."

Around that same time the Miami Dolphins, repeating as Super Bowl champions, had their "Mushrooms."

"They called us the 'Mushrooms,'" guard Bob Kuechenberg said, "because we were kept in the dark."

"Hogs" in the Mud

The Washington Redskins had their "Hogs," who blocked for quarterback Joe Theismann and running back John Riggins when they won Super Bowl XVII, 27–17, over the Miami Dolphins. During the Redskins' success, the Hogs joined Miss Piggy and the Three Little Pigs as the most storied swine in history. In height and weight the Hogs were huge:

> Left Tackle: Joe Jacoby, 6-7, 311.
> Left Guard: Russ Grimm, 6-3, 292.
> Center: Jeff Bostic, 6-2, 258.
> Right Guard: Mark May, 6-6, 295.
> Right Tackle: George Starke, 6-5, 270.

If those five Hogs were prodded into a stockyard, their weight would have added up to 1,426 pounds, give or take their latest meal. Their nickname developed one day during training camp in 1982 when Joe Bugel, the Redskin assistant coach in charge of the offensive line, stared at Grimm thoughtfully.

"You," said Bugel, "are a prototype hog."

Hearing that, the Redskin offensive linemen laughed at what they considered a compliment. Soon they were calling themselves the

Hogs. To show their admiration for Riggins, the linemen named their fullback an honorary Hog because, as Grimm says, "He's like us—he likes to get down in the mud." To be a good blocker, an offensive lineman must like to get his uniform dirty. To be a good blocker, there is no other way.

For an offensive lineman, however, there are two types of blocking—pass blocking and run blocking.

In pass blocking, which means backing up to protect the quarterback as he retreats to search for a receiver, an offensive lineman must be what coaches call a "dancer." He must use small, quick steps to stay between his quarterback and the defensive lineman who is trying to muscle past him. For some offensive lineman, accustomed to blocking mostly on running plays in college, it takes time to adjust to the pass blocking that NFL coaches demand. Every so often an All-America guard is unable to make the NFL because he can't make that adjustment.

When a block is missed, John Riggins faces the consequences.

In run blocking, which means trying to open a hole in the defense for a running back, an offensive lineman usually relies on what coaches call a "power" or a "drive" block. He comes off the line into the defensive player opposite him and tries to drive that player as far as possible. Depending on the matchup, driving that defensive player two or three yards is considered a good block. Sometimes even a standstill is enough for a running back to scoot past the defender. But if a blocker loses ground, he seldom succeeds.

One of the NFL's best offensive linemen was John Hannah, the 6-3, 270-pound guard of the New England Patriots, a consistent All-Pro.

"John's not just big, he's smart," said Dick Steinberg, the Patriots' director of personnel development. "You'll find that great offensive linemen are smart people."

For some reason offensive linemen often are misrepresented as big, strong blobs who aren't smart enough to play any other position.

The Anchor at Center

As proof that this isn't so, consider that in 1968, when Paul Brown took command of the Cincinnati Bengals as an expansion team, the first player he drafted was not a quarterback or a running back or a pass receiver or a linebacker. The first player was Bob Johnson, a center from the University of Tennessee.

"With this young man," Brown said, "we have a player who will anchor our offensive line for the next decade."

Johnson played twelve seasons, helping the Bengals develop into a consistent contender. Some coaches consider the center, aside from the quarterback, to be the most important player on the offensive unit. One of the most famous centers, Chuck Bednarik of the Philadelphia Eagles, was also a linebacker. When the NFL adopted two-platoon football in 1950, virtually every player concentrated on his role on either the offensive unit or the defensive unit. Although Bednarik was primarily a linebacker, occasionally he would fill in at center—two positions he had played as an All-American at Penn.

For the 1960 season the Eagles decided to use Bednarik at center in order to ease his physical burden as much as possible. But when their supply of linebackers was reduced by injuries, coach Buck Shaw asked him to finish a game at outside linebacker while remaining at center on offense.

As it turned out, Bednarik finished the season both as a linebacker on defense and as a center on offense. The only time he was off the field was during kickoffs, punts, and placekicks. When the Eagles defeated the Packers, 17–13, for the NFL championship that year, Bednarik not only played a total of fifty-eight minutes, but he also made the tackle on Jim Taylor in the final play that preserved the title. As he sat on top of the Packer fullback, the gun went off, ending the game.

"All right, Jimmy," he said, "you can get up now. The game's over."

Some of football's most legendary players have been offensive linemen. The 49ers once had an offensive tackle, Bob St. Clair, who ate raw meat. Not rare, raw. In a restaurant he once looked at the menu and then looked up at the waiter.

"I'll have the steak," he said. "Raw."

"Did you say rare, sir?" the waiter asked. "Did you say you want your steak rare?"

"No, I want it raw."

"Raw?" the waiter said.

"That's right," St. Clair said. "Take it out of the refrigerator and put it on a plate."

"Yes, sir," the waiter said.

Another offensive tackle, Bob Brown, a 290-pounder who played mostly for the Eagles before finishing his NFL career with the Rams and the Raiders, had powerful arms. The day he joined the Raiders at their training camp, he walked by himself to the goalposts at the far end of the practice field. Getting down into his stance, the man known as the Boomer rammed his taped right forearm into one of the uprights. After wobbling for a moment, the upright toppled backward, tilting the crossbar askew.

"He actually knocked down the goalpost," John Madden recalls.

Imagine what the Boomer did to humans he had to block. That's one reason so many coaches believe that their most important players are offensive linemen.

Tackling

"DEE-FENSE, DEE-FENSE"

Reggie White: too big and too quick for most blockers

THERE'S NEVER BEEN ANYBODY IN FOOTBALL QUITE LIKE Reggie White, a preacher who is also an intimidator.

An ordained minister who has preached in more than one hundred churches since he was seventeen, the Green Bay Packers' 6-5, 300-pound defensive lineman is known as the "Minister of Defense." The offensive linemen who must block him and the quarterbacks and running backs who hope to avoid getting tackled by him fear his assault, but he understands the contradiction in his life.

"I believe I've been blessed with physical abilities in order to gain a platform to preach the Gospel," he has said. "People look at athletes as role models, and to be successful as an athlete, I've got to do what I do—hard but fair. I try to live a certain way and maybe that's had some kind of effect. I think God has allowed me to have an impact on a few people's lives."

As the NFL's career sack leader he certainly has had an impact on a few quarterback's bodies. And on his teammates' attitude.

"He leads by example better than any player I've ever been around," said Fritz Shurmer, the Packers' defensive coordinator. "He never misses a turn in practice. And he has special leadership examples."

In all the commotion of a game White has never been heard to curse. Chew out his teammates, yes, but not curse.

"Every time we play these guys," he once said near the end of a loss to the Cowboys, "they kick our tails."

His stature shows how appreciated defense has become among college and high school teams as well as in the NFL.

Until 1950, when the NFL changed its rules to permit free substitution, a player was expected to play both ways—offense and defense. A quarterback usually was also a defensive back; a fullback was also a linebacker. But with free substitution, coaches began developing separate units for offense and defense as well as specialists, such as placekickers and punters. As it turned out, some players were better suited, through either ability or temperament, for defense. Those who thrived on the physical aspect of football usually enjoyed defense more.

The DEE-fense Chant

Soon those players on the defensive unit had their own following. Whenever a home team is ahead now late in a close game and the opposing team gets the ball, the chant of "DEE-fense, DEE-fense" is heard, with the accent on the first syllable.

The word, of course, is "defense." It is properly pronounced "de-FENSE," with the accent on the second syllable, and the first syllable is properly pronounced "de," as in "deliver." But now many people pronounce it "DEE-fense," the way the New York Giants' fans first did around the time of the team's 1956 NFL championship.

That year the Giants had a defensive unit that included two future Hall of Famers, Andy Robustelli at right end and Sam Huff at middle linebacker.

In previous years one of football's most popular cheers had been "Hold that line," but in beseeching their team to stop the opponent, Giant fans simplified it to "DEE-fense, DEE-fense." Hearing it on television, football fans in other NFL cities and in college stadiums began to use that cheer. So did fans of other sports, notably basketball.

Although DEE-fense is not the preferred pronunciation, when chanted at a sports event, especially a football game, somehow it sounds better.

The cheer also helped to identify the value of the defensive unit. According to coaches at all levels of football, a team won't be successful without a good defense. A team can't hope to outscore its opponents all the time. It must be able to *stop* its opponent from scoring.

In football a defensive unit has four groups of players—linemen, linebackers, cornerbacks, and safeties.

In a four-man defensive line, there are two ends and two tackles. In a three-man defensive line, there are two ends and what is called a nose tackle because he usually crouches across from the nose of the offensive center, who is about to snap the ball to the quarterback. With either four or three players, the defensive line is primarily responsible for the pass rush on the opposing quarterback.

The defensive line is also responsible for stopping running plays, but its ends in particular should be good pass rushers.

Through the years some of the NFL's most popular players have been those on a defensive line—the Steel Curtain of the four-time Super Bowl champion Steelers (L. C. Greenwood, Joe Greene, Ernie Holmes, Dwight White); the Fearsome Foursome of the Rams (Deacon Jones, Merlin Olsen, Roosevelt Grier, Lamar Lundy); the Purple People Eaters of the Vikings (Carl Eller, Alan Page, Gary Larsen, Jim Marshall); the Doomsday Defense of the Cowboys (George Andrie, Jethro Pugh, Bob Lilly, Larry Cole); and the New York Sack Exchange of the Jets (Mark Gastineau, Abdul Salaam, Marty Lyons, Joe Klecko).

Defensive ends usually are taller and quicker than defensive tackles, but not much. The taller the pass rushers are, the harder it is for a quarterback to see over them or through them in trying to find a pass receiver.

As big as defensive linemen are, they also must be quick, meaning they must be able to move with agility despite their weight. Years ago it was enough for some defensive linemen to be heavy. But with offensive players so much quicker now, the defensive lineman must be even quicker if he is to get around them.

Marchetti and Lilly

One of the quickest defensive ends was Gino Marchetti, who played on the Colt teams that won the 1958 and 1959 NFL championships. At practice one day Marchetti lined up against a rookie offensive tackle who was unable to cope with the All-Pro's moves. On one play Marchetti faked the rookie to the right, then sped past him on the left. Noticing that the rookie appeared discouraged, Coach Weeb Ewbank had a suggestion.

"Get lower," Ewbank said. "You've got to get your rear end lower if you expect to block Gino."

On the next play the rookie offensive tackle crouched lower. Marchetti faked him to the left this time and went by him on the right. Ewbank shook his head.

"Lower, lower," the coach said, "you've got to get lower."

On the next play the rookie offensive tackle was down even lower. Instead of trying to go around him, Marchetti put one of his hands on the rookie's helmet and leapfrogged *over* him. Startled and frustrated, the rookie looked around at Ewbank.

"What do I do now, coach?" he asked.

"Applaud," Ewbank said with a shrug.

Marchetti was 6-4 and 245 pounds, yet he was able to leapfrog over that husky offensive tackle as if the rookie were a fireplug. That's quickness. That's what offensive tackles must cope with in their man-to-man matchups with defensive ends. Offensive guards, meanwhile, match up with defensive tackles. One of the best defensive tackles was Bob Lilly, a member of the Cowboys' Doomsday Defense.

"Lilly," the Cowboys' coach Tom Landry said, "is the best player I've ever coached."

As a rookie Lilly was used at defensive end, but he floundered at that position. Switched to defensive tackle by Landry, he went on to a Hall of Fame career that included the Cowboys' victory in Super Bowl VI. Years later Landry explained why the 6-5, 225-pound Lilly was more suited to tackle than end.

Bob Lilly of the Cowboys simply hauled down ballcarriers.

"At tackle," the Cowboys' coach said, "Bob could be out of position and still get back to make the play because of his great quick-

ness, his agility, his balance, and his strength. At end he didn't have as much time to do that effectively."

Stories of Lilly's strength began at Texas Christian University, where he was known as the "Purple Cloud," after the color of the school's uniform. One day he was with a classmate who teased him about his strength and pointed to a Volkswagen that was parked nearby.

"If you're so strong," his classmate said, "let's see you lift that VW onto the sidewalk."

After walking around the little car to size it up, Lilly lifted the rear end onto the sidewalk. Then he walked around to the front end and lifted that onto the sidewalk. His classmate shook his head in disbelief. Afterward the story of Lilly's strength was exaggerated day by day.

"It got so," Lilly said later, "that some people were saying that I put the car up on the library steps. I'd have needed a crane to do that."

Lilly thrived in the four-three defense that Landry perfected with the Cowboys—four defensive linemen and three linebackers behind them. In recent years some NFL teams have preferred to use a three-four defense: three linemen and four linebackers. Whatever the defense, linebackers provide a triple threat. They must be able to rush the passer in what is called a "blitz." They must be able to stack up a running play up the middle or swoop out near the sideline on a sweep. They must also be able to stay with a swift running back moving out on a pass pattern.

L.T. and Butkus

To do this well, a linebacker often must rely on his intuition, an educated guess as to the opposing team's play. Lawrence Taylor is considered to have been one of the most intuitive linebackers.

"When the ball is snapped," the Giant linebacker once said, "I can kind of read everything up and down the line. It's an instinct that tells me where to go. I don't know how that is, but it is."

That's intuition, a sense of knowing what to do and how to do it.

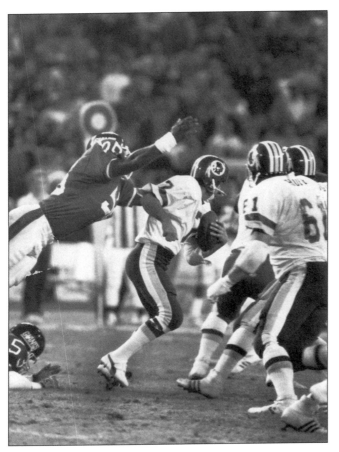

Lawrence Taylor about to sack Redskins quarterback Joe Theismann

At 6-3 and 245 pounds, Taylor had that intuition. Since he played in a three-four defense that used four linebackers, he was one of two outside linebackers—one outside the right end, the other outside the left end. Between them were the two inside linebackers. But when a team prepared to play the Giants, its coaches were mostly concerned with how to prevent Taylor from disrupting its offense.

"Taylor," said Dick Vermeil, once the Philadelphia Eagles' coach, "can cause you more problems in the preparation of an offensive game plan than any other single player I ever coached against."

In a four-three defense one middle linebacker is between two outside linebackers. Because he is able to roam wherever the play goes, the middle linebacker has been one of the most popular defensive players. The era of the middle linebacker began when Sam Huff was on the Giants' teams that inspired the "DEE-fense" cheer. "Huff, Huff, Huff!" the Giants' fans would yell, making a sound like that of a locomotive puffing. "Huff, Huff, Huff!" But he was only one of several outstanding NFL middle linebackers then. The others were Ray Nitschke of the Packers, Joe Schmidt of the Detroit Lions, and Bill George of the Bears.

As effective as those four were, Dick Butkus was even better. Joining the Bears in 1965 out of the University of Illinois, he quickly established himself as an All-Pro middle linebacker. He didn't just try to tackle a ballcarrier; he tried to make him fumble. He often succeeded. During his senior season at Illinois, he caused 10 fumbles, an extraordinary number.

"I want to get a good measure on a guy and strip him down," he once said. "If I can strip him down and make him drop the ball, that takes it out of guys."

The son of Lithuanian immigrant parents, Butkus grew up in Chicago with four older brothers, all of whom had played football but not as well as he would. Of the five brothers, however, Dick was the smallest.

"I'm nothing but little brother," he once said. "When they surround me, you can't even see the top of my head. They hide me completely."

But nobody hid Dick Butkus on a football field until knee injuries shortened his career. Unwisely he kept playing on those bad knees until he was unable to run properly. Just about the time he had to stop playing, another middle linebacker arrived who would be compared with him—Jack Lambert of the Steelers.

Dick Butkus lifts the Packers' John Brockington into the air.

As a rookie, Lambert took over at middle linebacker on the Steeler team that would win Super Bowl IX. The following season, as the Steelers repeated in Super Bowl X, all three of their linebackers were selected to the All-Pro team—Jack Ham and Andy Russell in addition to Lambert.

"I think that's what I'm proudest of," Lambert once said. "Imagine having all three of our linebackers selected as the NFL's three best linebackers—that's really a great honor. That never happened before. And who knows, it might never happen again. When all three make All-Pro like that, it means that each of us is doing a good job."

At 6-4 and 220 pounds, Lambert often was teased by his teammates for his aggressive style.

"Jack Lambert is so mean," defensive tackle Joe Greene often joked, "he doesn't even like himself."

But in serious moments Greene praised Lambert as the "spark" of the Steeler defense.

The Value of Cornerbacks

For all the headlines about linebackers and defensive linemen, Al Davis, who built the Raider organization into one of the NFL's best, believes that cornerbacks are the most important players on a football team. Not just on defense, but on the *entire* team.

"You start with cornerbacks," Davis says, "and then you build the rest of your team."

When the Los Angeles Raiders won Super Bowl XVIII in January 1984, they had what many football people considered to be the two best cornerbacks on any one team—Lester Hayes at left cornerback and Mike Haynes at right cornerback. The position of cornerback was established in 1952 by Dick (Night Train) Lane, who had played one season at Scottsbluff (Nebraska) Junior College and four seasons with the Fort Ord (California) team—as an offensive end. Discharged from the Army in 1952, he walked into the Los Angeles Rams' office. That year the Rams were the defending NFL champions, but they signed him as a free agent for a $4,500 salary—if he made the team.

Used as an offensive end at first, he was confused by the unfamiliar terminology. Switched to defense, he found himself covering pass receivers as no one else ever had.

As a rookie Lane had 14 interceptions, which is still the NFL record for one season. He also led the NFL in 1954 with 10 interceptions. In his career with the Rams, the Chicago Cardinals, and the Lions, he had 68 interceptions, the most of any cornerback. Two safeties have had more—Paul Krause of the Vikings with 81 and Emlen Tunnell of the Giants and Packers with 79.

"At cornerback," Lane often said, "you're going to get beat, but you've got to have a sense of recovery."

Night Train got his marvelous nickname as a rookie. During his trial as an offensive end in the Rams' training camp, he often visited Tom Fears, the Rams' best receiver, in his dormitory room to talk about pass patterns. Fears had a favorite musical recording, Buddy Morrow's rendition of "Night Train," which he often played on his phonograph. Whenever another rookie, Ben Sheets, stopped by Fears's room, Lane was usually there with "Night Train" playing in the background.

"Hey," said Sheets one day, "there's Night Train."

The name stuck. In the years that followed, it sometimes was shortened to Train by teammates and opponents alike. He was so feared as a cornerback that Vince Lombardi, the Packers' coach, once ordered quarterback Bart Starr not to throw a pass in his area.

"Don't throw anywhere near him," Lombardi said. "Train's the best there is."

The responsibilities of a left cornerback and a right cornerback are virtually the same—cover the wide receiver lined up on that side of the field. But the responsibilities of the two safetymen are much different. One is known as the strong safety because he lines up across from the "strong" side of the offensive team, the side with the tight end. On passing plays the strong safety is usually assigned to cover the tight end. The free safety meanwhile is exactly that—free, at least in man-to-man coverage, to roam wherever he thinks he should be, perhaps to join a teammate in double-covering a certain receiver. But in zone coverage, he is assigned to protect a certain area.

The free safety is also available for one of the most exciting plays on defense—the safety blitz.

What Larry Wilson Wrought

From about five or six yards behind the line of scrimmage, the free safety shoots past the offensive linemen as if he were a linebacker trying to sack the quarterback. When successful, this is a sensational maneuver. But every so often the free safety is stopped, usually by a husky running back assigned to remain as a blocker for the passer.

In one of his last games, Y. A. Tittle suffers the agony of a sack.

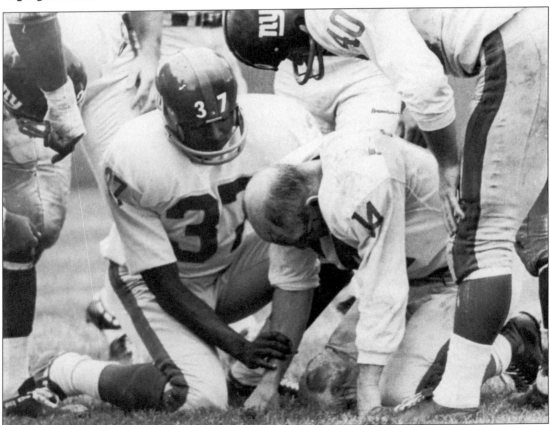

Larry Wilson, who was a free safety with the St. Louis Cardinals, is credited with inventing the safety blitz.

"It takes the soul of a linebacker," he often said with a smile, "and the mentality of a mule."

Wilson tried to time his blitz so that it coincided with the snap, making it more difficult for a blocker to stop him. When he timed it perfectly, he appeared to pounce on the quarterback as if he were a mountain lion leaping out of a tree.

"The first time I ever did it was against Charlie Conerly of the Giants," he recalled. "He didn't know where I came from."

Wilson was considered one of the NFL's toughest players. Not that big at 6-0 and 190 pounds, he had the eyes of a hawk under a shock of blond hair. His firm jaw symbolized his determination. He once actually played a game in 1965 with both hands in casts. From a distance he appeared to be wearing two white boxing gloves. He not only played but also intercepted a pass and returned it 34 yards for a touchdown in a 21–17 victory over the Steelers.

"Larry's not a 'holler' guy," one of his teammates, Jerry Stovall, once said. "Larry's a 'do' guy."

With today's more complicated pass defenses, most NFL coaches use five, six, and even seven defensive backs in certain obvious passing situations. In order to make room for another defensive back, a linebacker usually is removed. Defense has come a long way since the Giants' defensive unit in 1956 was the first in the NFL to be introduced before a game over the public-address system. Ever since then offensive players have had to share the headlines with defensive players.

"Championships," Vince Lombardi once said, "are won on defense."

COACHING IS TEACHING

In his houndstooth hat, Paul (Bear) Bryant was a Bear on the Alabama sideline.

IN THE ALABAMA FOOTBALL OFFICE, COACH PAUL (BEAR) Bryant dialed the telephone number for Auburn University, the Crimson Tide's state rival. Bryant wanted to talk to the Auburn coach, but when the switchboard operator took the call, she glanced at her wristwatch. It was shortly after seven o'clock in the morning.

"I'm sorry," the operator said, "but there's nobody in the coach's office yet."

"What's the matter?" Bryant asked. "Don't your people take football seriously?"

Few people have taken football as seriously as Bear Bryant did. When he finally retired at age sixty-nine after his 'Bama team concluded its 1982 season by winning the Liberty Bowl game, he had more victories than any other coach in college football history—323—against only 85 losses and 17 ties. But on January 26, 1983, he died suddenly of a heart attack.

"Football is my life," the coach in the houndstooth hat often said. "If I retired I'd be dead in a week."

College and high school graduates usually agree that their best teachers were the ones who worked them the hardest. And to Bryant a football coach was simply a "teacher, but he better be a leader, too." He'd better have some good players as well. Bryant had good players. He developed several outstanding NFL quarterbacks, notably Joe Namath, George Blanda, Ken Stabler, Vito (Babe) Parilli, and Richard Todd.

As the Bear, Bryant had one of America's most famous sports nicknames. He was a big man, at 6-4 and more than 200 pounds, but he earned his nickname for a dare, not for his size.

Growing up in Morro Bottom, Arkansas, one of eleven children in a poor farm family, he attended nearby Fordyce High School, where he played football. One day he walked into the town of Fordyce with his best friends, the Jordan twins. They were going to the movies at what he called a "picture theater" when they noticed a poster. It offered a dollar for each minute anybody wrestled a real bear inside the theater, owned by a Mr. Smith.

"They egged me on," he later recalled, referring to the twins, "and Mr. Smith lined it up with the fellow who had the bear. Mr. Smith agreed to let me and my friends into the picture free."

Inside the theater he was relieved to see that the bear was somewhat scrawny. Although he wrestled it to the floor, the bear bit his ear. He later went to collect his money, but the man with the bear had skipped town.

"All I ever got out of it," Bryant often said, chuckling, "was a nickname."

But that nickname enhanced his reputation as a football player. In high school he was a tackle; at Alabama he played end. The other end was Don Hutson, who went on to make NFL history with the Packers as a pass receiver. Bear Bryant went on to coaching. His teams were awarded six national championships and played in twenty-six consecutive bowl games.

"Get an Education First"

Another of football's true teachers has been Joe Paterno, whose Penn State teams earned the unofficial national college championships in 1982 and 1986 and were the first to win all four major college bowl games: Rose, Orange, Sugar, and Cotton.

"Joe Paterno has never forgotten," President Ronald Reagan once said, "that he is a teacher who is preparing his students not just for the season, but for life."

Going into the 1997 season, Paterno, the Penn State head coach since 1966, had guided the Nittany Lions to a 289-74-3 record, including undefeated but uncrowned seasons in 1968, 1969, 1973, and 1994. But for all his success he has always been aware that while more than 150 of his players, notably running back Franco Harris and linebacker Jack Ham (each now in the Pro Football Hall of Fame), have gone on to the NFL, thousands of others won't play football again.

Joe Paterno believes in "education first" at Penn State.

"His philosophy was that college was getting an education first," John Skorupan, a 1972 All-American linebacker, has said. "I think we always felt we had someone special in Joe Paterno. I was part of the 'Grand Experiment'—that football players can get an education, that they can talk, that they're not dumb jocks."

In an era when sports uniforms are flashier and more colorful than ever before, some people deride Penn State's uniforms as old-fashioned: a white helmet without a logo, a plain navy blue or white jersey without the player's name on the back, and high-top black shoes. But the uniform reflects Paterno's teachings.

"I think they say something to kids," he has said, "about team-oriented play and an austere approach to life."

That philosophy has earned Paterno four Coach of the Year awards from the American Football Coaches Association.

"More than anything else, coaches are teachers and educators," he has said. "We have the same obligations as all teachers at our institutions, except we probably have more influence over our young people than anyone other than their families. We're dealing with discipline, and loyalty and pride. The things that make a difference in a person's life—pride, loyalty, and commitment—are the things that make a difference in this country. We're teaching them the realities of the competitive life."

All Those Assistant Coaches

In football, a coach's first responsibility is teaching the fundamentals to players, especially to youngsters. Even in the NFL some players need to be reminded of various fundamentals, depending on their positions on the team. Footwork and technique for a running back, for example, are much different than they are for a defensive tackle. That's one reason why NFL teams, college teams, and even some high school teams have several assistant coaches—to teach players at different positions.

In addition to the head coach, an NFL or a major college team usually has a coach tutoring the quarterbacks, another working with the running backs, another with the pass receivers, another with the offensive linemen, another with the defensive linemen, another with the linebackers, and another with the defensive backs. Most teams also have an offensive coordinator and a defensive coordinator to tie everything together, along with another assistant coach who supervises the special teams.

The head coach, of course, makes the final decisions on which players make the starting team as well as the team roster. Selecting the players is not as easy as it sounds. Johnny Unitas, the quarterback who had a Hall of Fame career with the Baltimore Colts, originally was drafted by the Pittsburgh Steelers, who cut him as a rookie at training camp. At the time the Steelers had three other quarter-backs—Jim Finks, Ted Marchibroda, and a rookie, Vic Eaton.

In the NFL, rookies are drafted after the teams have scouted college players at games, on films, and sometimes at individual workouts. In the draft, each team is allowed seven selections each year; the team with the worst record during the previous season is the first to draft, the next worst team is second, and so on down to the Super Bowl champion, which is the last, or thirtieth, team to draft. Each team usually has more or fewer than seven choices because it is allowed to trade a choice, even in the first round, to another team.

After the draft is completed, an eligible player who has not been chosen is considered a free agent, meaning he may sign with any of the thirty teams.

In addition to recognizing talent, a coach must decide a player's best position. Some psychological studies point out that a player with an aggressive personality is more likely to succeed on defense. It's important for a coach to try to place a player at a position that fits his personality. A coach always tries to find a quarterback with the personality of a leader. But a team needs more than one leader.

"You need leaders every-where," John Madden, the former Raiders' coach, has said. "On offense, on defense, and on special teams."

Calling the Plays

Most quarterbacks resent having plays sent in to them. They prefer to call their own plays. As much

As the Raiders' coach, John Madden could get excited.

as Otto Graham, the quarterback on the famous Cleveland teams, respected Paul Brown, he disagreed with his coach's philosophy in this regard.

"We have eleven coaches on the field," Graham once said. "Various players will report to me on plays that might work. Paul Brown also got that information, but my criticism is that he might be one or two plays behind what I would have called."

As with today's quarterbacks, Graham had the option of calling a different play if he thought the play that had been sent in would not work. Usually such a change is made at the line of scrimmage in what is known as an audible: the quarterback barks new signals, usually a combination of colors and numbers. To do that well, the quarterback must be a quick thinker; his teammates also must recognize the new signals instantly.

During the 1983 season, Danny White of the Cowboys changed the play during an important game with the Redskins after he discussed the original play with Coach Tom Landry during a timeout. Watching from the sideline, Landry could be seen yelling, "No, no," in an unusual display of annoyance. White's play didn't succeed.

Landry had several reasons for preferring to send in plays to his quarterback, as do all the coaches who prefer this method. First, the coach feels he has a better knowledge of which play will work best in that situation. Second, by knowing what the play is going to be, he is better

Tom Landry discusses strategy with Roger Staubach.

able to watch how it develops. Third, by using a certain play at a certain time, he feels he might be able to set up the use of another play later in the game. Fourth, he is constantly being alerted to developments in the opposing team's defense by assistant coaches perched in a booth on the press-box level.

Another decision for a head coach, of course, occurs every time his offense is faced with fourth down.

In order to gain another first down, his team must advance the ball at least ten yards from where it began on first down. But if his team is close to a first down, say one yard or less, a coach has to decide whether to try to run or pass for at least the necessary yardage. If his team is close to a first down but within the range of his place-kicker, a coach must decide whether to continue the drive for a touchdown or be content with a field goal attempt. And in almost any other situation on fourth down, he must decide whether it is better to punt.

The Second Guess

No matter what the coach decides, if his decision doesn't work out to his team's advantage, he will be second-guessed by his team's fans for having made the wrong decision.

Anybody can second-guess a coach *after* the play is over or *after* the game is over. But the coach has only one guess—what will work best in this particular situation at this particular time. If the play of his choice turns out to be successful, especially if it wins the game, he is hailed as a genius. But if the play backfires, he is criticized for having made a mistake. For the fan it's fun to second-guess the coach for a mistake. But the coach also deserves credit when he makes a decision that is successful.

Just as a coach makes mistakes in judgment, players make mistakes in executing their plays.

Win or lose, coaches often say that "football is a game of mistakes," meaning that the team with the fewest mistakes usually wins.

**Don
Shula**

Quite often a player's mistake will result in a penalty—illegal motion by a running back, holding by an offensive lineman, defensive pass interference by a cornerback, to name only three. For many years one of the NFL's least penalized teams was the Miami Dolphins under Don Shula.

"You just don't make mistakes when you play for Shula—he won't stand for it," fullback Larry Csonka once said. "If you do, you're gone."

Instilling that determination in his players not to make mistakes is part of how a good coach motivates his team. His players concentrate on their assignments, no matter what position each plays. They don't jump offside. They don't forget to stay with a certain pass receiver.

Above all they don't forget the offensive play or the defensive coverage. Throughout football history that has been the trademark of the best teams and the best coaches.

In motivating players with words, the best coaches have all been a little different.

Some have been dramatic, as Knute Rockne was when he told his Notre Dame team to "win one for the Gipper." Others have been emotional, as Vince Lombardi was when he told his Packers before the first Super Bowl, "You're representing the entire National Football League." Others have been scientific, as Tom Landry was in explaining the Cowboys' game plan. Others have been sentimental, as Bear Bryant was when he told his Alabama players that they had "good mamas and papas."

Year after year the best coaches seem to have the best teams—not always championship teams, but usually winning teams.

Such success prompts a question—do the best coaches attract the best players, or do the best coaches make the players they have play better than other coaches could? The answer is, a little of both. In college football, where a player has a choice of what school he wants to attend, a famous coach will attract more good players than a lesser-known coach will.

"I went to Alabama," said Ray Perkins, once a Crimson Tide wide receiver and later their coach, "because I wanted to play for Bear Bryant."

Through the years other players have gone to Notre Dame, Oklahoma, Southern Cal, Grambling, and dozens of other famous football colleges to play for certain coaches. But in the NFL a rookie (unless he is a free agent) doesn't have a choice of teams. He must report to the team that selected him in the draft of college players. Even so, the same coaches have been able to produce some of the best teams—Don Shula with the Colts and the Dolphins, Chuck Noll with the Steelers, Tom Landry with the Cowboys, Bill Walsh with the 49ers, Joe Gibbs with the Redskins, Jimmy Johnson with the Cowboys and Dolphins, Bill Parcells with the Giants, Patriots, and Jets.

Obviously these coaches lift the skill level of their players, no matter what the turnover of the roster.

Emotion and Players

Because football is more of an emotional game than, say, baseball, the football coach seems to be more important to a team's success than a baseball manager is. One reason for the emotional

Bill Walsh in 1981, his first Super Bowl season with the 49ers

character of football is that it is played only once a week. Through several days of practice, a team builds to a peak for that game. Baseball, in contrast, is played almost every day on the major league level. With that daily schedule, emotional peaks and valleys would wear out players. But in football, players seem to react to emotion.

"Without emotion it's hard to win a football game," Tom Landry said. "If the other team has emotion and your team doesn't, chances are the other team is going to win."

For all the coaching and emotions involved, of course, a team still needs good players to win, usually better ones than the opposing team has. Without such players a good coach is helpless. He may make his men perform somewhat better than they otherwise would. But that doesn't mean he can make a team of poor players capable of beating a team with much better players. Perhaps that was never more clearly shown than in the years when Johnny Lattner, a Notre Dame halfback who later won the 1953 Heisman Trophy, was the best player on Frank Leahy's team. One day Leahy's wife, Floss, broke her leg in a household accident. At the hospital she phoned her husband during the second day of practice.

"Frank," she said, "I'm sorry to call you off the practice field, but I'm in the hospital."

"What's wrong, Floss?"

"I broke my left leg."

"Are you all right?" the coach asked.

"I'm all right."

The coach's wife paused, then said, "Frank?"

"Yes, Floss, what is it?"

"Better me than Johnny Lattner, huh, Frank?"

Yes, good coaches need good players. But without good coaches, good players don't always perform up to their potential. Despite the sometimes complicated vocabulary of football, it remains a game that depends on two basic elements—blocking on offense, tackling on defense. For all the mystique that surrounded his coaching, Vince Lombardi never pretended to confuse the issue.

"This game," he often said, "is blocking and tackling. If you do that better than the other team does, you win."

As with all outstanding coaches, Vince Lombardi also believed in the discipline that creates effective blocking and tackling, the discipline that helps a team avoid costly mistakes. That discipline, he knew, begins with the coach.

"The perfect name for the perfect coach," he once said, "would be Simple Simon Legree."

FOR SEVERAL YEARS NOW, FOOTBALL HAS SURPASSED BASE-ball as America's most popular sport.

One reason is that television, with its instant replays, has provided another look at action that often happened too fast to be fully appreciated by the spectators in the stadium. But perhaps the most important reason is that football is rooted in America on four levels—from neighborhood leagues for youngsters up through high schools and colleges and on to the National Football League.

Just about everybody can root for a team at one of those competitive levels, if not for teams on several levels.

Part of football's appeal is that it's a physical game. It's known as a contact sport, but Vince Lombardi once defined football properly. "Dancing is a contact sport," he said. "Football is a collision sport." In football, a collision sometimes produces an injury. That's why the players wear so much protective equipment, such as helmets and shoulder pads. But the collisions are what a real football player enjoys. The collisions are also what a real football fan enjoys.

Unlike most other sports, football is basically played by a team only once a week. As a result a football game is more of an event for its fans than baseball, basketball, or ice hockey, the other major spectator sports.

For many of those fans interested in college football or the NFL or both, television provides that event. Several college games are usually televised on a Saturday, two and occasionally three NFL games on a Sunday, with another NFL game broadcast on a Monday night.

More than most sports, football is subject to the second-guess by any fan worth the mustard on a hot dog.

With feet as quick as his arm, Joe Montana scores in Super Bowl XIX.

Anytime a play doesn't work, the fan in the stands or watching television will wonder why a different play wasn't called. The fan is always smarter than the quarterback or the coach, or so the fan believes. Down on the sideline the coach resembles a commander in combat. He stares out at what is happening on the field while evaluating the information supplied by his aides and his troops, visualizing the game films he has studied. But the fan is always smarter, or so the fan believes.

If fans didn't think that, they wouldn't be so interested in what was happening. In a sense that too is why football is so popular.

Much of the excitement in a close game is created by the final minutes flashing away on the scoreboard clock. The referee blows his whistle. Two-minute warning. Only two minutes remain for the team that is behind by four points to score a touchdown; for the team that is behind by two points, to kick a field goal. The very sight of those seconds flashing away...1:59...1:58...1:57...all the way down to :02...:01...:00...creates the tension that stirs the body and soul not only of the players and coaches but also of the fans.

On the field in those last two minutes, the players and even the coaches are part of the action. The fan must suffer from a distance.

Of the major sports in America, football also is the only one that has not departed on a round-the-world trip. Baseball has been an important sport in Japan for many years. Basketball is a worldwide sport, as is ice hockey. Basketball, baseball, and ice hockey are Olympic sports. Soccer, boxing, golf, tennis, and track-and-field have long been world sports.

But except for Canada (where it's played with slightly different rules) and the World League (where it's played in the spring in six European cities) football has remained an American sport, played by Americans (except for foreign soccer-style placekickers) for Americans.

As a result most Americans are able to identify with football players. Not that most Americans are as big or as fast as the best football players. But an American football fan may have attended the same college as his favorite wide receiver, or a fan will have grown up in the same town or area as her favorite linebacker, or a fan will root for a player simply because he is a member of that fan's favorite college team or pro team.

Football began obscurely on that field at Rutgers in 1869, developed slowly as a student activity on college campuses all over the nation, spread through the National Football League and other professional leagues into huge stadiums and onto television screens across the nation. Now, as the twenty-first century approaches, it is truly an American spectacle.

How to Reach 'Hard to Reach' Children

Improving access, participation and outcomes

Edited by
KA POMERANTZ
M HUGHES
D THOMPSON

John Wiley & Sons, Ltd

Other Wiley Editorial Offices

John Wiley & Sons Inc., 111 River Street, Hoboken, NJ 07030, USA

Jossey-Bass, 989 Market Street, San Francisco, CA 94103-1741, USA

Wiley-VCH Verlag GmbH, Boschstr. 12, D-69469 Weinheim, Germany

John Wiley & Sons Australia Ltd, 42 McDougall Street, Milton, Queensland 4064, Australia

John Wiley & Sons (Asia) Pte Ltd, 2 Clementi Loop #02-01, Jin Xing Distripark, Singapore 129809

John Wiley & Sons Canada Ltd, 6045 Freemont Blvd, Mississauga, ONT, L5R 4J3, Canada

Wiley also publishes its books in a variety of electronic formats. Some content that appears in print may
not be available in electronic books.

Anniversary Logo Design: Richard J. Pacifico

Library of Congress Cataloging-in-Publication Data

How to reach hard to reach children : improving access, participation and outcomes /
edited by KA Pomerantz, M Hughes and D Thompson.
        p. cm.
    Includes bibliographical references and index.
    ISBN 978-0-470-05884-8 (pbk.)
    1. Underachievers–Great Britain.   2. Children with social   disabilities–Education–Great Britain.
    3. Children–Services   for–Great Britain.   4. Child welfare–Great Britain.   I. Pomerantz,
    Kathryn Anne.   II. Hughes, M.   III. Thompson, D.
    LC4696.G7H68 2007

    378.772'95–dc22

                                                                                    2007002346

British Library Cataloguing in Publication Data
A catalogue record for this book is available from the British Library

ISBN: 978-0-470-05884-8

Typeset by Aptara, Delhi, India.
Printed and bound in Great Britain by TJ International Ltd, Padstow, Cornwall.
This book is printed on acid-free paper responsibly manufactured from sustainable forestry in which at
least two trees are planted for each one used for paper production.

Contents

List of Contributors

Peter Lloyd Bennett   Peter taught for 15 years in primary, secondary and special schools before studying educational psychology at University College London in 1990. As an Educational Psychologist and Researcher, he has written on a number of subjects within the areas of psychology and education. He is the book review editor for *Debate*, which is published by the Division of Educational and Child Psychology. He has four children and lives in Northamptonshire. He is currently employed in Peterborough as an Educational Psychologist.

Mary Chilokoa   Mary is an Educational Psychologist with the Leeds Psychology and Assessment Service. She is a member of the EdD Educational Psychology course at Sheffield University. A practising Buddhist, she has a keen interest in constructions of the self and reality, but especially in the vast potential of human beings. In this vein, her research interests include resilience and the factors that can promote it, peer support and the power of meaningful relationships to maximize the potential of young people in difficulty. Mary is also interested in the ways that perceptions of 'truth' may be challenged and deconstructed.

Joanne Catherine Holt   Joanne works as an Educational Psychologist for Lancashire County Council and has a specific professional interest in the education of children and young people with deafness. She is studying for an EdD in Educational Psychology at Sheffield University. Her research interests include multi-agency working and developing children as researchers.

Martin Hughes   Martin has worked in three educational psychology services in the UK, with the Ministry of Education in Singapore and is currently a Senior Educational Psychologist for Sheffield City Council. His research interests include multi-agency aspects of Children's Services, identifying vulnerability and young people's views of help and change linked to motivational interviewing. A member of the EdD Educational Psychology Course at Sheffield University, Martin also does occasional work as an expert witness.

Stephanie James   Stephanie is an Area Principal Psychologist at the Highland Council and editor of the Association of Educational Psychologists' professional journal, *Educational Psychology in Practice*. A former secondary school teacher, Stephanie's teaching and research interests focus on social inclusion and children's self-perceptions of competence, particularly as these relate to their willingness to engage with, and access, learning opportunities.

Jackie Lown   Jackie is Co-Director of Doctor of Educational and Child Psychology at Sheffield University and a Senior Educational Psychologist in the City of York. Jackie's doctoral thesis concerned the reintegration of pupils who had previously been permanently excluded. Her particular research interests include emotional and behavioural difficulties and the inclusion of pupils with such problems, and personal and social education.

Nic McGrath   Nic has worked for Calderdale Educational Psychology Service. She is currently an Educational Psychologist at Education Bradford. Her research interests include working with the most vulnerable groups, hybrid practice within multi-agency services, parenting in difficult circumstances and family change. She is a member of the EdD Educational Psychology Course at Sheffield University.

Jane McKie   Jane is an Educational Psychologist for Kirklees Metropolitan Council and a member of the EdD Educational Psychology Course at Sheffield University. Her research interests are mainly orientated towards discourse analysis and include how knowledge about Children's Services is produced and consumed, and for whose benefit.

Heather Northcote   Heather has worked in two educational psychology services in England and is currently an Educational Psychologist for Derbyshire County Council. She has a specialist role with the Youth Offending Team in Derbyshire for part of her work and is a member of the EdD Educational Psychology Course at Sheffield University. Her research interests include promoting well-being and resilience, perceptions of young offenders from within the community and effective processes in multi-agency working.

Kathryn Anne Pomerantz   Kathryn is Co-Director of Doctor of Educational and Child Psychology at Sheffield University and Specialist Senior Educational Psychologist for Derbyshire County Council. Her work, in addition to training, involves practising as an Educational Psychologist on behalf of children and young people who become permanently excluded from school. Her research interests include the links between language, discourse and challenging behaviour.

Michael Pomerantz   Michael is a Senior Educational Psychologist in Derbyshire and an Associate Tutor to the postgraduate doctoral programmes in Educational Psychology at Sheffield University. His teaching and research interests focus on social justice, children's emotional and behavioural difficulties, vulnerability, marginalization, supervision, professional well-being, research communities and underachievement.

Jane Reid   Jane was an assistant head teacher responsible for special educational needs in a north London comprehensive school. She has also worked for several years with particularly vulnerable asylum seekers and refugees (mainly single women and those with special needs) for Migrant Helpline, an organization in the south-east of England.

David Thompson   David is a Senior Lecturer in Educational Psychology at Sheffield University. His research interests include establishing anti-bullying policies in schools and training for the welfare professions.

Lynn Turner   Lynn currently works as a Senior Educational Psychologist in Leeds and has also worked in Canada and the United States as a school psychologist. For the last two and a half years, she has been seconded in order to coordinate the Behaviour Improvement Programme in Leeds, part of the Government's Street Crime Initiative, with a focus upon multi-agency working through the setting up of Behaviour and Education Support Teams. She graduated from the doctoral programme in Sheffield in 2006 and was a contributor to a previous Sheffield publication about children at the margins. Her research interests have focused upon pupil voice and school improvement issues.

Brian Willis   Brian has worked as a Maingrade, Senior and Acting Principal Educational Psychologist for over 30 years in the north of England. He has carried out specialist work in the areas of behaviour and parent support, including autism. He has worked for North Lincolnshire Council since March 2007, carrying out specialist behaviour and parent support work with Children's Centres. His doctoral thesis concerns listening to and making sense of parent experiences of bringing up a child with autism so that child, provision and professional reachability are considered.

Preface

This book is devoted to considering how professionals can work together more effectively for the benefit of children and young people who are among the most vulnerable in our society. Its contribution is timely now that the Government's agenda Every Child Matters (ECM) is becoming a reality. Most of the contributors to the book are educational psychologists and have worked for many years with children and young people in an educational context. The authors draw from their own research and practice to bring to the surface examples of working collaboratively with professionals from other disciplines. They highlight the views of children, young people and their families to provide some insights as to how the Government's 'five outcomes' (being healthy, staying safe, enjoying and achieving, making a positive contribution and economic well-being) *can* be realized by children who are hard to see, hard to find, hard to engage, hard to manage, hard to change or retain within systems set up to help and educate them.

The book aims to provoke thoughts about the concept 'hard to reach', while attempting to avoid stigmatizing some groups of children and their families. It aims to illuminate some of the complexity around the term 'hard to reach', while attempting to include the perspective of the user, whose experience may be in terms of services and professionals, who are themselves 'hard to reach'. The book is attempting to position the term 'hard to reach' within the discourse around children and families as clients, or service users. It tries to do this respectfully, acknowledging that professionals can unwittingly or otherwise create barriers to access, participation and outcomes.

This book aims to:

- raise awareness of some of the complex issues surrounding definitions, consequences and practice in relation to reaching 'hard to reach' children;
- deliberately problematize assumptions that professionals can reach 'hard to reach' children;
- draw on young 'hard to reach' people's constructions of their reality;
- look at the processes involved in achieving multidisciplinary teamwork at a time when professionals are simply expected to work together more effectively;
- encourage readers, especially service providers, to reflect on how they work with other professionals to access 'hard to reach' children;
- provide practical suggestions for accessing the most vulnerable children in society who often presently slip through the established net of support services.

The introductory chapter sets out some of the features of the current landscape in which professionals working with children in different contexts are attempting to help children deemed 'hard to reach' work in a climate of social and political change and make sense of the agenda that includes meeting the ECM 'five outcomes'. The meaning of 'hard to reach' is explored from a number of different angles and concludes by encouraging us to view the term as a process as opposed to a state.

The chapters that follow aim to identify examples of inter-disciplinary joint work as well as raise the voices of children, young people and their families to provide some insights as to how the Government's 'five outcomes' can be realized in relation to the 'hard to reach'. Early chapters address core underlying difficulties in schools relating to underachievement, disengagement and school avoidance and explore both the consequences of school exclusion and practices that can enhance the inclusion of pupils with social, emotional and behavioural needs. Later chapters offer new and creative approaches to promoting multi-agency teamwork in relation to working with 'looked after' children, refugees and asylum seekers and those with challenging behaviour and autism and their families. Although specific 'hard to reach' groups are the focus of individual chapters, readers should be encouraged to reflect on the principles and suggested interventions as broadly applicable to most 'hard to reach' clients and services.

The penultimate chapter is of particular relevance to those engaged in focus group conversations that attempt to elicit the views of 'hard to reach' children and takes a critical look at the methods employed. The concluding chapter reflects the emphasis throughout the book of multidisciplinary teamwork, collaboration and the validation of children's views. As practitioners and writers we are committed to exploring, reflecting and changing our own practice to meet the ECM agenda for change and in doing so hope to provide inspiration to others.

SOME FINAL POINTS...

Wherever readers see the word *parents* in this book, please treat this as sometimes meaning *carers*.

In order to preserve the anonymity of children and adults involved in the studies described, all names have been changed.

A glossary includes some of the terms currently used by those working with and for children, young people and families.

Appendix 1 provides a guide to some of the recent relevant legislation and documents related to ECM and, more broadly, the social exclusion agenda. Appendix 2 contrasts factors from the perspective of the client with that of an agency as a means of perceiving and explaining the concept 'hard to reach'. Finally, Appendix 3 suggests some principles from practice relating to the 'hard to reach' from which services can draw in their quest to develop their practice and improve client access, participation and outcomes.

ACKNOWLEDGEMENTS

We would like to thank the friends, colleagues and relatives who have helped to shape this book by commenting on various earlier versions of this work. We acknowledge members of the wider educational psychology doctoral community at the University of Sheffield, who have encouraged and supported us, especially our colleagues Pat Bennett and Katherine Selkirk, who have helped to facilitate our discussions.

Thanks are also due to Nick Axford and others at the Dartington Social Research Unit, who gave us permission to use some of the terms from their common language glossary and to Sheffield City Council for supporting this project.

We would especially like to acknowledge the young people, parents and professionals who helped us construct the essence of our chapters and also the artist and young people who contributed to the cover picture during a consultation exercise for Sheffield's Children and Young People's Directorate.

Finally, this project would not have been possible without the love and support of our families, so big thanks to Cherry, Liz, Sam, Myra, Mike and Charles for your patience while we have been a bit out of reach for a while!

Introductory Chapter
Every Child Matters: Setting the Context for the 'Hard to Reach'

MARTIN HUGHES

INTRODUCTION

The vision framed by documents in the United Kingdom such as Every Child Matters (ECM, Department for Education and Skills, 2003) is likely to shape the agenda for professionals working with children and families for some considerable time. It provides the initial part of the context for this introductory chapter, which explores issues relating to 'hard to reach' children and families and provokes thoughts, while attempting to avoid stigmatizing 'hard to reach' children and families. This introductory chapter aims to illuminate some of the complexity surrounding the term 'hard to reach', while attempting to include the perspective of the service user, who may have experienced services and professionals as being 'hard to reach'. A brief consideration of 'risk' is followed by a critical description of some of the themes that currently shape the work of the 'helping' professional in the United Kingdom. The section that follows offers perspectives from a multi-agency angle by briefly considering the term 'hard to reach' in relation to crime, housing, health, Connexions (careers service) and education. In addition to different definitions and meanings, a number of key questions are raised. The chapter concludes with an outline for the rest of the book.

The following 'quotation' represents, ideologically, a vision of how services in the future will have achieved improved access, participation and outcomes for 'hard to reach' children:

> All services that work with people in this country now have a good understanding of how to identify and address the needs of children, arising from the involvement of their own particular agency. Support workers, irrespective of their agency, are well aware of the need to consider how their involvement may need to link with that of other professionals. Social and mental health workers have worked hard, together with those in education and other health professionals, to develop clear and accurate ways of identifying the most vulnerable children and families. In contrast to the early part of this century, when there was a growing realisation that too much time and energy was spent on the identification and assessment of needs, we now collectively work more intelligently at collaborative efforts so as to address the needs of children and families who are most vulnerable and

most in need. After a few false starts, there is growing confidence that we now have the right structures in place which serve the needs of vulnerable children and families very well. After the freeing up of agency boundaries, the development of new roles (which started with notions such as social pedagogues) and new thinking about team practice (such as the development of transdisciplinary practice), we have moved well beyond the ECM five outcomes: being healthy; staying safe; enjoying and achieving; making a positive contribution; and achieving economic well-being. We have good links now with Children's Services in other European countries, and in the United Kingdom there has not been a serious case review for two years in the Greater London area and for five years in most of the other parts of the United Kingdom.

If such a vision of the future is to be more than fiction, then all of us involved in delivering services to children and families, in health, education, social care, youth justice, community and voluntary agencies, have our work cut out, for the next few years at least.

In this introductory chapter, we search for meanings in the term 'hard to reach', make links and associations with relevant areas of the literature and practice, from areas which reflect the current *Zeitgeist* in the form of the multi-agency agenda within Children's Services. A number of different considerations of children and young people are offered, for instance:

- by location (children out of school or rarely in school for various reasons);
- specific vulnerable groups (such as 'looked after' children, children excluded from school, children with communication difficulties);
- children who become 'hard to reach' due to family difficulties;
- by considering ways in which professionals can be 'hard to reach'.

In the chapters which follow, a number of possibilities are raised from which different definitions of and interventions for the 'hard to reach' may emerge.

KEY DOCUMENTS AND MODELS

What is shaping the direction of the future vision, represented by the fictitious quote at the start of this chapter? Core documents have set out a national, long-term programme of change and include *Every Child Matters* (Department for Education and Skills, 2003), the National Service Framework for Children, Young People and Maternity Services (described as a 10-year programme intended to stimulate long-term and sustained improvement in children's health and associated standards and targets) (see Department of Health, 2002, 2004a, 2004b), including the expectation that comprehensive mental health services for children and young people would be available in all areas by 2006.

Tiered models (NHS, (1995), which have become prevalent in the last 10 years, emphasize opportunities for preventative work (by professionals such as GPs, Health Visitors, School Nurses, etc.) at the pyramid base, perhaps the least intrusive level of intervention (see Figure 1.1), in the hope that fewer concerns escalate to the top of the pyramid (where tier 4 includes day units, highly specialized outpatient teams and in-patient units). Yet, it might be argued that it is the relatively few concerns at the top

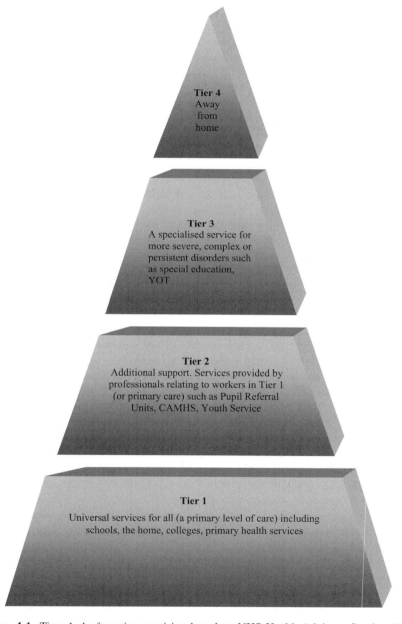

Figure 1.1. Tiers 1–4 of service provision based on NHS Health Advisory Service (1995) *Together We Stand, Chapter 10, p. 102, Figure 14*. To some extent, the tier is determined by where the service is offered and the severity and complexity of the problem. For instance, clinical child psychologists, child and adolescent psychiatrists and family therapy could all be offered at tiers 2–3, depending on whether or not these professionals had a community or clinic-based focus.

that cause the greatest stress in individual practitioners, in the system generally and amongst the public and media. In fact, one could criticize relatively recent thinking in the development of Children's Services for trying to shape and configure agencies so as to address the need to prevent these worst-case scenarios; after all, hard cases *can* make bad law. If we consider the extreme end of a distribution that relates to the risk associated with children, then in some sense we might say that the tail (of the distribution) is wagging the dog. Bullock (2003) makes a similar point when he questions whether the reason so many children are referred to the protection process (240 000 each year in England alone) is because of Children's Services' fears about the potential risk of harm occurring to children in extreme situations.

It could also be argued that it is at the boundary between tiers 2 and 3 where workers experience the greatest stress as it is here that they often have responsibility for children who have needs which are beyond their level of competency, but which do not trigger the criteria for referral to a higher tier and more specialized service.

Axford and Bullock make the point that through the modernization of Children and Family Services, although children deemed to be in need for a variety of reasons will be better protected in relation to 'unpredictable' incidents, those who have never been thus defined will 'remain difficult to reach' (Axford and Bullock, 2005, p. 61). It is worth noting that there are other frameworks for conceptualizing need in Children's Services besides the tiered model (Figure 1.1) (for instance see Hardiker *et al.*, 2002).

It is also important to remember the large numbers of underachieving (and disaffected) pupils in the British school system (which was intended to be a universal service for all children) who may be socially excluded because of the schools they attend. Some of these schools might be described as failing or suffering from a poor social mix (see Chapter 1). This is not to particularly criticize such schools or the dedicated staff who often choose to work in them but rather to point to the effects of what has increasingly been a market-driven education system, where schools have been encouraged to compete with one another in order to address the issues presented by 'parental choice'. While these issues and the schools involved also attract a lot of media and political attention, new developments in Children's Services embodied in documents such as ECM (Department for Education and Skills, 2003) do not seem to address whole-school improvement in quite the same way. ECM appears to address the social or welfare needs of individuals through the development of systems, rather than be concerned with the special *educational* needs of children, at an individual or cohort level. McNab (2005) draws our attention to an emphasis in *Every Child Matters: Change for Children* (Department for Education and Skills, 2004b) to 'the reconfiguration of services around the child and family in one place, for example, children's centres, extended schools and the bringing together of professionals in multi-disciplinary teams' (p. 4). *Removing Barriers to Achievement* (Department for Education and Skills, 2004a, p. 26) refers closely to ECM and includes: 'schools working together to support the inclusion of all children from their local community, backed up by good quality specialist advice from the local authority and health services, working in multi-disciplinary teams' and the 'greater integration of education, health and social care to meet the needs of children and families'. McNab argues that the emphasis on the inclusion agenda is not reciprocated in the ECM documents.

'HARD TO REACH' CHILDREN AND 'HARD TO REACH' PROFESSIONALS

Some vulnerable children grow up to be vulnerable adults and, in turn, raise vulnerable children of their own: the well-documented cycle of disadvantage repeated across generations. A disproportionately large amount of time, energy, resources and emotion is spent on trying to implement change in a relatively small cohort, which includes children and families who could be defined as being 'hard to reach', a term that resonates, certainly from the point of view of some professionals who struggle to engage *at all* with some of their clients. Even if it is possible to develop something resembling a working relationship with a 'hard to reach' young person and/or their family, our common experience is often that we quickly get to the end of our expertise, or that our theories and models of practice don't work with 'this kind' of client. Our services and ways of working are still not best suited to how children and families 'are'. The context where the current popularity is for 'customer-led' services, reflecting a marketplace mentality, seems to be predicated on beliefs about children and families who are willing and able to engage with help that is offered, whereas the reality for many professionals is quite the reverse. It is worth noting here that many practitioners are uncomfortable with the idea of 'the market' in relation to public services. Jordan (2006) makes the point, for instance, that services are not commodities but involve 'relational goods', such as affection, respect and belonging.

Consider the phenomenon of DNA (did not attend) in relation to some health professionals and their inability to reach families who fail to turn up for appointments, parents and carers who don't attend meetings based in schools where staff are concerned about their children and parents who are consistently not in, when professionals call, as arranged. These situations are familiar to many of us and can lead us to construct labels for families or clients, such as 'hard to reach', 'difficult', 'chaotic', 'dysfunctional' and so on. However, if we were to ask service users themselves, they may well describe some agencies or professionals as being 'hard to reach'. A client may not accept that they have the problem assigned to them by a professional. Being heard in this respect and getting their point across may lead a client to experience a struggle in reaching a professional. Even when more willing service users engage, their experience may be one of continued frustration, as they try to fit appointments into a schedule designed for the professionals, communicate aspects of their life story several times over, where the emphasis is on assessment rather than action, weigh up how trusting they can afford to be (as their personal and, at times, most intimate details are scattered across the locality), attempt to try out ideas that they haven't fully grasped (and are reluctant to seek clarification over) and retain some dignity throughout the whole process. Too often, agencies are arranged around the needs of organizations to deliver cost-effective services rather than shaped to meet the needs of children and families. This can be seen in the way that services are accessed (Griffiths, 2003) and in the professional language used in reports (Cranwell and Miller, 1987). Cranwell and Miller, for instance, found that words that were commonly misunderstood by parents included 'peers', 'self-image/concept', 'visual' (acuity, cues, defect...), 'cognitive' (development, functioning, skills) and 'social' (skills, interaction, reasoning).

CHILDREN AND YOUNG PEOPLE AT RISK

Children and young people who are 'hard to reach' are often vulnerable in some way or described as being 'at risk'. Roaf and Lloyd (1995) found that young people particularly at risk of 'falling through the net', in relation to multi-agency work, included those who were:

- carers;
- on the verge of criminality;
- having mental health problems;
- homeless;
- from minority ethnic groups;
- out of school for any length of time;
- experiencing education difficulties while in local authority care;
- from families in stress.

(Roaf and Lloyd, 1995)

The Department for Education and Skills (2005) lists certain groups of school pupils as being at particular risk, and there is overlap with the list above, although these groups are added: those with special educational needs, travellers, young carers, pregnant schoolgirls and teenage mothers, unaccompanied asylum seekers and children missing from education.

To this list might be added alcohol and substance misusers and those with refugee status. Clearly, this raises issues that some might label as being institutionally racist, as belonging to a minority ethnic group does not of course in itself put you at risk. However, history teaches us that there are institutional processes which can lead to children and families from minority ethnic groups becoming marginalized. For instance, one reason to explain a higher incidence of hearing impairment amongst some Asian children has been that programmes of immunization have missed parents whose first language is not English. Bernard Coard's book entitled *How the West Indian Child is Made Educationally Sub-Normal in the British School System* was published in 1971 and raised questions about the marginalization and exclusion of black boys in the British education system.

Risk factors can be identified for a number of different cohorts: 'looked after' children, pupils vulnerable to exclusion from school and children whose parents have mental health difficulties. However, there is overlap and a core of factors that seem to be identified throughout much of the research, which also relate to community (e.g. racism), family (e.g. substance misuse, poor parenting, parental conflict, lack of guidance, abuse, mental health issues) and child-based factors (e.g. developmental delay, learning difficulties, temperament and chronic illness).

Space does not allow for a fuller discussion here and 'the concept, method and findings emerging from an analysis of risk are fearsomely complicated' (Little, Axford and Morpeth, 2004, p. 111), but we also know that 'most children living in poverty, overcrowded conditions or in other stressful circumstances do not develop predicted problems' (Duncan et al., 1994, cited in Little, Axford and Morpeth, 2004, p. 107). Horwath (2001) makes the point that a risk factor will not automatically be followed by a consequence, although it does indicate the need for action to reduce vulnerability. This leads to the consideration of protective factors (which might be said to reduce the harmful effects of risk factors) and resilience. These concepts, in turn, offer methods for reaching the 'hard to reach', as an understanding of how children and young people come through difficult situations might enable professionals to develop more effective strength-based approaches to working with them.

France and Utting (2005) describe how prevention has become a major feature of policy concerning children and their families under the Labour Government. Sure Start was a key component in tackling social exclusion and child poverty, and the Home Office introduced On Track as part of the crime reduction programme. On Track's ethos links closely to cooperation and joint working and the provision of family services, which extend through to early adolescence (McKeown and Ghate, 2004). The Children's Fund was set up to pay for services for 5- to 13-year-olds at risk of social problems. Efforts have been made to make prevention a part of local authority and NHS mainstream services as well as a better identification of risk.

THE INFLUENCE OF LANGUAGE AND LABELS

The discourse, or type of language, used to describe children, families, clients, is of great importance to many writers and thinkers who grapple with understanding the ways in which children and families at the margins, the 'hard to reach', the excluded, are placed or positioned by themselves and other writers and thinkers. For instance, 'disengaged' is offered in preference to 'disaffected' (see Piper and Piper, 1998/1999). Williamson and Middlemiss (1999) and Williamson (2005) classify disengaged (in preference to disaffected) children and young people into the 'essentially confused' (not yet switched off in mainstream settings), the 'temporarily sidetracked' (by caring for others) and the 'deeply alienated', subdivided into the 'purposeful' (those with alternative careers) and the 'purposeless' ('in your face diamond white grunters'): different terms, different risks, but they give emphasis to a growing political realization that 'there are significant numbers of young adults disengaged from school provision who have established alternative "ways of living" in the informal and illegal communities' (Williamson and Middlemiss, 1999, p. 13). Living in a world so different from these young adults, how can professionals hope to reach them when they become clients?

Elsewhere, the discourse of risk has been deconstructed, where writers have explored the meaning of the language associated with risk in an attempt to understand the power that such language has over those it describes. Within the discourse of exclusion, a label such as 'special educational needs' (despite the original good intentions behind using this term) is criticized for placing emphasis on an individual's deficits. Thomas (2005) also believes that 'need' reinforces the concepts of disadvantage and deficit. For some support services, the culture of individual referrals can be contrasted with 'the whole school approach'. Similarly, using a term such as 'hard to reach' or 'at risk' emphasizes that the client (child or family) has the problem, rather than focusing on, as Lubeck and Garrett (1990) suggest, the institutional structures that create and maintain inequality. This relates to the earlier point about services being 'hard to reach' from the perspective of some clients. France and Utting (2005) also point to the 'dangers of stigmatising children and families if knowledge of relevant risk factors is used to target individuals from an early age and label them as "potential offenders" ' (p. 81). France and Utting describe the work of others who warn that such processes place families on the margins of society under more intensive monitoring and state control so that risk 'becomes a mechanism that gives the state authority for intervening in families that are deemed "dangerous" ' (p. 81). Elsewhere, France (2004) describes 'problem youth' and approaches to reduce future problem behaviour which involve a deficit model of youth that is seen as 'bad' and 'delinquent'. Hine (2005) lists some of the 'problematic premises' upon which the On Track model rests and also points to the problem-focused and deficit approach, 'with inherent notions of the likelihood of children and young people being problematic and the need for prevention' (p. 128).

Communities that care (Beinart *et al.*, 2002) support locally developed programmes in the United Kingdom using a survey which profiles risk and protective factors, an approach described by France and Crow (2005) as 'promising', and this type of approach looks set to be endorsed by the Government. *Reaching Out: An Action Plan for Social Exclusion* refers to 'groundbreaking new research' that 'examines the potential for different types of indicators to predict later adolescent and adult adverse outcomes' (HM Government, 2006, p. 27). While urging caution about the risk of labelling and stigmatizing families, this document states that 'those experiencing entrenched and deepseated exclusion are often harder to reach and harder to engage' and suggests 'such disengagement must be met with a redoubling of efforts to engage – personalisation with persistence' (p. 29).

Swadener and Lubeck (1995, p. 5) ask, 'how can those who exist at the margins of power gain more power and more control of their discourses and practices' rather than being controlled by them? Paulo Freire asked similar questions (see Freire, 1972). Rather than focus on deficit, Swadener and Lubeck place an emphasis on children and families 'at promise'. In so far as school is concerned, some writers exploring these ideas refer to the cultural compatibility theory, which assumes that children from different cultural backgrounds learn to behave competently in their natural cultural contexts. 'It assumes that children are not "at-risk" because of the cultural or linguistic community into which they are born, but they may be "at-risk" because other contexts into which they go, such as school, may require or expect different cultural patterns and values than those that they have learned' (Tabachnick and Bloch, 1995, cited in Swadener and Lubeck, 1995, p. 188).

A similar point is made by Cohen and Hagen (1997), who refer to discussion in Scandinavia of the term 'services', 'which, it is argued, implies a passive relationship in which children receive but do not assist in determining the care or learning experience' (p. 34). Schoon and Bynner (2003) note the increasing recognition within youth research of the need for attention to competencies, resources, skills and assets as well as the focus on risk and disadvantage.

Some of the points raised above might encourage professionals and parents to consider how they might reach out to each other, in developing teams of more responsive helpers who can work flexibly through relationships with children and families, relationships that are rooted in a different kind of reciprocal partnership. This is returned to later when we consider the skills necessary for this work.

CURRENT CONTEXT AND CONTEMPORARY THEMES

A vast number of documents have now been produced by central government and commentators on the need for improved cooperation and coordination between education and social care departments and Primary Care Trusts which deal with children and young people who are at risk or have special educational needs (Department for Education and Employment, 1997; HMSO, 1989 and 2003). Attempting to achieve 'joined-up thinking' has led to Children's Trusts, Children's Services and an emphasis on multi-agency practice.

The 'voice of the child' has become a theme, which has been heard more loudly over the last decade or so and, to varying degrees, written into legislation and service expectations. Calder and Cope (2003) interviewed over 900 young people aged between 14 and 25 years to determine their aims and ambitions in life and their perceptions of the barriers to achieving their goals. Most of the interviewees were from disadvantaged backgrounds: unemployed, educational underachievers, ex-offenders and serving prisoners and those in or leaving care. Their aspirations were very similar to those of most youngsters: family, interesting job, enough money to support their lifestyle, a nice house, good friends and to be in control of their own future (although the disadvantaged group were unsure about how they would achieve all of this).

Article 12 of the United Nations Convention on the Rights of the Child (UNICEF, 1989) states that children's views should be taken into account when making decisions that affect their lives. 'Involving young people in public decision-making demands a willingness to challenge deeply held assumptions about children's rights and the existing power relationships between adults, professionals, organisations and children and young people' (Partridge, 2005, p. 181). Children Now published a participation charter in June 2006. Linked to the UN Convention on the Rights of the Child, it stated that participation is a right, that children and young people are the best authorities on their own lives, that participation depends on mutual respect and honesty and that participation must be accessible and inclusive.

There is a growing trend for researchers to involve children and young people as co-participants or peer researchers; Triumph and Success is one such project (France, 2000). Young researchers were involved in designing questionnaires and undertook a survey with nearly 750 young people and face-to-face interviews with 60 young people from a range of backgrounds, including young people from ethnic minorities and 'hard to reach' groups.

Social and educational inclusion has influenced policy and practice for the past decade. The Government has strengthened parental rights to a mainstream education for their children, but this is a fight that is by no means over. A recent poll of (206) head teachers and (511) classroom teachers indicated that many believed that some of their pupils (perhaps up to 25 000) would be better placed in special schools (Bloom, 2005).

Multi-agency working is a very strong theme currently and many advocates write as if committed to the idea that it will solve many current problems. We are led to believe that working together will make things 'better' for the children and families with the severest of problems. However, it is worth questioning whether or not joined-up services do make a difference to outcomes for clients. Certainly, we know that providing a service, joined-up or otherwise, does not necessarily secure effective outcomes. There is also a growing awareness within the literature that casts doubt over the assumption that multi-agency working 'is a good thing', which should urge some caution and greater critical appraisal of this belief (Glisson and Hemmelgarn, 1998; Hughes, 2006).

The implementation of the Freedom of Information Act (2000) has encouraged professionals to consider how data might be shared and how to keep open records and has led to initiatives in health, such as copying letters. This links with the theme of common language, which emphasizes the cultures of different agencies and the associated vocabularies, and therefore mind-sets, of different professional groups. Many researchers and documents produced by government bodies stress common language as an important issue in supporting multi-agency work. While a common language places rightful emphasis on good communication and shared meanings, it is also important that individual professional identities are preserved so that we don't lose the richness and diversity of expertise and opinion necessary to improving multi-agency working.

WHAT DO WE MEAN BY 'HARD TO REACH'?

'We', in the context of Children's Services, includes those working in education (teachers, service managers, educational welfare officers, educational psychologists), social care (social workers, family support workers), the community and voluntary agencies, health (GPs, paediatricians, physiotherapists, occupational therapists, speech and language therapists) and in mental health (Child and Adolescent Mental Health Service, or CAMHS, workers, those in specialized settings, e.g. tier 4), but should also include the users of these services. In order to give a multi-agency angle to this section, what follows is a small selection of work drawn from these different perspectives to provide a flavour of some of the interpretations of what we mean by 'hard to reach'.

CRIME

Jones and Newburn (2001) highlight some of the problems of the term 'hard to reach', including its inconsistent and misleading use and stigmatizing effect and note 'a considerable amount of ambiguity – inside and outside the police service – about what is meant by the term hard to reach' (p. 7).

On Track was established by the Home Office in 1999 as part of its Crime Reduction Programme, and in 2001 it transferred to the Children and Young People's Unit and was incorporated into the Children's Fund. Doherty *et al.* (2004) report that 'hard to reach' is a powerful and well-used concept within On Track projects and found that how 'hard to reach' groups were defined was related to the particular agency that practitioners belonged to and their experience of working with different groups. Three main definitions were identified:

- 'minority groups', referring to the traditionally under-represented groups, the marginalized, disadvantaged or socially excluded;
- those 'slipping through the net', referring to the overlooked, 'invisible' or those unable to articulate their needs. This includes those caring for others, those with mental health problems, service users who fall just outside the statutory or usual remit of a provider or whose needs are apparently not so great as to grant access to a service;
- the 'service resistant', referring to those unwilling to engage with service providers, the suspicious, the overtargeted or disaffected.

Each of the three definitions led to different perceived needs and different actions on the part of practitioners.

HOUSING

Research into the area of housing (Watson *et al.*, 2003), looking at how the Supporting People programme might affect services for people with complex needs or those who are 'marginal' or 'hard to reach', found that housing, social services, health and probation service commissioners lacked agreed definitions of these terms. Among respondents, there were many interpretations of 'marginal', 'hard to reach' and 'high risk', and the researchers suggested a categorization that was intended to promote debate about who was included and the kinds of marginality or risk involved. Four general categories were used:

- *People with complex or multiple needs*, who are likely to need support from more than one source, or from a service offering generic and more specialist support. The combination of mental health problems, offending and substance abuse causes greatest concern;
- *People who are 'hard to reach'* in that they are resistant to services, or have perhaps already been excluded. This includes those who do not want to be drawn into, or are trying to get away from, the systems of care and support but remain vulnerable;

- *People who are 'high risk'*, in that they could pose a danger to others or to themselves, or may be at risk from others. Also included are those who are vulnerable to victimization, as well as people escaping domestic violence and those whose behaviour is threatening or disruptive;
- *People who are remote from services*, including those in certain minority ethnic communities which have little or no connection with formal services. Also included are those relying on informal support and people who live in private-sector accommodation and are unaware of services.

HEALTH

Rhodes, Holland and Hartnoll (1991) report on a model of HIV outreach intervention for sex workers and drug users in central London. Referring to a relatively small proportion of the total population, they use the term 'hard to reach' to refer to 'certain populations who are unlikely to be effectively reached by conventional HIV prevention strategies' (p. 1).

From a mental health angle, it has been suggested that 20% of children display some sign of poor mental health and that 10% of children and adolescents in England, Scotland and Wales aged between five and 16 suffer from some type of clinical or recognized disorder (Atkinson and Hornby, 2002; Green *et al.*, 2004). Five per cent have a conduct disorder, 4% an emotional disorder (anxiety or depression) and 1% are rated as hyperactive. According to Young Minds (the national charity committed to improving the mental health of all children and young people; www.youngminds.org.uk), the average secondary school of 1000 pupils will have on roll around 50 students with depression, 100 experiencing significant distress and between five and 10 affected by eating disorders. There is evidence that over time there has been a substantial increase in adolescent conduct problems affecting males and females, all social classes and family types and a recent rise in emotional problems (Collishaw *et al.*, 2004). While there is evidence that the situation in the United Kingdom appears to have deteriorated, this does not match the evidence from the United States and the Netherlands (Nuffield Foundation, 2004). Such studies suggest that it is becoming harder to reach youngsters experiencing difficulties related to mental health and well-being.

Griffiths (2003) discusses different patterns of engagement and the factors that appear to influence these. He reports that some studies show that less than 20% of youngsters with mental health problems receive appropriate services. A young person's acceptance of help is related to who has defined their mental health needs, so that adolescents are frequently in the 'pre-contemplative stage'. This is described as the earliest stage of change, where people are unaware of problem behaviour or are reluctant to look at changing it (DiClemente and Prochaska, 1998). Griffiths also refers to ways in which primary care services might be easier to reach from the perspective of young people, for instance in terms of increased confidentiality, being able to phone without giving names and having well-written information designed specifically for young people.

People with severe aphasia (those who are unable in some way to produce or understand speech) have been found to be excluded from the benefits of health, social care, residential and nursing services because information and instructions are inaccessible, activities inappropriate or unachievable and because of continuous communication breakdown in interactions. For these people, services become 'hard to reach' (see Parr, 2004). The same is likely to be true for those with other problems related to language and communication problems and mental health issues, and a similar case could be made for families where English is a second language and for those with sensory disabilities.

CONNEXIONS

Reaching and supporting socially excluded young people who are out of education, training and work is the *raison d' être* of the targeted Connexions Service. This cohort is referred to as the NEETs (Not in Education, Employment or Training). Recent research found that some young people in this category had serious problems, but those at high risk or with high needs would often associate with those with medium to low needs or levels of risk. Even projects aiming to intervene with young people of high risk or high need tended to work with less problematic members of their client's network because these young people often constituted potentially powerful influence and support systems (see Crimmens *et al.*, 2004).

Again, recent research into NEETs (Green *et al.*, 2001) asserts that in order to support 'young people at risk' it is necessary to know:

- how many there are;
- who they are;
- where they are;
- and from a policy perspective, what works with whom, where and how?

Green *et al.* (2001) reviewed a range of 'mapping' and 'tracking' systems from across different types of agencies in order to contribute to the debate concerning, and contribute to the agenda for, the Connexions Service and also raised issues of wider relevance to the research agenda on young people, partnership working, and mapping and tracking methodologies. The how, who, where and what works questions are just as valid and important for vulnerable and 'hard to reach' children, young people and their families under consideration in this book and are clearly questions that are being asked by practitioners involved with children and young people in a whole variety of settings.

The Neighbourhood Support Fund (NSF) was a DfES-funded programme, launched in 1999, aiming to re-engage 'hard to reach' young people aged 13–19 with education, employment or training. The pilot lasted three years and was evaluated by NFER in 2004 (see Golden *et al.*, 2004). The study described this group as 'hard to reach' young people who were either not in education, employment or training (NEET) or had characteristics which put them at risk of becoming NEET in the future. These characteristics included those young people who had:

- low levels of educational achievement (found in 55% of the young people who participated in NSF projects);
- long-term school non-attendance;
- been excluded from school (16%);
- become young offenders or were at risk of becoming so;
- special educational needs;
- alcohol/drug dependency problems;
- become homeless;
- been in the care of the local authority or were leaving it;
- mental health issues;
- taken on the role of young carers;
- experience of being refugees or asylum seekers;
- a disability (found in 2% of the young people).

Other research into the characteristics that could lead to a young person aged 16 to 18 becoming NEET indicated that people with poor GCSE results and those who had truanted in Year 11 were more likely to become NEET than those without these characteristics.

A study by Stone et al. (2000, cited in Golden et al., 2004, p. 24) outlined the 'triggers, each of which could be seen as providing the "right" set of circumstances for problem behaviours to occur' that could subsequently lead to a young person becoming NEET. These were:

- a dysfunctional family;
- personality and behavioural difficulties;
- confidence issues;
- a traumatic event, such as bereavement.

These characteristics have been shown in other research to be common among young people who are not engaged in learning or employment. They are also common to other agencies and inform the construction of the term 'hard to reach' across a range of professions.

EDUCATION

Children and young people who experience EBD (Emotional and Behavioural Difficulties) are described by some as sharing 'hard to reach' features. O'Brien and Guiney (2005) refer to such learners as existing on the margins, becoming defined as 'hard cases'. They contend that we can and should learn from the hard cases as they 'challenge the epistemology upon which systems are founded and thus problematise knowledge, its construction and its application' (p. 143). The term tells us something about the agency using it and its own particular epistemology, or knowledge foundation.

Bowers (2005) develops the argument that the term EBD 'does nothing to enhance our knowledge of young people's emotional states and how they may influence their learning and behaviour at school' (p. 86). He criticizes the way in which anger is frequently described as the predominant emotion and the way in which professionals do not delve deeply enough into important feelings that such a prototype masks. This would be an example of where the meaning of a term (in this case EBD and anger), is so frequently used and in so many different contexts that it takes on various meanings that render it, at best, oversimplified or, at worst, meaningless. The term in effect becomes 'hard to reach'.

Ofsted has produced guidance on inspecting vulnerable groups in schools. One group would include those with Special Educational Needs (SEN) as these are most likely to be excluded, especially boys. *Youth Matters* (HM Government, 2005), the Green Paper for youth, argues that many local teenagers, the 'hard to reach', are effectively excluded from provision and that too many youth services offer a poor service.

Although the idea of schools as therapeutic environments has had a long history, healthy schools, and the emphasis on all schools being able to develop emotional literacy, emotional health and well-being for all pupils, has been relatively recent. Such developments are likely to contribute to learning environments that may serve youngsters better. However, 'whole-school approaches' are not particularly aimed at preventing children at risk (although SEAL, Social and Emotional Aspects of Learning, attempts to do some of this at a universal level of intervention). For this, we need to look more at initiatives such as the Behaviour Improvement Projects (BIP) where, in an education context, 'hard to reach' has three typical definitions:

- those who have disappeared from education and therefore are physically 'hard to reach'. This might apply to travellers' children or school phobics, for instance;
- those who are in school but hard to engage (these young people may be in school but can't cope or they are in the cycle of school–Pupil Referral Unit; alternatively they may be pupils whose needs are severe but who are relatively invisible, such as those with mental health problems);
- those who are highly visible and are hard-core seriously disaffected in terms of behaviour and youth justice (perhaps as identified by the local Youth Offending Team or YOT, something along the lines of the most challenging 30–40 young people in an area).

Most educators would recognize these categories of pupils currently being failed by the education system. However, because 'hard to reach' can be defined in such different ways, there is a suggestion that there may be merit in seeing it as a process rather than a state of being. Lynn Turner (personal communication, 9/5/2006) refers to definitions used at one stage by BIP, where five separate aspects of working with 'hard to reach' pupils are suggested, each with their own set of challenges. These are:

- hard to see, the pupils who may be invisible in school but whose needs are nevertheless severe, such as children with mental health problems which manifest themselves in poor socialization;

- hard to find, the pupils who may have disappeared from education altogether. We know that they are out there but not sure where;
- hard to engage, the first part of the intervention process, which involves engaging the target group with the planned programme. We may have seen and then found the pupils but can we reach them in such a way as to begin work?;
- hard to manage or retain, the major stumbling block for many programmes catering for more extreme cases. Having engaged with pupils, there is no guarantee that they can be easily managed or retained on the programme;
- hard to change, the final hurdle, which can only be reached if the other stages have been successfully passed. Whether the planned intervention is going to change the existing patterns of behaviour.

SOCIAL CARE

Some of the 'hard cases' related to social care are represented by statistics. Let us consider children in public care where links with education are very apparent. Research indicates that in 2001/2002:

- 8% of children in care achieved five or more A*–C grades at GCSE, compared to half of all young people;
- children in care are about 10 times more likely to leave school without qualifications;
- children in care have poor results in Key Stage tests at age seven, 11 and 14;
- only 1% of children in care go to university;
- between a quarter and a third of rough sleepers were in care;
- young people who have been in care are two and a half times more likely to be teenage parents;
- children in care are 10 times more likely to be permanently excluded from school;
- children in care are also six times more likely to be bullied.
- around a quarter of adults in prison spent some time in care as children (Social Exclusion unit, 2001);
- children in care are more likely to have mental health issues (Dimond and Misch, 2002; Stanley, Riordan and Alaszewski, 2005).

(Office of the Deputy Prime Minister, 2003)

A Green Paper published in October 2006 describes the statistics relating to the education of children in care as 'shocking' where 'only 11% of children in care attained 5 good GCSEs in 2005 compared with 56% of all children', with similar performance gaps at all ages 'both before and after Key Stage 4' (Department for Education and Skills, 2006).

In writing about families who are hard to help, Lahiff (1981) notes that the term 'problem family' was used more than 60 years ago and that its definition relates to problem behaviour – that which contrasts with what is considered to be socially acceptable. Lahiff identifies the problems with any definition such as this, in that it relies on social values which change over time and are often determined by the opinions of society's most powerful groups. She states that 'social workers drew attention to personality difficulties' of those described with the problem (Lahiff, 1981, p. 35).

Child protection is a core activity for social work, and supporting parents links closely with this activity. The Webster-Stratton Incredible Years programme is a well-known example of how to both recruit and retain families who are hard to engage and high-risk. Webster-Stratton has written about 'hard to reach' families:

> Such families have been described as unmotivated, resistant, unreliable, disengaged, chaotic, in denial, disorganised, uncaring, dysfunctional and unlikely candidates for this kind of treatment – in short, unreachable. However, these families might well describe traditional clinic-based programs as 'unreachable'. Clinical programs may be too far away from home, too expensive, insensitive, distant, inflexible in terms of scheduling or content, foreign in terms of language (literally or figuratively), blaming or critical of their lifestyle. A cost benefit analysis would, in all likelihood, reveal that the costs to these clients of receiving treatment far outweigh the potential benefits even though they do genuinely want to do what is best for their children. Perhaps this population has been 'unreachable' not because of their own characteristics, but because of the characteristics of the interventions they have been offered.

> (Webster-Stratton, 1998, p. 184).

SOME KEY QUESTIONS

Issues that currently exercise the minds of some practitioners can be raised as questions:

WHY SHOULD WE WANT TO REACH THE 'HARD TO REACH'?

This question relates to why people choose particular professions and the motivations behind becoming a 'helper'. Lahiff (1981) considered the rewarding nature of helping (which related to gratitude) and the search for power. Perhaps professionals start their careers with ideals about helping the most needy. *Not* being (or not being able to be) helpful may invalidate some of the constructs that helpers hold about their professional identity, so that by not reaching some clients professionals invalidate their view of themselves. Perhaps this eventually serves to distance some professionals from their potential clients, in an attempt to preserve their professional sense of self. They might express a view of wanting to reach out, but are prevented from doing so by the need to limit their own pain: a difference perhaps between the espoused view and the theory in action.

WHY SHOULD WE REACH THE 'HARD TO REACH?'

Philosophical and moral issues relate to the ethics of care and education and the ethical challenges around choice, autonomy, fairness and justice. Surely the 'hard to reach' have rights and entitlements, including the option of refusing to engage? The fact that education is a statutory requirement fits uncomfortably with notions of the 'customer' where the locus of control is supposedly in their hands.

A contrasting argument is that resources are scarce or, at best, finite; so workers in Children's Services have to consider how best to deploy professional time. (Resources may also be poorly allocated, managed or located.) There are strong arguments for defining the 'hard to reach' in terms of those who are the most vulnerable and targeting services towards them accordingly, irrespective of the choice that they may or may not exercise. Often, the client has little or no choice anyway (for instance when an agency's statutory powers are used to protect children).

If we knew who to speak to and how, would we hear children and young people saying that they wished to be left alone, or would they explain that there was no one to ask or listen, that nobody tried to understand, that they weren't 'hard to reach' so much as invisible?

WHY DON'T WE REACH THE 'HARD TO REACH'?

It takes time, there are rarely any 'quick wins', it's hard, professionals can quickly get to the limits of their skills and services are often not configured adequately and have systems and procedures that do not reach the most challenging clients. Most services, for instance, are open during office hours only, not when some clients might need them the most. Services often have time limits for intervention where merely beginning to engage may exhaust these limited hours. Discussing interagency collaboration, Capper, Hanson and Huilman (1994) state that coordinated systems can lead to the centralization of services, resulting in 'organisational goals that meet organisation needs rather than client needs' (p. 336). Other problems related to collaboration include a tendency for client needs 'to be defined in terms of an agency's capacity to respond' (Mitchell and Scott, 1993, p. 89) and the placing of the professional agency network at the centre of the helping system, which highlights the administrative and organizational processes between agencies 'at the expense of a focus on how these processes actually promote better outcomes for the children and families served' (Walter and Petr, 2000, p. 497). Lahiff (1981) discusses the idea that 'hard to help families may be more "difficult to like"' (p. 61). In addition to the inability of professionals to relate to, communicate with and challenge some families and young people, effective challenging might be reduced due to the fear of being subjected to complaints procedures and other related formal investigations.

WHERE ARE THE 'HARD TO REACH'?

In considering home and family, we recognize that in order to access children and young people we generally have to engage with their families. Given this, perhaps age helps to define 'hard to reach' in that preschool children themselves would be 'undeserving' of the term as it is most likely to be their parents who are 'hard to reach'.

Some young people are 'hard to reach' by virtue of being young carers in their families.

By considering school location, we know that some children and young people are 'hard to reach' and in school permanently, in that they are physically present but absent from engagement in the process of education (perhaps by becoming disaffected by what is on offer or more specifically due to childhood depression, for instance). Some are in school sporadically (owing to patchy attendance, as a result of fixed-term exclusions, poor health or because they are travellers) or not in school at all (through their non-attendance, permanent exclusion or by being classed as 'missing').

WHAT CHARACTERIZES THE 'HARD TO REACH'?

The consideration here might be in relation to particular issues, such as children with autistic spectrum difficulties, emotional and behavioural difficulties, the permanently excluded, young carers, 'looked after' children and those with mental health problems. We might also consider those who are socially excluded in a more general way, in relation to race, disability, social class and intelligence. Within these groupings, there may be different characteristics of the 'hard to reach', for instance between white working-class mining (or ex-mining) communities and farming communities, and between first- and third-generation black African or Caribbean communities.

Responses to this question might equally be framed around issues relating to the professional. When a professional is challenged by and 'struggling' with their efforts to connect with a situation concerning a child or a family, they may choose to view that child or family as 'hard to reach', as such a term might serve to compensate for the professional's feelings of competence, expertise, their feelings and self-belief about being a skilled helper, all of which are in danger of being invalidated.

IS IT USEFUL TO CONSIDER DIFFERENT TYPES OF 'HARD TO REACH'?

This question might discriminate between situations where carers engage but the children or young people don't, where children or young people engage but the carers don't, or where children, young people and families are hard to engage. We could consider children who are out of school, lie low to avoid attention or who are not even on the school roll, or those who move around frequently and avoid the public gaze as soon as agencies develop greater awareness and knowledge of them. We might consider those who are unidentified and therefore unknown and out of reach, those who are known but not identified as being vulnerable and those who are known, identified but won't engage. We could also focus on professionals, for instance teachers, educational psychologists, social workers and doctors who are 'hard to reach', where professional misconduct or competency issues might influence our definition.

We might consider issues related to the capacity of a service and its finite resources, which could be being used by parents or carers who find it easier to engage with, or are more confident at finding their way around, systems.

Their ability to locate services might be enhanced by using the Internet or making phone calls, and they may access services by persistently pursuing professionals for appointments. This might mean that such processes create people with problems who are 'hard to reach' (or create problems for people who are then 'hard to reach'), simply because a service is stretched by existing clients and lacks the resources to reach out to others who are less confident or able to access systems.

WHICH PROCESSES, TOOLS AND SKILLS MIGHT HELP US TO REACH THE 'HARD TO REACH' MORE EFFECTIVELY?

If, as was stated earlier, we should be exploring ways of addressing the needs of those who are most vulnerable or at risk, this would lead us to consider how we might identify these individuals. Different agencies have their own tools. For example, the Youth Justice Board uses ASSET (a structured assessment tool for use by YOTs) in order to understand the reasons for a young person having committed a crime and to prevent them offending again, and Connexions uses the APIR (Assessment, Planning, Implementation and Review) tool. The search for a common vulnerability index could be worth while (Willms, 2002) as it seems particularly important to find ways of identifying the most vulnerable and those with the greatest needs, if joined-up services are to agree on which children and families to target. Without this kind of identification and a shared or common language of concern, services seem doomed to continue to duplicate work and leave gaps, with some children and families having too many professionals to deal with and some not having enough.

While an important area of inquiry, we should be careful to ensure that identification (or perhaps more specifically, assessment) does not take time away from acting. One might also wish to ask if the search for better identification is prompted by a lack of resources, which might require a different kind of response, perhaps a political one?

When working and planning with individuals facing a challenging or uncertain future, we might use tools to facilitate understanding, such as PATH (Planning Alternative Tomorrows with Hope) or MAPS (Making Action Plans) (Family Service Association of Toronto, 2004). These inclusion tools from North America have been used in the United Kingdom for about 10 years.

We need tools that can help children and adults to work together to improve outcomes, instead of adults solving the problems together with other adults. The ladder of participation (Hart, 1997; Kirby *et al.*, 2003), which moves from 'manipulation' to a position where a child or young person initiates and shares decisions with adults, is a tool that helps service providers to understand better the degree to which children and young people are more genuinely involved in decisions about service delivery.

There are approaches adapted for use with children, such as motivational interviewing, which are not predicated on the assumption that all people with problems want to change. Motivational interviewing is of particular relevance to the present inquiry and is described as representing a shift in focus from a trait perspective that promotes the blaming of clients and labelling to a more interactional perspective, better suited to individuals 'often categorised as "hard to reach", treatment resistant and unmotivated' (National Institute on Alcohol Abuse and Alcoholism, 2005). The idea that people with problems are unmotivated is thus challenged:

> You cannot convert clients into being motivated. Clients are always motivated. Sometimes (pretty often) they are not motivated for the therapist's goals or to do what the therapist thinks they need to do to get there – and they are labelled 'resistant' or 'low motivation'. These labels say nothing about the client. They only tell us that whoever put the label on the client doesn't know how to listen for what this client wants.

> (McNab, 2006)

France, Bendelow and Williams (2000) discuss the importance of not being seen as a 'proper adult' in order to secure involvement with young people, while constructing an acceptable identity built on 'naïve curiosity', honesty, openness and empathy, the avoidance of judgemental attitudes, creating opportunities for young people to present their own views and creativity and flexibility.

Many of the professional skills required to reach the 'hard to reach' are not necessarily professional competencies (i.e. the preserve of any particular professional group), but could be thought of instead as the skills of being an effective *person*, which have been employed within the professional domain. These 'human' skills facilitate 'real' encounters between people and experience of them, inform our judgements about the integrity of others and the degree to which we might view them as being helpful, warm, laid-back, nice and so on. Sharp (2003) reports that the perception of service quality received by parents and carers of young people with disabilities is influenced by the quality of the staff. The parents and carers felt very supported by staff who put the child at the centre of any involvement, built an effective relationship with the child and the family, were honest and open, did what they said they would do, were flexible (thinking laterally and creatively), respected the opinions and ideas of parents or carers, consulted the parents or carers to arrange a convenient time and location for meetings and appointments, didn't 'pass the buck' and communicated effectively. These skills are important to the further development of effective multi-agency practice. We could also include qualities such as integrity, bravery, humour, respectfulness, approachability and being imaginative.

The Pupil Attitude to Self and School (PASS) is proving to be a powerful tool for use with individual students as well as across the whole school (Williams, Whittome and Watts, 2003; Philpot, 2005). McLean (2003) has worked on understanding and changing the attitudes of teachers and students using the Motivating Learning Climate (described in his book *The Motivated School*) and SELF (Social and Emotional Learning Frame) in order to understand engagement in learning (Smart, 2005).

HOW MIGHT WE WORK EFFECTIVELY WITH ORGANIZATIONS?

For those working within education, we might think of organizational development with establishments, placing the focus on whole-school interventions, school improvement and using tools such as Soft Systems Methodology. There are a number of different systems theories, but one found to have particular relevance to working with schools is Checkland's Soft Systems Methodology, described as 'an approach which can be used to guide intervention in the kinds of ill-structured problem situations which crop up in the real world' (Frederickson, 1990, p. 2). Soft Systems Methodology (SSM) adopts a positive approach, focusing on the situation in which there is a perceived problem, or an opportunity for improvement, rather than the problem itself. Frederickson recommends SSM as a useful tool with which to tackle the fuzziness and complexity of many school-based problems. This fuzziness and complexity is not restricted to education settings alone and has led to these problems being described by some as 'wicked' (Rittel and Webber, 1973; Pacanowsky, 1995). Wicked problems, as opposed to problems described as 'tame', do not have definable outcomes and cannot be objectively solved using a linear process. Rittel and Webber describe 10 characteristics of wicked problems. Often applied to global warming, homelessness, drug dealing and racism, the term might equally be used in relation to most, if not all, of the 'five outcomes' of ECM. For instance, the outcome of children being healthy includes reducing the rate of teenage pregnancy, which relates to, amongst other things, education, class issues and attitudes, where the potential solutions are not well-described, where stakeholders have different views about whether a resolution is 'good enough' and where each problem can be considered as a symptom of another problem. Nixon, Walker and Clough (2003) state that 'thoughtfulness requires public engagement and a commitment to participation – to multiple voices, perspectives and experiences' and that 'our failure to think together, imaginatively and across boundaries, *is* the problem' (p. 102). The kinds of skills and qualities referred to earlier needed to tackle wicked problems and this failure to think together could be collected under the heading of 'thoughtful practice' (also see Chapter 7 of this book).

DEFINING THE 'HARD TO REACH'

Morpeth (2004) describes how the reluctance of the state to intervene in family life prevented the better protection of children until the late nineteenth century, when there was wider appreciation that relatives or parents might do their children harm, requiring the state to act in the child's best interest. She also notes that it was not until the identification of the 'battered child syndrome' in the 1960s and disclosure by women of abuse and rape that 'society at large was prepared to accept that some people may intentionally harm their children emotionally, physically, or sexually. Only then was the state considered to have a clear mandate to intervene' (p. 78). In the United Kingdom, child protection activity then rapidly became an important part of the social worker's role. Intervening in the lives of others is a core function of many other helping professionals.

As the Government has increased its awareness of and responsibility for citizens who are unable to care adequately for themselves or their families, we can see how the frustrations of those charged with supporting those who become 'clients' get discharged through the development of professional language and terms such as 'inadequate', 'problem families' and the 'hard to reach'. We have seen that the term 'hard to reach' has been used increasingly over the last few years in criminality, housing, health, education and elsewhere. We have also seen that defining the 'hard to reach' is problematic from a number of perspectives. This seems to stem from definitions that view 'hard to reach' as a 'state'. If instead we view 'hard to reach' as a 'process', we might avoid stigmatizing children, young people and families and might develop a more balanced understanding of how clients and professionals can engage more effectively with each other. The 'hard to reach' process starts whenever we see children as parental appendages rather than citizens in their own right, whenever we tolerate lower standards of care for some, when we are uncertain about the degree to which children should suffer at the hands of their parents and when we lack the confidence and assertiveness to challenge and engage with parents accordingly. When an initial child protection inquiry 'shows that the child is not at risk of significant harm, families are seldom referred to other services which they need to prevent longer term problems' (Cleaver *et al.*, 1998, p. 6) and they become a little further out of reach. Just as Bronfenbrenner's ecological model of human development (Bronfenbrenner, 1979) provides a framework for risk and protective factors, 'the ecological perspective reminds us that children do not develop in a vacuum but within a complex web of interacting, interdependent factors' (Bhabra, Dinos and Ghate, 2006, p. 4). Applying this to the concept 'hard to reach' means that we cannot understand the disengagement of those we are trying to help, without trying to make sense of the ways in which we have contributed to the distancing process. The way in which we intervene and support requires understanding. Scott (2006) refers to seven deadly sins that society and service providers commit to fail children. These include ignore what works, implement poorly and forget non-attenders. Scott contrasts these with our need to use proven programmes, promote programme fidelity and staff skill and pursue non-attenders.

CONCLUSION

Thomas (2005) asks what we mean by 'EBD' and I should like to conclude by applying his analysis to the 'hard to reach'. Thomas shows that in education the use of categories is alive and well and, in spite of an increased emphasis on the whole-school approach as a means of addressing emotional and behavioural difficulties, there remains a deficit model at work, based on the need of an individual child or young person. This provokes a helping or therapeutic response, designed to address behaviour that the institution finds unacceptable. In reality, it is the institution, the school, that often has the need to keep order. Whereas adult rule-breakers have their rights protected, there is no equivalent for children and young people as it is assumed that protection is 'automatically inherent in the beneficial action of the professionals acting on the child's behalf' (Thomas, 2005, p. 62). Professional helpers, such as educational psychologists, provide a clinical lens, often leading to the removal of a child from school. Building ideas about problem behaviour based on the language of need 'induces procedural responses whose main function is the appearance of doing something constructive. The mantra of need mechanically induces a set of reflexes from the school, but these are often little more than rituals – bureaucratic shows of willing' (p. 63). Thomas uses Foucault's ideas of the move from simple judgement and punishment to complex and unjustified judgements about the 'soul' of the wrongdoer, a move from 'naughty-therefore-impose-sanctions, to disturbed-therefore-meet-needs' (p. 64). To appropriate for the 'hard to reach' a quote from Thomas regarding EBD, there may be a lack of will to entertain the possibility that the 'hard to reach' may be a fiction constructed to escape society's insecurities and guilt about failing to keep order and include all of its citizens. To regard the 'hard to reach' as being in a state as opposed to a process emphasizes that there is something wrong with these types of clients, which relates to their character, upbringing and their deficits. Choosing to see 'hard to reach' as a process means that we as helpers can make choices about how to give choices to those we are trying to help. It could encourage us to understand and limit the unintended consequences of our deficit models so that we might narrow the gap between us, the helpers, and those we are trying to reach.

Discussion Points

- Should we always try to reach the 'hard to reach'?
- When might it be better not to reach them?
- What should be done if they continue to avoid being reached?
- If you do want to reach the 'hard to reach', what is your motivation?
- What is your or your agency's understanding of 'hard to reach'?
- What are the obstacles to you or your agency reaching the 'hard to reach' more effectively?
- Which processes, tools and skills might you or your agency develop in order to reach the 'hard to reach' more effectively?

REFERENCES

Atkinson, M. and Hornby, G. (2002) *Mental Health Handbook for Schools*. RoutledgeFalmer, London.

Axford, N. and Bullock, R. (2005) *Child Death and Significant Case Reviews: International Approaches*. Report to the Scottish Executive. Dartington Social Research Unit.

Beinart, S., Anderson, B., Lee, S. and Utting, D. (2002) *Youth at Risk? A National Survey of Risk Factors, Protective Factors and Problem Behaviours Among Young People in England, Scotland and Wales*. Communities that Care, London.

Bhabra, S., Dinos, S. and Ghate, D. (2006) Young people, risk and protection: a major survey of primary schools in On Track areas. *National Evaluation of On Track Phase Two*. Final Report to the Department for Education and Skills. Policy Research Bureau.

Bloom, A. (2005) Thousands 'better off' in special schools. *Times Educational Supplement*. 14 October 2005.

Bowers, T. (2005) The forgotten 'E' in EBD', *Handbook of Emotional and Behavioural Difficulties*. In: P. Clough, P. Garner, J.T. Pardeck and F. Yuen (eds). Sage, London.

Bronfenbrenner, U. (1979) *The Ecology of Human Development*. Harvard University Press, Cambridge, Massachusetts.

Bullock, R. (2003) Child protection post-Laming: The wider agenda. *Journal of Integrated Care* **11** (October), 13–17.

Calder, A. and Cope, R. (2003) *Breaking Barriers: Reaching the Hardest to Reach*. The Prince's Trust.

Capper, C., Hanson, S. and Huilman, R.R. (1994) Community-based interagency collaboration: a poststructural interruption of critical practices. *Journal of Education Policy* **9** (4), 335–351.

Cleaver, H., Wattam, C., Cawson, P. and Gordon, R. (1998) *Children Living at Home: The Initial Child Protection Enquiry. Ten Pitfalls and How to Avoid Them. What Research Tells Us*. Policy Practice Research Series, NSPCC, London.

Coard, B. (1971) *How the West Indian Child is Made Educationally Sub-Normal in the British School: System*. New Beacon Books, Ltd., London.

Cohen, B. and Hagen, U. (1997) *Introduction and Overview to Children's Services: Shaping up for the Millennium, Supporting Children and Families in the UK and Scandinavia*. In: B., Cohen U., Hagen (eds). The Stationery Office, Edinburgh.

Collishaw, S., Maughan, B., Goodman, R. and Pickles, A. (2004) Time trends in adolescent mental health. *Journal of Child Psychology and Psychiatry* **45** (8), 1350–1362.

Cranwell, D. and Miller, A. (1987) Do parents understand professionals' terminology in statements of special educational need? *Educational Psychology in Practice* **3** (2), 27–32.

Crimmens, D., Factor, F. and Jeffs, T. *et al.* (2004) The role of street-based youth work in linking socially excluded young people into education, training and work: findings. http://www.jrf.org.uk/knowledge/findings/socialpolicy/654.asp#top, accessed 11 September 2005.

Department for Education and Employment (1997) *Excellence for All Children Meeting Special Educational Needs*. DfEE, London.

Department for Education and Skills (2003) *Every Child Matters*. The Stationery Office, London.

Department for Education and Skills (2004a) *Removing Barriers to Achievement: the Government's Strategy for SEN*. DfES, London.

Department for Education and Skills (2004b) *Every Child Matters: Change for Children*. DfES, London.

Department for Education and Skills (2005) Advice and guidance to Schools and Local Authorities on Managing Behaviour and Attendance: groups of pupils at particular risk. http://www.dfes.gov.uk/behaviourandattendance/, accessed 26 July 2006.

Department for Education and Skills (2006) *Care Matters: Transforming the Lives of Children and Young People in Care*. DfES, London.

Department of Health (2002) Improvement, Expansion and Reform: The Next 3 Years, Priorities and Planning Framework 2003–2006. http://www.dh.gov.uk, accessed 2 September 2005.

Department of Health (2004a) Child and Adolescent Mental Health – National Service Framework for Children, Young People and Maternity Services. http://www.dh.gov.uk/PublicationsAndStatistics/Publications/ PublicationsPolicyAndGuidance/ PublicationsPAmpGBrowsableDocument/fs/en?CONTENT_ID=4094479&chk=ijOZ3N, accessed 5 February 2007.

Department of Health (2004b) The Mental Health and Psychological Well-being of Children and Young People (CAMHS Standard 9 of National Service Framework for Children, Young People and Maternity Services). http://www.dh.gov.uk/PublicationsAndStatistics/ Publications/PublicationsPolicyAndGuidance/PublicationsPolicyAndGuidanceArticle/ fs/en?CONTENT_ID=4089114&chk=CKZObO, accessed 6 November 2005.

DiClemente, C.C. and Prochaska, J. (1998) Toward a comprehensive, transtheoretical model of change: Stages of change and addictive behaviours. In: W.R. Miller and N. Heather (eds). *Treating Addictive Behaviours*, 2nd edn. Plenum Press, London, New York.

Dimond, C. and Misch, P. (2002) Psychiatric morbidity in children remanded to prison custody: a pilot study. *Journal of Adolescence* **25** (6), 681–689.

Doherty, P., Stott, A. and Kinder, K. (2004) *Delivering Services to Hard to Reach Families in On Track Areas: Definition, Consultation and Needs Assessment*. Home Office development and practice report.

Family Service Association of Toronto (2004) Tools for person-centred planning. http://www.fsatoronto.com/programs/options/path.html, accessed 05.02.07.

Forest, M. and Pearpoint, J. (2001) Common Sense tools, *MAPS and CIRCLES for Inclusive Education*. http://www.inclusion.com/artcommonsensetools.html, accessed 11 September 2005.

France, A. (2000) *Youth Researching Youth: The Triumph and Success Peer Research Project*. Published for the Joseph Rowntree Foundation by the National Youth Agency, Leicester.

France, A. (2004) Young people. In: S. Fraser, V. Lewis, S. Ding, M. Kellett and C. Robinson (eds). *Doing Research with Children and Young People*. Sage, London.

France, A., Bendelow, G. and Williams, S. (2000) A 'risky' business: researching the health beliefs of children and young people. In: A. Lewis and G. Lindsay (eds). *Researching Children's Perspectives*. Open University Press, Buckingham.

France, A. and Crow, I. (2005) Using the 'risk factor paradigm' in prevention: lessons from the evaluation of communities that care. *Children and Society* **19** (2), 172–184.

France, A. and Utting, D. (2005) The paradigm of 'risk and protection-focused prevention' and its impact on services for children and families. *Children and Society* **19** (2), 77–90.

Frederickson, N. (1990) *Soft Systems Methodology: Practical Applications in Work with Schools*. University College London.

Freire, P. (1972) *Pedagogy of the Oppressed*, Penguin, London.

Glisson, C. and Hemmelgarn, A. (1998) The effects of organizational climate and interorganizational co-ordination on the quality and outcomes of children's service systems. *Child Abuse and Neglect* **22** (5), 401–421.

Golden, S., Spielhofer, T., Sims, D. and O'Donnell, L. (2004) *Supporting the Hardest-to-Reach Young People: The Contribution of the Neighbourhood Support Fund*. National Foundation for Educational Research. Research report RR535.

Green, A.E., Maguire, M. and Canny, A. (2001) Mapping and tracking vulnerable young people: findings. http://www.jrf.org.uk/knowledge/findings/socialpolicy/411.asp#top, accessed 11 September 2005.

Green, H., McGinnity, A., Meltzer, H., Ford, T. and Goodman, R. (2004) *Mental Health of Children and Young People in Great Britain*. Office for National Statistics, London.

Griffiths, M. (2003) Terms of engagement: reaching hard to reach adolescents. *Young Minds Magazine* **62** (Jan/Feb). http://www.youngminds.org.uk/magazine/62/griffiths.php.

Hardiker, P., Atkins, B and Barker, M. *et al.* (2002) A framework for conceptualizing need and its application to planning and providing services. In: H. Ward and W. Rose (eds). *Approaches to Needs Assessment in Children's Services*. Jessica Kingsley, London.

Hart, R. (1997) *Children's Participation: The Theory and Practice of Involving Young Citizens in Community Development and Environmental Care*. UNICEF, New York.

Hine, J. (2005) Early multiple intervention: a view from On Track. *Children and Society* **19** (2), 117–130.

HM Government (2005) *Youth Matters*. The Stationery Office, London.

HM Government (2006) *Reaching Out: An Action Plan on Social Exclusion*. Cabinet Office, London.

HMSO (1989) The Children Act 1989.

HMSO (2000) Freedom of Information Act.

HMSO (2003) The Victoria Climbié Inquiry. Report of an inquiry by Lord Laming.

Horwath, J. (2001) *The Child's World. Assessing Children in Need*. Jessica Kingsley, London.

Hughes, M. (2006) Multi-agency teams: Why *should* working together make everything better? *Educational and Child Psychology* **23** (4), 60–71.

Jones, T. and Newburn, T. (2001) *Widening Access: Improving Police Relations with Hard to Reach Groups*. Home Office, London. Police research series paper 138.

Jordan, B. (2006) Well-being: The next revolution in children's services. *Journal of Children's Services* **1** (1), 41–50.

Kirby, P., Lanyon, C., Cronin, K. and Sinclair, R. (2003) *Building a Culture of Participation: Involving Children and Young People in Policy, Service Planning, Delivery and Evaluation. Research Report*. DfES, London.

Lahiff, M.E. (1981) *Hard-to-Help Families*. HM+M Publishers, Aylesbury, England.

Little, M., Axford, N. and Morpeth, L. (2004) Risk and protection in the context of services for children in need. *Child and Family Social Work* **9** (1), 105–118.

Lubeck, S. and Garrett, P. (1990) The social construction of the 'at-risk' child. *British Journal of Sociology of Education* **11** (3), 327–340.

McKeown, E. and Ghate, D. (2004) *The National Evaluation of On Track, Phase Two: Theoretical Overview of the Programme and its Evaluation*. Policy Research Bureau, London.

McLean, A. (2003) *The Motivated School*. Sage, PCP, London.

McNab, I. (2005) *A Good Model*. Seminar delivered to Educational Psychologists for Inclusion, 12 September 2005, Sheffield.

McNab, I. (2006) Message sent to EPNET@JISCMAIL.AC.UK, 30 April 2005 quoting Harry Korman.

Mitchell, D.E. and Scott, L.D. (1993) Professional and institutional perspectives on interagency collaboration. *Politics of Education Association Yearbook*, 75–91.

Morpeth, L. (2004) A study of organisation and outcome in children's services. Unpublished PhD thesis, University of Exeter.

National Institute on Alcohol Abuse and Alcoholism (2005). http://pubs.niaaa.nih.gov/publications/Social/Module6Motivation&Treatment/Module6.html, accessed 30 September 2006.

NHS Health Advisory Service (1995) *Together We Stand: The Commissioning, Role and Management of Child and Adolescent Mental Health Services*. HMSO, London.

Nixon, J., Walker, M. and Clough, P. (2003) Research as thoughtful practice, *The Moral Foundation of Educational Research: Knowledge, Inquiry and Values* (eds P., Sikes, J., Nixon W., Carr), Open University Press/McGraw-Hill Education, Maidenhead and Philadelphia.

Nuffield Foundation (2004) *Time Trends in Adolescent Well-Being*, The Nuffield Foundation 2004 seminars on children and families, London.

O'Brien, T. and Guiney, D. (2005) The problem is not the problem: hard cases in modernist systems. In: P. Clough, P. Garner, J.T. Pardeck and F. Yuen (eds). *Handbook of Emotional and Behavioural Difficulties*. Sage, London.

Office of the Deputy Prime Minister (2003) *A Better Education for Children in Care*. Social Exclusion Unit Report, London.

Parr, S. (2004) Social exclusion of people with marked communication impairment following stroke: findings. http://www.jrf.org.uk/knowledge/findings/socialcare/814.asp#top, accessed 11 September 2005.

Pacanowsky, M. (1995) Team tools for wicked problems. *Organizational Dynamics* **23** (3), 36–51.

Partridge, A. (2005) Children and young people's inclusion in public decision-making. *Support for Learning* **20** (4), 181–189.

Philpot, T. (2005) Downloading problems. *Young Minds Magazine* **77** (July/Aug). http://www.youngminds.org.uk/magazine/77/philpot.php.

Piper, H. and Piper, J. (Winter 1998/1999) Disaffected youth – a wicked issue: a worse label. *Youth and Policy* **62**, 32–44.

Rhodes, T., Holland, J. and Hartnoll, R. (1991) *Hard to Reach or Out of Reach? An Evaluation of an Innovative Model of HIV Outreach Health Education*. Tufnell Press, London.

Rittel, H.W.J. and Webber, M.M. (1973) Dilemmas in a general theory of planning. *Policy Sciences* **4** (2), 155–169.

Roaf, C. and Lloyd, C. (1995) Multi-agency work with young people in difficulty: findings. http://www.jrf.org.uk/knowledge/findings/socialcare/sc68.asp, accessed 11 September 2005.

Scott, S. (2006) Improving children's lives, preventing criminality: Where next? *The Psychologist* **19** (8), 484–487.

Schoon, I. and Bynner, J. (2003) Risk and resilience in the life course: implications for intervention and social policies. *Journal of Youth Studies* **6** (1), 21–31.

Sharp, S. (2003) Towards *More Integrated Services for Children and Young People with Disabilities in Sheffield*. Report to the Children and Young Person's Strategic Partnership Board, Sheffield.

Smart, S. (2005) Engaging work. *The Psychologist* **18** (9), 556–557.

Social Exclusion Unit (2001) *Consultation Document 'Raising the Educational Attainment of Children in Care'*. Social Exclusion Unit, London.

Stanley, N., Riordan, D. and Alaszewski, H. (2005) The mental health of looked after children: matching response to need. *Health and Social Care in the Community* **13** (3), 239–248.

Swadener, B.B. Lubeck, S. (eds) (1995) *Children and Families 'At Promise': Deconstructing the Discourse of Risk*. State University of New York, Albany.

Thomas, G. (2005) What do we mean by 'EBD'? In: P. Clough, P. Garner, J.T. Pardeck and F. Yuen (eds). *Handbook of Emotional and Behavioural Difficulties*. Sage, London.

UNICEF (1989) *UN Convention on the Rights of the Child* Office of the High Commissioner for Human Rights. UNICEF, Geneva.

Walter, U.M. and Petr, C.G. (2000) A template for family-centred interagency collaboration. *Families in Society* **81**, 494–503.

Watson, L., Tarpey, M., Alexander, K. and Humphreys, C. (2003) *Supporting People: Real Change? Planning Housing and Support for Marginal Groups*, Joseph Rowntree Foundation, York.

Webster-Stratton, C. (1998) Parent training with low-income families: Promoting parental engagement through a collaborative approach. In: J.R., Lutzker (ed.). *Handbook of Child Abuse Research and Treatment*. Plenum Press, New York, NY.

Williams, G., Whittome, B. and Watts, P. (2003) *PASS: Measuring Attitudes to Learning*. Research Report, Learning and Skills Research.

Williamson, H. and Middlemiss, R. (1999) The emperor has no clothes: cycles of delusion in community interventions with 'disaffected' young men. *Youth and Policy* **63** (spring), 13–25.

Williamson, H. (2005) *The Social Exclusion of Young People: A Reflection on Research, Policy and Practice over the Past Decade*. Seminar at the Centre for the Study of Childhood and Youth, Sheffield University, 9 March 2005.

Willms, J.D. (2002) *Vulnerable Children: Findings from Canada's National Longitudinal Survey of Children and Youth*. University of Alberta Press.

Young Minds (2005) http://www.youngminds.org.uk/whosecrisis/2/implications.php, accessed 17.09.06.

FURTHER READING AND RESOURCES

Children Now (2006) *The Participation Charter* (published in association with Participation Works). http://www.childrennow.co.uk/news/index.cfm?fuseaction=details&UID=df6cde71-e658-4488-ba3d-f823d89dae32.

Children Services Network, accessed at: http://www.csn.info/index.jsp

Communities that Care (CtC), accessed at: http://www.communitiesthatcare.org.uk/index.html

Dartington Social Research Unit, common language project is of particular interest, accessed at: www.dartington.org.uk/

Every Child Matters, accessed at: www.everychildmatters.gov.uk/

PASS Pupil Attitude to Self and School, accessed at: http://www.w3insights.pass-survey.com/home.htm

Research in Practice, accessed at: http://www.rip.org.uk/index.asp

Social and Emotional Aspects of Learning (SEAL), accessed at http://www.standards.dfes.gov.uk/primary/publications/banda/seal/

Street, C. and Herts, B. (2005) *Putting Participation into Practice. A Guide for Practitioners Working in Services to Promote the Mental Health and Well-being of Children and Young People*. Young Minds Good Practice, London.

Tools for Person-centred Planning (e.g. PATH, MAPS), accessed at: http://www.fsatoronto.com/programs/options/path.html

1 Underachieving Pupils, Underachieving Schools: What Pupils Have to Say

LYNN TURNER

INTRODUCTION

The school improvement movement, it can be argued, has been responsible for the drift away from inner-city schools to those perceived as higher achieving in that they are able to produce, with a given population, better results at GCSE, which are quite crudely described as percentage pass rates and published in respectable newspapers.

The progress that schools help individuals to make relative to their different starting points is usually referred to as 'value added', and more recently this has helped to temper the emphasis on results. However, it could be argued that this indexing is less likely to be taken into account by most parents than the bare facts.

The Government of the day in 1988 chose to introduce national testing to drive up standards; however, the effects on those schools that service our more deprived communities have been quite devastating. The emphasis on standards, combined with the Ofsted inspection regime, has led to the labelling of schools, which has seriously damaged the staff of those schools, the pupils who attend them and the communities where they are located. The effect of this policy has been to create a quasi-market (Gerwirtz, Ball and Bowe, 1995) where the concentration of pupils who may be described as 'hard to reach' (PricewaterhouseCoopers, 2004) has become higher in our inner cities than elsewhere.

The current Government, while propagating the standards agenda, has also unveiled what might be seen as a contradictory policy, where schools are seen as the hub of the community providing extended services in a climate where every child matters (Department for Education and Skills, 2003). The standards agenda and the resulting publication of league tables have led to a climate whereby schools compete with each other for pupils (the quasi-market). Extended services is the platform by which ECM (Every Child Matters), change for children, is to be delivered, and this is highly dependent on schools collaborating and working in partnership with each other as well as with other agencies and services. The

How to Reach 'Hard to Reach' Children: Improving access, participation and outcomes. Edited by K. Pomerantz, M. Hughes and D. Thompson. Copyright © 2007 by John Wiley & Sons, Ltd.

notion of a quasi-market is not conducive to such collaboration and, for some schools, makes the positive outcomes laid out in the ECM agenda that much more difficult to achieve.

This chapter explores some of the factors relating to contradictions in these agendas but, more importantly, seeks to explore the voice of the pupil in a school that has struggled, in a disaffected community, to meet government targets with the threat of Ofsted and HMI visits looming large. The views of some staff are also reflected here, as it is the interplay between these two sets of views that can be seen as pivotal to the process of becoming a more effective school and thus delivering better outcomes for young people.

THE CONTEXT OF THE SCHOOL

The school in question is located in a northern post-industrial city that has undergone much growth and restoration in recent years. With the expansion of service industries, good rail links to the capital and a thriving nightlife, it has also been described as a twin-track city, as not all parts of it have enjoyed this restoration or benefited from the economic growth.

The school itself is located in one of the inner-city areas that has not enjoyed the growth and prosperity described and so the social mix of the school has become skewed over time. Information from the Pupil Level Annual School Census (PLASC) suggests that the:

- eligibility for free school meals is in the highest benchmark group for social deprivation used by Ofsted and the DfES;
- percentage of pupils for whom English is not their first language is five times higher than for the city as a whole;
- percentage of pupils in public care is five times the equivalent figure for the city as a whole;
- proportion of pupils from black and minority ethnic groups (BME) is four times higher than for the city as a whole;
- proportion of pupils with special educational needs is higher than for the city as a whole.

On the Index of Multiple Deprivation for 2004, 55.5% of pupils lived in the 10% most deprived 'super output areas' (SOAs) in the country and 72.5% were resident in the 20% most deprived SOAs.

The school's results were below the Government's floor targets of 20% in all core subjects, and value added (progress made in those areas relative to the starting point of the pupils) was poor. The rate of attendance was 85.8%, and unauthorized absence above 5%. According to data available from the DfES, these rates of attendance lie in the tenth decile nationally (a way of ranking schools into ten groups).

THE COHORT

The group of pupils selected for this study all had SATs results deemed to be average at transfer to secondary school but failed to reach the levels predicted for them at the end of Key Stage 3. The group fairly reflected the ethnic mix of the school. Girls were over-represented in the cohort of underachievers (62%), whereas only 46% of the year group were female.

Pupils were interviewed in focus groups. Focus groups in themselves are not seen as unproblematic and some of the issues they raise are explored in Chapter 10 of this book. Issues around focus groups and the interpretation of data are also explored in some depth in Turner (2005). A small sample of staff interviews were also carried out to examine how far the pupil and staff views coincided or differed. This difference itself might be seen as a factor in underachievement.

THEORIES OF UNDERACHIEVEMENT

An analysis of literature relating to underachievement would suggest that explanations fall into four main categories that are:

SCHOOL EFFECTIVENESS AND SCHOOL IMPROVEMENT

The notion that schools can make a difference (Reynolds, 1976 Rutter *et al.*, 1979; Mortimore, 1991; Sammons, Hillman and Mortimore, 1995) also allows that schools can be blamed for not making a difference. When pupils underachieve, therefore, it is the school that has failed to add value and which will come under scrutiny. The pressure to raise achievement in order to meet targets and therefore raise standards became greater with the advent of notions of school improvement being linked to targets, where parental choice means that pupils can drift away from those schools seen not to be improving at an appropriate rate. Pupil achievement is therefore central to school improvement.

PSYCHOLOGICAL (PSYCHOSOCIAL)

Psychologists have looked for explanations of pupil underachievement in the research on motivation (Ausubel, 1968; Maslow, 1987; Howe, 1999), locus of control (Rotter, 1975; Bar-Tal *et al.*, 1980; Stipek and Weisz, 1981), self-efficacy (Bandura, 1986) and ego-identity (Erikson, 1963). Ideas about affiliation to social groups also play a part here. What is particularly pertinent here is the affiliation that pupils who are underachieving may feel to their peer group, particularly in a context where there is poor social mix, in that the predominant culture becomes a peer culture that is not pro-school.

SOCIO-ECONOMIC

Sociologists look to ideas about social class and socio-economic status to account for educational underachievement. The idea of social mix in schools is discussed (Willms, 1992; Thrupp, 1999), a lack of which has been brought about in part by the school improvement agenda with its emphasis upon parental choice to drive up standards, leading to a drift away from inner-city schools by those in a better position to make such choices (Gerwirtz, Ball and Bowe, 1995). It is argued by some sociologists that school effectiveness research has served to remove socio-economic status from the debate about educational standards (Hatcher, 1996; Mac an Ghaill, 1996).

BIOLOGICAL/GENDER

Ideas about biology and gender are also presented in the debate about underachievement. There has been much focus in recent years on the underachievement of boys, with some biological explanations including shorter attention span and less facility with language being put forward (Bleach, 1998), as well as gender-related ideas about 'laddishness' and masculinity (Covington, 1992; Connell, 1995; Jackson, 2002).

WHAT WE DID

A group of educational psychologists (EPs) worked with the school to identify the cohort of pupils in Year 10, set up two focus groups of one hour's duration and carried out a semi-structured group interview for each, with the focused topic of underachievement. The project was inspired in part by the work carried out by Pomerantz and Pomerantz (2002) focusing on 'able underachievers', where young people were given the opportunity to reflect on the causes of educational underachievement.

All participants in this study were given an option of whether to attend and were assured of individual and group confidentiality. Because of issues that arose in the second group, a third group was set up which was much smaller but gave some girls a voice that had not been heard in the second group because of the dominance of the boys. The interview material was transcribed and subjected to analysis using a method known as 'grounded theory' (Strauss and Corbin, 1998). This method of analysing data has its origins in the field of sociology and emphasizes the development of theory. The theory, however, is grounded in data drawn from actions, interactions and processes. Concepts and hypotheses from the field can then be used to generate theory. Such analysis goes beyond language and takes into account processes at work, in a group for example. As a method of analysis it moves from description to conceptual ordering to theorizing. Originally an empirical, positivist method where theory emerges from data, the Strauss and Corbin method recognizes the role of the researcher in making deductions from the data and brings into that process the researcher's own knowledge and experience. The researcher then plays a creative role, and there is a legitimate interplay between data and researcher. The method itself has three stages, those of:

- open coding, where concepts are uncovered and named;
- axial coding, where categories found at the first stage are related to each other at the level of properties and dimensions;
- selective coding, where the theory is integrated and refined.

As this was an action research project the school was consulted at each stage. It was decided that it would be useful to ask a sample of school staff the same questions about underachievement as had been put to the pupils. The sample included a newly qualified teacher (NQT), a head of year (HOY), who was also a teacher of humanities, a learning mentor (LM), a behaviour support worker (BSW) and a special needs assistant (SNA).

The two sets of views were compared around the key themes that emerged.

WHAT THE PUPILS TOLD US

The key themes that emerged from the focus group interviews to account for under-achievement were as follows:

- teaching and learning;
- relationships with adults;
- relationships with peers;
- climate and environment.

TEACHING AND LEARNING

ISSUES IDENTIFIED

Some of the pupils in this study felt that the quality of teaching that they received was not of the same quality as in other schools, and that other schools not only had better teachers but also had better facilities. It was also felt that support staff did not always know the subject area to which they were designated.

Relevance of the subject being taught was also raised as an issue, either they could not see the point of what was being taught or they felt that a topic had been covered previously at primary level and they did not understand why it was being revisited.

Boredom was an issue with too much teacher talk and too much copying being cited by some as a barrier. On the other hand, it was felt that better explanations by teachers would help them to understand the topic better, and so a lack of adequate explanation was cited as a barrier, and this also ties in with their ideas about quality of teaching (initials 'LT' denote the researcher):

Pupil   They're not fully qualified. Mr X – he teaches maths but he doesn't teach it.
Pupil   He just has us copy examples.

Pupil	He gives us a piece of paper and tells us to copy examples.
Pupil	I don't like writing a lot really.
LT	So writing's not good? Anybody else agree with that? That writing isn't. . .
Pupil	All we do is copy off the board.
Pupil	And my hand starts to hurt.
LT	So copying and writing you're not too keen on at all?
Pupil	It's not that I don't like writing, it's that I don't like copying.
LT	What kind of things could help you do better at school or achieve better results?
Pupil	To have proper teachers instead of supplies.
LT	So to have permanent teachers instead of supply teachers?
Pupil	Yeah.
Pupil	To have easier work.
Pupil	And hard work.
Pupil	They give us stuff what we've already done.

OVERCOMING BARRIERS

The pupils describe teachers who explain subject content well, guide them along rather than just writing information on the board and favour a step-by-step approach. This is not the same as a lot of teacher talk but rather is about the teacher giving structured guidance. Another example was cited where the group was small and the pupils were able to sit round the teacher while he explained things to them 'to a T':

LT	What do you think helps you to learn? Can you think of. . .?
Pupil	Decent teachers.
LT	Tell me what you mean by decent teachers.
Pupil	That they explain it good enough.
LT	OK, so a decent teacher means they explain it well to you.
Pupil	Explain it more than once.

Many pupils cited practical lessons as their favourites, and there was clearly a greater sense of engagement for subjects like PE, IT, drama and art. Demonstration, as in science, was seen as helpful when it occurred. Pupils felt that having some 'fun' in the lessons helped them to learn. There was a clear view that they would only work if the work was enjoyable. Some pupils felt that doing a lot of writing, although not copying, helped them to learn but recognized that others in the group did not agree with this. In coursework, there seemed to be a lot of variety where different methods of learning could take place, and to some extent the pupils could do their own research and work more independently. Some pupils felt that they needed to be given more work than they currently had.

RELATIONSHIPS WITH ADULTS

ISSUES IDENTIFIED

Pupils raised the issue of support and how they felt that they did not get enough support from staff. This, in turn, tied into feelings of fairness and unfairness. There was a strong perception in one group that support was directed mainly to those pupils who did well at school (the teacher's pet) or pupils with special needs. For this group, who were neither, they felt that their learning needs were largely unmet. They felt that some teachers did not give them adequate explanations in terms of what they needed to do in a lesson.

Responses from all of the groups suggest that they felt that they needed more support from teachers and support staff:

Pupil   No, but the teachers, they're always around other pupils in your class like and you're shouting your teacher and they're always around the teacher's pet. They're getting it so you're not getting attention because the teacher's pet's getting it.

LT   Can we say what kinds of pupils teachers give most attention to?

Pupil   The ones that are already on the second book in class.

Pupil   The ones that have got two exercise books and stuff like that.

LT   They're doing better and so they get more help?

Pupil   It's basically who they want to help.

LT   How do they make the choices?

Pupil   They're trying to say they don't want to help the second class.

OVERCOMING BARRIERS

Support is a key issue here with pupils feeling that it can come from various sources: teachers, non-teaching staff, parents and peers. Mentors are also recognized as helping with learning. Pupils felt that more support in lessons would help them to learn but that this should be given by a teacher qualified to teach that curriculum area and that the non-teaching staff should also be familiar with the subject matter. There was also an implication that support should be given in a more even-handed and fair way.

RELATIONSHIPS WITH PEERS

ISSUES IDENTIFIED

Pupils often saw peers as a source of support, and several expressed the view that they liked to work with their friends in class. For some, friends were synonymous with those pupils working at the same level, but when a friend who was not working at the same level needed help in class they would give it. Peers were mentioned equally with family as a source of support.

Others held the view that friends ought to be split up in lessons because they could be a source of distraction. The behaviour of other pupils in class was a negative influence, and the girls particularly cited the behaviour of boys.

Teasing and name-calling by boys was an issue for some girls but they also said that girls would intimidate them too. There was a mixed view about whether this was bullying or not. One of the boys, who wanted to work for GCSEs, revealed that other pupils often called him a 'geek':

LT   So, when you are there, what gets in the way?
Pupil   The boys.
LT   Boys? What is it the boys do that gets in the way?
Pupil   Teasing, calling you names.
LT   Are they teasing you?
Pupils All of us.
LT   Do they tease the girls generally?
Pupils Yaah.
Pupil   Especially me.
Pupil   Some of the girls intimidate you.
LT   Some of the girls? So there are some girls who also behave like the boys? What do the girls do?
Pupil   Just start on you, like two of them.
Pupil   Depends what side you get on them: some of them are all right.
LT   Are they intimidating in lessons or out of lessons?
Pupil   Out of lessons sometimes.
Pupil   Both.
LT   When the boys are behaving badly in lessons and girls are being intimidating, what do the teachers do?
Pupil   Nothing. They just stand there watching.

The influence of friends was raised when they would try to get another pupil to truant from school or from a lesson.

OVERCOMING BARRIERS

Peers could be a useful source of support, and some favoured working in groups – although this was not a universal view. Pupils preferred to choose their own groups and work with other pupils to whom they could relate. For some, this meant working with pupils at the same learning level as themselves.

CLIMATE AND ENVIRONMENT

ISSUES IDENTIFIED

Pupils felt that there was not a relaxed enough atmosphere in some lessons and that teachers needed to 'chill out' more. They also perceived a lack of praise and positive rewards and felt that a greater emphasis was placed on punishment.

Some pupils talked about 'bad people' getting in the way of learning, and by that
they meant those pupils who misbehaved in class. They also complained about people
coming in from the corridors and running around making a noise:

LT	What gets in the way of you working or learning? What does distract you?
Pupil	Bad people.
LT	So what do people do to distract you?
Pupil	Just talk.
Pupil	Throw things at you.
Pupil	Constantly make noise.
Pupil	Flick bogies at you.
Pupil	And they call me 'geek'.
Pupil	Lots of people from the corridors, they come in.
Pupil	They open the doors.
Pupil	When they're running about and making noise as well.

OVERCOMING BARRIERS

Some pupils felt that a quiet, tidy classroom helped them to learn. There was some
difference in view as to whether it was better to allow a degree of talking amongst
pupils, that there was a balance between too much talking and no talking at all.
Listening and concentration were seen as important to learning. A teacher making a
pupil sit on his or her own was sometimes seen to be an advantage, while other views
favoured working with friends or in groups.

There was a view that teachers spent a lot of time on disciplinary issues (always
yelling at someone) and that some classes were not strict enough. Although they felt
that in school as a whole there were lots of rules, this did not apply to some lessons.
This was particularly attributed to young or new teachers. Some pupils felt that they
did better when there was a more relaxed atmosphere in the class, when the teacher
was calm.

Some pupils felt that they would be motivated by more rewards in school. Stickers
and tickets to football matches were both mentioned as tangible rewards.

STAFF VIEWS ON UNDERACHIEVEMENT

The key themes emerging from interviews with staff were:

- behaviour;
- outside influences/background/neighbourhood;
- motivation and goals;
- ethos;
- confidence – both staff and pupil;
- teaching and learning.

BEHAVIOUR

Staff raised some key issues about behaviour in the school. Managing behaviour was seen as a distraction for the teacher, which affected the quality of teaching in the classroom. The overall impact of staff absence was noted, and this affected the general atmosphere around school, allowing 'hot spots' (areas of the school building where problems occur most frequently) to exist in terms of movement around school and an atmosphere of indiscipline, which would spill over into lessons.

Staff readily acknowledged the importance of pupil image amongst their peers. It is acceptable neither to be seen to be doing well nor to have difficulty in learning. Both of these may lead to non-engagement in the lesson and, at its most extreme, create reasons to escape from the lesson by using misbehaviour as a mechanism to this end.

> Issues with other kids – look at kids who achieve more, they cover up so not to be teacher's pet. This opens the door to bullying.
>
> (Behaviour Support Worker)

These issues are explored in-depth in Chapter 2 of this book.

OUTSIDE INFLUENCES

Outside influences were generally viewed in a negative way by staff, with home and parents not seen as supportive of their child's education.

> So whereas in primary school the parent would sit down, help them with their homework and their understanding, when they come to the high school that has gone out of the window: the kids do not get that influence at home. The children get more responsibilities at home, i.e. looking after siblings, more cleaning, etc. They are rushing their homework, or sometimes they are too tired, they come to school in the morning bad-tempered and not ready to work because they have not gone to bed early enough.
>
> (Learning Mentor)

MOTIVATION AND GOALS

Broader, societal issues were acknowledged that are particular to the area of the city in which the school in question is situated, lack of suitable jobs and the lack of positive role models in the community. More specifically, staff pointed to the competitive nature of the pupils as a motivational force and the idea that assessment was not only a competitive element but also a way of ensuring that pupils knew where they were and how they were doing in relation to school work. Staff enthusiasm was seen as an important factor in motivating pupils in a subject area.

> Some are from disadvantaged backgrounds – no good role models out of school. Some boys can't see the point and there are no jobs.
>
> (Behaviour Support Worker)

The enthusiasm of the staff, if the staff are enthusiastic about their work, about their teaching, it is infectious and the pupils go the same way.

(Learning Mentor)

ETHOS

Getting the classroom ethos right was seen as a balance between managing behaviour and setting out expectations regarding standards of work.

For me it has been getting that sort of culture that within this lesson you will be expected ... there are certain standards that you have got to meet. Not just behaviours but work as well, the work ethic within the classroom.

(Teacher/pastoral and Humanities)

CONFIDENCE

Staff recognized that some of the key issues for pupils related to their image within the peer group and its impact upon learning and accessing support. It is seen as unacceptable, in simple terms, to be either too bright or not bright enough. Pupils tread a fine line in trying to cover up either their enthusiasm for learning or their difficulty in understanding.

Some of the older children do not want to do any work; they think it is 'cool' to get sent out of the class rather than work. They also do this to avoid the work when they do not understand it: if you then offer them help, they do not accept it.

(Teaching Assistant)

Again, these issues are further explored in Chapter 2.

TEACHING AND LEARNING

Staff views on teaching and learning centred around two areas: preferred learning styles of the pupils and issues of confidence, both teacher and pupil. It was readily understood that many pupils prefer practical lessons where they are actively involved and where time spent listening is limited.

The reticence of pupils to engage in question-and-answer type lessons may be related to a lack of confidence in being able to give a correct response and opening themselves up publicly to being wrong or, on the other hand, being right and being seen as a 'geek'.

A lot of kids can't be bothered with English, maths, history and geography. They are not very good at communicating with adults and they hate to get anything wrong. With question and answers, they will not give you the answers in case they get it wrong; they think they might say it in the wrong way or in the wrong manner so it's understanding that.

(Learning Mentor)

Teacher confidence also plays a part here as a lack of confidence may lead to the planning of lessons that feel safe and may therefore be rather more dull than where teachers are prepared to take a risk in planning something interesting and participative.

> I think a lot of staff, especially that are new to school or new to teaching, will probably have issues regarding their [own] confidence and their ability, which has a massive effect on what you are prepared to do in the classroom.

> (Teacher/pastoral and Humanities)

DIFFERENCES IN VIEW BETWEEN STAFF AND PUPILS

In some cases, the staff's and pupils' views broadly coincided. This was the case with many aspects of teaching and learning, classroom ethos and to some extent peer group influence. It was also of interest to note where pupils raised concerns that were not alluded to by staff and vice versa.

PUPILS' CONCERNS OVER RELATIONSHIPS WITH ADULTS

The issue of lack of support was a significant concern to pupils, and there were grounds for saying that this was a relationship issue because it was perceived as unfair or equating to a lack of attention or even protection from teachers and support staff. For staff, pupils did not access support because of peer group influences (too embarrassed to ask for help or concerned about being seen as too academic):

LT   Are there any things that would help you?
Pupil   If the teachers were more supportive.
LT   Tell me what that supportive would look like. In what way could they be more supportive to you?
Pupil   Like notice that people are saying things to you and helping you with your work more and being more kinder.

Pupils' Concerns Regarding Fairness

Although an important issue for pupils, staff did not perceive their behaviour or the behaviour of other adults as unfair, although they did recognize that pupils may deliberately get into trouble to avoid being exposed when work was too difficult.

> You could just be sat there and that's how you get in trouble. You're just sat there and you don't know what you're doing. You ask the teacher and they just don't listen to you.

> (Pupil)

Pupils' View that Peer Influence Can be Positive or Supportive

Some staff acknowledged that pupils (mainly girls) could be a source of support for each other but perceived staff as giving pupils most support with their work, whereas pupils viewed peers as a key source of support:

Pupil   I've got loads of friends.
LT   Have you?

Pupil   Yeah.
LT   So when you are with them, you mean just if they're in the same room as you or do you have to be able to work with them?
Pupil   Yeah. 'Cos they help you as well, don't they?
Pupil   'Cos in subjects as well, they help you.

Adults' View About Home Background as Negative or Unsupportive Influence

While a staff view emerged that pupils did not get the support they needed at this age from home, some pupils mentioned home as a source of support in their work.

Adults' View that Learning Difficulties or Lack of Understanding Play a Part

While some staff believed that pupils would not ask for or accept support because of protecting their self-image, pupils felt that support was withheld from them because it was focused on other pupils (those with special educational needs or those who were higher achievers or more hard working).

Adults' View that Lack of Confidence Plays a Part

Confidence was raised by staff as a factor for both pupils and staff (see staff views on teaching and learning above), while this was not an area that pupils ever touched upon.

> Learning needs to be more personalized. Individual learning would overcome difference in academic levels – affects confidence. Confidence is important.
>
> (Learning Mentor)

Figure 1.1 illustrates the degree to which the key themes for staff and pupils coincided and in which areas they differed. While there a was common view in relation to teaching and learning, climate and environment, behaviour and the negative aspects of peer group relationships as all having an impact upon achievement, there were also key differences. The pupils in this study clearly had a more negative view of relationships with adults in the school and the impact of this upon their levels of achievement, and were also able to attach more positive benefits to peer relations in supporting their learning. The staff highlighted confidence as an issue for both pupils and staff, the lack of goals and motivation of pupils as affecting performance and outside influences (both familial and in terms of the wider community) as either unsupportive to learning or as detrimental to achievement.

The process of examining views of both groups in this study was enlightening, and decisions had to be made during the process about the meaning of certain statements and about the key themes that could be inducted (concepts are uncovered and named) and deducted from the data. Strauss and Corbin (1998) maintain that in their approach to grounded theory analysis the interplay between researcher and data is recognized and that at the heart of theorizing lies an interplay between induction and deduction.

Pupil view	Shared Pupil and Staff View	Staff view
⊙ Relationships with adults in school (negative perceptions) ⊙ Peer relationships (as key source of support)	⊙ Teaching and Learning ⊙ Climate/environment/ ⊙ Ethos ⊙ Behaviour ⊙ Peer relationships/ ⊙ Influences (emphasis on negative)	⊙ Confidence (lack of) ⊙ Goals/motivation (lack of) ⊙ Outside influences (negative perceptions)

Figure 1.1. Overlap and separateness in pupils' and staff's views of key factors in achievement and underachievement.

The researcher therefore has an important role as part of the process and cannot be seen as neutral. The researcher is legitimately more than a witness in the process and plays an active part in constructing a particular understanding of phenomena.

THE IMPORTANCE OF SHARED MEANING

The construction of meaning is an important element in this study when we consider the overlap and separateness of pupil and staff views on key factors in achievement and underachievement. There are significant differences in the key themes in the study that equate to the very areas which create our sense of self; relationships and confidence are central to this.

Frederick Erickson asks:

> What are the conditions of meaning that students and teachers create together, as some students appear to learn and others don't . . . How is it that it can make sense to students to learn in one situation and not in another? How are these meaning systems created and sustained in daily interactions?

> (Erickson, 1986, p. 127)

This highlights for us the importance of developing shared meanings and, therefore, it could be argued, the shared value systems so important at this crucial stage of development, which are based upon daily interactions that we can translate into interpersonal relationships, the building blocks of identity or sense of self. In a climate where pupils are not succeeding in school or where they cannot see its relevance, or where relationships are not positive, values may be constructed with peers that may be frowned upon by the adult community of the school. Farrell (1990) argues that students cannot value the opinions of those who do not give them positive reinforcement and will value those who do. He points out that values cannot be imposed but must be co-constructed. The issue of rewards and positive reinforcement was one raised by pupils in this study and also by staff, and so these pupils may have had stronger affiliations to their peer groups, who do reinforce them in some way.

THE ISSUE OF SOCIAL MIX

School effectiveness research, it is maintained (Thrupp, 1999), gives explanations for underachievement that are about 'blaming schools' for not making a difference because if it can be demonstrated that schools can make a difference, they are clearly doing something wrong if they can't. This body of knowledge and the School Improvement Movement, it is argued, are socially decontextualized, little account being taken of issues such as social mix, with 'the new right' holding schools directly accountable for their outcomes with little or nothing to say about the interactions between student culture, the culture of the community and the official culture of the school. As described earlier in this chapter, the culture of the school has to be co-constructed and cannot be imposed by one group upon another. For some schools, this imposition has become an uphill struggle. Marketing and league tables have led to a further imbalance in social mix (Gerwirtz, Ball and Bowe, 1995) and the cultural capital brought to some schools by the middle classes is missing from others, thus creating a very different kind of pupil culture where the 'self as my work' and 'self as student' are not integrated with the 'self in peer group' or 'self as loyal friend' (Farrell, 1990). The pupils must be able to see a working life beyond school, to see themselves as a student engaged in the academic life of the school and its relevance to the working life beyond school, while integrating these two with a view of themselves as a member of a peer group, being a good 'mate'.

Farrell identifies students who were from the same socio-economic background as his 'drop out' students (students who did not remain at high school) but attended an elite high school in the same city. The difference he drew from their pro-school attitude was that these students had a peer group support system that constantly validated their belief in education. This elite school had therefore developed a culture where staff and students shared values and had a similarly constructed reality. As hypothesized earlier in this chapter, perhaps the schools with the most successful outcomes have a greater degree of overlap between staff and pupils (see Figure 1.1 above) than did the groups in this study, who had areas of similarity on some important issues but also had significant areas of difference.

Farrell also makes the point that schools are not just a physical space but also a mental space where meaning systems, what we might call the culture of the school, are constructed but not necessarily co-constructed by the key groups: staff and pupils.

> The two groups obviously share part of an everyday reality, but there may be no overlap whatsoever in the mental spaces of school that constitute part of their circles of reality.
>
> (Farrell, 1990, p 147)

ESTABLISHING SHARED VALUES

If we accept that members of the school community must share a broadly similar set of values in order to live and work productively alongside each other, then we must ask what possible processes might help to arrive at such a point.

Systems based on Restorative Justice can become a way of life in an organization and should positively influence the entire school ethos if adopted. Restorative Justice was originally founded as a way of bringing together offenders with victims but has been widened beyond actual offending to look at ways of managing conflict in schools. It is defined as:

> A systematic response to wrongdoing that emphasizes healing the wounds of victims, offenders and communities caused or revealed by criminal behaviour.
>
> (Restorative Justice, 2006)

Restorative approaches in the educational setting include such activities as peer mediation and circle time (healing circles) and stresses relationships over and above rules. According to the organization Transforming Conflict (www.transformingconflict.org) there are profound implications for school communities and they are strongly linked to citizenship. Restorative approaches are founded on philosophy and ethos, involve key skills such as active listening and problem-solving and entail key processes. These processes can be light touch, such as restorative enquiry and corridor conferences, through to community conferencing, setting up circle time activities and mediation systems. Restorative pedagogy is also advocated where teachers model the values and skills necessary for restoration. Wachtel (1999) describes a restorative practices continuum, which has at one end 'affective statements' and at the other the formal conference. The term 'restorative practices' is used to describe any response to wrongdoing that is both supportive and limit setting. Therefore, restoration does not have to be a system incorporating many formalized procedures but is intrinsic to the ethos of the establishment and must be seen within the whole context of the school's behaviour policy and approach to discipline. Like our criminal justice system, schools often adopt a punitive approach, with the ultimate punishment being exclusion from school. It is a major philosophical shift to embrace a restorative approach but one that puts the person and the relationship at the centre rather than the concept of punishment or consequences. This connects very directly with school ethos.

The process of examining views as a joint exercise between staff and pupils can lead to a greater shared understanding of the issues on both sides. This kind of dialogue, in my experience, rarely if ever takes place in schools in any kind of formalized or structured way. Collaborative exercises between staff and pupils can help to establish a set of shared values, rather than one group imposing a set of values on another. This also opens up the possibility of involving parents in such a process so that values are truly established between staff, pupils and families.

Having established a set of shared values, it is important to keep those values alive and to refer to them frequently, and to ensure that they are active in shaping policy and any decisions that are made about the life of the school. Wood (2005) states:

> If ever there was a time when schools should be re-asserting simple, common values it is now. In our community school ... we start by asserting that we value learning. That is our purpose as an institution. We value respect for self and others, so that we can learn together. We value co-operation because we can achieve more together than we do separately. We value courtesy as a sign of our mutual respect. We value fairness, justice and tolerance, which create equal opportunities and reinforce respect. We value truth and honesty, the keys to trustful relationships. We value kindness, compassion and generosity because we are all made better by giving and receiving these virtues. We not only proclaim these values – from every notice board, in every classroom – but we teach them and we do our best to live them.

(Wood, 2005, p 5)

What is so refreshing about the statement made above is the emphasis on values rather than the trend that has grown in education of asserting a set of rules as part of a behaviour policy, often developed by staff and imposed on pupils, and sometimes written only by one person or a small group. Values have so much more potential to underpin discussion and decision-making and influence the way we live and learn than do a simple set of rules or expectations. Unfortunately, the latter became received wisdom in the world of behaviour management over the last decades. One of the clearest examples of this was the popularity of assertive discipline (Canter and Canter, 1982, 1992) in British schools in the post-Elton (1989) period.

IMPLICATIONS FOR PRACTICE

Billington (2005) clearly articulates the view that professional practice must reflect the synergistic nature of feeling, thinking and learning. There are therefore new models to be drawn in the way that the profession of educational psychology supports schools, not only in considering individuals but also in looking at overall systems. For example, the way that educational psychologists (EPs) support schools by developing behaviour policies and putting them into practice must necessarily take into account a complex set of human interactions that go on within a school, and that have not always been taken into account in the simplistic 'rules, praise, ignore or consequences' models that were widely promoted following the Elton Report (1989).

EPs are well positioned in their work with secondary schools to promote a model of adolescent development (Erikson, 1963; Kohlberg, 1981), which takes account of all aspects of feeling, thinking and learning and how these coincide with issues around transition linked to a decrease in motivation and an externalizing of locus of control. EPs have long promoted models of early childhood development, which have been helpful to parents, carers and those working in the early years' sector, but there has been a dearth of work that equally illuminates adolescent development.

EPs are also well positioned to promote activities in secondary schools that emphasize the importance of shared values and meanings between young people and adults in the school, as these are central to enjoying and achieving in the world of education.

Some of the vehicles for such work may lie in supporting schools in action research, including seeking pupils' views through focus groups and other research mechanisms, and in promoting restorative approaches in schools that value the emotional world of the individual. At the simplest level, these can be initiatives such as Circle Time and Peer Mediation. These last two are certainly not new to the work of EPs but may be part of an audit of what we already do which underpins the values of a profession that gives equal emphasis to feeling, thinking and learning and one that recognizes the need for a gestalt in the approach we take.

It is also important to recognize that, as the profession becomes part of the wider children's workforce, psychology is not solely the preserve of the EP but is shared by many other disciplines. What is important is what can be added by the application of psychology rather than who applies it. Much of the important work that is carried out in schools is undertaken by advisers, national strategy consultants, multi-agency support teams such as BESTs (Behaviour and Education Support Team) and education welfare officers, to name but a few, as well as by EP Services. The profession needs to find its place within a wider children's workforce rather than pondering for too long the age-old questions regarding unique contribution.

CONCLUSION

It is important that, in this chapter, the voices of the young people involved are heard. Ruddock, Chaplain and Wallace (1996) argue strongly that many failing schools could have been turned round if the views of pupils had been heard and acted upon, and ensuring that such action is taken is a challenge for researchers. Where schools are in challenging circumstances, whether recognized as an official category of concern or not, the sheer weight of day-to-day challenges may mean that acting upon pupil views is not a priority. In the case of this research we feared that action might not be taken, but the increased impetus of a new head teacher who values research and national drivers such as ECM and the new school Self Evaluation Form (SEF), which demonstrates that pupils' views have been taken account of and acted upon, have all helped to ensure that some action has been taken. The results of the case study school, as expressed in A–C GCSE grades, have risen through a combination of factors but we would want to attribute some of the success to the voice of the pupils themselves.

> We study people and we feedback our findings to those we have studied. Those people may or may not agree with what has been said about them. But whatever the outcome, the act of being studied makes people more aware and sensitive to those aspects of themselves that have been the subject of scrutiny. Increased self-awareness can lead to changes in values, attitudes and behaviour.
>
> (Buchanan and Huczynski, 1985)

It may be difficult sometimes to see the direct impact of research, but it is suggested above that being part of a study in itself and having feedback from that study creates a heightened awareness, which in turn promotes change.

Giving pupils a voice is the first step towards understanding their thoughts and feelings and therefore their values. It is argued that in many schools the values of pupils, staff and community do not coincide, or at least do not coincide enough in order to share the physical, social and mental space which is the school. It is proposed that in creating a climate where values are shared, learning will take place. This can be an important starting point to break into the cycle of underachievement, whereas it is often more common to begin with teaching and learning or by examining behaviour and attitudes.

It can further be argued that the School Improvement Movement itself has done much to skew the social mix of our inner-city schools by creating a quasi-market based upon published league tables. This drift away from certain schools upsets the social mix and reduces the cultural capital of the school so that the prevailing culture is one of dominant peer group values, which are not pro-school or pro-learning.

In terms of the PricewaterhouseCoopers' (2004) definition of 'hard to reach' (see introductory chapter), these young people may be hard to see and hard to engage. They may not be immediately apparent as underachievers unless due weight is given to levels of attainment prior to transition. It is the evidence of the possibility of achievement, arising from outcomes at Key Stage 2, that gives a fuller picture of the unrealized potential of this group. They may then become hard to engage because of the many and complex issues around the culture of the school and of adult and peer relationships. The third category of 'hard to reach' might be hard to change, but at the same time one must allow that it is not the pupils who need to change first but the many elements of the context within which they are expected to learn. Pomerantz (Chapter 3) poses a number of questions or key messages for professionals, which resonate in part with the findings of this research, on how to ensure positive outcomes for young people who do not fulfil their educational potential because of the risk of exclusion.

The issue of being hard to see is relatively straightforward to address in that it requires rigorous systems of monitoring and tracking to be in place and for appropriate questions to be asked of available data. At a time when electronic contextualized PANDAs (Performance and Assessment Reports now known as RAISE on-line, Reporting and Analysis for Improvement through School Self-Evaluation) are available to all schools and Local Authorities, the close interrogation of such data should be an integral part of the educational landscape. Being hard to engage with reference to this group of underachieving pupils presents a more complex challenge, and engagement will ultimately depend upon the nature of relationships that are established between adults in the school community, young people and their families, a welcoming and positive school ethos, good-quality teaching and learning experiences, a sense of purpose in education and a safe and supportive environment in which to learn. Adolescent identity, it is argued, is at the heart of this complex set of factors, and is impinged upon by factors around the identity of adults in the school. So who or what should change? The cycle of underachievement can only be broken if a number of factors change, including school mix, how relationships are built and maintained in schools and the way in which we give young people a voice in their own education.

When every child matters (Department for Education and Skills, 2003) in reality rather than in political rhetoric, we should see positive outcomes achieved in all five defined areas. A developing sense of identity, if negotiated successfully, should have as an outcome a healthy individual in the sense of being emotionally and mentally healthy, and we cannot dissociate physical health from this when we appreciate the interconnectedness of mind and body. Relationships, where they are positive, should bring about outcomes that support feelings of safety, for example being safe from bullying and intimidation, and should at the same time contribute to good emotional health. Teaching and learning, when successfully established, should allow all young people to enjoy school life and achieve their full potential. Where a positive ethos exists in a school, making a positive contribution to school life and to the community is more likely to be achieved. What lies outside of the immediate circle of the school is an environment where young people will be expected to achieve economic well-being, in the community and in the world of work. This will be more likely if the relevance of school life can be clearly demonstrated, so that young people achieve their full potential. If every child and young person really *does* matter, they should matter regardless of postcode, or 'super output area', and they should not have a better chance of achieving each of the five outcomes if they live in one part of the city or another, or attend one school or another. The very issues which underpin school improvement currently, and the need to drive up standards, may actively work against these positive outcomes as schools 'fail' to raise standards and 'fail' to add value because of issues of social mix that this very drive to raise standards has created.

REFERENCES

Ausubel, D.P. (1968) *Educational Psychology: A Cognitive View.* Holt, Rinehart and Winston, New York.

Bandura, A. (1986) *Social Foundations of Thought and Action.* Prentice-Hall, Englewood Cliffs, NJ.

Bar-Tal, D., Kfir, D., Bar-Zohar, Y. and Chen, M. (1980) The relationship between locus of control and academic achievement, anxiety and level of aspiration. *British Journal of Educational Psychology* **50** (1), 53–60.

Billington, T. (2005) First principles of feeling, thinking and learning: research and theoretical bases for professional practices in children's services. University of Sheffield, Unpublished paper for the 'Children's Services and Psychologists' conference, 1 July 2005.

Bleach, K. (1998) *Raising Boys' Achievement in Schools*. Trentham, Staffordshire.

Buchanan, D.A. and Huczynski, A.A. (1985) *Organizational Behaviour*. Prentice-Hall, Hertfordshire.

Canter, L. and Canter, M. (1982) *Assertive Discipline: A Take-Charge Approach for Today's Educator*. Canter and Associates, Los Angeles.

Canter, L. and Canter, M. (1992) *Assertive Discipline: Positive Behavior Management for Today's Classroom*. Canter and Associates, Santa Monica CA.

Connell, R. (1995) *Masculinities*. Polity, Cambridge.

Covington, M.V. (1992) *Making the Grade: A Self Worth Perspective on Motivation and School Reform*. Cambridge University Press, Cambridge.

Department for Education and Skills (2003) *Every Child Matters*. The Stationery Office, London.

Elton, L. (1989) *Discipline in Schools: Report of the Committee of Enquiry Chaired by Lord Elton*. HMSO, London.

Erickson, F. (1986) Qualitative methods in research on teaching. In: M.C. Whitrock (ed.). *Handbook of Research in Teaching*, 3rd edn. Macmillan, New York.

Erikson, E. (1963) *Childhood and Society*. Norton, New York/London.

Farrell, E. (1990) *Hanging in and Dropping Out: Voices of At-Risk High School Students*. Teachers College Press, New York.

Gerwirtz, S., Ball S. and Bowe, R. (1995) *Markets, Choice and Equity in Education*. OUP, Buckingham/Philadelphia.

Hatcher, R. (1996) The limitations of the new social agendas: class, equality and agency. In: R. Hatcher, K. Jones, B. Regan and C. Richards (eds) *Education After the Conservatives*. Trentham Books, Stoke on Trent.

Howe, M.J.A. (1999) *A Teacher's Guide to the Psychology of Learning*, 2nd edn. Oxford, Blackwell.

Jackson, C. (2002) Laddishness as a self-worth protection strategy. *Gender and Education* **14** (1), 37–51.

Kohlberg, L. (1981) *The Philosophy of Moral Development*. Harper and Row, San Francisco.

Mac an Ghaill, M. (1996) Sociology of education, state schooling and social class: beyond critiques of new right hegemony. *British Journal of Sociology of Education* **17** (2), 163–76.

Maslow, A.H. (1987) *Motivation and Personality*, 3rd edn. Addison-Wesley, New York.

Mortimore, P. (1991) The nature and findings of research on school effectiveness in the primary sector. In: S. Riddell and S. Brows (eds). *School Effectiveness Research: Its Messages for School Improvement*. HMSO, Edinburgh.

Mortimore, P., Sammons, P., Stoll, L. et al. (1988) *School Matters: The Junior Years*. Open Books, Wells.

Pomerantz, M. and Pomerantz, K.A. (2002) *Listening to Able Underachievers: Creating Opportunities for Change*. NACE/Fulton Restorative Justice at www.restorativejustice.org, London.

PricewaterhouseCoopers (November 2004) Hard To Reach. Unpublished LLP (Limited Liability Partnership) paper produced for the Department for Education and Skills.

Restorative Justice (2006) Restorative approaches and practices, http://transformingconflict. org/Restorative_Approaches_and_Practices.htm, accessed 3 February 2007.

Reynolds, D. (1976) The delinquent school. In: P. Woods (ed.). *The Process of Schooling.* Routledge and Kegan Paul, London.

Rotter, J. (1975) Some problems and misconceptions related to the construct of internal versus external control of reinforcement. *Journal of Consulting and Clinical Psychology* **43** (1), 56–67.

Ruddock, J., Chaplain, R. and Wallace, G. (1996) *School Improvement: What Can Pupils Tell Us?* Fulton, London.

Rutter, M., Maughan, B., Mortimore, P. and Ouston, J. (1979) *Fifteen Thousand Hours: Secondary Schools and Their Effects on Children.* Open Books, London.

Sammons, P., Hillman, J. and Mortimore, P. (1995) *Key Characteristics of Effective Schools.* Ofsted, London.

Stipek, D.J. and Weisz, J.R. (1981) Perceived personal control and academic achievement. *Review of Educational Research* **51** (1), 101–137.

Strauss, A. and Corbin, J. (1998) *Basics of Qualitative Research: Techniques and Procedures for Developing Grounded Theory*, 2nd edn. Sage, London and CA.

Thrupp, M. (1999) *Schools Making a Difference: Let's Be Realistic.* OUP, Buckingham/Philadelphia, Transforming Conflict at www.transformingconflict.org.

Turner, L. (2005) An investigation into pupils' views on underachievement and the implications for school improvement. Unpublished EdD thesis, University of Sheffield.

Wachtel, T. (1999) Restorative Justice in Everyday Life: Beyond the Formal Ritual. Paper presented at the 'Reshaping Australian Institutions Conference: Restorative Justice and Civil Society', Australian National University, Canberra, 16–18 February 1999.

Willms (1992) *Monitoring School Performance.* Falmer, London.

Wood, A. (2005) Positive spin. *Seced* **73**, 5.

2 Impression Management: Understanding and Enabling Children's Perceptions of Competence

STEPHANIE JAMES

INTRODUCTION

'All he's got is his swagger.' This was the observation of someone trying to offer a friend an explanation for the behaviour of the youth who was strutting along the footpath, apparently oblivious of the needs of others and, in a very resolute manner, sweeping aside all before him. The youth's baseball cap was sitting atop a determined, brow-furrowed face. The rest of his gear appeared to signal the young man's attempt to appear 'cool' – in essence, to give an impression of a person whose status was clear through his designer-label gear and whose defining gesture was the swagger. He didn't look happy.

The messages that the onlookers took from their observations were very different and produced quite different emotions. In the one, the boy was a threatening lout; while, for the other, the boy was the summation of all his missed opportunities.

Neither observer may have been entirely correct, perhaps not even near the mark. However, what is clear is that the interactions each of us has are shaped by the messages we think that we give, and those which we receive. In turn, these perceptions affect and perpetuate the way we continue to think and, by inference, have an impact upon subsequent interactions in similar encounters.

What might we take from this young man as an example? Is it not true that we all swagger in our own different ways? Children in the playground discuss their conquests, their reflected glory in 'my dad's car's better than your dad's'; at dinner parties when guests exchange stories of holidays, past and future, of new kitchens and cars, recount encounters with shop assistants, garages or bemoan the long wait on the end of a telephone and the amusing way in which the subsequent discussion with the call-centre operator finally gave them the upper hand, or as adults standing at the school gate waiting among other parents to greet their children, we want to be accepted, to be normal; as interviewees seeking employment we need to appear

How to Reach 'Hard to Reach' Children: Improving access, participation and outcomes. Edited by K. Pomerantz, M. Hughes and D. Thompson. Copyright © 2007 by John Wiley & Sons, Ltd.

competent; as we prepare our child's birthday party for her young friends we need to compete with the brilliance of all those other birthday parties she's been invited to; as we engage in casual small talk in those daily encounters with acquaintances, friends, colleagues, we want to give the right impression; are we not all motivated in some way to want to make the 'right' impression? Life, for many, may be a social minefield. Some of us may ask why do others swagger about, particularly when they have not obviously achieved much in life. Perhaps the swagger is born from a realization that they are bereft of legitimate accomplishments and so have created a defensive posture as a means of dealing with the highly competitive nature of the world – a competitiveness that begins in the nursery and continues through school and beyond into the world of work.

Most importantly, the constant theme running through this is the need to distance ourselves from implication where failure is concerned. So, if failure is threatened, how can we offer an appropriate excuse so as to minimize the sense of personal responsibility, which might imply incompetence?

And what if we fail? What part does failure play in our willingness to engage in subsequent encounters? Are our motivational drives affected by our previous experiences such that subsequent motivation is not so much to be able to succeed but, rather, to further avoid, at all costs, the humiliation that subsequent failure might become?

As adults, if we can place ourselves in the shoes of others, it is possible to reflect upon our thoughts and feelings before deciding on which course of action to follow. Imagine that you are a child or young person in a classroom where achievement and attainment is apparently the goal, spoken or unspoken. Imagine that every day is filled with a fear of failure. How would that make you feel? How would it make you think? How might it make you act or behave? Might you become harder to reach with every experience of failure?

In a school climate of assessment and testing, many children routinely experience a sense of failure with a corresponding self-perception of incompetence. Research suggests that this perception of failure is internalized by the children as a failure to give the 'right impression' (of competence) and therefore to appear unable or 'stupid'. Subsequent expectation of further failure, in turn, affects children's willingness and ability to engage successfully with the learning process, since avoidance of additional failure then becomes a major goal of learning for the child.

This chapter is concerned with the many ways in which children become 'hard to reach'. Clearly, if children's energies are consumed with avoiding failure, then it is likely that they will miss vital learning opportunities. This, in turn, makes them ever harder to reach since their relative poorer achievements, given the resultant gaps in knowledge of the missed learning opportunities, will require ever greater presentational ingenuity to avoid them being perceived as failing.

The content of this chapter is based upon a study undertaken as a result of the author's developing interest in the role of attributions upon pupil learning and school effectiveness. A literature review suggested that the attributions which people make to explain success or failure appeared to be related to behaviours that were deliberately designed to prevent a failure experience or to present the person in a positive light.

Behaviours related to attributions of failure were described as 'self-handicapping' in that they prevented successful engagement with tasks so that, in the event of a failure experience, this could be attributed to the behaviour and not to the ability or competence of the individual. An example of this is deliberately 'forgetting' to revise for a school test so that this, the lack of revision, offers an explanation for subsequent poor performance.

Gaining an understanding of the factors involved might help inform teachers, parents, other professionals and perhaps governments about ways of re-engaging those youngsters who have become 'hard to reach'. Better still, it may inform and prevent failure experiences from occurring in the first place.

WHAT DOES RESEARCH TELL US?

CONSTRUCT OF SELF-HANDICAPPING

We have already acknowledged that negative feelings can often lead to behaviours which are designed to protect us from the experience of failure in the future: self-handicapping behaviours. In turn, these behaviours often prevent us from engaging with experiences where we might learn how best to proceed. The concept of a young person being 'hard to reach' can be all too easily envisaged where the child is locked in a chain of behaviours, motivated by fear of failure and apparently barricaded behind tried and tested methods for avoiding failure. These children are at risk of missing opportunities, such is their need to avoid the risk of failure.

Snyder and Smith (1982) define the term 'self-handicapping behaviour' thus:

> Self-handicapping may be understood as a process wherein a person, in response to an anticipated loss of self-esteem, resulting from the possibility of inadequate performance in a domain where performance clearly implicates ability or competence, adopts characteristics or behaviours that superficially constitute admission of a problem, weaknesses or deficit, but assist the individual in controlling attributions (made by oneself or others) concerning performance so as to discount the self-relevant implications of poor performance and augment the self-relevant implications of success, avoiding the threatening evaluative situation entirely, or, maintaining existing environmental conditions that maximise positive self-relevant feedback and minimise negative self-relevant feedback.

(p. 133)

EXCUSES

Within Western culture it appears that each of us has a repertoire of excuses (attributions) we offer to ourselves or to others as explanations or reasons for our actions or inactions.

There are three prerequisites for an excuse-making process. First, an action must be attributable to the person offering the excuse; secondly, the action must have some unfavourable connotation; and, thirdly, there must be an observer who is making some value judgement. The observer in this context may in fact be an inner conscience rather than some third party who actually sees the action or omission.

PHILOSOPHICAL BACKDROP TO THE 'EXCUSE MASQUERADE'

Snyder, Higgins and Stucky (1983) use the term 'excuse masquerade' (p. 9) to capture the notion of the pretence, pretext, cover up, subterfuge, ruse and deception that is inherent in many of the self-handicapping behaviours which contribute to the excuse-story. Of particular importance to the excuse-making process is the understanding that the person offering the excuse has some choice about how to proceed. In essence, those who are forced into a particular course of action are absolved from responsibility for their actions and therefore need not offer an excuse to explain themselves. What is inescapable is that never before has there been such an apparent proliferation of choice in almost every walk of life. This places a further burden of responsibility on the actor and so makes the offering of plausible excuses ever more necessary (Berofsky, 1996).

The lesson that excuses must be offered for poor performance is given to children in every social arena. They are likely to have heard parents, carers and other significant people in their lives offer a range of excuses for everyday occurrences. It is therefore unsurprising that children themselves become so proficient at making excuses. Some of these excuses are undoubtedly benign in intent and effect, for example excuses for not tidying one's bedroom, while others may have more far-reaching consequences.

Within the school arena, what may be of most interest is discovering the cognitive processes by which pupils feel the need to offer excuses for poor performance and what impact this has upon the teaching and learning process across contexts, including the social context.

SELF-IMAGE, SELF-CONCEPT AND SELF-ESTEEM

ISSUES OF TERMINOLOGY

One problem with discussing issues that examine the effects of perceptions about the self as they relate to behaviour is the general lack of consensus in the use of the terms 'self-image', 'self-concept' and 'self-esteem'. Burden (1996) suggests that one of the main reasons for many of the contradictory research findings surrounding associations between achievement and self-esteem is the inaccurate comparison of very different constructs. Burden notes the interchangeable use of the terms 'self-esteem' and 'self-concept', among others, in the literature and suggests that, in the absence of an agreed definition of the terms, 'self-regard' may be the most appropriate generic term.

It may be useful to consider two contrasting interpretations to illustrate the dilemma. Coopersmith offers a succinct definition in terms of self-esteem being a *product* of perceptions of self over time.

> By self-esteem we refer to the evaluation an individual makes and customarily maintains with regard to himself: it expresses an attitude of approval, and indicates the extent to which the individual believes himself to be capable, significant, successful and worthy. In

short, self-esteem is a personal judgement of worthiness that is expressed in the attitudes the individual holds towards himself.

(Coopersmith, 1967, p. 5)

Others suggest that self-esteem is a *process*, rather than a product, of evaluation:

Self-esteem is the process by which the individual examines his performance, capacities and attributes according to personal standards and values which have been internalised through society and significant others.

(Burns, 1979, p. 68)

This suggests that the process is affected by perceptions the individual has regarding performance, reflected in feedback from the self and others. In this process-model there is an assumption that self-esteem is flexible, with esteem being raised or low-ered, not unlike a thermometer recording changing temperature. This contrasts with Coopersmith's (1967) suggestion that self-esteem is 'customarily maintained' over time and circumstances. This difference in perspective is reflected in much of the research, which, as previously noted, has partly explained contradictory research findings (Burden, 1996).

Taking this into account, if it is argued that excuses are reasons offered to explain performance then it follows that the performance must have some impact upon the self-perception of the actor. The concept of the perceptions of self being 'played in the theatre of the mind' (Snyder, Higgins and Stucky, 1983, p. 36) is an established analogy to be found in ancient as well as modern literary and philosophical thinking (Schlenker, 1980). The basic tenets are that there are three main components of the self-image: the actor, the performance and the audience. How one (the actor) perceives one's performance (actions or inactions) and what the audience (self and others) makes of the performance defines the self-image (Goffman, 1959). In addition, one's performance in a variety of arenas has a compounding or moderating effect and so informs the overall self-concept.

It has been suggested that, within a school context, perceptions which pupils hold regarding their social competence are associated with motivation and attributional style. Other variables concern pupils' beliefs about intelligence and academic per-formance and, particularly, the extent to which the performance is associated with ego-relevant outcomes. Additionally, the individual's locus of control – that is, how far a person perceives that what happens to them is within their control (internal locus of control) or outside their control (external locus of control) – is a further variable. Those who are judged to have an external locus of control are likely to choose chance activities where there is an inbuilt range of excuses to explain failure.

As suggested, strategies that children adopt to avoid failure include 'self-handicapping' strategies, such as refusing to comply with teacher requests to begin or complete work. The aim of such strategies is to avoid any task where failure is a possibility.

At the extreme, children may adopt the ultimate self-handicapping and avoid-ance strategy, avoidance of school altogether through school refusal (truancy) or by engineering their exclusion and thus compounding the cycle of failure. These children are not so much 'hard to reach' as impossible to reach.

Understanding the factors that exacerbate, or ameliorate, these defensive but self-defeating behaviours is crucial. Thereafter, creating a climate that supports and enables children to appear competent and to present themselves in a positive light to peers is essential if professionals are to improve access, participation and outcomes for all children.

HOW MIGHT WE REACH THE 'HARD TO REACH'?

THE CHILDREN'S VOICE

In order that we might answer this question, it is crucial that the voices of the young people themselves are heard. For this the author draws upon research conducted with young people in Year 6 as part of a study undertaken to look at the link between children's perceptions of their academic and social competence, their locus of control and their need to present themselves in a positive light. Particularly, the research suggested that what was crucial to all children was the need and desire to manage the impressions of competence.

The following quotations are transcripts from interviews where children gave their views about their feelings and behaviours associated with feelings of competence and fear of failure. Particularly, the young people felt a great need to present themselves in a positive light, especially to peers.

> Well, there's me and A and D. I'm not as clever as other children, neither is J. I'd like to be as clever as them but then I might be as bad as them and say 'you're stupid, you're useless, you're thick' . . . I think I'm quite a nice boy . . . but I use the wall as a punch bag at home.

For this boy, the dilemma was between the frustrations of being *perceived as 'stupid'* and the desire to be *'as clever as everyone else'* but then be as unkind as others.

> I'm about the same as everyone. If they're not clever, they might behave badly. They might mess about because they think they might get shown up. This doesn't happen to me.

Here there is an empathy for those who might be *'shown up'* if they feel that they are *'not as clever'* as others, particularly the shame attached to being 'shown up'. If even 10-year-old children are aware of this, what excuse have governments for embarking upon, and perpetuating, the 'showing up' of young people *through their failure to meet national attainment targets*?

> They [pupils] want to know they can do it. They worry about what other people think but they mainly worry about what they think about themselves. Sometimes children laugh at other children. I'm sensitive. I sometimes cry. My Mum says I need to give myself confidence. Some people think I'm boasting but I'm not.

This young person's mother sounds to be very supportive. What of the young people for whom such support is lacking? In any case, should the role of parents be to give confidence to their children in the face of institutionalized 'showing up'?

> I think I'm not as clever [as others]. I can't read good or write good. I can write but I'm not good at spelling. (Interviewer: Do you mess about when you can't do the work as well as you would like?) No . . . well, sometimes.
>   I'm not that clever. I'm OK but I'm not that clever. Some people are frightened of getting things wrong. I'm like that. I think that they'll laugh at me and then I'd feel upset and get embarrassed.

The observations of these young people are almost universal in that they fear ridicule.

> Once I answered a question in maths and I got it wrong and D laughed at me and I felt embarrassed.

For others, the shame of failure reaches further.

> If you get shown up [by your friends], it's awful . . . like, my shoes cost £8 . . . my shoes are OK but it upset me when they said they were rubbish.

Are the institutional structures and demands adding to the burdens some young people feel by being routinely bullied for their so-called idiocy?

> Some children pick on me in the playground . . . they call me names . . . lots of people . . . they call me an idiot . . . this makes me feel sad . . . I feel sad most of the day . . . I feel quite miserable.
>   Other children laugh at me when I get things wrong . . . when the teacher asks me a question and I get it wrong . . . this makes me sad and I say 'shut up'.

Even the young person who didn't 'mess about' in class observed the need to prove himself to others by managing the impression he gave in the playground.

> I don't mess about in class, but in the playground people say I'm a 'goody goody' so I mess about there to prove I'm not.

What all these examples have in common are the children's need and desire to present themselves in a positive light, especially to peers.

Other examples concerning *self-presentation* include:

- If they're not clever they might behave badly . . . mess about because they might think they might get shown up.
- We want to show off to our mates.
- They do it because they want to be like their friends.
- They want children to think they're clever.
- They think they're big . . . above other children in the class.
- To show off . . . to look cool . . . to try to be 'it'.
- They do it to show off but it doesn't work because the teacher tells them off.

Although the transcripts of the pupil interviews indicated that there were many different reasons offered by the pupils for the way they behaved, almost all were associated with impression management and the avoidance of failure.

In summary, young people are concerned with social acceptance, fear of failure and rejection and fear of put downs. They feel a need for sameness and normality and want to be included.

Children are acutely aware of peer ridicule and peer pressure to conform. Fear of social incompetence and taunts can lead to feelings of resignation and hopelessness. Feelings of difference affect youngsters' overall sense of competence.

It hardly needs stating that such feelings are inevitably going to affect pupils' willingness and ability to successfully engage in either the social or academic curriculum, which in turn perpetuates a cycle of failure and denying youngsters opportunities to succeed. The more entrenched that such failure experiences become, the more difficult it will be to reach such children.

IMPRESSION MANAGEMENT

The core and defining feature of all the young people's comments was the over-riding need to manage the impressions they gave to others, particularly to peers. Impression management may therefore be seen as a universal need, as discussed in the opening paragraphs of the chapter.

The real question is concerned with exploring the implications of this knowledge, both in terms of practice and also for future research: particularly, how the context of education can affect the ability of youngsters to successfully manage the impression they give so as to appear to others to be worthy and competent. Aspects including the role of classrooms as enabling environments in helping children succeed will be explored, against the background of legislation and current educational philosophy. Additionally, the findings will point the way to further research that may now be necessary.

SO WHAT CAN WE DO ABOUT IT?

PROMOTING EFFECTIVE IMPRESSION MANAGEMENT

What has been highlighted so far is the need to help youngsters to proactively and effectively appear able and worthy, 'cool', especially in front of peers. Research has suggested that having a particular status and social identity among peers is important for all children (Carroll *et al.*, 1999) and so this problem is one of universal importance.

While, for some, academic achievement and effort may have been successful in attaining a positive social status and image, for others it may have been more important to have a non-conformist image (Nurmi, 1991; Houghton and Carroll, 1996). It may also be hypothesized that this latter desire may result from the compounding effects of failure to achieve status through more pro-social or traditional achievements. In this respect, achieving status through non-conformist actions and attitudes may be the only strategy available, hence the story recounted at the beginning of the chapter of the young man with the swagger. It may be important to attempt to generate a culture within schools so that pro-social and appropriate academic targets are also perceived by young people to be 'cool'.

STRATEGIC INTERVENTIONS

Of crucial importance to the educational process is the range of strategies that may be employed by teachers and schools in an attempt to help youngsters manage the impressions they give in a functional and positive way. Particularly, it is important to identify ways in which teachers and educators can enable youngsters to appear worthy and competent to others, to give the 'right' impression.

Although many interventions in schools may be specifically designed, for example, to prevent behavioural difficulties, increase motivation and so forth, what will be especially important to identify are those which also target the prevention of failure and maintenance of self-esteem, since these may be the keys to successful impression management and the prevention of dysfunctional self-handicapping behaviours. It has been suggested that a significant minority of teachers do not generally recognize the self-handicapping purpose of behaviours without prompting (James, 1998a) or, by inference, the importance placed by youngsters on managing the impressions which they give.

It is therefore possible that interventions which target only the behaviour, and not the impression management motivation behind the behaviour, will meet with only limited success. In effect, any reduction in self-handicapping behaviour, as a function of impression management, is likely to be almost randomly achieved. On the basis of this, teachers would be advised to ensure that any intervention designed to remediate behavioural difficulties has as its principal aim the protection, and enhancement, of the self-image, which in itself is a feature of impression management. For example, an intervention to remediate off-task or disruptive behaviour should have as its primary purpose facilitating opportunities for the child to present a preferred image and to enhance his or her self-esteem. This may be achieved by facilitating the demonstration of competence and autonomy, rather than by increasing on-task behaviour per se, since the former is likely to affect the child's overall on-task behaviour across contexts (Deci and Ryan, 1985; Connell and Wellborn, 1991). In this way, the youngster will be enabled to manage the impression he or she wishes to make.

CURRENT LEGISLATIVE FRAMEWORK

Interventions to target any discrete difficulty that interferes with the teaching and learning process cannot stand in isolation from the political and philosophical mores of the time. Indeed, as previously noted, some national targets and collective aspirations do not sit comfortably with the suggestion that the prime motivation for some children is the avoidance of failure and the management of the impression they give to peers (Dweck, 1986; Dweck and Leggett, 1988; Elliott and Dweck, 1988; James, 1997).

The series of government initiatives spanning the last decade and including *Excellence for All Children: Meeting Special Educational Needs* (Department for Education and Employment,), *Every Child Matters* (Department for Educatio n and Employment, 2003), *Children Act 2004* (HMSO, 2004) and *The Children's Workforce Strategy* (Department for Education and Skills, 2005a) reflect the current political belief that education can, and should, be centrally important to a thriving and civilized society. The philosophy suggests that excellence for all should be reflected by a high quality of education, beginning in the early years, with commitment to achievement. What is termed 'a new approach' in *Excellence for All Children* (Department for Education and Employment, 1997a) elaborates on the theme in expecting 'zero tolerance' of poor standards with a partnership between all those with an interest in education, working for the benefit of all.

None of the vigour, verve and rhetoric has been modified over the years; rather, successive government initiatives have sought to 'drive up standards'. The education White Paper *Higher Standards, Better Schools for All* (Department for Education and Skills, 2005b) argues that the past decade has seen wide-ranging reforms across the education sector in order to provide each child with the high-quality education they need as an individual to fulfil their potential. To this end the White Paper acknowledges that the main measure has been test and examination results.

Unless the new approach also takes into account the pupils' primary need to present themselves in a positive light, that is to manage the impression they give to others, it is likely to remain just one more inadequate intervention. The main measure of test and examination *results* is testing and measuring of *children*, not of the delivery of high-quality education. In the impression management stakes, children will assume that it is their worth (ability) that is being assessed and not the competence or ability (worth) of the teacher to teach. While this is the case, children will continue to fail in their own self-image as competent individuals.

ASSESSMENT AND MONITORING

This is not to say that teachers are immune from assessment. Underpinning the new educational philosophy is a combination of carrot and stick to manage the disparate interest groups. Teachers and schools are the subjects of rigorous inspection through the auspices of Ofsted, with winners and losers being given equally high profiles. At the same time, children are subjected to regular testing against subjective norms, often presented as objective criteria, with failures in both school and child being catalogued and recorded for all to see.

School results are packaged to inform parents so that they are able to make *choices*. Where are parents able to access information about a particular school's attributes which are enabling? What are the measures of esteem-raising and competence-enhancing? In short, how are parents able to gather information to enable them to make informed choices about a school's ability and willingness to enable young people to feel autonomous and manage impressions of competence?

The impact of government initiatives upon the ability of pupils to manage the impression they wish to achieve, upon their self-esteem and, ultimately, upon their behavioural functioning may be significant. An environment that increases pupils' doubts about their basic worth or competence will also increase the incidence of self-handicapping behaviour (Ames, 1992) as a consequence of trying to manage the impression they give. Teachers, who are pressured into pursuing excellence in the guise of exam results, may see as peripheral the need to help pupils create, manage and maintain a positive impression. However, neglect of this crucial area may lead to cyclical problems of a failure experience affecting behaviour which, in turn, may provoke a further failure experience.

AFFECTIVE AND MOTIVATIONAL FACTORS

It has been suggested that most of the time people monitor the ways in which they present themselves at a non-conscious or pre-attentive level (Hogan, 1982). Additionally, some are seen as high self-monitors while others are less aware (Snyder, 1974). Again, personality factors have been suggested (Avia *et al.*, 1998) as affecting the extent to which individuals engage in monitoring the ways in which they present.

An additional factor is possible in that anxiety may be provoked by multiple failure experiences. Those who are least able, across contexts, to manage the impressions they wish to give may go to ever-increasing lengths to hide their perceived failures. Those who are motivated to belong, for example, to the football team, gang or other in-group, but lack the relevant skills or attributes, may be even more motivated to compensate for this so-called failure. Within a school context, where escape from peer scrutiny is impossible, it may be little wonder that some youngsters go to desperate lengths to try to successfully impression manage. Discrepancy between the desired and perceived image is therefore likely to trigger the excuse-making process. Ultimately, some children will vote with their feet and truant from school. Others will become one of the 9440 permanent exclusions or one of 220 840 fixed-term exclusions (figures for England 2004/5; Department for Education and Skills, 2006). There is also a clear link between exclusion and crime, with a third of all prisoners having been regular truants from school and half of all male prisoners having been excluded from classes (Social Exclusion Unit, 2001). Thus the spiral of failure and exclusion from mainstream society continues, making these youngsters even more difficult to reach.

In an arena where peer audience is crucial and where youngsters perceive that they fall short of the desired impression, excuse-making will be employed. If this is in conflict with the aims of the school, or society as a whole, it is likely that the need to present a positive image to peers will prevail. Therefore, it is important to ensure that the context allows successful impression management, preferably through cooperative structures (Ames, 1992) as outlined in the following section.

INTERVENTION AND REMEDIATION STRATEGIES

Against this background, what other practical strategies are possible that might help children to positively impression manage, reduce self-handicapping behaviour, maintain self-esteem and so reduce motivation to avoid failure? Which strategies might work best and in what context?

ASSESSMENT AS AN INTERVENTION MODEL

One method for increasing attainments may also include a target to help children to manage the impression they give so as to be viewed positively by peers, which, in turn, may foster a positive self-image. Teachers are now used to applying criteria for assessing whether pupils have reached a level of competence in individual subject areas. What they may also incorporate may be another measure, albeit subjective, about the impression management strategies youngsters are adopting that, again, affect their self-confidence and self-esteem.

As teachers become more familiar with the markers that define competence, autonomy and relatedness (Deci and Ryan, 1985; Connell and Wellborn, 1991), they may more readily anticipate the difficulties arising from negative self-perception and the resultant impression management problems which may provoke dysfunctional self-handicapping behaviour. Particularly, it may be useful for teachers to know that there is a relationship between those whom they regard as having behavioural difficulties and poor social skills and the use of self-handicapping behavioural strategies which pupils use in an attempt to manage the impressions they wish to create (James, 1999). It may then be possible for teachers to take proactive measures to enable pupils to be successful in giving and maintaining the 'right' impression.

RESPONSE TO FAILURE

A particular model might be thus: the teacher should first identify the learning objectives of the lesson and then consider the impact that the means of delivery may have upon the impression management needs of the pupil. For example, if the taught element is interactive and relies upon oral feedback from the pupil, the teacher might consider the possible impact on the impression a pupil wishes to give and maintain in being required to risk giving the wrong answer. What might be the usual teacher response to this, and what of the response of peers? Is getting the answer wrong likely to diminish the pupil in the eyes of his or her peers or would he or she think this might be the case? What might be the subsequent impact on the child's behaviour? Answers to these and related questions may help a teacher focus upon small but significant interactions between the pupil, teacher, peers and subject content, each of which may exacerbate or remediate the need for a pupil to use self-handicapping strategies to manage an impression of competence.

LEARNING PROCESS

A further intervention might be the modification of the delivery of the curriculum by the teacher to emphasize the value of the *process* of learning. This may be one initiative to encourage and support pupils in taking the risk of failure that self-handicapping behaviour, to manage the impression one gives, often prevents. One intervention strategy may be to rehearse with the pupil the inevitability of failure in some situations and, even, its potential merits. The teacher may, for example, analyse the interaction of thoughts, feelings and behaviour that may have led to the error in an explicit attempt to identify further, or different, teaching strategies. It is likely that, within this process of assessment, the teacher will recognize the need of the pupil to manage the impression he or she wishes to create or maintain.

It may then be useful to help the student reframe the error so that it may be seen as helpful and part of a process-orientated approach to learning rather than overemphasis being placed on performance of the task itself. Pupils may be encouraged to accept failure not only as an integral and benign fact of life but also as a useful indicator of how best to proceed. The experience of failure may then be perceived, by pupils and teachers alike, as less of a reflection of worth or competence. In this way, the impression created by the pupil will be one of a competent problem-solver. However, this view is made more difficult to assert in an era of measuring success in terms of product-orientated exam passes. None the less, pupils and teachers may be encouraged to focus on the positive aspects of discovery and evidence that the greatest inventions often emerged from apparent failure (James, 1997).

PRODUCT OR PROCESS?

As previously noted, failure of effective impression management strategies may lead youngsters to become disaffected with the learning process and may lead to the ultimate self-handicapping strategy, truancy, so as to avoid failure (Jones, 1989). If this is to be avoided, early intervention is crucial to help minimize the compounding effects of repeated failure experiences (Ames, 1992). In this context 'failure' is perceived as a failure of effective impression management.

Many initiatives that have attempted to look for solutions in the content of the curriculum (Archer, 1998), allowing more flexibility to offer work-related programmes aimed at increasing motivation, are likely to have been initiated after prolonged failure experiences. Understanding the relationship between the need to impression manage and behaviour, with early intervention to help youngsters to positively manage the impressions they wish to create, may prevent the need for such remediation in the future. Meanwhile, these initiatives are to be welcomed as a practical attempt to reduce the self-handicapping effects of disaffection. However, the philosophy of these schemes appears to focus almost exclusively upon *what* is taught rather than *how* it is taught. Presumably, those schools that routinely omit proactive opportunities within their teaching methods to allow pupils to demonstrate their competence – that is to present a positive image – may also do so for the new curriculum (James, 1998a).

Additionally, if the pupils' main aim is to manage the impression they give, it may be useful to explore precisely what that impression is.

It may be pertinent to ask whether the success of these initiatives relies more on an increase in helping the pupils maintain an impression of self-confidence, of autonomy and competence than necessarily being solely related to the curriculum content.

What may be hypothesized is that self-selected and self-instigated learning, allied to successful impression management, must involve the pursuit of competence, absence of self-handicapping and maintenance of a positive self-concept. What may be important in any learning situation is to try to establish, and then replicate, the contextual factors for individual pupils, modelled on their own self-initiated goals and achievements. This may necessitate teachers identifying with the pupil those factors that each recognizes as either having the potential to assist or to prevent successful learning. To some extent tracking individual pupils' achievements should happen through personalized learning planning. However, it is not clear that the self-presentational needs of children are routinely recognized by teachers (James, 1997). Of particular importance in any personalized learning planning is ensuring that the needs of the child are identified, especially in terms of the impression they wish to manage, rather than the needs of the school or society as a whole.

LEARNING SKILLS

When children are engaged in classroom-based activities, working at similar tasks, competition between them is inevitable, even in largely cooperative environments. As Dweck and Bempechat wryly note:

> Low ability pupils perceive themselves as failures because they are frequently praised for work which is neither praiseworthy nor of intellectual merit.

> (Dweck and Bempechat, 1983, p. 72)

Further, if teachers identify errors in the work of such children, they frequently minimize the importance of these for fear of upsetting the child. This attitude may perpetuate the failure that it was designed to remediate. Indeed, the pupils may perceive this as clear evidence that the impression they wish to manage has been unsuccessful; this, in turn, may provoke dysfunctional self-handicapping behaviour.

SELF-ASSESSMENT AND MOTIVATION

By implication, judgements that pupils make about their performance have a motivational effect (Weiner, 1985); for example, those who attribute their successes to personal attributes and their failures to lack of effort may be able to persist when they encounter failure. By contrast, those who attribute failure to innate lack of ability are far more likely to give up. While young children ordinarily attempt all tasks with enthusiasm and are not inhibited from further endeavour if they see that success is not possible, once they understand that to try and to fail reflect on ability, and that to be perceived as having low ability is anathema, then they are likely to disengage from the learning process (Nicholls, 1984; James, 1997). Clearly, another key variable in this motivational conundrum may be successful impression management strategies.

Stipek and Gralinski (1996) suggest that pupils' perception of their intelligence and performance is a powerful predictor of achievement outcomes regardless of the effect of goal-orientation and problem-solving strategies. This presumes that teachers need to identify differential aspects of intelligence and not only those associated with, for example, the tasks of numeracy or literacy in order for pupils to be able to demonstrate their different and relative competencies. To suggest, as the National Curriculum and attendant assessments indicate, that there is one standard measure of competence and, by definition, of worth, implies that many pupils are going to be disenfranchised and resort to dysfunctional ways of managing impressions, including self-handicapping behaviour, in order to disguise their inability to compete successfully.

Although many recent initiatives have apparently been designed to address the social and emotional aspects of learning (SEAL; Department for Education and Skills, 2005c), it is not yet clear that this will entirely support those youngsters for whom academic failure continues to affect their ability to maintain a sense of competence.

It is incumbent upon teachers to enable pupils to manage the impression they give through demonstrating their relative strengths, with equal value being placed upon academic, social and practical skills in a context where these skills are perceived by pupils as being 'cool'. Teachers must make their own judgements about how this can practically be achieved but the aim should be enshrined in school policy.

POSITIVE TEACHER EXPECTATIONS

One factor in the successful functioning of children who have previously exhibited significant self-handicapping behaviours, allied to failure to manage the impression they give, may be the teacher's commitment to influencing the children's development (Bond and Feeney, 1986). This suggests that intervention with pupils who had low self-esteem, who had experienced significant social deprivation and who demonstrated poor interpersonal skills effected outstanding change, both academic and social.

The important variable was an acknowledgement that the negative expectations of the teacher could, unwittingly, be transmitted to the child and so reinforce a negative self-concept and confirm in the child that their ability to manage the impression they wish to give has failed. By contrast, a willingness by the teacher to acknowledge the part which he or she could play in raising the child's self-esteem, and acceptance by even a small number of peers, could begin to effect change. Even within the constraints of the National Curriculum, individual teachers can be powerful influences for change. Such initiatives as Circle Time (Mosley, 2001) and Circle of Friends (Newton, Taylor and Wilson, 1996) may play an important role in enabling pupils to give a positive impression.

ASSESSMENT AND INTERVENTION MODEL

The success of any intervention to enable youngsters to manage the impression they give, especially to peers, is likely to be dependent upon careful assessment of that child's strengths and needs. Particularly, the identification of aspects of both the academic and the social curriculum, and contextual factors, will have an impact upon successful intervention. What may further assist teachers and educators in selecting appropriate methods for increasing pupils' abilities to successfully impression manage is a model of assessment and intervention. This model (Figure 2.1) may be used to assess the needs of children who are presenting with behaviours, including self-handicapping behaviours, whose aim is to successfully impression manage but for whom this is unsuccessful. The model may be used as both an assessment and intervention tool.

CONTEXTUAL FACTORS

In any assessment of a pupil's behavioural functioning, it is first important to consider the impact and role of contextual factors. These may include any legislation that constrains or enables schools to meet pupils' needs. Examples of this include the legislation contained within the 1997 Education Act, which focuses on behaviour management, as well as curriculum constraints, such as the literacy and numeracy hours. Clearly, the same legislation may have varying impact upon different pupils.

Pupil functioning also cannot be divorced from the school context, which may include physical and structural factors as well as philosophical and stated aims. Examples may include the actual structure of the classroom as well as the covert or overt climate of competition or cooperation within the school. The particular inter-relationships of the pupils as a whole are also likely to have an effect upon the individual class members. Additionally, teacher expectation, experience and teaching style are all likely to have an impact. It may be useful to remember that impression motivation and impression construction are also likely to be key factors in teachers' behavioural functioning, no less than in the population as a whole.

A further contextual factor that should be considered is the environment in which the school operates, including the cultural, societal and parental aspirations that are evident. This is not to imply that expectations should be constrained by cultural or sociological factors but rather that their impact should be considered before any intervention or remediation is attempted. Some parents, for a variety of reasons, might not share a school's ethical or moral standpoint. In these circumstances, the conflicting messages that children are likely to hear must be taken into account.

Assessing the constraints and opportunities afforded by the context in which the teaching and learning take place may allow a better focus on what is most or least amenable to change.

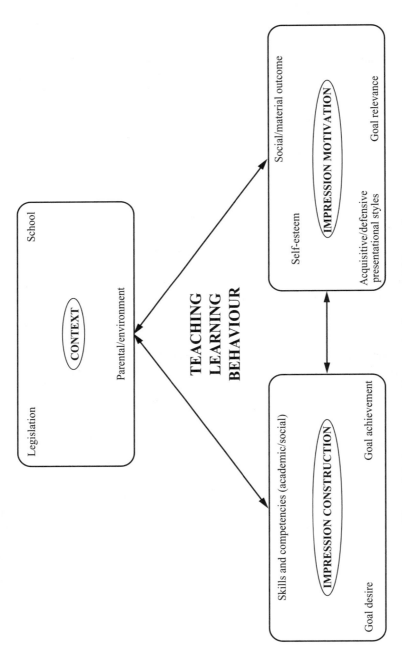

Figure 2.1. Assessment and intervention for successful impression management.

IMPRESSION MOTIVATION

Inevitably, the context in which teaching and learning are taking place will have an impact upon the outcome. Equally important is the need for teachers to identify the impression motivations of each youngster. Helpful in gaining insight into this area may be questions asked about pupils' self-esteem and about the goals and aspirations of all youngsters. Additional motivational considerations may be their acquisitive or defensive presentational styles, all of which may help inform decisions about how next to proceed. Knowing whether a young person is primarily motivated to achieve success or to avoid failure may require subtle changes by the teacher to the task requirements, which then enable the individual pupil to present their preferred image. In any case, the careful observation and assessment of each child's style should become an integral part of any teacher's assessment repertoire.

Although it is arguable that this is an onerous responsibility, this is not a plausible reason for not attempting it. Schools now have access to learning mentors and teaching assistants, part of whose role might be to engage children in identifying threats and opportunities that might affect their self-image and, as a consequence, their engagement with learning opportunities.

IMPRESSION CONSTRUCTION

Having identified the motivations behind the impression that youngsters wish to create, teachers may attend to the constraints placed upon successful impression construction. These limitations will include the skills and competencies (or lack of them) of the youngster which are likely to hinder or assist in successfully constructing that impression. Possible constraints will also include the likelihood, or not, that a pupil can achieve the desired goal, and whether the desire to achieve the goal is strong enough to sustain the impression which it is hoped to achieve. Again, it is incumbent on the teacher to identify strengths and limitations in both the child and the environment so as to design appropriate interventions to allow pupils to construct a favourable impression.

INTERACTION BETWEEN VARIABLES

The variables so far discussed do not stand in isolation and are constantly being affected and effected by the interaction between context, motivation and the construction of the impression in behavioural terms. As stated, the role of the teacher is crucial and requires insight and skills, perhaps beyond what can be reasonably expected of any one individual within a classroom. It is therefore incumbent upon all for whom the education of our youngsters is important to play a part. Teachers, parents, mentors, teaching assistants and others who have a responsibility for education all need to work cooperatively to enable youngsters to find constructive ways of demonstrating competence and skills (that they are 'cool'), not only to each other but also to themselves. In this way, youngsters may be able to give the right impression.

CONCLUSION

This chapter has been concerned with the implications of the theory of impression management within an educational context. It has also looked briefly at wider societal implications in the context of offending behaviour and school exclusion. Particularly, it has looked at possible assessment and intervention strategies for teachers to help youngsters to successfully manage the impressions they are motivated to create, and so to prevent dysfunctional self-handicapping behaviours. This may be problematic when pupils profess to have aspirations that conflict with the teachers' expectations of what is desirable or possible. Teaching youngsters to negotiate successfully may be a useful by-product of this system. However, it may be more likely that oppositional or defiant behaviour, so often the result of compounding failure experiences, is likely to be minimized by early intervention to actively seek pro-social ways in which pupils can successfully manage the impression they wish to give (Winkley, 1996).

The link between what we ask children to do and how we enable them to respond has been investigated. Particularly, we have examined the link between enabling children to manage successfully the impressions they give, particularly to peers, and their corresponding feelings of competence and worth.

All too painfully we have listened to the children's's stories when they have been made to feel failures: 'stupid', 'shown up', 'not as clever', 'idiots', 'ridiculed', 'sad' and 'shamed'. These are not descriptions that the children gave of some extreme life event. Rather, these were descriptions of how life is in ordinary classrooms for many children. We also heard of their overwhelming desire to 'look cool in front of their mates' and 'to be like their friends'. If, as a society, we wish educational opportunities to reach all children, we must ensure that structures are in place for all children to experience social acceptance and so free them from fear of failure.

Unless we are able to actively address these issues, more and more children will become 'hard to reach' with all the lost opportunity that this involves.

REFERENCES

Ames, C. (1992) Classrooms: goals, structures, and student motivation. *Journal of Educational Psychology* **84** (3), 261–271.

Archer, M (1998) Affirmative action. *Special Children* May (111), 27–29.

Avia, M.D., Sanchez-Bernardos, M.L., Sanz, J. *et al.* (1998) Self-presentation strategies and the 5 factor model. *Journal of Research in Personality* **32** (1), 108–114.

Berofsky, B. (1996) *Free Will and Determinism.* HarperRow, New York.

Bond, J. and Feeney, D. (1986) Has anybody here seen Kelly? The effect of positive teacher and clear expectations on pupil disaffection. *Pastoral Care* **4** (3), 187–193.

Burden, R.L. (1996) Pupils' perceptions of themselves as thinkers, learners and problem solvers. Some preliminary results from the myself-as-a-learner scale (MALS). *Educational & Child Psychology* **13** (3), 25–30.

Burns, R.D. (1979) *The Self-Concept: Theory, Measurement, Development and Behaviour.* Longman Press, London.

Carroll, A., Baglioni, A.J., Houghton, S. and Bramston, P. (1999) At-risk and not at-risk primary school children: an examination of goal orientations and social reputations. *British Journal of Educational Psychology* **69** (3), 377–392.

Connell, J.P. and Wellborn, J.G. (1991) Competence, autonomy and relatedness: a motivational analysis of self-system processes. In: M. Gunnar and L.A. Sroufe (eds). *Minnesota Symposium of Child Psychology*. University of Minnesota Press, Minneapolis.

Coopersmith, S. (1967) *The Antecedents of Self-esteem*. Freeman, San Francisco.

Deci, E.L. and Ryan, R.M. (1985) *Intrinsic Motivation and Self-determination in Human Behaviour*. Plenum, New York.

Department for Education and Employment (1997a) *Excellence for All Children: Meeting Special Educational Needs*. The Stationery Office, London.

Department for Education and Employment (1997b) *Education Act*. DfEE Publications, Nottingham.

Department for Education and Skills (2003) *Every Child Matters*. The Stationery Office, London.

Department for Education and Skills (2005a) *Children's Workforce Strategy*. DfES Publications, London.

Department for Education and Skills (2005b) *Higher Standards, Better Schools for All: More Choice for Parents and Pupils*. DfES Publications, London.

Department for Education and Skills (2005c) *Social and Emotional Aspects of Learning: Improving Behaviour . . . Improving Learning*. DfES, London.

Department for Education and Skills (2006) *Permanent and Fixed Term Exclusions from Schools and Exclusion Appeals in England 2004/5*. DfES Publications, London.

Dweck, C.S. (1986) Motivational processes affecting learning. *American Psychologist* **41** (10), 1040–1048.

Dweck, C.S. and Bempechat, J. (1983) Children's theories of intelligence: Consequences for learning. In: G. Paris, G.M. Olson and H.W. Stevenson (eds). *Learning and Motivation in the Classroom*. Erlbaum, Hillsdale, NJ.

Dweck, C.S. and Leggett, E.L. (1988) A social-cognitive approach to motivation and personality. *Psychological Review* **95** (2), 256–273.

Elliott, E. and Dweck, C. (1988) Goals: An approach to motivation and achievement. *Journal of Personality and Social Psychology* **54** (1), 5–12.

Goffman, E. (1959) *The Presentation of Self in Everyday Life*. Doubleday Anchor, New York.

HMSO (2004) *The Children Act 2004*. HMSO, London.

Hogan, R. (1982) A socioanalytic theory of personality. In: M. Page (ed.). *Nebraska Symposium on Motivation*. University of Nebraska Press, Lincoln.

Houghton, S. and Carroll, A. (1996) Enhancing reputations. *Scientia Pedagogica Experimentalis* **33** (2), 227–244.

James, S.C. (1997) The Relationship between Self-handicapping and Behavioural Difficulties in the Primary School Child. Unpublished doctoral research, Sheffield University.

James, S.C. (1998a) Developing the Theory of Methods of Intervention to Reduce Self-Handicapping Behaviour. Unpublished doctoral research, Sheffield University.

James, S.C. (1998b) Assessments of Pupils' Perceptions. Unpublished research.

James, S.C. (1999) Teachers' Assessment of Pupils' Perceptions of Academic and Social Competence and Locus of Control. Unpublished research.

Jones, N. (1989) Educational psychology, primary schools and pupil alienation. In: J. Docking (ed.). *Education and Alienation in the Junior School*. Falmer Press, London.

Mosley, J. (2001) *The Circle Book*. Positive, Trowbridge.

Newton, C., Taylor, G. and Wilson, D. (1996) Circle of friends. *Educational Psychology in Practice* **11** (4), 41–48.

Nicholls, J.G. (1984) Achievement motivation: conceptualisation of ability, subjective experience, task choice and performance. *Psychological Review* **91** (3), 328–346.

Nurmi, J.E. (1991) How do adolescents see their future? *Developmental Review* **11** (1), 1–59.

Schlenker, B.R. (1980) *Impression Management: the Self-concept, Social Identity and Interpersonal Relations*. California Brooks/Cole, Monterey, CA.

Snyder, C.R., Higgins, R.L. and Stucky, R.J. (1983) *Excuses: Masquerades in Search of Grace*. John Wiley & Sons, Chichester.

Snyder, C.R. and Smith, T.W. (1982) Symptoms as self-handicapping strategies: the virtues of old wine in new bottles. In: I.G. Weary and M.L. Mirels (eds). *Integrations of Clinical and Social Psychology*. Oxford University Press, New York.

Snyder, M. (1974) The self-monitoring of expressive behaviour. *Journal of Personality and Social Psychology* **30** (1), 526–537.

Social Exclusion Unit (2001) *The Truancy and School Exclusion Report*. Cabinet Office, London.

Stipek, D. and Gralinski, J.H. (1996) Children's beliefs about intelligence and school performance. *Journal of Educational Psychology* **88** (3), 397–407.

Weiner, B. (1985) An attributional theory of achievement motivation and emotion. *Psychological Review* **92** (4), 548–573.

Winkley, L. (1996) *Emotional Problems in Children and Young People*. Cassell, London.

3 Containing the Emotional Needs of Adolescent Boys 'at Risk of Exclusion' in Mainstream Schools

KATHRYN ANNE POMERANTZ

INTRODUCTION

Raggy, a 13-year-old boy, sits in the group on a cold Friday morning in November, his shoulders hunched over, his contribution to the conversation on 'experiences of being fixed-term excluded from school' limited. The researcher can only imagine the reality of Raggy's lived experience in the last 24 hours: being in the school isolation room for failing to comply with teachers' requests, feeling frustrated and angry, returning home to his mother, with whom he has a raging argument with expletives bandied on both sides, grabbing his daily nourishment of half a packet of custard creams before heading out to play football for at least four hours with his brother Dodge and returning home to a broken night of sleep with his sister's baby two feet away from his head on the other side of the bedroom wall.

Waking up today on that cold Friday morning feeling like the frost is biting into his toes (no heating again and his winter coat is too small and beyond repair), Raggy reluctantly drags himself to school. Friday is often a day of excuses to attend, avoidance of work or protesting so vehemently that he will be internally excluded or sent home from school. However, this is a project Friday and Raggy, despite his hunched, quiet presence in the group, is present and contributing in a small way, a wry smile on his face as he comments, 'I could stay in the project all day.'

Raggy is one of eight boys in one of two secondary schools invited by the author to take part in a year-long inclusion project. The descriptions given are far from fiction. He is the youngest of 13 children living with a mother who has found services 'hard to reach' over many years – a mother suffering from depression, who would describe herself as a victim, blinded in one eye as a result of a bullying incident she experienced as a young child, raped as a teenager and now desperately trying to recover contact with her son who was given up for adoption 30 years ago. Raggy's problems at school are low on her list of priorities and are exacerbated by her belief that he should support and stand up for himself.

How to Reach 'Hard to Reach' Children: Improving access, participation and outcomes. Edited by K. Pomerantz, M. Hughes and D. Thompson. Copyright © 2007 by John Wiley & Sons, Ltd.

There are many Raggies ie in our secondary schools, adolescent boys who become 'hard to reach', eventually disengaging themselves completely from the school system and becoming permanently excluded. The purpose of this chapter is to highlight the domestic lives, daily school experiences and anxieties disclosed by Raggy and seven other boys who worked with the author (hereby referred to as the researcher) on an inclusion project in order to shed light on what parents and professionals can do to address the emotional needs of these young people to sustain their 'in school careers' (Turner and Waterhouse, 2003).

The inclusion project involved two closely located secondary schools in a large rural authority, where a group of boys identified as being 'at risk of exclusion' by senior school staff in each school had access to a group intervention with the researcher over a period of 12 months. Boys in secondary education were identified as participants in the project as they were continually over-represented in local and national exclusion figures.

The project aims were as follows:

- to increase the resilience, confidence and self-esteem of the identified group of boys leading to a reduction in behavioural concerns;
- to develop a set of key questions that can be addressed by teachers and other professionals and applied in a systemic and preventative way to reduce the need to exclude pupils.

The group sessions were relaxed and informal and took place in small rooms away from teaching areas. A hot drink and snack were provided by the researcher on arrival and each one-hour session involved focus group discussion and activities around themes: first impressions of each other, first impressions of school, experiences of fixed-term school exclusion, general behaviour in school, living in a family, being healthy, staying safe, enjoying and achieving, making a positive contribution and economic well-being. The last five themes in the list above relate to the 'five outcomes' framework taken from *Every Child Matters* (Department for Education and Skills, 2003), and information from all the themes discussed was used by the researcher to construct the set of key questions established as one of the aims of the project. To meet the other aim of the project, it was intended that the boys' experience of participating in the group intervention would improve their confidence and self-esteem and should demonstrate improved behaviour over the course of the project. In this sense, the aims of the project as a form of research were to achieve both informative effects for the researcher and therapeutic effects for the participants.

Information was also derived from interviews that took place with the boys' parents and other relatives at the beginning and end of the project and through meetings with teachers and other professionals working with these pupils. However, the identified key questions were mainly constructed as a result of the first-hand experiences and stories that came from the themed focus group discussions involving the researcher and the pupils. The key questions are included at the end of each section in this chapter relating to the 'five outcomes' and are intended for those working in Children's Services to reflect on and develop their working practice with 'hard to reach' adolescent boys and their families. It is hoped that improved access, participation and outcomes for adolescent boys at risk of exclusion will result from the wider dissemination of these findings.

SETTING THE CONTEXT FOR SCHOOL EXCLUSION

In order to generate a deeper understanding of what it is like to grow up male in twenty-first-century Britain, in a society where the helping professions fail to reach out to some young people and their families to the point where many adolescent boys become excluded from school, it is useful to consider the wider political context. The media perpetuates the view that indiscipline is a rising tide in our schools and in our communities in such a way that young people have become criminalized. The political solution to this appears to reside in increasing measures to deal with deviance, as seen in the following statement made by Ruth Kelly, former Education Secretary:

> It is a zero-tolerance policy because any incident and any level of bad behaviour is dealt with promptly and appropriately and parents and pupils appreciate that the word of the head is law . . . There needs to be: support for teachers in the classroom; quality on-site provision within schools for those who can't be in class – such as learning support units; schools able to exclude where they need to; quality off-site provision for those who should not be in school – such as pupil referral units or other alternative provision; and sensible local arrangements to get excluded pupils back in class when they are ready to return and schools are ready to take them . . . The aim for excluded pupils is that they can eventually return to the classroom, their behavioural problems having been addressed.

> (Kelly, 2005)

The over-riding discourse in the above quote reinforces notions of control and exclusion and the simplistic idea that once behaviour is 'sorted out' children can eventually return to mainstream classes. Such political discourses are singularly absent in recognizing that it is often the school systems 'at local level' and those that work within them that perpetuate the need to exclude some young people while failing to recognize or address the *emotional* needs that have led to the behavioural difficulties in the first place.

All schools have discipline policies and well-developed practices and procedures for excluding pupils for disruptive or deviant behaviour. Mostly, these involve what the researcher would call 'physical means of containment': concrete, overt procedures such as report cards, behavioural targets, removal from lessons, restrictions on where pupils can be and when, before being picked up on the 'radar of exclusion' (C. Curtis, educational psychologist, personal communication, 31.08.06), a discipline procedure as inevitable and consequential as being targeted by a nuclear missile. However, an equivalent set of procedures for driving the inclusion of pupils with social, emotional and behavioural needs is less explicit either nationally or at local school level in many schools, although the principles of inclusion may be implicit.

THE SIGNIFICANCE OF EMOTIONAL NEEDS

A key theme to emerge during the life of the project was that of the variability, vulnerability and emotional fragility of the young people involved. Some pupils made great strides early in the project but then began to show an increase in behavioural concerns as the project came to a close. Others became permanently excluded along the way. One pupil came to the end of the road in one school and experienced a managed transfer to the other school involved in the project, and just one pupil out of eight made steady, consistent progress throughout the project. Although one of the two schools involved retained all but one of their project pupils, most of the young people continued to present as emotionally needy as the project came to a close.

What does this tell us? The groups of boys in both schools had caring and committed key senior teachers, similar systems in place for managing behaviour, experienced behaviour support teachers working directly with them and the same group intervention and home visiting by the researcher. In order to understand this phenomenon we should consider some of the literature and research findings relating to behavioural concerns that draw attention to terms such as 'attachment' and 'containment'. There exists considerable evidence to suggest that early infant attachment experience (that is to say the quality of the infant's attachment to their main carer) considerably influences the child's later behaviour and performance in school (Geddes, 2006). The quality of the relationship between teacher and pupil and especially the communications that exist between them is also found to play an important part in behavioural outcomes.

Geddes (2006) explains that on entry to school most children, those with secure attachments, are able to explore and learn with relative confidence when support is consistently and reliably available both from the professionals around them and from parents or carers at times when children encounter distress or uncertainty. Secondary school teachers and parents of adolescents could learn much here from colleagues in early years and primary education. Hargreaves (2000), for example, found that the relationship between teachers and very young children is often characterized by an emotional intensity where teachers talk about loving their pupils and feel rewarded when children show affection towards them. In contrast secondary school environments are characterized by strings of disconnected interactions and differences that give rise to emotional misunderstandings. Secondary school environments can, therefore, become 'affective deserts' (Edwards, 1976).

Coupled with this, Luxmoore (2000), from his extensive experience of youth work, found that young people, especially boys, tend to joke around as a means of articulating feelings of anger and loss and this is seen in particular when boys transfer from primary to secondary school. At this point of transition boys desire to be both big and little, attached and separate at the same time. They can feel a strong sense of loss in leaving behind their primary school teachers who are mostly able to *contain* the strong emotions, fears and anxieties they experience in growing up, even when attachments with parents are less secure. Paradoxically, it is, therefore, hard for professionals and parents to emotionally attach themselves to adolescent boys at a time when they are developmentally emotionally vulnerable and anxious. Adults may retreat from attempts to do so, thinking that by creating a distance between themselves and the young person they are respecting the young person's right to take responsibility in creating their own 'grown up' identity. The reality for so many young men of secondary age is that they consequently underachieve, become disaffected and eventually experience both social and school exclusion (Geddes, 2006).

The term 'container' arises from psychoanalytic theory and from the work of Bion (1962). During infancy, the parent or carer functions to process the infant's raw emotions, returning them to the infant in a digested form and in doing so he or she performs a containing function for the infant. The carer's response to the infant enables them to feel understood and helped. Applied to schools, 'containment' refers to the institution's capacity to be able to keep within itself parts that arouse anxiety. As all agencies are now more than ever primed to work to improve the emotional well-being of children, institutions such as secondary schools can and should begin to see themselves as capable of performing an *emotionally containing function* for groups of adolescents.

If we attempt to link these ideas together, we can begin to see that as children with insecure attachments progress through the education system they continue to project these raw emotions such as fear, anger and hurt on to the adults they encounter, often pushing teachers into becoming increasingly punitive and negative (Shearman, 2003). However, where the family or school setting itself is emotionally secure, the adults within are better able to absorb these strong emotions without engaging in counter-transference (unconsciously projecting back feelings of anger and rejection to the child). One of the main findings of the inclusion project on which this chapter is based is the need for professionals to improve the emotional health and well-being of boys 'at risk of exclusion' who tend to express these raw emotions within the school context. The spoken experiences of the young people involved in the project will now be discussed in relation to the 'five outcomes', with particular emphasis on 'being *emotionally* healthy'.

BEING HEALTHY

In the outcomes framework (Department for Education and Skills, 2003) each of the 'five outcomes' is further subdivided and will be considered here in turn in relation to meanings and experiences attached to each aspect by the young people involved in the project, namely Raggy, Tazzer, Spud, Scotty, Spike, Buster, CJ and Jay.

BEING PHYSICALLY HEALTHY

Interestingly, amongst the eight boys involved, the need to be more physically healthy than they were already was not identified as a concern. The exception to this was Raggy, who was described by his mother as being reluctant to eat or drink from the time of his birth to the present day. Raggy's mother, on closer questioning, had to admit that her son's eating habits occurred in fits and starts, sometimes he would eat all day then would eat very little for days. Tazzer had a voracious appetite but was harder to pin down at meal times on account of his demanding social life. Consequently, he would often catch something to eat in the early hours of the morning. Attempts by school staff or parents to instil the virtues of healthy eating in these adolescents were largely lost on them, although these young people were well aware of which foods were healthy and those that were not. These boys were often hungry on entry to school and discussion of biscuits, crisps and a good English fry-up had great appeal. The researcher soon discovered that choices between grapes and biscuits as a snack for group sessions were never competitive and she played to their likes, always having a supply of favourite biscuits and hot chocolate available on arrival, which was eagerly welcomed on cold mornings.

HAVING A HEALTHY LIFESTYLE

As above, the young people did not express concern in this area but saw themselves as having physically healthy lifestyles. All the young people were very active in pursuing sports and showed great interest in being physically engaged. Jay was a very experienced football player who, the previous year, had played for several local teams. However, the consequences of taking medication for ADHD were adversely affecting Jay's ability to maintain his participation in sport:

> During the day I'm knackered because I have my tablets . . . I'd like to have more time doing football because I used to do training about four times a week. I ain't been feeling a bit like I used to be. Mum thinks the key to my problems is the medication. I know I don't need it.
>
> (Jay)

During the project, Spike set up a football league and was keen to learn elaborate ball tricks he could put to use in indoor football. Jujitsu and kick boxing were also favoured pursuits. CJ was also interested in kick boxing and weightlifting. Scotty had just started boxing and was also involved in playing basketball, also a favoured sport of Buster. Tazzer liked cross-country running and on occasions when he visited his father would jog from his mother's house to his father's on account of his mother being at work and his father not having a car.

These young people could be said to be fitter and more actively engaged in sport than many boys their age who live in warm homes containing many material comforts and with parents who drive them to school or to social engagements. However, *perseverance* on activities to enable these pupils to achieve and feel good about themselves was another matter. During the life of the project, all pupils were encouraged to identify a goal to work towards in any area of their choice. Nearly all the young people chose a goal related to their interest in sport. The term 'resilience' is gaining currency in education, meaning that if young people are resilient they will be better able to recover quickly from setbacks in their lives. Resilience can be engendered in many different ways: by having a secure base, good educational attainments, social competencies, positive values, friendships, and talents and interests (Daniel and Wassell, 2002). Attempts were made to exploit the talents and interests of the young people during the project as a way of improving their resilience. However, there were a number of setbacks to this. As these activities occurred mainly outside of the school day, they were dependent on the encouragement of families and people in the local community.

As it transpired, Jay became detached from his previously high achievements in football as a result of the effects of his medication (the taking of which was demanded by his mother in collusion with school staff). Scotty, who lived in an outlying village with limited access to public transport, lost his means of attending boxing lessons. Spike and CJ were prevented from continuing to engage in their interests by parents who had grounded them for misbehaviour. Tazzer's arrangements for visiting his father had become sporadic, and Raggy experienced a long fixed-term exclusion from school, during which time he became depressed and reluctant to get up to face the day ahead. Buster's progress was difficult to ascertain as he drifted further into a pattern of truancy and non-attendance. Spud, on the other hand, began attending Air Cadets, through which he became highly motivated to attend well and engage in all activities in order to go flying.

It seems, therefore, that most of these young people did not lack the talents or initial desire to engage in an active, healthy lifestyle but that they were unable to persist due to a lack of opportunity, motivation and the interference of adults, and as such the development of resilience skills was not realized:

> I've got six footballs but not many people to play with round here ... Well, yeah, but I never play out.

> (Spike)

> He's always in trouble you see ... I prefer him to stay in. He started Cadets but something builds up and he lets himself down. He'd started kick boxing then he was in trouble at school. You give him something and he seems to chuck it back at you.

> (Spike's stepmother)

Being proficient at sport appears to reinforce a strong macho image amongst these young people, who often compared themselves to, or offered comments about, fathers, male relatives or their fathers' mates (e.g. by describing them boxing or going to the gym). Such comments appear to be a recurring theme amongst the conversations of adolescent boys, who are searching for what they appear to desperately seek, a respectable masculine identity. This theme of engaging in healthy sports was also mirrored in the boys' aspirations to gain eventual employment in physically demanding jobs (such as construction work, car mechanics and engineering).

BEING MENTALLY AND EMOTIONALLY HEALTHY

By far the most significant area of *being healthy* relates to the emotional health of these young people. The young people were unanimous in describing areas of stress in their lives through which they expressed frequent angry episodes. At home, siblings were significant in the list of irritants, especially younger sisters who appeared to be favoured by parents far more consistently than their brothers. Annoying experiences included siblings being able to stay off school at the slightest sign of illness, siblings taking their brother's belongings and siblings taking over personal space in the house, such as bedrooms.

A high level of stress was described by the young people in relation to their school experience. Conversations with the young people produced a long list of stresses: classroom activities that involve writing, especially where the task has to be repeated or where the purpose of the task is not made clear; getting blamed straight away for the misdemeanours of others; feeling that they were not always treated fairly as individuals or as a group; being in large class groups; having arguments with teachers whom they perceived to be sarcastic; being subject to systems of internal exclusion; confusion about who they are and how adults perceive them; and having difficulty keeping swearing in check when in conflict with teachers as swearing is commonly used during interactions with parents:

Jay	Yesterday Mr Lord asked me where I was because I was 20 minutes late, and I goes 'I went to the medical room', and he pulled a face at me taking the mick out of me being sarcastic . . . I do what I'm told sometimes, but if a teacher gets on my nerves, because this happened this week as well, the teacher says, 'Why did you hurt Andrew?' when I never. It was Jack Smith.
Researcher	Mmm?
Jay	I got done for it and then he told me to take my jumper off and I goes not until you say sorry and then he just had a right go at me.

The young people found it difficult to relax in school, especially when they felt under constant suspicion or felt they were being discriminated against, as indicated above. At this crucial time of identity development for young people they were often troubled and confused by labels and others' perceptions of them:

CJ	You're not worse than me, 'cos I've never seen you kicked out like. I know you've got anger problems like me and you've got ADD or whatever it is.
Jay	ADHD.
CJ	ADHD or whatever that is. I've got ADHD.
Researcher	Attention Deficit Disorder.
Buster	I've got some of that!
Researcher	You all think you've got a bit of that?
Jay	I have.
Researcher	You definitely have?
CJ	I checked average for it.
Jay	I've got Asperger's syndrome.
Buster	What's that?

Jay   A bit confusing life. I don't know how it is, but it confuses you. I don't
know how it is. Somebody says something to you. Either you don't
listen or you take it another way or it's confusing. Somebody tells you
to stab somebody. You either won't listen or you take it the wrong way.
I don't know what it's like.

It is clearly difficult for these young people to establish themselves as anything
other than labelled or deviant although at the same time trying to defend themselves
as having a favourable reputation and a positive identity:

> Tazzer, I know he can be naughty at school but he'd never take anything that wasn't his. I
> know he wouldn't. I think because Tazzer has been in trouble often, it does happen once
> you are in trouble, something happens and I suppose some people say, 'Oh it must be
> them.'

(Tazzer's mother)

> The first time wasn't my fault though, because when me, Tom and Ricky were down
> on the field over there, Tom called Jo 'gay' and I got the blame for that homophobic
> behaviour and that was Tom who said it. When Tom grassed me up I wasn't allowed to
> say my side of the story. They just called my Mum and I was suspended.

(Spud)

Being in internal exclusion represents a form of punishment – a type of *physical
containment* – and it evoked strong feelings of discomfort and anger amongst the
boys both at home and at school. Internal exclusion can involve being in the school
isolation room for behavioural incidents or being grounded at home. One pupil
described being locked in his bedroom by his stepfather. Another described being in
the school isolation room and prevented from being allowed to use the toilet:

Researcher What is it about being in isolation that really winds you up?
Raggy   It's just the feel of it – you know? – just horrible.
Researcher The feel of it?
Spud   Small room.
Tazzer   Just like being in prison but not quite as horrible.

Typical responses to forms of isolation included refusal to go in isolation, jumping
out of the window and absconding. Consequently, avoidance is one strategy used
by young people when they are emotionally stressed. The young people valued
opportunities to develop anger management strategies, especially those that allowed
them the time and space to calm down before having to have a conversation with
an adult about the situation. The build-up of anger is so intense that if they are not
able to act to avoid the situation emotions are likely to spill out in aggressive and
destructive acts:

> When she tells me off, I just sort of end up punching the wall or hitting mirrors, and
> sometimes, most times, I just go out.

(Tazzer)

Repeatedly mentioned by the young people was the need to learn ways of managing their anger, and this type of intervention was highly valued by the young people when it occurred through work with behaviour support teachers or psychiatrists. When Jay's psychiatrist changed and he encountered a professional who just prescribed him medication (as opposed to his previous psychiatrist, who 'did anger management' with him), his ability to trust adults and cope with his emotional stress plummeted. Support from other young people (often girls) in helping these boys to manage their anger was also highly valued, especially as this was reinforced by some peers out of school as well.

While the range of stresses outlined may seem surmountable to most, for young people at risk of exclusion they were often enough to trigger a violent or non-cooperative response, especially in the school context. In marked contrast, these young people took a fairly positive view of living within their families (despite encountering conflicts with siblings and some parents who were overly negative of them) and perceived emotional stresses as being mostly related to their experiences of school. This is an interesting point, which merits further exploration. The researcher, in talking recently to a fellow professional who herself had been 'hard to reach' as a child due to living in a family where she experienced poverty and neglect, was struck by this colleague's insistence on defending her family. Some young people, it seems, may not recognize they are 'hard to reach', may consider that their own family experiences are typical of others and are unlikely to attribute blame to their parents. Unlike the stereotypical view often held by professionals of children living in abusive and oppressive homes as vulnerable and at risk, the young people in this project did not perceive themselves as such. Out of school there appeared to be fewer demands and far more opportunities to engage in calming activities, such as time alone, being with small groups of friends, watching favourite TV programmes or going fishing. Such opportunities were, however, restricted for Spike, CJ and Jay, who had very controlling parents.

Most of the young people tended to avoid having conversations with their parents, and where interactions occurred with adults in school these were often strained. Paradoxically, while using the strategy of avoiding conversations with adults wherever possible, by the end of the project some pupils had begun to re-engage in talking to their mothers and were also expressing the need to have closer relationships with key adults in school:

I have been able to talk a bit more. I feel closer to my Mum.

(Scotty)

The project made a difference. He calmed down after your meetings. He did talk about it and the other children in it, which is very unusual for Raggy.

(Raggy's mother)

It appeared that the desire to feel close to someone became stronger as the project progressed. During an activity involving pictures of people in group settings, all the young people chose pictures of themselves in close proximity to others and in some cases being hugged. However, during discussion about family life, few of these young men could recall being able to talk about how they felt or being hugged at home and saw this as fairly typical.

For professionals in schools or those supporting families of 'hard to reach' boys:

'BEING HEALTHY' KEY QUESTIONS

- Do secondary schools have breakfast clubs or have hot and cold food available to purchase during the morning break in addition to lunchtimes?
- Could staff in secondary schools who select vulnerable young people for individual or small group sessions provide a hot drink or snack for pupils?
- To what extent do parents or professionals avoid prohibiting young people at risk of exclusion from engaging in activities for which they express interest or talent?
- How can parents and professionals seek new opportunities for these young people to access physically demanding and fast-paced activities where they can be encouraged to persevere, achieve and develop their resilience?
- Can professionals provide adolescent boys at risk of exclusion *early* broad discussions about careers where a vast array of possible vocations are considered?
- Parents and professionals should consider reflecting on methods of physical containment (or confinement) that they may use. Whose interests do these systems really serve?
- What steps are taken in schools to audit fairness in the organization, for example how are the views of the most vulnerable pupils heard and are there opportunities for young people to put their side of the story when incidents occur?
- Do parents and professionals invest time attaching labels to young people (or reinforcing labels given by others) or do they actively help young people at risk of exclusion identify their strengths and skills in order to explore and promote a positive identity?
- What restorative practices exist in schools, for example 'relationships policies' or 'relationships for learning policies' and where is the practice of enabling young people to have problem free, non-judgemental conversations?
- Do professionals spend time with young people to map out their emotional support networks by identifying key adults and peers who are in a trusted position to help?
- Do parents and professionals have facilities available to enable young people to relax (e.g. their own bedroom, a safe haven in school, calming activities)?
- Do schools have available anger management workshops for young people on a self-referral basis?
- Do teachers allow students to legitimately employ avoidance strategies (such as 'time out') before the need to process incidents?

- Can professionals support parents in recognizing that their adolescent sons desire and need closeness in their relationships with family members and find ways to achieve this?

STAYING SAFE

The general view was that these adolescent boys are very aware of what it means to stay safe but did not perceive safety as a main concern in relation to their own social practices and experiences. However, they were concerned about aspects of discrimination and loss. Similar concerns are voiced in Chapter 5 in relation to the needs of migrant children.

SAFE FROM ACCIDENTAL INJURY AND DEATH

Experiences of family bereavement were mentioned spontaneously by Tazzer, who disclosed that there had been three people who had died in his family: his baby sister about four months previously, his grandfather about three years ago and his uncle, who had been murdered in the local town centre. He explained that while he did not feel too troubled personally about these events other family members had been more affected. In the last few days of the project, the researcher had attempted to meet with Jay and his mother for a closure interview. This did not take place as the family had just experienced bereavement. This aspect of 'staying safe', as stated by the DfES (2003), highlights the need to avoid injury and death but fails to highlight the impact of loss as experienced not just through bereavement but through divorce and separation, *a very significant feature* of the lives of all the boys involved in the project. Loss seems to be of considerable importance in predisposing adolescent boys to anger and violence leading to school exclusion as seen by the inclusion project and other studies (Pomerantz and Graham, 2005; Geddes, 2006).

SAFE FROM BULLYING AND DISCRIMINATION

The young people described the confusion they felt by being wanted and cared for some of the time and then feeling rejected. They generally felt unjustly discriminated against by parents, step-parents and teachers, especially as they perceived their siblings and peers as being equally challenging at times. During a picture activity where they had to choose from pictures depicting people in groups, some being included and others rejected (Sunderland, 2000), it became clear that these boys vacillated between positioning themselves as being included and being discriminated against:

> The one on the third row across, people telling him, like, 'Get out, go away, we don't want you', or summat like that. Like you've been in trouble, the head teacher, like, when I've been in trouble, he's said, 'Go, you're not part of this school anymore', like that.

(CJ)

I can do really good and then they'll say, 'Why are you being like that?' and when I'm feeling bad and when I'm in trouble I feel left out and they all pick on me. Or I can be that one, I can be medium.

(Jay)

In respect to bullying, the young people felt that, despite the anti-bullying work that was being promoted in their schools, bullying was still a problem (although they did not perceive themselves as adopting the bully role). However, the bullying of teachers was another matter and one which they raised on several occasions, showing an awareness of this phenomenon and the need for it to be tackled. Tazzer declared feeling uncomfortable when the whole class appeared to be bullying the teacher. Tazzer's peers reminded him that he was often in on the act, but he retorted with examples of him making humorous remarks in class that were not intended to upset the teacher and were often said out of the teacher's earshot. The boys were quick to distinguish between 'razzing' (having a bit of a laugh at someone's expense) and cruelty.

SAFE FROM CRIME AND ANTI-SOCIAL BEHAVIOUR

The boys generally showed great awareness of 'life on the street'. This included knowledge of drugs, vandalism, fights, Anti-Social Behaviour Orders (ASBOs) and dealings with the local police leading to having a criminal record. Some had been in court and cautioned but appeared to keep themselves on the outer edges of criminal behaviour in the community while being witness to it. This did not deter most of the boys from being out late at night. They had established their own protective mechanisms: always being in a group, carrying a mobile phone and an emergency number, carrying a penknife and being wary of people who dress smart because 'they might do drugs'. The topic of crime and anti-social behaviour was of particular interest to these young people, who found frequent opportunities to share the latest stories – either fact (directly witnessed or appearing in the press) or fiction (such as those occurring in *Eastenders*).

HAVING SECURITY AND STABILITY AND BEING CARED FOR

None of the young people were in (or had been in) the care of the Local Authority, although CJ had been cared for by his grandparents for some months the previous year, Raggy had experienced a lot of domestic upheaval and transitions and Spike described contrasting experiences of being cared for lovingly by his mother (whom he saw for only two weeks each year) as opposed to the tensions of living with his father and stepmother. CJ's parents were outspoken about their desire to have him sent away to boarding school, 'a military school or a school for kids with ADHD with the proper input' (CJ's mother). With these particular boys, it emerged that their mothers or stepmothers were all experiencing major family stresses or mental health needs (such as depression) that were further isolating them from nurturing a close relationship with their sons or stepsons. So while concerns over stability and security were not made explicit by the pupils, they existed in the lives of the young people and emerged during home visits.

For professionals in schools or those supporting families of 'hard to reach' boys:

'STAYING SAFE' KEY QUESTIONS

- To what extent do schools and other services provide attractive visual displays to signpost young people to support services and voluntary agencies, for example in the area of domestic violence?
- How easy is it for young people at risk of exclusion to access counselling services where they may wish to talk in confidence?
- Do schools recognize the need and have materials available to address the topics of loss, change and bereavement both through the curriculum as a whole but also with individuals who may be suffering the impact of this, especially pupils who are at risk of exclusion?
- To what extent do anti-bullying schemes address the need to tackle the bullying of teachers?
- Are narratives of crime and anti-social behaviour relating to national, local or soap-opera stories made use of to stimulate healthy discussion amongst adolescents about ways of keeping themselves safe?
- To what extent do professionals take time to explore and support the well-being of parents to reduce the impact of negative relationships building up between parents and adolescents as a result of depression and stress within the home?

ENJOYING AND ACHIEVING

ATTEND AND ENJOY SCHOOL

Surprisingly many of the young people involved in the project were academically able and had experienced a range of achievements. Spike had acquired a governor's award, Tazzer had gained high grades leading to his initial placement in top sets (a status that was gradually eroded) and CJ was especially good at maths. Jay was recognized in the community as being a skilled football player. Some of the other boys had mild learning needs, such as Scotty, Jay and Raggy, who found aspects of literacy demanding. Those pupils who had no learning needs described a sadness and feeling of dissatisfaction with themselves despite their achievements. Where was the enjoyment of school, or a sense of pride in themselves?

It appears, then, that for these 'hard to reach' young people there is little correlation between achieving in school and enjoying the experience. This is most likely related to the boys' self-concept, their self-esteem, their lack of belief in themselves as worthy young people and above all their emerging 'deviant' identity. Where is the intrinsic value in enjoying school achievements when you are seen and see yourself as an irritation within the system? In contrast, discussions around enjoying and achieving released a wealth of talk around the extrinsic material pleasures of going on holidays and buying designer clothes, with the exception of Raggy, Jay and CJ, who lived in families experiencing significant financial constraints. This situation was exacerbated by Tazzer's and Spud's parents, who appeared to provide almost unlimited financial incentives. In school, these pupils had gone to enterprising lengths to fuel their material habits, such as buying sweets cheaply in town and then selling them on for a profit, an activity they clearly enjoyed. Also, when asked to provide an example of achievements, pupils were more likely to report on their progress with behaviour rather than learning, Spud in particular. Despite Spud making the most significant progress of all the pupils in the project, he still found it difficult to shake off his negative identity, that he perceived himself as being typecast in relation to certain peers:

Spud	It's the first year since I've been at school that I've not been on report.
Researcher	That's definitely something to be proud of, that fact.
Spud	I don't know why but the teachers have never liked me. They've always put me on report since Year 3, since I started school with you (looked in the direction of Tazzer).

For pupils like CJ, their notion of attending and enjoying in school was at the basic level of being fed and the merits of school dinners: chips especially (sorry, Jamie Oliver!) were very appealing. Buster also described truanting some mornings but timing his activities to arrive just before lunch and in time for the afternoon PE lesson.

ACHIEVE NATIONAL EDUCATIONAL STANDARDS AT SECONDARY SCHOOLS

About half of the pupils in the project were performing in line with national standards at the beginning of the project, but for some these achievements went into decline as their change of placement into lower sets as a result of misbehaviour began to have an effect on this. Time spent away from school during periods of exclusion further exacerbated the problem as work was not always set and the class and topic had moved on following the pupil's return with no hope of being able to catch up.

Of those pupils who experienced some anxieties over learning, they expressed a concern over missing work, mainly as a result of being excluded for fixed periods or being excluded from a specific lesson due to relationship problems with a certain subject teacher. This resulted in a drastic loss of confidence. Help with following instructions and spelling, reduced expectations of having to listen for long periods in class and working in smaller groups were all cited as interventions that these young people valued.

For professionals in schools or those supporting families of 'hard to reach' boys:

'ENJOYING AND ACHIEVING' KEY QUESTIONS

- Do parents and professionals recognize the links between self-esteem and enjoying and achieving and, if so, how can 'hard to reach' young people be encouraged to think positively about themselves as a necessary prerequisite to enhancing their school achievements and enjoying their experience of school?
- Can parents be helped to motivate their children by ensuring they earn pocket money and learn the responsible management of finances rather than an over-reliance on parents simply giving financial and material rewards?
- Do parents and professionals sufficiently acknowledge and praise improvements in behaviour, however small?
- Is realistic work always set for pupils who are excluded from lessons and opportunities provided for mentoring, coaching and catching up in areas of the curriculum missed?
- How best are pupils with challenging behaviour and additional learning needs supported in class, and have the views of pupils been taken into account in making such provision?

MAKING A POSITIVE CONTRIBUTION

ENGAGE IN DECISION-MAKING AND SUPPORT THE COMMUNITY AND ENVIRONMENT

In practice it seems that the most vulnerable, 'hard to reach' and marginalized young people remain largely silent within the institutional walls of schools and local authorities. Wise (1999) reports that the views of pupils with behavioural problems are often dismissed through suspicion and distrust. To elaborate, Street and Herts (2005) remind us that participation *should* involve young people proactively so that they have the power to shape events as they work alongside adults where their views are given equal weight. In reality, this participation rarely happens in a culture where such young people are seen as deviant and untrustworthy.

The young people in the project were unanimous in stating that being involved in the focus group discussions had helped them make positive changes in their behaviour and, in particular, they valued the opportunity to have someone with whom to talk. However, as seen in the research of Wise (1999), they gave frequent examples of being misjudged and being unable to tell their side of the story. Despite these feelings, most of the pupils gave spontaneous examples about ways they had helped others and ideas of ways in which their schools could be improved, suggesting that these 'hard to reach' young people have a strong desire to make a positive contribution. Examples given were: helping their classmates with reading and spelling, giving a friend a hug because he had just lost his younger brother in a car crash, giving ideas to others in the project group to help with their behaviour, making pupils clear up their lunch litter to help midday supervisors, installing CCTV to catch smokers and creating a football league for younger pupils.

ENGAGE IN LAW-ABIDING AND POSITIVE BEHAVIOUR IN AND OUT OF SCHOOL

The young people in the project can be said to be experts in the field of law-abiding behaviour. Talking with young people can reveal insights both to enhance their own understanding and the understanding of professionals when engaged in (no blame) discussion about such topics (Ravenette, 1999).

Although the young people were knowledgeable about receiving warnings or being charged for offences and being subject to Acceptable Behaviour Contracts (ABCs) and ASBOs, they were also curious to find out more about police enforcement of these methods. The general understanding amongst the young people is that ASBOs, for example, are yet another form of physical containment, involving restrictions on their movements and exclusion from activities in which they engage with their peers. In a way that mirrors the young people's concerns that adults in school are quick to make judgements of their behaviour and actions, the same applies to the way some adults interpret their behaviour and actions in the community. Tazzer was most indignant about his recent experience when the group were discussing ASBOs:

Tazzer	I was going to get one of those last week. I nearly got done by the police on Wednesday.
Spud	For what?
Tazzer	Intimidating an old lady.
Spud	(laughs)
Tazzer	It's not funny intimidating an older person. I was sitting outside the toilet and this old lady was in there but she didn't dare come out. She thought I was going to hit her.
Researcher	Was that because of anything you said to her when she went in there?
Tazzer	No. We were sitting outside and she thought we were going to hit her when she came out.
Spike	Have you got a hoodie, because that creates a lot of misunderstanding?
Researcher	So how you dress is going to affect how people might feel threatened?
Spike	Yeah because the police are saying 'Watch out for youths' now.

In exploring these themes the young people themselves are raising critical questions about how young people can be perceived, highlighting that in fact these perceptions may detract from closer surveillance of those who may be committing crimes. Spud himself and also Jay had both experienced being questioned by the police and in Jay's case appearing in court for crimes they did not commit. Again such examples provide further evidence of young people having entrenched negative identities that place them under constant suspicion. Resentment about young people being misunderstood was also strongly expressed by some parents. Spud's mother relayed the story of her son being arrested for allegedly hitting another pupil (resulting in his fixed-term exclusion from school). When Spud's views were eventually taken into account, it transpired he had been bullied by the pupil (repeatedly kicked and spat at) for over a year and eventually a witness had come forward to substantiate his story.

Dent (2006) reminds us that very young people are now becoming demonized and develop an early criminal identity, which positions them in society as deviant. The use of ABCs, ASBOs and electronic tagging provide further examples of physical forms of containment that are both aversive and counter-productive to solving the problems which they are intended to address (Bell, 2006).

In respect to perceived anti-social behaviour occurring in school, most of the pupils in the project at some point expressed the view that they had been misjudged or unable to give their side of the story:

> Teachers don't believe me since I started getting into trouble; so I'm not bothered about them any more.
>
> (Spud)

> Sometimes they just ring up or they call you and tell you to come to the office and they just exclude you, they don't even ask you.
>
> (Raggy)

Despite examples of being misunderstood and unfairly punished, there were clearly other times when the young people admitted engaging in behaviours that they saw as legitimately leading to school exclusions. However, there were some interesting observations on this point. First, the group were unanimous in stating that internal school exclusion was far more of an unpleasant punishment than a fixed-term exclusion from school. Paradoxically, for most of the pupils, the latter experience often made them feel better about themselves (feeling calmer, less stressed) and for some provided them with opportunities to be more trusted by adults and make a positive contribution! Both Raggy and Tazzer had been gainfully employed by relatives during their exclusions, for example by helping a family friend move house or by working with a relative doing up houses. Being set academic work by teachers during exclusion was a variable experience amongst the group. Experiences ranged from having no work set at all to having work set in every subject. Surprisingly, most pupils felt that having work to do from school during periods of exclusion was important in helping them keep up. Where work wasn't set, it may, therefore, have been perceived by some pupils that their teachers did not much care about their achievements.

All the pupils in the project experienced time away from school as a result of exclusion and two pupils found themselves in a difficult position in respect to their return. Raggy, for example, remained away from school for several weeks, beyond the period of his exclusion because he failed to sign a behaviour contract as part of the procedure required by the school for his return. Jay also experienced a long period away from school. On this occasion he had refused to take his medication and the school staff in consultation with his mother felt that his return to school should be dependent on him taking this in order to prevent further misbehaviours occurring. Jay, on the other hand, had felt that his behaviour had improved and wanted to prove that he could manage his difficulties without the need for tablets, a view endorsed by his father. Situations like these place young people in an impossible bind as the power of parents, professionals and institutions over-ride any attempt or right of a young person to feel they can influence important decisions that relate to themselves, make choices or develop confidence in themselves.

Finally, the experience of exclusion can for some mean that they are caught up in a procedure over which there is only one outcome. Spike, who had escaped permanent exclusion to experience a transfer to another school, was pessimistically fatalistic over his future:

Spike: I won't be able to get fixed-term excluded. I'll just get expelled straight out.
Researcher: Well, I'm not so sure about that.
Spike: I got expelled from . . . I came here; so I've only got one chance.
Researcher: Is that what you've been told?
Spike: I might not be here for the next project meeting anyway.
Researcher: You are a bit doom and gloom again today. Are you suggesting that you are going to get kicked out before our next meeting?
Spike: I think so because I've got to see the governors before the next meeting.
Researcher: And that was for talking in class?
Spike: Yeah.

DEVELOP SELF-CONFIDENCE AND DEAL WITH SIGNIFICANT LIFE CHANGES

For young people like those in the project, who are largely distrusted by adults and sometimes overly controlled, it is hard to see how they can develop self-confidence and deal with significant life changes when they are prohibited from making important life choices as seen in the discussion about choosing subject options for Key Stage 4 below:

Scotty: I sat down with Mum and . . . picked a couple and she said, 'I don't think you would enjoy that.'
Researcher: So you might have had a discussion with your mum about helping you make that choice but she allowed you to make the choice, did she?
Spike: I don't think I would be allowed to choose.
Researcher: Why is that then?
Spike: Because my Dad wants me to do certain things.
Researcher: Do you think it's fair of your dad to make those choices for you?
Spike: No, it's whatever I want to do, then they will say what I've got to do. They won't give me the piece of paper to let me choose.

DEVELOP ENTERPRISING BEHAVIOUR

This topic rarely emerged during the group discussions, perhaps as a result of the young people feeling they had few opportunities to be enterprising other than in areas that fitted their perceived identities (e.g. as previously mentioned, selling off goods in school for profit to unsuspecting pupils). One example came from Spike, who revealed that he was trying to set up a football league and spoke of other boys chipping in to buy the kit and how he was designing the logo. However, when asked if his father was helping him with the enterprise he replied by saying that he had not told his father anything about it.

For professionals in schools or those supporting families of 'hard to reach' boys:

'MAKING A POSITIVE CONTRIBUTION' KEY QUESTIONS

- What emancipatory practices and opportunities exist in schools, homes and community settings that enable the 'hardest to reach' young people to give their views and actively create change and so prove themselves as valued citizens, so that adults will think about them differently?
- Can professionals think of examples of where a pupil at risk of exclusion was actively encouraged to help another student and then praised for his or her efforts? Do professionals know whether such pupils feel they can make a positive contribution and in what ways?
- How can professionals take action to support those working in the youth justice system to influence the Government and public opinion as to the need to perceive young people differently?
- If young people at risk of exclusion have difficulty making relationships with adults, to what extent do adults recognize that *they* have difficulty making relationships with some young people and look for ways of interacting differently?
- How many schools have critically reflected on the effectiveness of their behaviour and inclusion policies to determine the extent to which the systems and procedures adopted actively reduce exclusion?
- How can professionals best support parents and pupils at risk of exclusion in considering important life choices in a way that reflects respect and trust in the views of the young person?
- How can young people at risk of exclusion be encouraged and supported by both parents and professionals to develop enterprising skills?

ACHIEVING ECONOMIC WELL-BEING

Many professionals considering how they might work with young adolescents might choose to overlook this aspect of the 'five outcomes', perceiving this area as the remit of those working at Key Stage 4 or the Connexions Service. However, the researcher was interested to explore with the young people a positive view of themselves, their skills, strengths and aspirations both at the beginning, during and in the final stages of the project. During the project, the young people were encouraged to self-reflect, to acknowledge a positive perception of themselves that came from the researcher, their peers and ultimately themselves so that they left the project with a vision of where they were going in life in respect to achieving economic well-being. The researcher would argue that work of this kind is a crucial intervention to undertake with 'hard to reach' young people and should take place at the earliest opportunity.

ENGAGE IN FURTHER EDUCATION, EMPLOYMENT OR TRAINING ON LEAVING SCHOOL

All the boys in the study, despite their general lack of interest in the school curriculum, low self-esteem, brushes with criminality and their feelings of being distrusted by many adults, could all identify jobs they would like to aspire to on leaving school, some of which would involve further education. These ranged from being a car mechanic to training to be a policeman. A hypothetical suitcase (inspired by the visual tools of Sunderland, 2000) was constructed by each pupil to take away with them into the future in which were stored their vocational goals and identified skills and strengths that would enable them to meet those goals.

ACCESS TO TRANSPORT, MATERIAL GOODS, DECENT HOMES AND SUSTAINABLE COMMUNITIES

At least three of the boys in the study experienced living in homes where there were financial difficulties. Voluntary services, such as Barnardo's and Community Voluntary Services, were working with these families to improve their economic well-being. For Raggy and CJ these difficulties affected their daily lives in relation to overcrowding, sleeping arrangements and access to basic needs (food and clothing), and these two boys were two of the three boys who became permanently excluded. This further highlights the impact of economic deprivation on successful outcomes for young people.

For professionals in schools or those supporting families of 'hard to reach' boys:

'ACHIEVING ECONOMIC WELL-BEING' KEY QUESTIONS

- To what extent do professionals work with young people at the earliest signs of them becoming 'hard to reach' to identify realistic vocational goals, to encourage a sense of purpose and direction and to highlight strengths and skills that will enable them to achieve these goals?
- How best can professionals work to ensure they signpost families to services who can support them in improving aspects of basic economic well-being?

CONCLUSION

This chapter has attempted to signal to those working in schools and to other professionals working to support 'hard to reach' adolescent boys and their families a range of ways that can improve access, participation and outcomes for these young people. The inclusion project has highlighted, within the 'five outcomes' framework, the significant need to focus on improving the *emotional* health and well-being of adolescent boys at risk of exclusion. However, there is a wider message here beyond the key questions provided that individual readers may consider. There is a need for adults to plan in a *strategic* way and take into consideration the voices of these young people in a way that influences the delivery of support services and the policy, planning and practice that take place within schools to improve inclusion.

In an interesting, parallel study to that described in this chapter, McBlain (2006) worked with groups of adolescents in three secondary schools and found significant differences in the schools' capacities to function as an 'effective container' in addressing the emotional needs of these pupils leading to outcomes that either prompted inclusion or exclusion. The same outcomes were found in the inclusion project that has informed this chapter, where one school was successful in continuing to include their project pupils and one was not. Research concludes that much depends on the head teacher and senior management team and the systems they establish.

Finally, to place responsibility on parents in addition to professionals I close this chapter with my personal reflections and a letter to my own son (affectionately known at home as 'Mr C'), who was a very 'difficult to bring up' child, presenting many behavioural challenges both at school and at home:

Dear Mr C

Now that you are approaching your sixteenth birthday I want you to know that my work with a group of boys in secondary schools has helped me reflect on the struggle I felt in bringing you up and my great pride in the young person you have now turned out to be.

When I was summoned to your infant school, junior school and secondary schools to discuss incidents of misbehaviour, I felt humiliated and ashamed and resorted to punishing you at home. When you were bullied on the school bus, I talked to you about sticking up for yourself and resented being late for work because I had to drive you to school. When you refused to go to school and had panic attacks, I became angry and stressed and considered giving up my hard-earned career to teach you at home.

But when, at aged 13, I gave up the fight, stopped trying to control you and let you make decisions for yourself, our relationship changed. My response to your emotional needs was to feel sorry for myself when all the time you needed greater emotional support, reassurance and acceptance than I seemed able to give. I also look back at the meetings I had with your clinical psychologist and my surprise (and now my delight) that he did not feel it appropriate to label you. I have learnt so much about myself from being with you. I just hope those parents, like me, who put their own emotional needs first can recognize that small changes in their relationships with their sons can lead to enormous rewards. If the parents and teachers of challenging adolescent boys can take the same steps as I did as a parent with you, then the world would be a far more peaceful place.

All my love

Mum

My own reflections have led me to believe that successful outcomes with challenging adolescent boys depend on the ability of adults to contain the young person's *emotional* needs by:

- being less punishing and more understanding;
- acknowledging that the adult's own emotional needs can influence their behaviour towards a young person;
- taking pride in a young person's emerging identity and avoiding labelling the young person;
- recognising that the young person's well-being can depend on changes the adult makes in relating to the young person;
- imposing less control and encouraging more autonomy.

REFERENCES

Bell, M. (2006) Are Asbos the only answer? *The Guardian*, 21 September 2006.

Bion, W. (1962) *Experiences in Groups and Other Papers*. Tavistock Publications, London.

Daniel, B. and Wassell, S. (2002) *Adolescence*. Jessica Kingsley, London.

Dent, J. (2006) Expert calls for complete overhaul of youth justice system. *The Guardian*, 22 September 2006.

Department for Education and Skills (2003) *Every Child Matters: Change for Children*. The Stationery Office, London.

Edwards, A.D. (1976) *Language in Culture and Class*. Heinemann, London.

Geddes, H. (2006) *Attachment in the Classroom: The Links Between Children's Early Experience, Emotional Well Being and Performance in School*. Worth Publishing, London.

Hargreaves, A. (2000) Mixed emotions: teachers' perceptions of their interactions with students. *Teaching and Teacher Education* **16** (8), 811–826.

Kelly, R. (2005) 'Behaviour is the toughest issue of all' speech by the education secretary, Ruth Kelly, to the secondary heads association in Blackpool. *The Guardian*, 1 February 2005.

Luxmoore, N. (2000) *Listening to Young People in School, Youth Work and Counselling*, Jessica Kingsley, London.

McBlain, A. (2006) The place of psychoanalytic theory in working with schools at a systems level to manage challenging behaviour: concepts and literature. Paper submitted as Part I of a doctorate in educational psychology, University of Sheffield.

Pomerantz, K.A. and Graham, V. (2005) *A Detailed Study of the Pupils with Statements of SEN, Permanently Excluded in the Last Academic Year*. Derbyshire County Council.

Ravenette, T. (1999) *Personal Construct Psychology*. Whurr Publishers, London.

Shearman, S. (2003) What is the reality of 'inclusion' for children with emotional and behavioural difficulties in the primary classroom? *Emotional and Behavioural Difficulties* **8** (1), 53–76.

Street, C. and Herts, B. (2005) *Putting Participation into Practice*. Young Minds, London.

Sunderland, M. (2000) *Draw on Your Emotions*. Speechmark, Bicester.

Turner, E. and Waterhouse, S. (2003) Towards inclusive schools: sustaining normal in-school careers. *Emotional and Behavioural Difficulties* **8** (1), 19–31.

Wise, S. (1999) *Listen to Me*. Lucky Duck, Bristol.

4 What Works in Reintegration Following Exclusion: Supporting the Parts Only Peers can Reach

JACKIE LOWN

INTRODUCTION

In August every year, we have come to expect media interest in GCSE and A-level results; this is becoming part of the British calendar, akin to the grouse-shooting season. Another area of annual media interest is also beginning to emerge with the same predictability: the published annual figures for permanent exclusion. For a few days each year, the topic elicits temporary interest from local and national press. Contrary to the flavour of these annual media headlines, however, the reality is that the incidence of permanent exclusion in England is mercifully low. Parsons and Howlett (2000) suggest less than 1% of the school population is permanently excluded at any one time. Of this excluded group, the authors indicate that one- to two-thirds is subsequently returned to a new mainstream school placement. We know very little indeed about the long-term outcomes for those 'hard to reach' excluded pupils returned to new mainstream schools; reintegration is a relatively new concept and the numbers involved are very small. It therefore becomes very important to learn from the experiences of those who have returned, in order to inform evolving understandings of successful reintegration, thereby shaping future developments in educational policy and practice in relation to these pupils, their families, support services, receiving schools and Local Authorities.

This chapter aims to:

- outline the patterns of exclusion in England over recent years;
- consider the rationale for returning permanently excluded pupils to new mainstream placements;
- give a brief overview of a recent, detailed study by this author, exploring participant perceptions of the experience of reintegration;

How to Reach 'Hard to Reach' Children: Improving access, participation and outcomes. Edited by K. Pomerantz, M. Hughes and D. Thompson. Copyright © 2007 by John Wiley & Sons, Ltd.

- identify and discuss the factors which emerged from the study as important in determining the sustained success of reintegrated placements following permanent exclusion;
- explore in some detail one particular factor found to be important in successful reintegration, namely peer support processes.

The *Special Educational Needs: Code of Practice* (Department for Education and Skills, 2001) highlights the importance of listening to pupils' views regarding their own learning needs. The view is reiterated in this chapter: it is essential to reveal pupils' views about returning to mainstream school in order to become informed about, learn from and act upon what we as educators are told by children and young people and what we go on to tell others.

THE POLITICAL CONTEXT

Referring to the Labour Government, which took office in 1997, Fisher (2001) writes:

> The present Government, so delightfully tempting to criticise for many of its education policies, has, during its period in office, poked a stick into a number of hornets' nests, including this one [exclusion], which have lain buzzing and undisturbed for long years, and it deserves credit for so doing.

(Fisher, 2001, p. 1)

The present Labour Government has made a serious issue of 'education, education, education' and has raised the profile of those children who have proved more vulnerable to failure in the past. Alongside this changing focus, there has come increased debate, guidance and legislation about inclusion for vulnerable pupils. This chapter will pay attention to a particular group of vulnerable pupils who can be 'hard to reach', namely those who have found themselves outside the mainstream education system as a result of adult decisions to intentionally exclude them from school. Hopefully, the Government incorporates this sub-group of youngsters in its exhortations to Local Authorities to work towards inclusion for all pupils.

There have probably been exclusions from school since schools first came into existence, though it wasn't until the 1944 Education Act that such action was formalized as a right for head teachers. It seems that the subject of exclusion from school raised little political interest for nearly 50 years after its introduction. It was in the early 1990s that political interest was stirred: probably driven by the advent of the first public national data. Drawing attention to the rates of exclusion in England, through the publication of data, created an accompanying climate of mild panic as exclusion rates were observed to be rising rapidly, along with growing concern about the social costs of such a trend.

Many authors have commented on the explosion in exclusion figures during the 1990s, although it has to be recognized that national exclusion figures were not kept prior to 1990, and rates were known to have been under-recorded by the National Exclusions Registration System in 1990/1 and 1991/2. Parsons (1999) traced the

Table 4.1. Excluded pupils in England 1990–2004

Year	Number permanently excluded
1990/1	2910
1991/2	3833
1992/3	8636
1993/4	11 181
1994/5	12 458
1995/6	12 476
1996/7	12 668
1997/8	12 300
1998/9	10 440
1999/2000	8320
2000/1	9140
2001/2	9540
2002/3	9290
2003/4	9880

Adapted from Parsons (1999) and Department for Education and Skills (2006) *National Statistics Bulletin*.

growing number of permanent exclusions in England between 1990 and 1998. These figures are noted in Table 4.1, with the years 1997–2004 added by reference to the *National Statistics Bulletin* (Department for Education and Skills, 2006). The figures show the numbers of pupils permanently excluded from maintained primary, secondary and special schools in England between 1990 and 2004:

According to the 2006 *National Statistics Bulletin*, in 2003/4:

• 84% of all permanent exclusions were secondary age pupils;
• By gender, 20 in every 10 000 boys and five in every 10 000 girls were excluded;
• 68% of all permanent exclusions were of pupils aged between 12 and 14 at the start of the school year;
• By ethnicity, rates ranged from two in every 10 000 Indian pupils being excluded to 41 in every 10 000 black Caribbean pupils. 80% of all permanent exclusions were white.

In addition to the increasing incidence of permanent exclusion, political interest in the subject of exclusion was raised during the 1990s because of growing public concern about the 'dangerousness' of children with emotional and behavioural difficulties spending time outside of the confines of the school system, with consequent concern about their alternative activities (Hayden and Dunne, 2001). During the late 1990s, there was growing evidence linking absence, exclusion from school, criminal activity and anti-social behaviour (Parsons, 1999; Audit Commission, 1996).

Jones (2003) charts the changes in the meaning of 'emotional and behavioural difficulties' over the last 50 years. She describes three distinct phases of development:

(i) Emotional and behavioural difficulties were defined as 'maladjustment' prior to the 1981 Education Act; in this medical model, responses would be construed as 'treatment' for the individual.

(ii) An educational interpretation followed, viewing emotional and behavioural difficulties as special educational needs. The logical response to difficulties defined in this way would therefore be framed in terms of special educational provision.

(iii) Next came an interpretation of emotional and behavioural difficulties as disaffection or disorderly behaviour. Within this construction, the goal becomes one of the 'inculcation of disaffected individuals into the social–moral order of the school' (Jones, 2003, p. 148). For permanently excluded pupils, reintegration to new schools could be viewed as an attempt to re-absorb them into this social–moral order. One area of focus within this chapter will be the factors that act as 'enablers' to this re-absorption, with specific reference to peer support systems.

The political agenda creating pressures for inclusion and the growing awareness nationally of the wasteful nature of educational and social exclusion in Britain combined towards the end of the 1990s to bring the plight of children and young people permanently excluded from school sharply into focus. As a direct result, the possibility of returning these children into new mainstream schools started to become a reality, for more children and young people. In my experience, working as an educational psychologist within Local Authority (LA) settings since 1985, reintegration following permanent exclusion was once a rare occurrence encountered as a one-off situation. Now, LAs are much more likely to have systems in place that are designed to support children, families and schools through the process. An interesting adjunct to this is that the *Social Inclusion: Pupil Support* document (Department for Education and Employment, 1999) introduced the idea of 'managed moves'. The document sets out an outline process for reintegrating pupils to a new school prior to permanent exclusion, if circumstances suggested that a fresh start would be the most fruitful course of action. This may, of course, be related to the slight downturn in exclusion figures reported in 1999–2000 (see Table 4.1).

Billington (2000, p. 2) reminds us that children can be 'placed elsewhere ... although usually there will be a paucity of evidence to suggest that this will result in any kind of success'. It is foolhardy to assume that permanently excluded pupils should always be returned to new schools because of commitment to the idea that children and young people are bound to be better off included in mainstream settings. We can probably all think of examples where this has not been the case; indeed, Parsons (cited in Fisher, 2001, p. 3) goes so far as to say, 'the reintegration of permanently excluded children back into mainstream school is known to be a difficult process meeting with limited success'. Schools can be reluctant to accept previously excluded pupils, and therefore lack commitment to the placement. This can be caused by a whole range of reasons: schools may feel unfairly pressured into accepting pupils, the level of support needed to make such a placement successful may be viewed as inadequate and there may be a sense of injustice created by a perception that other schools are excluding many and reintegrating few.

It is therefore interesting to ponder why reintegration of permanently excluded pupils into mainstream schools should be viewed as a desirable end to work towards.

The commitment to social and educational inclusion, resulting from social, philosophical or political belief systems, has undoubted importance. Further, with permanently excluded pupils particularly in mind, the commitment to return these children and young people to mainstream schools rests on an assumption that such an education somehow results in better outcomes than if they were not reintegrated, instead receiving home tuition or placement in a pupil referral unit, for example. The definition of 'better', and for whom it is better, raises tantalizing questions. Is returning to mainstream better because it means more exam passes at SAT/GCSE or A level? Is it better because of a rise in the percentage of school leavers who go on to further education, training or employment? Is it better because it somehow benefits the other pupils in the school? Or is it better because the resources of the nominated school improve? Is it better because of the improved profile of the school as a 'community resource'? The list could go on and on; hard evidence for the answers to these questions is sadly lacking. Tootill and Spalding (2000) provide one of the few studies exploring the outcomes of reintegrated placements. They conclude the article by saying:

> The systems and attitudes, which saw the pupils excluded in the first instance, can be the same barriers to their inclusion on their return. Therefore . . . we have to challenge and improve these systems and find the vision and resources to change them if we really believe we should move towards a more inclusive education and society for all young people.

(Tootill and Spalding, 2000, p. 117)

CHILDREN'S VOICES

Garner (1996) acknowledges the need to see 'how the social reality called education exists in the lived world' (p. 189). Strong arguments can be made about the potential benefits of exploring children's perspectives on education, not least because, as the consumers of the education service, they are likely to have views about those services received. Pomeroy (1999) emphasizes the importance of gaining pupil views about their educational experience:

> As the recipients of policy-in-practice, they possess a knowledge of the educational system which is not necessarily known to teachers, parents or policy makers . . . Too often, the viewpoint of the student remains unheard.

(Pomeroy, 1999, p. 466)

The *Special Educational Needs: Code of Practice* (Department for Education and Skills, 2001) reiterates a point made in an earlier code that 'the views of the child should be sought and taken into account' (p. 7). There are, in my view, even more compelling arguments to be made for seeking the views of pupils who have experienced such problems coping in the school environment that they become excluded. This group of children and their families, as well as their teachers, are highly likely to have relevant opinions and views about the aspects of schooling that presented particular difficulties to them and aspects which did, or could have, helped them be more successful. Similarly, we should take the time to explore the views of pupils who have been returned to new schools following permanent exclusion in order to learn from their experiences about the positive and negative forces in the process. Listening to child and family views, as well as the views of professionals involved, would inform future planning, policy and practice at the levels of the LA, the school as an institution and individual professional practice.

Norwich, Kelly and Educational Psychologists in Training (2006) contend that the views of pupils across the education system, including those with special educational needs, are becoming increasingly accessed in order to inform educational practice and school development. Despite the principle outlined in the UN Convention on the Rights of the Child that young people should be consulted about decisions which affect them, there are only a small number of studies investigating the views of pupils with social, emotional and behavioural difficulties about their own educational experiences. Gersch and Nolan (1994) recognized the potential contribution that could be made to understanding the process of exclusion by pupils who had experienced it, and undertook a study to elicit their views. The authors assert, 'there are good moral, pragmatic and legally supported reasons for listening to pupils, if plans are to be successful for them' (p. 37). Only a small number of researchers have explored this specific area (e.g. Osler *et al.*, 2002; Goodenough *et al.*, 2003), which represents an unfortunate underutilization of insight and suggestion.

THE STUDY

In 1996, I became part of a four-year initiative tackling emotional and behavioural difficulties, exclusion and disaffection in a city in the north of England. One of the aims was to raise the number of permanently excluded pupils returning to mainstream schools. Several years later, I decided to follow up some of the pupils who had been reintegrated during the project years. My research interest lay in exploring the factors that had enabled successful and sustained reintegration into new mainstream schools from the point of view of the participants involved, namely the excluded pupils, parents, receiving schools and supporting professionals. However, it was necessary to determine what was meant by the terms 'successful' and 'sustained' in order to select pupils to follow up. For this I could find no precedent in the literature or in government documents. National data were only available for return rates following permanent exclusion, failing to give any indication about how long a pupil would need to remain in a new placement for it to be deemed 'successful'. Inevitably then, I needed to develop a rationale for this decision. Having played an active part in supporting excluded pupils returning to mainstream settings, I made a judgement to opt for three terms following return. I was aware that support systems would gradually reduce after about a term, on the assumption that the pupil had been successful in settling into the new school context. Examination of exclusion and reintegration rates within the particular LA showed that rates of reintegration of permanently excluded pupils varied year on year; however, it was apparent that the number returned for reintegration was often considerably higher than the numbers remaining in new placements beyond three terms. In other words, although within this particular LA reintegration to new schools would occur on average in just over a third of cases, only half of those returned remained within new placements for longer than three terms. Of the pupils who met the criteria for selection into the sample for study, only five were prepared to become involved in the research. By definition, this group determined themselves 'hard to reach'.

The participants included in the study shaped up as five clusters, each made up of the pupil, parent, receiving school and supporting professional. Semi-structured interviews were carried out with the pupils themselves and the specified 'others' involved in their reintegration. The intention was to explore each participant's views about the process of reintegration and the factors perceived as contributing to success.

Interviews with the pupils, parents, receiving school staff and support professionals took place, and at the end of the individual data-gathering period a focus group interview was held with eight members of the behaviour support team. The purpose of the focus group interview was twofold: first, to open up more general discussion amongst the team about their perceptions of factors important in sustained successful reintegration and, secondly, to feed in some of the themes that had emerged from individual interviews in order to gather further views about these issues.

All interviews, including the focus group interview, were tape-recorded and subsequently transcribed. Data were analysed using grounded theory (Strauss and Corbin, 1998), and indicated that three core dimensions played a critical role in initial and maintained success. The findings were recognized to have direct relevance for: school practice, educational psychology and other supporting professionals' practice, and LA procedures and practice. The psychological and social processes deemed important in enabling success were identified as:

- support;
- pupil characteristics;
- relationships.

These three dimensions will be discussed here, then implications for practice will be explored. Following on from this, the particular dimension of peer relationships will be scrutinized more fully.

SUPPORT

All parents interviewed viewed the preparation and support of academic processes for their children as important, mainly from the point of view that they did not want academic pressure to jeopardize new placements. Receiving staff in mainstream schools echoed similar views, namely that having academic support available at the beginning of placement was helpful 'just in case', rather than through necessity. The issue was not raised by pupils, in fact they hardly mentioned it, though of course it is possible that they did not become aware of academic pressure precisely because they were supported in the early stages of placement. The messages of support given to pupils by their parents were seen as important by pupils; these ranged from the transmission of subtle messages about valuing the placement and wanting it to work through to more concrete support, such as visits to school. School staff made surprisingly little reference to the support they had received from LA support services, apart from their role in organizing direct assistance to pupils in classrooms. One reason for this appeared to be that the person who had received initial support from services, in the form of placement preparation, did not turn out to be the person with day-to-day contact with pupils; so they were unaware of the placement preparation support offered by LA services.

PUPIL CHARACTERISTICS

This dimension refers to those aspects of the pupil that largely come into the new school situation with them, for example abilities or aspects of personality. Of course, it is acknowledged that situations and contexts have a hugely important part to play and will undoubtedly affect the manifestation of such 'within child' characteristics. What is interesting is that this theme came out strongly as an aspect in successful return to mainstream school, and yet allows the least possibility for assigning success to matters within the control of adults.

One such 'within child' aspect concerned ability. Some adults suggested that good intellectual ability might in fact play an important part in facilitating successful and sustained transfer to a new school. The focus group raised the possibility that intelligence helps pupils to understand and fit into social and academic aspects of school life – to know how to play the school game successfully: 'Brighter helps, it does . . . it helps you fit, doesn't it?' said a focus group participant. I am reminded here of the work by Luthar, Cecchetti and Becker (2000), in which the authors debate the nature of the construct of resilience and its usefulness in understanding the processes influencing at risk individuals.

Another aspect of 'pupil characteristics' recognized as important within this study relates to goal motivation. Goal motivation has been recognized as an important aspect of self-efficacy and educational performance (Galloway *et al.*, 1998; Hufton, Elliott and Illushin, 2002). Did the pupils in the present study naturally have, or did they acquire, different goal motivations during the process of school change? Khan (2003) suggests that those with motivation related to task goals, that is those who want to get the best out of education for intrinsic value rather than for external reward, are more likely to succeed.

RELATIONSHIPS

The dimension of relationships greatly overlapped with the 'support' dimension and featured in three combinations: adults with adults, adults with pupils, pupils with peers.

Relationships: Adults with Adults

Parents spoke about the importance of the relationships they had formed with other adults in the process of supporting their children back into mainstream school. The support they had received themselves, from school staff and support workers, was important to them. Parents weren't necessarily demanding high levels of direct support; what they reported was that they needed to feel they *could* call on known people for support, if they felt they needed it, even though such a request may not be activated. This enabled them to feel more secure during the process of reintegration.

In terms of the relationships between adults, comments reflected the importance of positive *initial* contacts between parents and school staff. However, findings also suggested that sustained placement may be affected by *ongoing* adult relationships, determined by the quality and effectiveness of continuing channels of communication.

Such channels needed to, at the outset, provide secure pathways for information flow between parents, school staff and support staff; this was likely to heighten the quality of placement preparation and initial information sharing. Once a pupil's placement was established, these communication channels could not be neglected; they needed to *remain* effective and open as the placement progressed in order to facilitate processes such as: rapid response to emerging difficulties including non-attendance, the facility to make adjustments and alterations to arrangements, sharing strategies and making strategy changes, and information exchange regarding emerging vulnerability in the placement. From their continued relationships with school staff, parents reported feeling involved, informed and reassured. I wonder whether we overlook the importance of the quality of initial and *continued* relationships with these adults at our peril?

Relationships: Adults with Pupils

There is nothing new in the idea that the quality of relationships between adults and pupils in school is a hugely important factor in promoting positive school experiences. The present study revealed strong feelings about the importance of adult–pupil relationships, from the perspectives of both adults and pupils. Pupils talked about the importance to them of feeling liked by adults, supported by them and having an adult there for them. The pupils viewed positive relationships with adults as having a direct impact upon feelings of belongingness and comfort within the school environment.

Many of the adults in the present study recognized the critical importance of the adult–pupil relationships in school, and the benefits of being able to form these relationships quickly. Importance was attached to school staff recognizing the need to be proactive in building relationships with students, rather than waiting for pupils to make the first move. Pupils who felt well supported were in situations where adults in the new school acknowledged that it was their responsibility to make this happen and be proactive about it.

Relationships: Pupils with Peers

Many of us can remember our teenage years. Some will have a rosy glow when thinking about teenage social relationships; others will cringe as they remember the embarrassment and unhappiness of uncomfortable or hurtful social networks. Most of us would recognize, from our own memories or everyday observation, that relationship networks between young people are tremendously important to them in all aspects of their lives. Yet it seems that this fundamental aspect of young people's lives is rather underutilized in the world of education. Even so, I was surprised at how powerfully the dimension of peer networks emerged from the data in the present study. Peer networks were found to be one of the major elements in the success of reintegrated placements for pupils. All pupils raised the critical importance of their emerging, developing and existing friendships in assisting (and sometimes jeopardizing) new placements. Such issues were also raised by all adults involved, and were discussed at length within the focus group interview. The pupils in this study gave insights into the 'force field' created around them by social networks, and how these worked to support them in new placements or, alternatively, shake their stability, for example through bullying.

Khan's (2003) study proposes a model describing adult–child relationship vulnerability for excluded pupils in pupil referral units (PRUs). This raises for me the question of whether there is a similar vulnerability for some students in relation to social relationships with peers. If Khan's model is accepted (put simply, that long-established negative pupil–teacher relationships contribute to disaffection), it is possible that these same students also have vulnerability in peer relationships and have less ability to access, contribute to and maintain social networks that are supportive (this possibility is also raised by Cullingford and Morrison, 1997).

IMPLICATIONS FOR PRACTICE

The limited literature available on the subject of reintegration has suggested several factors that may affect the success of pupils accessing new school settings (INCLUDE, 2000; Parsons and Howlett, 2000; Fisher, 2001). These factors will now be outlined before moving on to the implications for practice arising from the particular study detailed earlier.

At the strategic level, the literature informs us that it is important that LAs have clear policies and procedures in relation to prevention of exclusion, early intervention and reintegration, with shared understanding across LA departments about what support each can provide. The literature suggests that systems need to be in place to allow the LA to identify and secure new placements, and these should be operational within one term. Alongside these policies and procedures, multi-agency systems (such as data sharing, mediation and parent support schemes) appear to be important. In order to permit the creation of individual packages to support reintegration programmes, the LA's approach to budgeting needs to be flexible; this may become increasingly possible as a result of the move towards pooled budgets within Children's Trusts.

The literature raises several points that will signal successful reintegration, at the school level. Schools should have effective pastoral care and behaviour policies in existence. Alongside these should be effective multi-professional working practices, encompassing clarity and understanding of roles and responsibilities for all professionals connecting with schools, for example education support teams, youth offending teams and social workers. The issues of school culture and ethos have emerged from the literature; these need to be conducive to learning and good behaviour and provide the flexibility to adopt a variety of strategies to support reintegrated pupils.

At the case level, the literature indicates that placement preparations have implications for the outcome of placements (Hayden and Dunne, 2001; Parsons and Howlett, 2000). It appears that excluded pupils may need to be provided with support to ensure the maintenance of basic skills while not attending school, in addition to curriculum-support reintegration packages during the period of exclusion, at the point of reintegration and in the early stages of new placement to ensure curriculum access (Fisher, 2001). On a related theme, liaison between previous placement (school, home tuition, PRU) and the new school also seems to be important, since the quality of this liaison could affect the fluency of curriculum transition.

The themes of pupil involvement in decision-making and the importance of involvement in the process of reintegration also emerge as potentially critical issues, as does the quality of the working relationships between parent, school and support workers. A further factor seems to be the need for a nominated individual to champion the needs of the pupil, drive the process and coordinate professional involvement around the young person, ensuring frequent reviews of progress in the early stages of new placement.

Another factor arising from the literature is the nature of the support that returning pupils need to receive to make a new placement more likely to succeed. There are several strands to this. Curriculum support has already been mentioned. In addition, there is the need for emotional support from an adult in the early stages, as the pupil lets go of earlier networks. As the new placement progresses, the importance of peer support and acceptance grows as the pupil creates new peer networks of social and emotional support.

As can be seen, there are several areas of overlap between the points raised as important for successful reintegration arising from a search of the literature and the dimensions arising from my own research of participant perceptions. However, there do appear to be important differences in emphasis. It appears to me that the factors arising from the literature may translate the concerns and perspectives of those most usually asked about these processes, that is adults within LAs. Existing literature generally does not reflect the views of pupils and families about the particular theme of successful and sustained return to new mainstream schools following exclusion. Acknowledging pupils' and families' views about reintegration extends and refines current understandings; it is time to emphasize the importance to sustained success of adult–pupil relationships, support and pupil characteristics. My research study carries further implications for practice at several levels. These have been reported elsewhere (Lown, 2005) but are worth repeating here.

LAs and support professionals could support the process of reintegration for pupils following permanent exclusion by ensuring a number of processes are given attention. LAs and support staff should ensure:

- accurate records continue to be kept of exclusion and reintegration rates. In addition, rates of sustained reintegration (i.e. placements lasting a year or more) should be recorded within LA databases;
- pre-placement preparation is undertaken with teaching assistants and pastoral staff (e.g. year head) as well as with senior managers or head teacher in the new school;
- sources of emotional support, and academic support if necessary, are identified and made explicit to the pupil; the significance of the quality of these relationships needs to be understood by those identified as providing such support;
- effective communication systems are facilitated between school staff and parents or carers at the beginning of the placement, as well as sustained over a longer period than is usual;
- that the significance of pupil opinion and choice in school factors is understood, for example choice of school, and acting upon these views where possible and appropriate;
- that the significance of entering new peer networks is understood and that all possible methods to ease entry to them are created and acted upon by the school. In addition, the importance of maintaining social networks needs to be understood and assisted;
- that systems are in place between the school staff, parents and carers and support professionals to recognize emerging difficulties quickly, thereby raising the possibility of improvement, for example attendance difficulties, bullying issues;
- support processes such as those above are maintained for a period of at least three terms, and vigilance maintained beyond.

Schools receiving pupils following permanent exclusion could become better prepared for their arrival and sustained success by ensuring:

- consistent, good, close communication with parents or carers, which is maintained over a long period (probably more than three terms);
- communication channels are clear and explicit, and ideally school staff should take the initiative about maintaining contact with parents and carers, rather than waiting for contact from them;
- identification of a member of staff who will ensure that strong personal links are forged with the incoming pupil, again sustained over a period of time (at least three terms). As with parent communications, time would need to be invested into the relationship, and the member of staff should take the initiative in seeking out the pupil in order to take the time to continue to build and strengthen the relationship thereby strengthening the connection between pupil and adult;

- good, clear communication systems within school to allow for preparations and swift modifications to placements to be effectively transmitted to all staff and communicated with parents and pupils themselves;
- direct involvement of a pastoral teacher or support assistant in pre-placement preparations;
- the ability to predict and address an in-coming pupil's needs for access to social networks. Receiving schools may need to take the initiative in developing access routes to social networks for new pupils (the basis of the remainder of this chapter).

PEER SUPPORT SYSTEMS: PROVIDING PLANNED INTERVENTION

This section briefly considers the nature of peer social networks and their importance, and then looks towards interventions that can be made by school staff and support professionals. Gibson's work (2005) has contributed to our current understanding of the importance of peer social networks, and is drawn upon here.

The following issues are raised within the context of the importance of peer social networks for pupils reintegrating to new schools following permanent exclusion. However, the points may be equally relevant for consideration within the context of the needs of any vulnerable pupil in the position of accessing a new school at an unusual time or in unusual circumstances.

Peer relationships can be considered as important in the developmental sense of having an impact upon the social skills required for social interaction, such as effective communication, competencies to moderate aggression, sexual socialization, forming moral values and the development of social perspective-taking skills. Of course, a young person would not usually express the wish to make secure friendships for these reasons. However, they might recognize the desire to construct meaningful peer relationships because they contribute to a sense of social support and security, reduce anxieties and fears, contribute to the development of self-concept and self-esteem, inform on behavioural norms and assist in learning skills for self-presentation and impression management.

It is recognized (Gibson, 2005) that in the middle childhood years, friendships and friendship cliques stabilize, with notable popularity and power hierarchies, and children become more concerned with group belonging. In-group and out-group membership can evoke anxiety and make the social climate tricky for some. Perhaps these complex issues concerning childhood social networks go some way towards explaining why they have been identified as being of fundamental importance to pupils entering new school environments. It seems there is so much potential for things to be difficult or go wrong. So how can vulnerable pupils who have little choice but to enter a new school context be supported in accessing, forming and maintaining positive social networks with peers? What interventions are open to the adults who are in a position to facilitate such support processes? There are two main types of intervention to be addressed:

(i) interventions that are embedded within whole school initiatives and are accessed by any pupils;
(ii) interventions targeted in such a way that they are open to access by specific groups of pupils or are targeted towards individual pupils.

WHOLE SCHOOL INITIATIVES

Cowie and Wallace (2000) concur with Gibson (2005) in recognizing that the systems of peer support for pupils to access with the greatest ease are those which have a profile within schools as being everyday, normal arrangements and resources. Such initiatives include:

- effective, visible and frequently reviewed anti-bullying policies;
- cooperative group-learning activities embedded within general curriculum delivery, recognized by individual teachers for their value in promoting social networks;
- formal schoolwide systems for peer support, such as peer listening schemes, peer counselling schemes, peer mediation schemes, 'buddy benches', peer mentoring schemes and peer learning schemes (such as paired reading). Schemes need to be well-publicized around the school, with carefully thought out access arrangements to encourage use;
- effective organizational approaches to the development of social and emotional aspects of learning, embedded within curriculum approaches, such as the SEAL material (Department for Education and Skills, 2005).

INTERVENTIONS FOR SPECIFIC GROUPS OR INDIVIDUAL PUPIL-FOCUSED APPROACHES

Organizing support for social networks through specific group intervention can be a powerful tool (Lown, 2001). Again, access to such systems is smooth, when regarded as part of everyday school arrangements.

Circle Time is one such class or group intervention that has been found to be effective in enabling pupils to get to know each other better and forge better relationships (Lown, 2002). There are many Circle Time materials available on the market, many containing specific sections relating to building friendships and peer support processes (e.g. Bliss and Robinson, 1995). Direct intervention to teach social skills within a small group context could be an extension of a Circle Time-type approach to skill development for specific pupils identified as needing this type of input.

Befriending schemes can be a useful form of regular support when multiple befrienders are used for multiple recipients; variations on this theme can be developed whereby befrienders are around in school during social times and initiate contact with pupils who appear to be isolated or rejected. Mentoring systems are likely to work in a more formal way to identify particular mentors for particular mentees, and care should be taken to match pairs effectively. On a similar theme, buddying systems are a useful way of bridging the initial days of a pupil's arrival in a new school, though adults should think carefully about how to match up the buddy with the new pupil – areas of shared interest might be more productive than choosing the most socially skilled and apparently most responsible pupil for the task.

A well-established and evaluated method of incorporating vulnerable pupils into social networks is Circle of Friends (Frederickson and Turner, 2003; Newton and Wilson, 2003). This can be a highly useful technique in its usual form, but also lends itself to adaptation for use with groups of pupils to introduce the need for other peer support systems, such as befriending or peer listening schemes. The No Blame Approach (Maines and Robinson, 1995) to bullying is a group-support process that has some parallels with Circle of Friends.

Several schemes and approaches to supporting the positive development of peer networks have been outlined above. However, it is worth bearing in mind that these methods may have a time cost; several will require input, for example from an adult to run circle meetings for Circle of Friends or for peer mediation training. For schemes such as peer listening, it will be necessary to train participants in particular skills, such as active listening, and also in potentially problematic areas (e.g. confidentiality or becoming over-responsible). Supporters will need to have skills developed and maintained, and also have access to a supportive adult themselves. A further issue to consider is how to attract boys into becoming involved in such initiatives, as they tend to be under-represented.

Individual pupils will vary in how much they feel the need to access such systems, and vulnerable pupils entering a new school system will need to be made fully aware of the possibilities for support and how to access them. It will be very important to ensure that the pupil feels that his or her voice is heard in identifying the type and level of support he or she requires.

CONCLUSION

Billington and Pomerantz (2004), in their discussion of children excluded and marginalized from schools, remind us that 'there is something deeply offensive to social justice in witnessing fellow human beings pushed out through overt or covert marginalization' (p. 6). There is a paucity of evidence concerning the reintegration of excluded pupils. The limited literature has been filtered and synthesized to identify a range of factors at authority, service and school levels that have an impact upon reintegration. In the knowledge that previous work has tended to reflect the views of professionals, the present research study was used as a vehicle to supplement these factors, bringing into focus the perception of the participants in such processes, namely pupils, parents, receiving school staff and supporting professionals.

This chapter has looked at issues of exclusion and the case for reintegrating, with care, pupils excluded from schools following adult decisions to remove them. The issues of support, pupil characteristics and relationships have been explored in terms of their relevance to supporting the process of reintegration. Peer support systems have been given a particular focus; the importance of this theme emerged from the research study with such clarity that it was felt to merit particular examination. Peer support intervention approaches have therefore been outlined as methods to increase the likelihood of success in reintegration arrangements.

Perhaps, following adult-sponsored exclusion, adult action that supports reintegration, through the factors identified in this chapter, can help to repair some of the psychological damage which may have been experienced by those children and young people who have been 'pushed out through overt or covert marginalization'.

REFERENCES

Audit Commission (1996) *Misspent Youth . . . Young People and Crime.* Audit Commission, London.

Billington, T. (2000) *Separating, Losing and Excluding Children.* Routledge Falmer, London.

Billington, T. Pomerantz, M. (eds) (2004) *Children at the Margins.* Trentham, Stoke.

Bliss, T. and Robinson, G. (1995) *Developing Circle Time.* Lucky Duck, Bristol.

Cowie, H. and Wallace, P. (2000) *Peer Support in Action.* Sage, London.

Cullingford, C. and Morrison, J. (1997) Peer group pressure within and outside school. *British Educational Research Journal* **23** (1), 61–80.

Department for Education and Employment (1999) *Social Inclusion: Pupil Support.* DfEE Publications, London. Circular 10/99

Department for Education and Skills (2001) *Special Educational Needs: Code of Practice.* DfES Publications, Nottingham.

Department for Education and Skills (2005) *Social and Emotional Aspects of Learning.* DfES Publications, Nottingham.

Department for Education and Skills (2006) *National Statistics Bulletin.* www.statistics.gov.uk/ (accessed September 2006).

Fisher, D. (2001) *Lost and Found: Effective Reintegration Programmes for Excluded Pupils.* EMIE (NFER), Slough.

Frederickson, N. and Turner, J. (2003) Utilising the classroom peer group to address children's social needs: an evaluation of the circle of friends intervention approach. *Journal of Special Education* **36** (4), 234–245.

Galloway, D. (1998) *Motivating the Difficult to Teach.* Longman, London.

Garner, P. (1996) A la recherche du temps perdu: case-study evidence from off-site and pupil referral units. *Children and Society* **10** (3), 187–196.

Gersch, I.S. and Nolan, A. (1994) Exclusions: what the children think. *Educational Psychology in Practice* **10** (1), 35–45.

Gibson, C. (2005) Fostering Peer/Social Relationships to Promote Successful Reintegration of Looked After Children. Unpublished EdD essay, Sheffield University.

Goodenough, T., Williamson, E., Kent, J. and Ashcroft, R. (2003) 'What did you think about that?' researching children's perceptions of participation in a longitudinal genetic epidemiological study. *Children and Society* **17** (2), 113–125.

Hayden, C. and Dunne, S. (2001) *Outside, Looking In.* The Children's Society, London.

Hufton, N.R., Elliott, J.G. and Illushin, L. (2002) Educational motivation and engagement:

qualitative accounts from three countries. *British Educational Research Journal* **28** (2), 265–289.

INCLUDE (2000) *This Time I'll Stay*. Ely, INCLUDE.

Jones, R.A. (2003) The construction of emotional and behavioural difficulties. *Educational Psychology in Practice* **19** (2), 147–157.

Khan, K. (2003) Teacher–Student Relationships and Motivational Goals: The Evidence for a Simple View of Disaffection Gained from the Perceptions of a Small Sample of Excluded Students. Unpublished MSc dissertation, Sheffield University.

Lown, J. (2001) *Circle of Friends*. Positive Behaviour Management, Merseyside.

Lown, J. (2002) Circle time: the perceptions of teachers and pupils. *Educational Psychology in Practice* **18** (2), 93–102.

Lown, J. (2005) Including the excluded: participant perceptions. *Educational and Child Psychology* **22** (3), 45–57.

Luthar, S.S., Cecchetti, D. and Becker, B. (2000) The construct of resilience: a critical evaluation and guidelines for future work. *Child Development* **71** (3), 543–562.

Maines, B. and Robinson, G. (1995) *The No Blame Approach*. Lucky Duck, Bristol.

Newton, C. and Wilson, D. (2003) *Creating Circles of Friends: A Peer Support and Inclusion Workbook*. Inclusive Solutions, Nottingham.

Norwich, B., Kelly, N. and EPiTs (2006) Evaluating children's participation in SEN procedures: lessons for educational psychologists. *Educational Psychology in Practice* **22** (3), 255–272.

Osler, A., Street, C., Lall, M. and Vincent, K. (2002) *Not a Problem? Girls and School Exclusion*. NCB, London.

Parsons, C. (1999) *Education, Exclusion and Citizenship*. Routledge, London.

Parsons, C. and Howlett, K. (2000) *Investigating the Reintegration of Permanently Excluded Young People in England*. INCLUDE, Ely.

Pomeroy, E. (1999) The teacher–student relationship in secondary school: insights from excluded students. *British Journal of Sociology of Education* **20** (4), 465–482.

Strauss, A. and Corbin, J. (1998) *Basics of Qualitative Research*. Sage Publications, California.

Tootill, R. and Spalding, B. (2000) How effective can reintegration be for children with emotional and behavioural difficulties? *Support for Learning* **15** (3), 111–117.

5 'Hard to Reach' Migrant Children

PETER LLOYD BENNETT AND JANE REID

INTRODUCTION

This chapter focuses on the particular needs of migrant families and children who are seeking or who have been granted asylum in the United Kingdom. These families come from a vast number of countries with different languages, customs, religions and institutions. The children of these families will have much in common with some established ethnic communities in the United Kingdom. They will also have much in common with some of the poorest of the indigenous populations: poverty, inadequate housing, poor health and so on. Already there are some families with children from European Union (EU) states settling in the United Kingdom and the numbers are likely to grow in future as the EU expands. Workers from the new accession states, for example, will have the right to housing and benefits in this country after one year of work and many may choose to bring their families to live here. However, there may be some ways in which asylum seekers and refugees have specific problems that could make some of their children 'hard to reach' in several ways, and these children are the main focus of this chapter.

There are several terms related to migrant children and their families in current use (as outlined at the end of this chapter). A key distinction can be made between families who have been given Indefinite Leave to Remain (ILR) and are therefore eligible for all benefits and processes as a UK citizen and those who are still awaiting an outcome of their asylum claim. Until then they are regarded only as temporary residents, often with recourse to emergency services only. These asylum seekers will be given temporary accommodation and subsistence provided by a department of the Home Office, usually outside London and the South-East. There are various complexities in the law, including an appeals system, but as a generalization they are able to stay in that accommodation until a definite decision is reached regarding their future country of residence. All immigration matters are detailed and complicated and come within the remit of specialist immigration lawyers or agencies such as the Refugee Legal Centre, and legal aid is usually provided.

How to Reach 'Hard to Reach' Children: Improving access, participation and outcomes. Edited by K. Pomerantz, M. Hughes and D. Thompson.   Copyright © 2007 by John Wiley & Sons, Ltd.

ORGANIZATIONS

There are two main organizations: the Refugee Council, which is a charitable organization, and the National Asylum Support Service, which is statutory. There are also a number of voluntary and additional smaller services. The Refugee Council provides practical help and specialist advice as well as campaigning and lobbying for refugees' voices to be heard. This organization suggests that it is virtually impossible for people fleeing persecution to reach Britain without resorting to false documents, which does not mean that their case lacks credibility (Refugee Council, 2004). In some countries simply applying for a passport may put an individual's life at risk, let alone visiting a foreign embassy. Asylum seekers, including children, can be detained in detention centres at any time during their application and for any period without being given any reasons for their detention. Some asylum seekers are interviewed as soon as they arrive in the United Kingdom with no opportunity to get legal advice, and many asylum seekers are issued a 16-page Statement of Evidence Form (SEF) to complete within 10 days of receipt. This form is extremely complicated and can only be completed in English. If the SEF is not returned in time, the Home Office will not consider the merits of the claim and the application will be refused outright.

The National Asylum Support Service was established in April 2000 in order to provide financial support and housing for asylum seekers. In the past, asylum seekers have tended to settle in areas where they first arrive or where they have family or friends, and this can lead to an increased demand for local housing and resources. This has led to a practice of dispersing asylum seekers to other parts of the country where they tend to be housed in hard-to-let properties in socially deprived areas.

In general, refugees are able to stay in emergency accommodation until they have been granted permission to stay or are forced to leave. Adults are not normally allowed to work until they have a positive decision, but children have access to available education and health provision. Kralj and Goldberg (2005) suggest a discrepancy between best practice and policy and recommend that child welfare legislation should be fully implemented for all children. Once adults are granted refugee status, they need to apply for housing and transfer their means of subsistence to Income Support or Job Seeker's Allowance.

There are counselling agencies for children and adolescents who are known victims of torture, such as the Medical Foundation for Victims of Torture – its main centre is in London but other centres have opened in Leeds and Glasgow. Other counselling agencies exist, but referring can be difficult and initial diagnosis equally so. Referral would normally be through a doctor.

LEGISLATION

The United Nations 1951 Convention on refugees (Office of the High Commissioner for Human Rights, 1951) describes a refugee as a person who has left his or her country and cannot return because of a well-founded fear of being persecuted for reasons of race, religion, nationality, social group or political opinion and is not protected. If they have a choice, asylum seekers apply for refuge in a country where they may have historic links, the escape or journey has been arranged by others, they have relatives or friends, they can speak the language or they are attracted to the social and economic prospects of the country. Under international law anyone has the right to apply for asylum in the United Kingdom, though there has been a reduction in applications due to measures preventing people from getting to the United Kingdom to apply for asylum.

Under the Immigration and Asylum Act 1999, asylum seekers were to be paid for by the National Asylum Support Service (NASS) until they had a definite decision on their asylum claim from the Home Office. Newly arrived asylum seekers were to be housed in emergency full-board accommodation while their claim for government support was processed.

Once processed, asylum seekers are dispersed throughout the United Kingdom to government-acquired accommodation, and they have no choice as to where they are going to be housed. Family or community networks are not recognized as sufficient reason for a person not to be dispersed. However, these are thought to be key factors in children adjusting and achieving in schools and avoiding isolation (Kao, 2004; Pallon et al., 2001). When accommodated, they would be given slightly less funding than Income Support. Full access to education and health services would be provided once dispersed.

Alternatively, some asylum seekers choose to live with families or friends, but in those cases financial support for living expenses is given, but not rent. In certain cases, immigration authorities have the right to compulsorily detain entrants in detention centres. Usually, families are not detained, although occasionally the male head of family might be.

Asylum seekers are allowed to appeal against decisions made by the Home Office, and there are considerable rights of appeal that can take some time to work through (Coker et al., 2004). If all appeals are negative, the Government has the right to return failed asylum seekers to their countries of origin and support will be terminated. Where there are children, however, support will be taken over by Social Services. Children of failed asylum seekers have the right to go to school until removal orders are instituted. Failed asylum seekers may be detained in detention centres, but this would be unusual in cases involving families.

Unaccompanied minors (children under the age of 18) are the responsibility of Social Services and have the same rights as other children in care. They may be placed in foster homes or in residential homes. After the age of 16, they may live in independent accommodation in the care of Social Services. On leaving care they have the same rights under the Children (Leaving Care) Act 2000. They also have the same rights to claim asylum. Unaccompanied minors are not sent back to their countries of origin until the age of 18 when their cases are considered alongside adults who are also seeking asylum.

Although the structure may be rickety and in need of strengthening, there are some measures in place for those seeking refugee status in this country. The children of dispersed asylum seekers and refugees alike have access to education and medical services.

However, we would argue that some children of refugee families have specific problems that may make them 'hard to reach'. Some children will have been victims of torture, forcibly enlisted in armies (where drug addiction may be encouraged), taken by armed groups as camp workers or for sexual purposes. Others may have witnessed terrible atrocities, perpetrated perhaps on parents, family members or friends, or may have been caught up in the dreadful consequences of war.

THE ROLE OF THE MEDIA

The media is sometimes responsible for the perpetuation of myths and can encourage a tendency to scapegoat other people as violent aggressors and 'welfare spongers' or as innocent victims of bureaucracy and hostile forces (Gilmore and Martin, 2005). There is some evidence indicating a link between media reporting of asylum issues and race-related crime (Information Centre about Asylum and Refugees in the UK, 2004) suggesting that negative newspaper coverage of migrants in the community may result in race-related crime.

Asylum is an important issue to the British public and is rarely out of the newspapers and is the subject of intense political and public debate. The Refugee Council (2004) claims that media reports and commentary about asylum seekers is often hostile, unbalanced and factually incorrect.

Asylum seekers arrive in the United Kingdom, where there is a free market economy and commercial enterprise can achieve economic rewards. The initial experiences of new arrivals are likely to differ from people born in the country as they may be subject to certain hardships and exploitation. Struggling to learn a foreign language or dealing with bureaucracy abroad can provide us with insights to some of the difficulties experienced by asylum seekers.

THE NATURE OF THE DIFFICULTIES

Melzak (1999) proposes that children who have suffered traumatic events including torture may hold the secret as closely as victims of sexual abuse. They are 'hard to reach' because no one knows the problem is there. Sometimes, these children will be travelling on their own as unaccompanied minors, possibly living in care homes or with foster parents and tend to be older children. Others may be with parents who may themselves find the topic hard to discuss and are suffering from post-traumatic stress disorder (PTSD). The traumatic event may be consistently re-experienced by distressing recollections, dreams, suddenly feeling or acting as if the event is recurring or triggers that are associated with the trauma. Individuals can have difficulty falling asleep, experience outbursts of anger, difficulty concentrating and hypervigilance.

Some schools have initiated programmes to overcome the effects of PTSD on children, which include the use of play activities and providing opportunities for children to talk about their experiences. Women interviewed by one of the authors at Migrant Helpline expressed a feeling of release after being 'allowed to talk'. Such schemes in schools might allay problems before they become critical.

Even where the child's disturbances may be acknowledged, sometimes the parent may find the child 'hard to reach'. One woman travelling with her 14-year-old son and a younger child had been recently reunited with the older boy. He had been abducted into a rebel army in his home country where he had been forcibly addicted to heroin. Before reaching the United Kingdom, he had been treated with Subutex but very quickly went missing in the United Kingdom. I contacted the police on her behalf, her son was found and returned to her but she felt she was already losing the battle for the child. This anxiety might be familiar to the parents of drug-using UK children, but is compounded for new arrivals by their lack of understanding of the culture, institutions and language of their new country.

Not all children will have directly experienced some of these terrors for themselves, yet family experiences may have an indirect influence. Parents may have been imprisoned, tortured, suffered long-term harassment, been sexually abused, lived in fear of a knock on the door or the sudden arrival of a marauding army. They may have been caught up in battles that were none of their concern, lived in refugee camps or simply been the victims of poverty. Some arrived in the United Kingdom as babies or were born after arrival. They will suffer from the parents' anxieties in struggling with a new culture and language, poverty and loneliness. Some of these very young children may be the result of rape, their mother may have AIDS, they may have single mothers or fathers, but all will be suffering some form of anxiety and stress.

Many young people have their age disputed by the Home Office, which may disregard overseas documents, such as passports, and Social Services are asked to carry out an age assessment, which can take several months. There is a margin of error up to five years of age (Levenson and Sharma, 2004), and age assessment is not thought to be conclusive.

The very diversity of refugees is in itself a problem and can make stereotyping hard to avoid. There are a considerable number of families from educated professional backgrounds with a high standard of living who have been forced to seek asylum on political or religious grounds. On the other hand, there are families who are poor, illiterate and dependent on others and who were swept up in civil wars or revolutions. There are an increasing number of single women with children, some of those born in this country. There are also children, travelling alone, whose family's whereabouts are unknown.

The needs of such a range of people are widely different, but there are similarities:

- Most refugees, whatever their family wealth, will be impoverished.
- Some will be facing the shock of poverty for the first time.
- Asylum claimants face overwhelming uncertainty about their claim.
- Refugees are uncertain about their long-term future.

- All experience a huge culture shock.
- They may experience or fear hostility and racism.
- They have to learn about new institutions.
- They have to adapt to a new language.
- They all experience grief and homesickness.
- Some may face the horror of bereavement, loss of children, past torture and imprisonment.
- Some will be in ill-health, the result of torture, imprisonment, rape or possibly an accident.

INVOLVING PARENTS IN THEIR CHILDREN'S EDUCATION

Any activity which brings mothers and families into the school so that they feel more relaxed and at home there is invaluable. These activities are not easy to run but examples might be basic English or maths classes, cookery, art and craft activities. The parents themselves often have a great deal to offer. Many have skills that are worth sharing. In their country of origin they could have looked after their children, cooked, run a home, run a market stall, worked in offices, schools, hospitals, universities and in government. They were engaged socially, and perhaps with older women looking after children while the younger members of the family worked. They belonged to churches, choirs, football clubs, debating groups or political parties.

With their change in status to a country where they feel supplicants for everything, that their culture has no place here, that family and friends are gone, possibly for ever, that they are parted from husbands, wives, children or parents and are having to ask for everything in an unknown language and an unknown country, self-esteem may plummet. The effect of that loss of self-esteem on children is very hard to bear.

Despite the problems families face, there is usually one constant: they all wish their children to be well-educated. In a survey on newly arrived single women carried out by Migrant Helpline in 2003, the 25 women all said that a good education and a better life for their children was their main aim (Reid, 2004). They were prepared to put up with all sorts of sacrifices to attain this. Education was seen as a key to a better life.

However, the concept of education differed. How or what children were taught, by what means or in what circumstances was hardly known by the parents who were not involved in their children's education. School itself was the important factor, but the idea of parental involvement in education was rarely seen. School was a safe haven where children would learn and that was it.

Some refugee children do very well at school, of course, and more data are becoming available. However, it is likely that all children suffer tremendous pressures, and these may be exacerbated where there is a single mother or a sick father. These pressures can be particularly difficult if a single mother is from a small ethnic minority.

A refugee mother, suffering depression, had been in the United Kingdom for five years with her two children (Reid, 2004). She lived in a suburb where there were no other people from her previous country. She had learned no English in that time and avoided going out. She said she had never been to the school but that her children were doing well. Speaking of her older daughter, she said: 'I feel she is the mother and I am the child.' She did not like her children going out and longed for them to come home from school each day. This woman's husband had been killed and she had been raped in front of her children. I asked her if anyone knew the children had suffered this and she was astonished. She didn't think so: the children were doing well at school.

This case history raises many questions including cultural perceptions of a child 'doing well' at school. For many parents 'doing well' may mean simply not being in trouble. It is difficult to know.

In some cultures there is a distinct separation between home and school. Children go to school and they come home. The children's education is the school's responsibility and just by being at school they are felt to be safe and educated. In areas where there are long distances to walk to school, there is no school-gate culture and no ease or familiarity with the school itself. 'I do not go to the school. My son tells me what happens. He is a good boy,' said another mother. But her son could not sort out the problem of his bus fares. By chance this was mentioned to the mother's refugee organization, which was able to contact the school on her behalf – she could not read or write in English.

On the other hand, a former university professor from Iran, who had escaped with his wife and three children after terrible experiences in prison, worried that he was depending too much on the school. Two of his three children were thriving, he said, but the third was suffering what he described as PTSD, including bed-wetting and lack of concentration at school. The father, who spoke good English, felt that he was pestering the school with his worries but, none the less, an educational psychologist had been brought in and this was helping to reduce his concerns. The father told us that his son had not directly witnessed his experiences as he was in prison, but suffered the effects of his own PTSD. In this case, the school had supported the family's request to be accommodated within its catchment area. This was a good example of one agency cooperating with another. Yet the key to this outcome was probably the ability of the father to understand the education system, express his views in clear English and have the confidence to speak to teachers about his concerns.

ISSUES AROUND LANGUAGE

Language is perhaps the main factor in understanding a child's or parent's concerns and the frustrations of the language barrier are as difficult for the practitioner as for the client. However, it is unwise to rely on children to interpret for their parents, because they may have difficulty understanding some of the concepts and there are various interpreting agencies, some using telephones. There is some improvement in the provision of interpreters and interpreting agencies, and practitioners should become aware of these and the methods of contacting them. Sometimes local community groups will supply interpreters, or perhaps a friend may act in this role, yet this is not always satisfactory. Interpreters may have their own agendas, and the system is unfortunately open to abuse. Interpreters may vary in terms of their skill in explaining the views of the client and their sensitivity to the issues being discussed. Translation of reports by professionals may be difficult to achieve as costs vary considerably and some of the terms may not translate easily. For these reasons the use of an interpreter to feed back on an assessment to the parents may not be a viable option.

Culturally, some women may prefer female interpreters and to speak to a female teacher or social worker. Equally, it may not be appropriate for the child to have a parent or even a family friend act as interpreter. Lastly, complexities in overseas countries may even mean that the child or parent refuses to see anyone from their own country. This may make asylum seekers seem difficult or obstinate to school staff, but there may be very real political, religious or social reasons for this. It is not unusual. There are a range of skills required in working with interpreters in a way that inspires trust and confidence on both sides, and courses are occasionally available. It may be worth while pressuring providers to arrange such courses.

MULTI-AGENCY WORKING

There is often more than one agency involved with refugee families, some professionals may know the family well and accessing this multidisciplinary network could be crucial to a satisfactory outcome. However, the refugees themselves do not necessarily realize the linking between agencies, in fact, may regard it as something to be hidden. For example, they could be in touch with a social worker, a lawyer, a refugee agency caseworker, a place of worship, a community organization and a network of friends.

A multidisciplinary approach can help tremendously if a network is successfully evolved. An example was a refugee woman and two children living with her brother, sister-in-law and their three children. A home visit was made by an under-five social worker, who was worried by the overcrowding. She telephoned the Homeless Persons Unit (HPU). The HPU had already refused to offer further housing as an earlier offer had been refused. By chance she was given a card with the refugee caseworker's name. That caseworker was already trying to rectify the problem with the HPU. When the three agencies worked together, the problem was quickly solved – but it happened in this case by chance. Coordination and a key worker could make a huge difference.

We would also argue that much can be done in advance so that problems do not become those of crisis management. It is useful for professionals to know the address of the local refugee agency, which is often able to signpost or point towards the issues involved, taking into account confidentiality. It is worth asking if there is a lawyer involved or a social worker and so on. A directory of local community groups is invaluable.

THE EDUCATION OF MIGRANT CHILDREN

Children's Services support provision for migrant children in schools by drawing on funds from the Vulnerable Children Grant (VCG) and the Ethnic Minority and Achievement Grant (EMAG). Migrant children are one of many groups, including ethnic minorities, 'looked after' children and students with English as a second language, who draw upon these resources. Services need to gather information about migrant pupils and at the same time avoid stigmatizing them as problems. There appears to be very little coordination between government bodies involved in the dispersal of migrant families (e.g. the Home Office) and those responsible for arranging educational provision (the DfES and Children's Services). This means that schools and teaching staff may be ill-prepared to meet their needs (Arnot and Pinson, 2005). Britain like many other countries is in a dilemma between meeting its humanitarian responsibility to provide asylum and concern over the impact, as reported in the media, of immigrant populations (Bauman, 2004) together with concerns over potential terrorist groups and racial tensions.

Schools are at the forefront of trying to resolve these tensions and provide an education for the diversity of all their pupils. Children may be provided with additional adult support and may also be assigned another child to act as a befriender. Schools are allowed to exclude pupils who have been in the country for less than two years and do not have a good grasp of English from their published examination results. This means that there is very little official data on the performance of migrant children who have to adjust to their new environment following possibly traumatic experiences, grapple with a new language, may also feel unwelcome in the new culture and can experience racial harassment.

Newly arrived migrant children are likely to respond well in schools where pupils are included in class teaching and learning and where there is a culture of praise, support groups (which avoid the need to take pupils out of lessons such as English and mathematics), there is targeted intervention, homework and breakfast clubs (Peterborough Children's Services, 2006). New arrivals may include highly motivated and achieving pupils and are unlikely to be a homogeneous group. Speaking a minority language does not imply a special educational need but requires an appropriate response from schools.

A recent unpublished survey of newly arrived bilingual children in one primary school found that children reported the following factors as helpful: being with other children who have the same first language (though some children may not want to engage in their first language), having access to dictionaries, there being written words around the school, story tapes in different languages, being shown around the school on the first day, opportunities to play and develop friendships and not too much pressure of work when they first start (Fletcher, 2006).

Key aspects in successful outcomes appear to be being good at literacy and numeracy, positive relationships with the teachers, support and strategies for managing the negative behaviour of peers, positive feedback on their progress and friendships.

ISSUES IN THE ASSESSMENT OF MIGRANT CHILDREN: A PSYCHOLOGIST'S PERSPECTIVE

Gaining an accurate picture of a pupil's past history, present circumstances, current levels of achievement and abilities can be difficult. There are many factors to take into account when assessing a young child with special educational needs whose family has recently come from another country. Meeting professionals can be an intimidating experience for parents who may be distrustful of people they see as part of the Local Authority (LA) and in a position to influence decisions regarding their family's future. Parents' anxieties can be reduced by professionals clearly explaining the precise nature of their role. A number of professionals may have been involved prior to the assessment, and a diagnosis may have been made or labels applied such as attention deficit and hyperactivity disorder, autistic spectrum disorder or oppositional defiant disorder. Signs of distress or unusual behaviour in children could be the result of previous negative experiences or signs of a family attempting to adapt to a new situation and cope with previous possibly traumatic experiences. A child who cries, has difficulty sharing toys and engaging in social interaction, uses minimal spoken language and engages in repetitive behaviour with cars and aeroplanes could be responding normally to a new situation or the behaviour could be seen by some professionals as indicating that he or she is on the autistic spectrum.

A period of assessment may be needed in the child's new setting to monitor his or her developmental progress as the child becomes more settled in school and develops social relationships with adults and his or her peer group.

Individual assessments can be seen as temporary signposts regarding the child's developmental pathway rather than as definitive points indicating his or her future educational progress. The child's responses to school and the learning environment can be influenced by a variety of factors, including culturally accepted means of children's expression, trauma-related anxiety or short-term defence mechanisms to help deal with new situations, such as learnt helplessness. Though these factors can be difficult to measure, they may be influential in children's behaviour. Professionals may also observe children's avoidance of direct eye contact and reluctance to express personal views.

Using an interpreter with the parents can enable professionals to gain some insight into the conditions of society in the previous country without engaging in excessive information gathering, which could cause the parents some distress. Families may be reluctant to put their trust in professionals and have contact with other families or neighbours. In cases where families have had negative experiences with people who share their ethnic background, they may even be reluctant to leave the familiarity of their own household or form relationships outside the family with people who can speak their first language.

Accurately identifying the nature of a child's needs when he or she has been accepted into a school takes time and care as there is likely to be a wide range of family, cultural and language issues that impinge on a child's ability and willingness to access the curriculum and develop social relationships. Schools are likely to vary in their willingness to receive migrant families, and it can be more comfortable for the child if there are similar newcomers in the school and they can access additional adult support.

IMPLICATIONS FOR PROFESSIONALS WORKING WITH MIGRANT CHILDREN

The following checklist may be helpful:

- Use interpreters but use them carefully (e.g. check the accuracy of the comments being recorded).
- Use specialized refugee agencies (local where possible) for advice, bearing in mind confidentiality.
- Promote multi-agency working.
- Make yourself aware of cultural and political backgrounds.
- Be vigilant for signs of PTSD and refer to appropriate professionals.
- Provide opportunities for talking and listening or find out where these are available locally (e.g. bilingual support services).
- Make use of training courses in working with refugees.
- Keep a list of local community groups.
- Encourage parents to come into schools (e.g. a special room could be made available).
- Provide opportunities for parents who want to learn English.
- Avoid the use of misleading labels when assessing children.

CONCLUSION

Key factors in successful outcomes for migrant children who may be 'hard to reach' include access to sympathetic schooling, being liked, an absence of racist abuse and violence as well as the ability to access the language of local communities (Fletcher, 2006). The inclusion of migrant pupils is assisted by knowledgeable professionals who have links with specialist support agencies and are accustomed to working flexibly with ambiguities and changing circumstances. No final assessment of needs is possible, and situations need frequent reviewing and updating – and the valuable input of parents and other professionals as partners in the process should never be underestimated.

TERMS IN USE

Asylum seeker: A person whose asylum claim is being processed by the Home Office, including those who may be appealing against negative decisions. Usually, asylum seekers are supported by the National Asylum Support Service (NASS), a department of the Home Office, for both accommodation and subsistence, though some asylum seekers may be accommodated by family or friends and receive subsistence only.

Refugee: A person who has been granted Indefinite Leave to Remain (ILR) in the United Kingdom by the Home Office. If they wish, they may apply for British citizenship after five years in the United Kingdom. A refugee has full rights to education, healthcare, benefits and so on as a UK citizen.

Unaccompanied minors: Children under the age of 18 who have travelled alone to the United Kingdom and claimed asylum. They remain under the care of Social Services in residential homes or foster care until 18, when they would normally be transferred to the NASS. (Exceptionally vulnerable cases may remain with Social Services.) Asylum claims will be processed on becoming 18.

Failed claimants: Asylum seekers whose claim has been refused and who have no further appeals available. Under certain circumstances they may apply for further NASS support. Social Services may take over where children are involved. Failed claimants may be deported or detained in a detention centre.

Illegal immigrants: Those who have never claimed asylum and have no documents or papers. They are not able to claim benefits or access any amenities, although emergency medical care would normally be available.

European Union (EU) members and economic migrants: Workers from the EU are subject to EU law and are able to work in this country. There are usually reciprocal benefits within the EU. People from new EU states need a year in full-time work before benefits are allowed.

REFERENCES

Arnot, M. and Pinson, H. (2005) *The Education of Asylum Seeker and Refugee Children*. Faculty of Education University of Cambridge, Cambridge.

Bauman, Z. (2004) *Wasted Lives: Modernity and its Outcasts*. Polity, Cambridge.

Coker, J., Farbey, J., Finch, N. and Stanley, A. (2004) *Asylum: A Guide to Recent Legislation*. ILPA Resource Information Service, London.

Fletcher, M. (2006) Perceptions of newly arrived bilingual children in one primary school. Tavistock Clinic, London. Unpublished MSc dissertation.

Gilmore, I. and Martin, L. (2005) Albanian hell for family the UK rejected. *The Observer* 16 October 2005, p. 24.

High Commissioner for Human Rights (1951) Convention relating to the Status of Refugees, Geneva, OHCHR. http://www.unhchr.ch/html/menu3/b/o_c_ref.htm, accessed 1 February 2007.

Information Centre about Asylum and Refugees in the UK (2004) *Media Image Community Impact*. Commissioned by the Mayor of London. www.refugeecouncil.org.uk

Kao, G. (2004) Social capital and its relevance to minority and immigrant populations. *Sociology of Education*, **77** (2), 172–175.

Kralj, L. and Goldberg, D. (2005) UK government policy and unaccompanied adolescents seeking asylum. *Child and Adolescent Mental Health*, **10** (4), 202–205.

Levenson, R. and Sharma, A. (2004) *The Health of Refugee Children: Guidelines for Paediatricians*. Royal College of Paediatricians and Child Health, London.

Melzak, S. (1999) Psychotherapeutic work with child and adolescent refugees from political violence. In: Lanyado, M. Horne, A. (eds). *The Handbook of Child and Adolescent Psychotherapy*. Routledge, London.

Pallon, A., Massey, D.S., Ceballos, M., Espinosa, K. and Spittel, M. (2001) Social capital and international migration: a test using information for family networks. *American Journal of Sociology* **106** (5), 1262–1298.

Peterborough Children's Services (2006) *Conference on developing a local authority policy on ethnic minority achievement*. Peterborough.

Refugee Council (2004). *Refugees: Renewing the Vision*. www.refugeecouncil.org.uk

Reid, J. (2004) Sometimes I feel that she is the mother and I am the child. *The British Psychological Society, Debate* **112** 14–20.

FURTHER WEB SITE RESOURCES

www.dgteaz.org.uk – Letters to parents in many different languages.

www.omnilot.com/languages/phrases – Foreign phrases in approximately 80 different languages.

www.hants.gov.uk/education/ema/advice/Icr/home – A source of information about Chinese, French, Portuguese, Turkish and Urdu languages.

www.leicester.gov.uk – Multi-cultural resources.

http://www.qca.org.uk/8476.html – Pathways to learning for new arrivals.

www.qca.org.uk – Assessing English as an additional language linked to English National Curriculum levels.

www.standards.dfes.gov.uk/primary/publications/inclusion/newarrivals/pns_incl138105new arrivals.pdf – Materials to support schools in meeting the needs of newly arrived learners of English as an additional language. Disclaimer: This information was gathered from a variety of sources in good faith and is thought to be accurate at the time of going to press.

6 A Seminar Approach to Multi-Agency Collaboration, Team-Building and Therapeutic Group Problem-Solving Where Some Attendees Might be Described as 'Hard to Reach'

MICHAEL POMERANTZ

INTRODUCTION

This chapter will tell a story about a journey that begins with a problem involving a pupil called Dan with Asperger's syndrome and associated challenging behaviour. It concludes with some suggestions for team-building and the resolution of many behavioural problems by appreciating the value of studying factors that are both inside and outside the child. It is inspired by real narratives associated with helping to understand why some people can be described as 'hard to reach'.

I would define 'hard to reach' as children, young people and particularly adults who are resistant or reluctant to participate with others for all sorts of reasons, both conscious and unconscious. There are many explanations for this phenomenon despite our good intentions. Some people are cautious or suspicious, some have felt let down in the past and are reluctant to trust others, some are defensive about being judged and some are overworked or stressed with too many demands. Some may be able to tell you why they are 'hard to reach' and others will not. We need to study this.

Many years ago, I was asked as an educational psychologist to see a boy called Dan, a secondary age pupil. He was described as having Asperger's syndrome and had a Statement of Special Educational Needs.

Dan would be a good example of a 'hard to reach' client in that he was capable of avoiding eye contact and was well versed in manipulating adults who questioned him about his behaviour. He could be evasive, argumentative, immature and withdrawn when it suited him. He was skilful at denial ('I did not do that'), minimization ('it was no big deal'), rationalization ('it is caused by my condition') and the projection of responsibility on to others ('he made me do it'). People helpers found him inaccessible,

How to Reach 'Hard to Reach' Children: Improving access, participation and outcomes. Edited by K. Pomerantz, M. Hughes and D. Thompson. Copyright © 2007 by John Wiley & Sons, Ltd.

difficult to assess and non-responsive to normal interventions. Otherwise he could be quite likeable, charming, intelligent and relatively normal when he felt comfortable and so inclined. I learned a lot from working with him. Staff were concerned about his unacceptable behaviour and the serious safety risk he posed to others within the school community. Without going into great detail, it would be fair to say that he was hurting others and generating high levels of anxiety around his school. Behind the outward behaviour was a very anxious child. I was fascinated to hear the various colourful descriptions and explanations that staff offered about the behaviour in question. Having considered the normal range of potential responses that an educational psychologist could have made, I decided to listen to what this pupil, his parents and the staff had to say and then proposed that we convene a seminar to delve deeper into the assessment and to locate some practical solutions that might be valued and put into operation.

The term 'seminar' was initially chosen carefully and was designed to overcome some of the inherent problems often associated with many traditional meetings that I was attending in a wide variety of settings, like schools, special schools, offices, clinics, homes, hospitals and so on. I suppose I had developed a slightly disappointed or pessimistic attitude towards meetings and was seeking something new and more powerful for Dan. I wanted to experiment with a different way to hear voices and to engage the creativity that is often missing in traditional school-based meetings in particular (Pomerantz and Pomerantz, 2002; Billington and Pomerantz, 2004). Some people have said that the word '*seminar*' could be considered off-putting for some, with connotations of a threatening academic exercise. I wanted the work to be serious, experimental and innovative and to avoid many of the common pitfalls associated with other meetings that I have attended. If readers can identify a better word for these alternative meetings, please feel free to use it. It is not the activity label that is crucial but the inherent process.

There are many different reasons why traditional school-based meetings are convened. One is the annual review (AR) for a statemented pupil with special needs and another is the case conference convened when a child is close to exclusion. I have attended ARs that have been empowering, enlightening and productive for all parties. However, some of these AR meetings are overly scripted and most of the precious time is underutilized, listening to various people rehearsing their prepared reports. While one person is speaking, others are shuffling their papers in preparation for their turn to speak. I sometimes wonder how much listening occurs. Complicated questions seem to be out of order. There is potential and justification here to support someone deciding to become 'hard to reach'. Some cynics have been prone to speculate that some meetings are convened to meet other needs like loneliness, boredom or helplessness. Sometimes the convener books the meeting specifically because he or she is stuck and hopes a meeting will sort out the problem. Sometimes it works and sometimes it doesn't.

One gets the feeling that the AR ritual is usually designed to persuade the parents to endorse all the good work that is occurring for their child with little opportunity from the start for anyone to raise issues that are problematic, time-consuming or confrontational. This is how strong emotions can be contained. Some parents find this unhelpful when the allocated time is running out and they have not really been asked at the start whether there is anything problematic that they want addressing. My tendency is to ask that this potential agenda-generating question be addressed at the beginning so that parental voices, and hopefully the child's, are actually heard. I suppose I am seeking some assurance that there will be time for more dialogue and less reporting. Sometimes this is effective and sometimes it is resisted as it breaks the tradition.

MEETINGS

Lots of us are quite familiar with the architecture and the landscape of the social event we call 'meetings'. Some meetings work and others do not for a variety of reasons, many of which are unexplored. It is possible for some attendees to feel that the meeting achieved its aims while others would doubt this. There is rarely an opportunity to process a meeting or to conduct a post-mortem on how attendees actually felt about the event. Most of these meetings are not evaluated. I can recall attending a number of child-protection conferences where a follow-up event might have been therapeutic and might have allowed for some repairing of relationships when conflicts arose. There is no doubt that with the evolution of Children's Services there will be more invitations to attend meetings, which I greet with mixed feelings. Applied psychology can offer insights into the processes underlying meetings. The initial meeting about Dan was the original stimulus for writing this chapter.

Many meetings are structured with invitations, seating patterns (obvious or subtle), scripts (explicit or implicit), tasks to complete, agendas (hidden or explicit), traditions, specified roles like the chairperson and the minute taker, timetables, deadlines and so on. These can help or hinder the process. Occasionally, refreshments are offered but this is certainly not the norm, nor are comfort breaks unless the meeting is very long. Some more experienced people appear to have a better understanding of what is happening than others. Some attendees arrive late and some leave early. Some send in apologies that may or may not make a significant difference to the outcomes of the meeting. I worry about those who look uncomfortable from the start (potentially 'hard to reach') and are not given enough support to believe they are really a valued part of the process. They sometimes look as if there is a game in operation and they are struggling to make sense of it.

Productive meetings tend to make all attendees feel welcomed, valued and heard. They are safe, supportive, reflective, efficient, open to new ideas and engage the talents and the motivation of the participants. They tend to be purposeful, protected with boundaries and safeguards, achieve targets, address individuals and systems, aim for the inclusion and participation of those attending the meeting, attempt to reach the 'hard to reach', overcome barriers, add value, utilize appropriate language and meet human needs. They can contain and address strong emotions competently and sensitively. More people get a fair share of contributing. They focus upon the generation of knowledge. They support agreed and shared values about how we can best work together, which is a restorative justice principle. In the meeting about Dan, many of these features were present.

Less productive meetings can be boring, unsafe, confusing, non-supportive, competitive, closed to new ideas, confrontational, unpredictable or too predictable, inefficient and relatively unsuccessful. Some associate this with bureaucracy. They can involve time-wasting and work-avoidance; they can lack motivation and can perpetuate power and control imbalances that fail to harness the gifts and the talents of all those in the room. They tend to focus on knowledge dissemination or briefings rather than knowledge construction. The voice of the child is less likely to be heard. People leave some meetings feeling they have not been heard, valued or acknowledged. In some cases it appears as if the script and the subsequent activity was written previously and the result is an empty ritual that accomplishes little, although someone may have completed a tidy paper document or form as one outcome or performance indicator. Some meetings simply cannot contain strong emotions and so they are suppressed or simply ignored. A few participants tend to dominate the discussion. Some parents have complained that the person in the chair tended to speak too quickly and with a raised voice. This might make a parent feel 'hard to reach'. Some women have noted a tendency for men in suits to dominate these discussions, although this is not always the case. I was trying to avoid all this with Dan's parents.

NEW MEETINGS OR SEMINARS

Having asked attendees lots of questions about how meetings work and what steps could be taken to make meetings more productive and efficient, I elected to try to sell the idea of convening a seminar for the benefit of helping Dan. This had not been a regular part of the service that we had been offering schools and families. I wanted the parents to feel heard and thought that by introducing the notion of a seminar with a large chart at the front we might begin with a fresh start and a chance of achieving a better resolution. I wanted the parents to feel prepared and not intimidated by confronting a group of professionals with the unspoken assumption that collectively they alone held the archived expertise we needed to understand their Dan's serious difficulty in coping with the school environment.

Invitations were extended to several staff (including the year head, the special needs coordinator, the form tutor and a teaching assistant), the parents, the speech and language therapist, the community paediatrician, the social worker and the clinical psychologist. I would have liked for Dan to join us but on this particular occasion the majority of the attendees had deemed this to be inappropriate. This meeting took place many years ago. It is encouraging to note that nowadays families and school staff feel much more confident including rather than excluding pupils from gatherings like this. Normally, we should be advocating the gains to be achieved by having the pupil present for all or most of the meeting. I am always interested in the arguments offered as to why a pupil should not be invited and the subsequent debate amongst attendees about the merits of the arguments. I would feel most uncomfortable if the matter was not discussed, as still happens occasionally.

We met in a comfortable room sitting in a semicircle with a chart for about 90 minutes. Someone mentioned that it felt like 'being back in school again'. After introductions I explained that it might be helpful for each participant to offer their own perspective on a plausible explanation that would account for Dan's challenging behaviour. Predictably, there was considerable variation, but I recall something like the list that follows. The actual spoken responses are no longer available but this list attempts to convey something of the flavour of the contributions offered on this occasion. Everyone had an opportunity to present as many explanations as they could generate. No one chose to opt out of this exercise. They volunteered that Dan's behaviour:

- is a characteristic of Asperger's syndrome;
- is imitative of a known or unknown role model;
- occurs because something is reinforcing or rewarding it;
- occurs because something is precipitating or stimulating it;
- is triggered by negative thoughts or feelings;
- is simply an expression of his free will and his creative personality;
- is caused by a medical or a psychiatric condition;
- has been exaggerated and blown out of proportion;
- is caused and sustained by the peer group perhaps unconsciously;
- is caused by his simply going through a developmental phase;
- is a non-verbal language problem that needs to be interpreted;
- must be comprehended as occurring within a much wider social context;
- is a political gesture nested within a host culture;
- is a learned habit that could be unlearned;
- is caused by the curriculum on offer at school and how it is taught;
- is caused by his lack of ability (social intelligence);
- is caused by an undiagnosed special educational need;
- is caused by an inappropriate school placement;
- is due to a lack of impulse control;
- is due to a lack of learned positive values;
- is due to a deficit in moral tuition;
- is symptomatic of a family problem;
- is symptomatic of a power struggle.

It is important to stipulate here that many attendees would have felt that they could have spoken on behalf of Dan, but since he was not present we do not have his authoritative account or explanation to add to the list. We simply have a series of contributions by those made either for themselves or on his behalf.

I then asked the group to identify if there was anything problematic about our having produced such an imaginative and lengthy list within the seminar. They all quickly agreed that there were too many explanations and that a lack of agreement on a way forward would create big problems. They could see that some of the behaviours might well be associated with inconsistent responses given by the adults in the room and other staff not present. They agreed that each explanation could well be associated with a different intervention or a treatment programme and that it would be best to agree on one consistent course of action even if there were doubts or hesitations as to whose perspective was the best.

ATTRIBUTION

One of the basic questions that can attract the attention of many traditional meeting attendees is the presumed location of the cause of the behavioural problem. There is the perennial debate about whether that cause (if it can be found) is intrinsic to the child or extrinsic or a combination of both internal and external factors. This tension can promote a culture of unhelpful blaming (expressed or hidden) with some individuals forming up on either side of an unseen line. Often these differences of opinion are not made publicly explicit within meetings but are salient in the minds of the attendees. They can guide thinking. Some want to plant responsibility within the home rather than the school setting and look to alleged handling difficulties, inconsistency, overprotection, lack of care and so on.

Those who are attracted to 'within child' explanations often seek a medical diagnosis that would prove that the child has brought a personal problem or deficit into the school. That is why the child or the family may be 'hard to reach'. The child and the family might be tempted to put up defences, become awkward, resist help, be unforthcoming, be negative, feel persecuted, stigmatized or blamed, seek a school change, file a complaint and miss appointments or arrive late.

Those who are attracted to 'outside the child' explanations are normally less interested in a 'within child' diagnosis and feel that we should look elsewhere for a practical cause and a resolution to be identified. They might suggest that a scrutiny of the school setting, the curriculum, the individual educational programme (IEP), the staff, the peer group, bullying, scapegoating, prejudice, racism, lack of appropriate staff training, the school host culture, the pastoral system, the disciplinary system, the support services, the senior management team and the whole socio-emotional community environment might hold the clues that explain or make sense of challenging behaviour. Unless this perspective is adopted, the child and the parents might find some of the school staff and other professionals 'hard to reach' in that they want the school staff to look more broadly and resent the implication that the problem lies within the child. To avoid appearing 'hard to reach', staff need to be open to all possibilities.

Some professionals attending meetings express a preference for an agenda that primarily addresses solutions and are less interested in laborious historical journeys seeking causes which may prove unsuccessful in contributing to change. They would propose another effective way to convene a different type of meeting but this will not be elaborated upon here.

TEAMWORK

The main outcome of this particular seminar many years ago was the perceived need to establish a sense of substantial teamwork in the best interest of the child. The attendees thought this was even more important given Dan's diagnosis of having Asperger's syndrome, where a consistent approach would be desirable. By the end of the seminar participants felt empowered, energized and less inclined to think of one another as 'hard to reach', which had been a potential cause of concern at the outset. They even thought the pupil might become less 'hard to reach', although this was not a term that would have been used at the time.

The teamwork was created and it lasted. The adults agreed on a shared course of action that carried a strong measure of endorsement despite competing theoretical explanations or paradigms to account for the challenging behaviour. All the adults agreed to a protocol or a social contract in which there was shared creation, essential ownership and confidence. No one went away feeling his or her voice had gone unheard. Within the seminar we examined each perspective and especially the intervention implications and practicalities. Some hypothetical causes or explanations simply did not lend themselves to workable ingredients within the final plan. Dan managed to navigate successfully throughout his secondary education without being permanently excluded. Everyone was able to take some measure of credit for the team and what it accomplished. The actual agreed programme was a compassionate synthesis that had behavioural and non-behavioural components. The staff and parents agreed to take steps to remove or minimize aversive antecedents or stimuli while setting clear limits and consequences for Dan's actions at school. There was an emphasis on increasing staff training about Asperger's syndrome and maintaining very positive home-to-school communication.

The secret that contributed to the success of the seminar was the format, the ground rules and spoken language encouraging full participation, the spontaneity witnessed within the room, the respect demonstrated and the use of questions posed by myself, and especially by others, rather than a more traditional meeting script that marginalized questions and creativity. The seminar had the characteristics of an academic inquiry without anyone feeling that his or her contribution was peripheral. It addressed the issues that can create and sustain the 'hard to reach' phenomenon and took a course of action that minimized this happening. When social relationships are threatened within a meeting, this needs to be addressed so everyone feels safe, welcome and valued. We ignore this at our peril.

AUTISTIC SPECTRUM DISORDER SEMINARS THAT ARE TAKING PLACE NOW

Since that single seminar took place many years ago, we have subsequently experimented with the seminar format in several other schools and settings, including homes. Some seminars have been convened for pupils with others types of problems as this intervention is not restricted to one particular type of difficulty. The formula for the seminars has undergone many modifications and can be flexibly applied to a wide range of contexts. The work has been informed by research, participants, students and colleagues, who have all contributed to the bank of questions that stimulate and motivate the seminars. Some will be demonstrated below. You would not have to identify this as a seminar per se in your setting especially if you can find a better or more useful word to describe the activity.

In essence, the seminar is simply a place to convene a special group conversation. It assumes that the facilitator is confident, assertive and familiar with group dynamics and some of the games that people like to play in groups. The facilitator needs to engage attendees to co-create a small community that values listening to one another, practises fair play, shows respect and tolerance, promotes democracy, safety and care and demonstrates empathy, warmth and genuiness, which are Rogerian ideals (Rogers, 2003, 2004). Within this unique context, social justice and knowledge-generation can thrive as participants can begin to trust one another and form a team with some aspirations. Under these conditions the 'hard to reach' phenomenon is less likely to be seen. More people tend to feel genuinely included.

In some instances participants have requested a second, or even third, follow-up seminar. One school seminar actually met on 10 different occasions over the course of an academic year for one child with a core group and a few occasional attendees. This was their choice and I never felt we were wasting time. These sessions lasted between one and two hours and were held after school. Time is precious and we cannot afford to waste it. Anyone attempting to sell and convene a seminar will have to convince participants that it is a good use of time. In the first instance it could be treated as an experiment. Evaluation is always recommended especially if the facilitator wants to improve local practice.

To convey some of the flavour of how seminars can actually work and the essential language that is employed, I offer below something of an introduction or an invitation that could be distributed to people thinking of either convening or simply attending a seminar. This would give potential participants some idea of what might happen, but remember that the seminar questions should be specific to the focus child and problem. Someone needs to do logistical planning and prepare the questions and take initial responsibility.

INVITATION TO THE SEMINAR

Let us imagine that a hypothetical, secondary-aged, statemented pupil with Asperger's syndrome called Billy is mentioned as someone creating difficulties, as often happens, and staff are requesting further assessment and recommendations for improving his conduct at school. Perhaps he is not the only pupil presenting with behavioural difficulties. He is definitely 'hard to reach' and is the focus of numerous conversations involving the school's pastoral team and the family, but these are not resulting in substantial new thinking and planning thus far.

He is most challenging and his acting-out behaviours (spitting, kicking, throwing, tripping, hitting, running off, hiding, destroying, etc.) pose a serious health and safety risk to other pupils and himself. His current school placement could be considered risky, although I am confident that we could all work together to improve the situation. Thus far, I am most impressed by all that the staff are doing under difficult circumstances and by the professional way that teachers have embraced the preliminary questions that I have asked. Normally, I start to compose some messages to those who would attend the seminar. What follows conveys some of that thinking. I have written and circulated messages containing these same or similar suggestions to potential attendees as a way to focus attention, recruit participation, facilitate preparation and provide a menu of possibilities so that when we do meet everyone has a good idea of what we might address and what we might actually accomplish. Here is a script to demonstrate the process. It represents what I might say or write to potential professional attendees, which would be modified in a version for parents or carers:

> My inclination at this stage is that we begin to meet together and start a collaborative group process designed to inform our practice with Billy. There are many agencies involved and some positive initial signs of teamwork are in evidence. We may need a series of seminars or workshops to help us gain a better grasp of Billy's behaviour, to build upon the evolving teamwork, to arrange some negotiated professional development, to examine problem identity, interpretation and ownership and to look at the problematic behaviour from some behavioural and non-behavioural perspectives. By doing this we ought to increase both the range and the depth of our collective understanding as a measurable outcome of group consultation. We would also look at how much genuine compliance we can achieve with a team effort at helping Billy.

> I hope that soon we can launch our next gathering. I have tried this seminar approach in several schools and would value any contribution that you and others can make both to the agenda and the processes whereby we construct some better plans to address Billy's special educational needs. I intend to do some further research myself and to consult with the family and colleagues before we meet. We have some reference and training materials available that may be of use before the seminar. [Examples of what might be useful for attenders are listed at the end of this chapter under further reading.]

> Preparation is a personal matter and individual needs and motivation vary, but in my experience anything we can do to reduce the knowledge gap and share information amongst participants before the seminar will increase the probability of a successful outcome. When parents arrive with their considerable historical perspective, they may sometimes feel initially intimidated by the presence of professionals each arriving with briefcases, qualifications and perhaps a reputation. That is where background preparation can be facilitative. One of my initial tasks is to make sure that participants feel prepared and 'warmed up'. Some value conversation more than paper documents and really appreciate an opportunity to talk about their feelings and needs outside the seminar. I always tend to look at what attendees bring into the room and how they greet one another. Some participants find parents arriving with books or papers slightly discomforting as if the parents are taking on a superior or defended role. I see this as preparation and an asset.

I like to ask myself: 'What can I do make certain that this particular meeting is going to be successful?' There is normally an abundance of talent, insight and energy within any group. The trick is to make certain that it blossoms.

The sorts of issues (a sample) that I hope all of us can address are listed below. These can be used like a menu by staff and the parents as advance organizers for future deliberations. I hope they are reasonably self-explanatory. They have been developed for use within similar staff training and seminar sessions in other schools over the past 10 years. Each question has a specific purpose and can be read within the 'hard to reach' framework. Normally, I tend to modify the construction of this list with vocabulary, the number of questions and question length to suit all the participants. This is intended to present something that is accessible and useful. Occasionally, the questions might be simply presented orally if the parents or the pupil would find the language particularly challenging. These questions are designed to highlight the expertise that Billy and his parents can bring into the seminar and to redress any appearance of a power imbalance.

Seminar Questions Part I: Exploring the context in which the behaviour takes place

INTRODUCTION

What are the agenda issues that meeting attendees want us to address? Which of the questions listed below are judged to be the priorities for attendees? How can Billy participate in some or all of the seminar? How could we justify excluding him? How could we best prepare him for his attendance? Does he want or need an advocate?

ASSESSMENT OF BEHAVIOUR QUESTIONS

What specific behaviours are of concern today?
What happens when Billy is having a really bad day at school?
What happens when Billy is having a really good day at school?
Why does Billy's behaviour vary over time and between adults?
Do the behaviour patterns in evidence shed any new light on our beliefs?
Are there any possible antecedent events or triggers that we have failed to assess as yet?
Is the current behavioural protocol or individual educational programme (IEP) proving effective? Has everyone present got a copy and have they read it? Who compiled it? Is everyone confident in using it?
Can we tighten up the communication between home and school so as to take advantage of behavioural strategies that the parents or carers have discovered to work in the past year?

Are we in full agreement with what we are expecting of Billy academically and socially?

Should we expect more or less and within what specific context or target?

Can we modify or differentiate the National Curriculum further?

How does Billy explain his behaviour?

Are staff prioritizing Billy's behaviours as:

- irritating actions but we can live with them?
- actions that the team can live with but need urgent attention?
- actions that must be addressed and resolved first?

What is the function of his behaviour at present? What does Billy gain by it for himself?

What acceptable or alternative behaviours can meet this function or need?

Can we help him to unlearn some of his anti-social behaviour?

Do we understand his avoidance of requests or demands and do we always respond with a common and consistent agreed plan?

Can we expand the repertoire of rewards currently employed to reinforce positive behaviour at school? Are we relying mostly on external rewards or does Billy reward himself intrinsically?

Can we try to resolve his conflicts with staff without a winner and a loser?

TEAM-BUILDING AND ROLES QUESTIONS

What is the role and the lists of tasks for each adult working with Billy?

- How and when is each adult involved?
- Is there a key worker?
- Who is the key worker?
- How do team members communicate in a difficult situation?
- What happens if the key worker or regular worker is not present?

What is the exact composition of the day-to-day team looking after Billy?

- How often do they meet and what is the structure of their meeting?
- Do the parents understand the training that staff have?

How will the parents be involved with these meetings?

- Is the current system of school-based record-keeping informing our practice?
- Is there an agreed strategy for recording behaviour positively?

Does the paper trail help us to improve our practice with Billy?

Are the staff strategies working when Billy shuts down and refuses to comply?

- Are they consistent?

Are all staff following the agreed behavioural protocol or contract?

- Is there an agreement amongst all staff as to who is in charge of a situation?
- How would that person ask for help?
- When should other staff intervene?
- How will other staff react to Billy?
- What actions will they take?
- How is all this recorded?
- Who reads the records?
- Are they accurate?
- Are they helpful?

ENVIRONMENTAL QUESTIONS

Have we taken into consideration sensory aspects of the environment that may upset Billy, such as visual stimuli, sounds, tone of voice, glare, allergies, temperature, touch, fabrics, seating arrangements, physical space, smells and so on?
Have we considered and established his unique position in the classroom?
Are strategies being used consistently and by all staff?
Are the adults reacting in a positive and a calm manner to whatever the behaviour is?
Is anyone not surprised or shocked by Billy's behaviour?
Do all adults, such as visiting speakers or supply staff, understand Billy's difficulties and his programme?
Does Billy have an alternative place to be when he is stressed?
What does Billy need to work at his best? Are these needs met?
Are there one or two staff who are particularly struggling with Billy?
Does Billy react to one member of staff and why? Can we build on this?

STAFF DEVELOPMENT QUESTIONS

Is it Billy who has to change or is it the adults who have to adapt the environment, the language and the strategies to change the situation so that Billy can initially succeed?
Have we taken into account all of Billy's communication strengths and difficulties both in relation to his understanding and use of language but also adults' use of language with him? This should include his preferences.
Is it useful to consider using social stories and comic strip conversations?

Within the seminar, I hope we can widen our approach beyond the behavioural strategies that focus so much on antecedents and the consequences like rewards, ignoring and sanctions. There are a collection of other psychologies that might inspire us to look in other directions and to ask other questions, as seen below. We must be vigilant in that there are many adults who could all attempt to represent Billy's best interests but we are somewhat disadvantaged in that Billy himself may not be a full participant in the processes that we plan to use. Any steps that can be taken to maximize our listening to whatever he is trying to communicate ought to help us all. Asking Billy what leads up to difficulties and what helps should be useful.

Seminar Questions Part II: Exploring less obvious solutions

NON-BEHAVIOURAL PARADIGM QUESTIONS

What do we know of how Billy thinks and feels? Can we empathize with his position?
How adequately do we assess his self-esteem?
What is the role of fear and anxiety reduction in understanding his behaviour?
Does he have unmet needs that we could help to fulfil?
Can we teach him new roles or acts to play when faced with whatever he finds challenging?
Is there any way to better engage the social friendship resources of his peers at school so he feels more included and valued and acquires more support and resilience?
Are we in full agreement about the use of restraint or physical contact?
Should Billy have any special rules or privileges not applicable to his peers?
How would we explain these to other pupils who might say 'it's not fair'?
Do we have any concerns that Billy may be bullied at school?
What skills do his peers have in responding to his behaviour and in keeping themselves safe?
How is Billy's identity (or his self-image) constructed for him by the adults and by himself?

LANGUAGE QUESTIONS

Do the staff have an agreed language or phrasing of instructions to use when Billy is stressed? (Where the language is kept simple and minimal.)
Are all adults using precise, small-step instructions and are they being consistent?
Is Billy always being given adequate time to process the language?
If the instruction is repeated, is the wording the same?
Are the words we use with Billy supported by visual clues?
Do we fully understand his intentions and his feelings?

Are we in full agreement about the social interpretation of his gestures, facial expressions and non-verbal behaviours and his efforts to express himself? Do we fully appreciate his meanings, however expressed? To what do we attribute his behaviour?

Do we feel that Billy would appreciate how we are addressing and answering these questions?

Have the school's drama staff been consulted about our questions and, if so, do they have any suggestions to offer? (I often find that drama teachers have a great deal of experience to contribute in giving pupils opportunities to rehearse new behaviours in a safe setting.)

EVERY CHILD MATTERS, OR THE FIVE OUTCOMES QUESTIONS

Will what we are proposing help to keep Billy healthy?
Will our plans ensure that Billy will stay safe?
Will Billy be able to enjoy himself and to achieve both at school and in the community?
Will Billy now be more likely to make a positive contribution?
In the end will Billy achieve economic well-being?

(Department for Education and Skills, 2003)

EVALUATION QUESTIONS

How will we know that the planned improvements are having their intended effect?
How can we improve the staff-support structures that are in place so that everyone feels they are working in an emotionally healthy environment?
Have we assembled the appropriate levels of support, resources, training and supervision?
Do all stakeholders feel they have a part to play in this programme for Billy?
Do all staff feel valued and respected?

It would be reasonable to conclude that the above list of questions would be well beyond the appetite of most people but remember that this is only a preparatory menu of possibilities to give the seminar a vision. It is certainly more comprehensive than the possibilities on offer during most traditional school-based meetings. We normally begin seminars with introductions and then co-construct the agenda, which specifically targets perhaps half a dozen of these questions. We would include additional contributions from participants that were not on the pre-circulated menu. Ideally, there would be an owner or presenter attached to each question. If all these questions are addressed and answered, we might well find that no one is deemed to be 'hard to reach'. The seminar would close with an evaluation.

CONCLUSION

The seminar approach described in this chapter represents a means of reaching the 'hard to reach' and a means of prevention. In communicating with seminar attendees I have been asking further questions about the 'hard to reach' construct, and predictably they have generously offered a rich description of personal reactions. Without a doubt they feel it is better to prevent someone becoming 'hard to reach' than to attempt to cure or repair the problem once it is hatched and matures. To minimize the chances of producing a 'hard to reach' person, they would be inclined to recommend the following suggestions to those facilitating or simply attending a seminar:

- Attend to the arrival and the welcome so as to make everyone feel comfortable and establish rapport. Having to wait isolated for more than a few moments upon arrival can be daunting and communicates a strong message about who is valued. Have you found a quiet room that is appropriate for what you want the seminar to accomplish? Will you be interrupted? How will you warm up the group? Does anyone have special needs and, if so, how will these be addressed?
- Consider the seminar language and the vocabulary to minimize miscommunication. This is essential. Avoid creating barriers, social and status divisions, a climate of negativity, pessimism, helplessness, mistrust and confusion. You do not want anyone to feel outclassed by the process or the people in the room. The most brilliant insights and contributions often come from the least likely people in the room. When someone who is normally quiet and inarticulate plucks up the courage to speak out, this should be treated as a blessing rather than a threat to the group. Listen to what is behind that voice.
- Attend to what is not being said within the seminar.
- Have you considered the effect a multicultural make-up to the seminar will have on the language you plan to use?
- Think about who receives an invitation, who is consulted about the invitation list and the timing and venue decisions. Are the timing and the venue more convenient for some than others? Be flexible. Set reasonable time boundaries and maintain them. A clock helps. A time or process manager can help.
- Take steps to ensure that the seminar is truly multi-agency in scope with a conspicuous 'joined-up' public impression.
- Ask everyone to contribute to the ground rules for the seminar.
- Acknowledge that some participants may well arrive with unfinished business or baggage from when they were pupils in school. They may have been frightened about school or challenging with school themselves. They may have been in a dispute with someone else in the room. You may know this or you may not.

Someone might have been previously excluded from school. We are currently generating a bumper crop of parents with this legacy.

- Plan to attend to the different emotional needs of seminar participants knowing that how someone feels may not be immediately apparent. Some may arrive feeling frightened, angry, needy, depressed, entrenched, unmotivated or anxious. Alternatively, they may be dependent, threatened, resentful, patronized, competitive, lost, pessimistic, controlling or manipulative for reasons that might not be readily apparent.

- Avoid appearing judgemental yourself and attempt to discourage it in others as it can seriously damage the fabric of the session. I recall a friend who once told me that every time he greeted a certain colleague at work he was confronted with a facial expression suggesting he had something on the sole of his shoe. I knew his colleague and could appreciate exactly how he felt. His colleague would have had no idea that she communicated this impression frequently. This is a story I have always wanted to tell. Apologies if it appears judgemental.

- Never forget the importance of power, which is expressed either subtly or blatantly. Parents or carers often arrive expecting an 'us and them' situation based upon previous meetings outside your control. They may well be anticipating blame or projected responsibility for their child.

- Adopt a position of neutrality for attendees to feel safe and to believe that someone is in charge. A seminar is not a leaderless activity drifting through a vague agenda. Participants have a right to know that there are negotiated boundaries and that someone is watching out for boundary violations like overextending the finish time or allowing someone to monopolize the discussion. It is also definitely not a private club that the parents or carers are allowed to visit.

- Establish and maintain a respectful host culture that is conducive to listening and problem-solving. People should not be punished for getting it wrong within the seminar. The group needs to feel some collective ownership of the process.

- Trust your intuition and the notion that the collective expertise contained within the group ought to find some solutions to problems that surfaced at the beginning of the seminar.

- Construct knowledge rather than just disseminate it, and give due credit.

- Consider the research potential within the group and the value of work done outside the session and perhaps arrange to meet again if anyone believes this to be desirable.

- Give the group permission to experiment and try new strategies so as to gain the evidence necessary to support or refute whatever hypotheses the seminar constructs.

- Be bold. Blame systems rather than people. Be restorative and fair.

- Finally, celebrate effective collaboration and accept the fact that you are expendable and even redundant over time. Someone else could convene and chair the next seminar with the next child's problem. This should effect an appropriate closure.

- Can you still now identify someone who is 'hard to reach'?

Finally, I would like to emphasize that colleagues who have been using this approach have stressed that these procedures are actually applicable to a wide range of problematic behaviour within schools and the community. They have read earlier versions of this work and their editorial suggestions have been implemented over the past two years. Their comments and critiques have also been studied in compiling the version that you are reading. I owe them a large debt of gratitude.

REFERENCES

Billington, T. and Pomerantz, M. (2004) *Children at the Margins: Supporting Children, Supporting Schools.* Trentham Books, Stoke on Trent.
Department for Education and Skills (2003) *Every Child Matters.* London, The Stationery Office.
Pomerantz, M. and Pomerantz, K.A. (2002) *Listening to Able Underachievers.* David Fulton Publishers, London.
Rogers, C. (2003) *Client Centred Therapy: Its Current Practice, Implications and Theory.* Constable and Robinson, London.
Rogers, C. (2004) *On Becoming a Person.* Constable and Robinson, London.

FURTHER READING

Attwood, T. (1998) *Asperger's Syndrome: A Guide for Parents and Professionals.* Jessica Kingsley Publishers, Ltd, London.
Attwood, T. www.tonyattwood.com/
Baron-Cohen, S. www.jkp.com/mindreading/
Essex County Council (2000) *Introducing Real People: Understanding Asperger Syndrome.* (This is a videotape with pupils talking to the camera.) Copies can be purchased from Essex County Council Learning Services, Information and Publications, PO Box 47, Chelmsford. CM2 6WN; ISBN: 1 84194 013 5.
Haddon, M. (2004) *The Curious Incident of the Dog in the Night-Time.* Vintage, London.
Holliday, L. (ed) (2003) *Asperger Syndrome in Adolescence: Living with the Ups, the Downs and Things in Between.* Jessica Kingsley Publishers, Ltd, London.
Ives, M. (1999) *What Is Asperger Syndrome, and How Will It Affect Me?* Autism Asperger Pub Co, Toronto.
Jackson, L. (2002) *Freaks, Geeks & Asperger Syndrome: A User Guide to Adolescence.* London, Jessica Kingsley Publishers, Ltd.
Sainsbury, C. (2000) *Martian in the Playground: Understanding the Schoolchild with Asperger's Syndrome.* Lucky Duck Publishing Ltd, Bristol.
Welton, J. (2003) *Can I Tell You About Asperger Syndrome?: A Guide for Friends and Family.* Jessica Kingsley Publishers, Ltd, London.

7 Reaching Pupils on the Autistic Spectrum: Parents' Experiences, Provision and 'Professional Reachability'

BRIAN WILLIS

INTRODUCTION

This chapter explores parent experience of bringing up a child with autism, through both individual accounts of mothers and parent support groups. This group of children is notably 'hard to reach', hard to understand and hard to include. The chapter is based on an evaluative research study and considers the impact of professionals in all agencies on parents and pupils, where autistic spectrum disorder is the primary need. This term is used to include pupils with more severe learning difficulties and autism, as well as those with greater cognitive strengths in mainstream settings. An interpretative approach is adopted in making sense of the experience of six mothers. Elements of action research methods are used, where the views and concerns expressed by parent support groups, which included fathers, were taken forward to a multidisciplinary Local Authority (LA) policy group, which led to the setting up of a joint parent professional group. Political and provision tensions and dilemmas are highlighted in this discussion.

The introductory chapter has emphasized the *Every Child Matters* and *Children Act* agendas, where multi-agency work and 'hard cases' are highlighted. Exclusion is common for pupils with autism, and Barnard, Prior and Potter (2000), in a National Autistic Society publication, suggest that mainstream pupils with autism are 20 times more likely to be excluded than their peers. Children with autism are also more likely to end up in a special school, disproportionately more than any other child with a disability or special educational need (Barnard, Prior and Potter, 2000). Budgetary expense for LAs arising from pupils with autism is considerable, with many extremely expensive out-of-area placements being sought. The introductory chapter also mentioned schools working together in line with *Removing Barriers to Achievement* (Department for Education and Skills, 2004), to improve practice for this group and the need for services to be suited to families, not

How to Reach 'Hard to Reach' Children: Improving access, participation and outcomes. Edited by K. Pomerantz, M. Hughes and D. Thompson. Copyright © 2007 by John Wiley & Sons, Ltd.

organizations. This chapter will extend dialogue on these themes for this specific vulnerable group.

We will also consider how the interpreted experience and voice of mothers represent the child, better ways of working with this vulnerable group, mental health, coping and protective themes, and whether parents experience a mutual reaching out with professionals and how this might be developed. The study has used qualitative research methods, both interpretative and critical, which have enabled careful listening to the parents of this group. Many current service evaluation methods lack depth in their analysis and do not readily consider factors such as individual feelings and thoughts, as well as resistance operating in organizations.

The overarching research question of the study was 'How can parents' experiences of bringing up a child with autism inform provision?' Attempts were made to derive policy implications from the research work and link tentative theory with desired good practice. The main method used involved semi-structured interviews with six mothers, where individual accounts were combined into a joint account using Interpretative Phenomenological Analysis (IPA). Reid, Flowers and Larkin (2005) stress that the 'increasing confidence in IPA is reflected in the accelerated rise in published studies across a wide range of psychological inquiry' (p. 23). Briefly, IPA aims to explore the research participant's experience from his or her perspective, yet recognizes that such an exploration must necessarily implicate the researcher's own view of the world, as well as the nature of the interaction between the researcher and the participant.

Parent-involving action research approaches were also used, through initial focus groups, to consider research and interview questions and embed the study in a local context, to enhance quality, by providing purposive and political elements. Ideally, according to Carr and Kemmis (1986), action research essentially involves a self-reflective spiral of cycles of planning, acting, observing and reflecting. The study had elements of this desired approach and longer-term use of such approaches is required.

The study also attempted to adopt Wolfendale's (1999) Code of Conduct for Cooperative Research with parents, where the main elements of the partnership model are rights and entitlement, equality, reciprocity and empowerment. Partnership also extended to my LA, which supported the project in such a way that implications were drawn from the enhanced understanding and experiential essence that were developed from listening to parents.

POWER, DISCOURSE AND PARENT SUPPORT GROUPS

Billig *et al.* (1988) describe how teaching, equality and authority dilemmas are prominent in the field of education. With regard to the field of autism, issues and dilemmas around experts and non-egalitarian roles and categorization are particularly pertinent and are likely to feature in discussions with parents. Discourses and dilemmas around pathologization have been considered, as well as social power relations in a partnership context.

Burman *et al.* (1996) describe how psychology functions to determine knowledge in shaping and governing our lives and hence to maintain current institutional structures of inequality. Psychology can function to create and preserve inequalities through gate-keeping, labelling and categorization activities. Research also needs to recognize the possibility of dislocating institutional boundaries through resistance to categorization and institutional definitions. Billington (1996) argues that psychology has adopted a medicalized, symptom-definition approach that relates to the allocation and distribution of resources and confirms pathology in individual children.

Thus, mothers' accounts and parent support group discourse were interpreted with recognition of these methods. The psychoanalytic approach of Hollway and Jefferson (2000) provides a useful background for understanding mothers' experience and parent group discourse. Many of the Hollway and Jefferson principles of interviewing were adopted, such as encouraging mothers to tell their story, following their lead and retaining the structure of the interview questions in a less intrusive way. Interviewees are often guarded, anxious or defensive and possibly misleading in what they say, and such techniques assist with producing more open and meaningful accounts.

Thus, while an interpretative methodology was used to make sense of parent experiences, critical and reflexive approaches were used that recognized the research context, individual interviewee background and attempted to take forward issues and concerns arising at a provision, policy and political level. Furthermore, individual parents were given the opportunity to develop the individual interview transcripts and combined interpretative account and agree content.

Thus, I interacted with parent groups, listened to their concerns and helped to set up a parent professional group to address these concerns. This more critical aspect of the research is described later and, while not intended to be a major part of the enquiry, it emerged as a necessary, natural, moral and ethical component when doing research in a real LA context as a practising professional.

THE STUDY

PARTICIPANTS

The children had a wide age range and attended mainstream and special schools in Samsara LA. I will later draw on text from the individual interviews; some basic details are provided in Table 7.1 .

RESEARCH QUESTIONS

Stemming from the overarching research question given above, the main component research questions were as follows:

- How did mothers make sense of their experiences of bringing up a child with autism?
- What were the life impacts of these experiences on mothers and their families?

Table 7.1. Study participants

Mother	Child(ren)	Child's age	Siblings	School
Carol	Linda	15	Brother 13	Mainstream Secondary
Donna	James	6	Brother 19 and Sister 17	Special School
Louise	Simon and Alan	12 and 10		Special School
Mary	Terry	5	Sister 11	Local Infants and Special School dual placement
Sheila	Adrian	10	Sister 11	Mainstream Primary
Steph	Kelly	14	Brothers 18 and 17 and Sister 15	Mainstream Secondary

Table 7.2. Themes and domains rsulting from analysis

Domains	Key themes
Deconstructing self and expectations	Unfulfilled wishes and desires
Life impacts and restrictions	Child as central focus
Reconstructing self and expectations	Control and self-reliance
Provision quality and equality	The listening professional

- How did mothers achieve control, coping and resilience?
- How do mothers' experiences inform our quest for both equality and quality of provision?

Aspects of this last question were also considered in the light of the parent support group discussions and developments.

FINDINGS

The master themes or domains emerging from the analysis, with their key underlying themes are shown in Table 7.2

In many ways, experience was ordinary in that it resembled our reactions to more stressful events, such as bereavement, and yet it was also individual and varied, with convergence and divergence. The above domains and themes will be discussed in the following sections.

CHILD REACHABILITY AND LIFE IMPACTS

The nature of autism is such that not only does the child have difficulties appreciating their own and others' feelings but also the parent is unsure about the child's feelings, their response to situations and the reactions of others. For example, Carol said of her older, secondary school daughter:

> She doesn't seem to feel it. When she kicks off, when she's had one of her outbursts, particularly now that she is nearly six foot and approximately 14 stones. She is a big girl and very strong and I have back problems because of it. But when she kicks off big time, people don't understand, because she looks very aggressive and very angry and they are shocked by her actions. People are very ignorant and they tend to misjudge the situation. They make comments and try to get involved. I just need them to leave it to me, because she has never ever hurt me, never.

The theme of 'all pervasive constant battle' provided an interesting parent conceptualization of the generally acknowledged extreme demands imposed by a child with autism. Louise, who had two boys with autism and severe learning difficulties, talked of this very challenging experience:

> Initially, the challenges affect everything. They hit your marriage, your relationship, the friends that you think you have, your life – you know? It affects where you go and what you do.

Donna provided some interesting examples of the complications and necessary adaptations that arise in everyday situations, for example when arranging contact with the dentist or the doctor for her child, who had major anxieties about seeing these professionals. Mothers described extreme demands related to unpredictability, lack of response to danger or correction and extreme behavioural difficulties. Mary explained: 'He was standing on my windowsills, diving over the chairs – it was just outrageous. He was completely uncontrollable and you couldn't discipline him . . . he completely ignored it.'

For Steph, 'The worst thing is that she latches on to someone who she thinks will support her, but she wears them out. She uses them as people who can sort things out for her.' Carol also needed to adapt the way she asked Linda to follow requests, as she did not do that readily, for example: 'If the door was open and I said, "Linda, close the door", she wouldn't. If I mentioned that the door was open, she probably would, in her own time.'

Transition, for example or change of school, was a general concern for mothers, as this could involve separation, feelings of rejection, anger and loss for the child and parent. Mothers spent a great deal of time investigating suitable placements and often had to battle with schools and the LA to establish plans.

CHILD AS CENTRAL FOCUS

Some illustrative comments from mothers included those from Steph and Donna, who pointed out, 'The whole family know that *we* have to change, not Kelly, and that things are easier that way.' Donna said, 'Your whole life revolves around James; everybody's life revolves around James in our house and keeping him happy. He has to come first, because if he doesn't he lets you know about it.'

A major linked theme of the study concerned how mothers cognitively rebuilt or reconstructed themselves and their expectations and appeared to gain confidence and mastery. A role as expert was assumed, with a central focus on the child developing, and this was possibly linked to labelling and external locus of control. Consistency in child management appeared hard to establish and was a 'constant battle', with mothers sometimes seeing others as lacking understanding and being harsh. Fathers, on occasions, were absent or lacked involvement, and schools and other professionals were not always viewed as supportive.

Carol referred to her divorce, saying, 'Linda had been a great strain on both of us ... I know, having been divorced once, when I meet someone it is very difficult, because they have to understand Linda, because she is my first priority.' Carol also pointed out, 'She is on my mind 24 hours a day; basically, when I am at work, I wait for a phone call.'

PARENT REACHABILITY: SHATTERED AND RECONSTRUCTED EXPECTATIONS

Rowe (1991), a clinical psychologist, following Buddhist principles, views the notion of pride or an exaggerated sense of self-importance as underlying our negative feelings when faced with life experiences, which are not acceptable to how we see ourselves, how we think others see us and how secure we feel in the world. Taylor (1983) describes how we seek new meaning, control and self-esteem; and the experiences of the mothers in the study have shown how these three elements of reconstructing self are interlinked. Essentially, through fighting a strongly controlled 'constant battle' with the child as central focus, a fierce independence can emerge, as the mothers' accounts demonstrate. Such reconstructions may be part of motherhood generally, but seem to provide an exaggerated or more extreme change in self or identity, so that there is a new or different interpretation of reality.

MENTAL WELL-BEING

Where such negative experiences are concerned, mothers are vulnerable to mental health concerns with reduced emotional reachability. Donna described isolation and depression, following several professional interviews and inaccurate diagnoses. Health visitors had recommended hearing tests for James and a community paediatrician investigated autism at his mother's request and concluded that this was not present. Her feelings of self-blame and isolation were exacerbated by the reactions of her older children and husband, who was in denial.

> Basically, she [the paediatrician] made me feel that I was being a neurotic mother really, and the line of questioning that she was taking suggested she was either trying to find out whether I had been shaking James, perhaps giving him brain damage or whether I was a Munchausen-by-proxy sort of mum.

I was still insisting that I felt there was something wrong with James. My husband and the other children were getting fed up with me and said that the doctors had told me James was fine, but I still felt there was something wrong with him.

Like Donna, Steph also highlighted the way in which mental well-being was affected:

I would get the children settled and just sit and cry. Kelly was exhausting. She hurt me physically and mentally and probably still does. Certainly, physically things haven't changed, although it is harder punches now. I am a lot stronger now, mentally, and can accept so much more.

ISOLATION AND REACTIONS OF OTHERS

An avoidance of family gatherings emerged as a general theme for parents, perhaps encouraging the use of other support networks and independence and control. Some mothers developed a special friend.

The isolation involved in bringing up a child with autism is heightened by the lack of experienced childcare, as Sheila drew out, 'My Mum became ill and I didn't have any childcare and Alex wasn't able to go anywhere, as he was such a disruptive child. So I still don't work.'

The mothers generally commented on remarks from others about how they managed their children, no doubt influenced by the normal appearance of a child with autism. Sheila saw this as a particular concern:

Always having to apologize for the behaviour of my son. Going somewhere ... it's just been very, very difficult bringing up Adrian. He is a demanding little boy and he has no understanding of danger or sense of how he should act socially. We used to go to play areas or whatever and had to deal with a lot of comments from parents, who obviously didn't understand and just thought he was a naughty little boy. That to me has been one of the greatest difficulties.

CERTAINTY, DIAGNOSIS AND LOCUS OF CONTROL

Dilemmas exist around the implications and usefulness of a diagnosis. Mothers seemed to see diagnosis as useful in that it brought them more certainty and helped with self-perception, so that self-blame was reduced and difficulties were more easily externally attributed. The mother is helped to be more accepting of herself, and her view of herself in the eyes of others is enhanced, giving rise to a more secure perception of the world. Donna improved in her emotional well-being and Sheila also described how resources for the support of Adrian were made available at school entry following diagnosis, which was required by the LA as one criterion for additional support. Carol also seemed to gain esteem and pride from the diagnosis after a lengthy search and saw caring, dedicated and skilled support as following.

Billington (1996), in considering parent–professional discourse concerning labelling, categorization and resourcing, notes the circularity of knowledge, in that professionals and parents see provision coming from diagnosis and this is made dependent upon categorization. Dilemmas of regulation and resistance are present as psychology is seen to pathologize children by categorizing them so that opportunities and resources can subsequently be regulated or managed.

Along similar lines, Oakley (2004) sees labelling and diagnosis as disempowering for children, parents and teachers through externally attributing control, which can remove personal responsibility and the need for change. The diagnosis of autism was wanted for the provision it brought, but not for the stereotyped perceptions and constraints associated with the label. Mothers in my study (Carol, Steph, Donna, Mary and Sheila), however, described the need for a new beginning, which they perceived as stemming from the diagnosis, so that they were able to seek information about the condition and progress emotionally from this position of increased certainty. The belief in an external attribution can also be seen as a cognitively helpful positive illusion (Taylor 1983), especially in a local context where professionals and fellow parents appear to share the same illusions or beliefs.

RECONSTRUCTING SELF: SELF-RELIANCE AND CONTROL

Being the Voice for the Child

For mothers in the study, reconstructing self seemed to go alongside heightened control; thus, by taking charge, a new self is developed, with shattered expectations, burdensome and constant life restrictions being managed, so that self-reliance and coping is achieved. The reconstruction process involves being organized, planning, being in charge, developing coping strategies and taking the initiative. Donna pointed out that 'You have to become slightly autistic yourself in order to . . . understand him better.' Reading the literature was often seen as a starting point for getting in charge.

Following diagnosis, all of the mothers spoke of a strong emphasis on organization and control within daily life, often with a set of rules and procedures that governed the way the household was run. The *cognitive adaptation theory*, described by Taylor (1983), seemed to mesh with much of what the mothers described, and forms part of their self-reconstruction process, so that phenomena and our experience of them depend on how we construct or look at them. This, of course, is the essence of Buddhist philosophy, in that 'all our actions of body, speech and mind are causes and all our experiences are their effects' (Geshe, 2003, p. 42). The essence of cognitive adaptation theory is that the impact of an event is dealt with psychologically by reordering beliefs and attitudes and perhaps adding new ones to deal with real-life events. Some beliefs and attitudes that are not shared by others may be adopted to deal with this traumatic event. By adapting our beliefs and attitudes or actions of body, speech (language) and thought (mind), our experience is changed.

Carol emphasized her role as a mother, saying that she checked that others were dealing with Linda in the right manner:

> At the end of the day, she is mine and I need to make sure that they are coping with her and that she is coping with them. When I return from work, I will take over with the

children. When Linda has spent time at her father's, I remain in charge and, as a mum, I keep checking that they are dealing with her in the right way.

I keep thinking and focusing on the good things and what her talents are. I truly believe that she will become an independent person. I will always be there and she will not be very far from me, but she will be independent. She will work with people, who need her, where she is in control of what she is doing, as with the disabled or elderly people that need her to do things for them, that is her niche. It's about finding where she fits best.

You cannot educate everybody out there. I have to keep trying with Linda; I get involved in every conversation she has, putting things right . . . saying they mean this or what she means is this. That is constant.

ORGANIZED AND IN CHARGE

Sheila commented:

Finding information out, reading information and trying different strategies. You just learn to cope with your own child, how to deal with their behaviour, and you know them so well that you can foresee problems that may arise . . . something that may trigger your child. You tend to cope . . . I've mentioned support from my mother and my friend, but apart from that you've just got to get on with it yourself really, unfortunately.

MOTHERHOOD AND IDENTITY

The participant's story represents a part of their identity and psychological world, and Smith (1999) has looked at changes in identity of mothers during pregnancy. Mothers have provided their interpretation of reality, where control and child focus has affirmed their identity. They sought to become the ever-present voice for the child, helping others to understand the child and working hard to obtain the best resources possible. They also saw themselves as the expert on the child, by providing this voice.

PROFESSIONAL REACHABILITY

When discussing professional reachability and the difficulties involved in multi-agency working, Brimblecombe and Russell comment:

Although each [professional] will be committed to helping the child as best they can, the sheer scale of numbers and different disciplines and agencies involved sets the scene for conflicting advice, duplication in services, confusing input to the family, as well as rivalry between colleagues. Contact with suitable support services may be random and dependent upon the knowledge or goodwill of individual professionals to make appropriate referrals.

(Brimblecombe and Russell (1988), p. 281)

The professional may also mirror the stress within families, and this may show itself in a number of defence strategies or coping methods used to minimize distress. According to Dale (1996), these might include 'detachment, avoidance, selective attention, inappropriate cheerfulness or false reassurance' (p. 290).

Sheila commented on similar denial or a lack of knowledge on the part of the professional:

> When I mentioned it to the health visitor, she said that I only had one child and I didn't realize that it was just something that he was going through.

Donna had earlier described her isolation around the time of diagnosis and the denial with which she was faced, both within the family and from professionals. Not surprisingly, she mentioned bewilderment and isolation and how mental health difficulties can result.

> I didn't know where to turn. They [the professionals] should know that stress is placed on families with a child with autism and how it can easily lead to depression.

CERTAINTY AND UNCERTAINTY

With regard to professional input, false trails were described, delays were experienced and some particular assessment processes were disliked. Parents generally felt unhappy and uncomfortable in the child development clinic (CDC), where diagnoses were often made. Donna felt under the microscope and judged as a parent:

> It was very uncomfortable for parents. I know they're watching the child through the two-way mirror and I don't know whether they are watching the parents and how they interact with the children, but that's the way it felt to me. It felt as though we as parents were being watched, which made me feel uncomfortable. I don't know whether that could be improved in any way by re-arranging the seating because the way it is at the moment you can't even talk to other parents that are there. One group of parents sits here and another sits over there. You feel quite on your own. I know I was just sitting there wishing that James would behave normally in some ways and I wasn't quite sure whether they were watching me and it made me feel guilty and as if perhaps I wasn't interacting with James or that it was my fault.

Donna required certainty, because of the isolation she felt:

> All I wanted was for somebody to say, 'Yes you're right and here's what we do and here's where we go from here.'

PROFESSIONAL SUPPORT FOR PARENT REACHABILITY

Mothers of children with autism may not be easy to reach and may have developed defences and their own illusions, theories or attributions, which could include pregnancy, delivery and family interactions issues. Appropriate parental expectations about potential are a key area and linked to subtle denial. The gradually unfolding symptoms of autism dictate that professionals need to tread a delicate path when working with parents, so as to provide help, which is in keeping with their needs and conceptualizations at different stages. When parents become too adrift from reality in terms of their defences, greater pain may ensue at a later date.

Oakley (2004) follows Selfe (2002) in developing the 'medical diagnosis related parental passivity' argument, in both the attention deficit and autism spheres. Law's (1997) notion of children 'growing down' is seen as a consequence of external locus of control, following external attributions of control. For Oakley, the diagnosis of ADHD or autism appears to have partly absolved the parent of responsibility for the child's actions.

DEFENDED SUBJECTS, PREPARATION AND READINESS

Interviewees are likely to have invested in particular positions or beliefs about their child. These can be seen as defences, and mothers may not know why they experience things the way they do. Furthermore, they may be unconsciously motivated to disguise the meanings of their feelings and actions. Taylor's (1983) notion of positive illusions and the useful function they serve helps us to understand these processes.

Parents may not be cognitively and emotionally prepared for diagnosis; as Mary recalled:

> I wasn't aware of autism, didn't even know what it was. There was no preparation for the diagnosis in all the sessions we went to, and when we went to the CDC feedback session the following week our new health visitor came with us. There were probably about 13 professionals in the room with us round the edge . . . they just said . . . yes, there was something and described what their findings were and just passed us a book, a blue autism book and that was the diagnosis. We were shell-shocked.

PROVISION EQUALITY AND QUALITY: PROFESSIONAL VARIABILITY AND BOUNDARIES

PROVISION BEWILDERMENT

Early parental uncertainty and lack of knowledge about support and provision have been mentioned. Donna had feelings of guilt about receiving a special placement, while for Mary the mainstream school did not feel competent to meet her son's needs. Professionals appeared to vary in the extent to which they were able to help, and this was related to feelings about personal and professional boundaries and levels of expertise so that egalitarian provision was not always present. The mothers felt there needed to be recognition of them as 'expert', though the extent that this linked with the child being their central focus and the possible difficulties involved with detached child management approaches, should also be considered.

Participants described varied professional understanding and handling; for example, Mary commented, 'The child development clinic assessment was like a conveyor belt, seeing one professional after the other.' Professionals there could be encouraging, as Mary found, when the mainstream support teacher said, 'It's manageable; you can put things in place; it's not the end of the world, but I wouldn't imagine you know that now.'

Mary, Carol and Sheila described how mainstream support teachers had provided the most useful support, sometimes with personal telephone contact regarding concerns and a willingness to challenge schools. Experience of school support seemed to fluctuate with teacher and support assistant variability. For Carol, perceived support effectiveness involved close personal attention to her child, possibly linked to the child as central focus.

Experience with health professionals was also varied. Louise experienced consultants positively and negatively, yet she liked her contact with a community nurse, who cheered her up, and a helpful speech and language therapist, while a social worker was not seen as approachable.

INCLUSIONARY SCHOOL PRACTICE

Steph was positive about school efforts: 'She is aiming to get some GCSEs. She should achieve some with difficulty, but the school have been wonderful really.' Sheila described school adaptations, often after considerable personal effort. Examples included complex swimming supervision arrangements, menus being sent home in advance, so food choices could be made, and introducing computer time reward systems. Regular planning meetings were established and release planned for Adrian's support assistant to help him settle into secondary school. The school had always been honest with the children in Adrian's class and they had discussed his needs and reactions with the other children, 'who just accept that Adrian is Adrian'.

Carol usefully contrasted the differing experience of two secondary schools her daughter had attended and the degree of identification with Kelly:

> Her present school see her as a challenge and want to succeed with her, whereas school N didn't really want her there ... she was a hindrance they could do without. Sad but true.

> [Her present] school is doing everything to keep Linda there. For example, they established ways that Linda can pass her exams, without affecting the other children ... that's a school that cares ... they put together a personal timetable for her, starting in the Learning Support Unit for a short time and finishing the day there ... When she is not coping in class, she goes there.

EXCLUSIONARY PRACTICE

Exclusion as an area of concern for pupils with autism has been mentioned in the introductory section, and Carol has already alluded to this above. Donna raised concerns about a lack of structure and inconsistency in practice within the special school autism provision, which her son had attended, while recognizing the skills of the teacher in charge of the overall provision. Her son was about to move to another special school with autism provision and she said, 'James needs a lot of structure in his day and they didn't seem to stick to any one programme . . . they seemed to try something for a week and if it didn't work it was scrapped and then they'd move onto something else . . . if there's one thing an autistic child doesn't like [it's] change.'

Carol and her daughter Linda were caught up in exclusionary interactions with her first secondary school. She said:

> N school was horrendous . . . a bad school for Linda . . . far too big and the buses arrived at once, which was chaotic. The teachers seemed constantly under pressure and were more interested in academic results than Linda's needs, in a nutshell. They gave up on her and my biggest plea was 'Please don't give up on her'. She did nearly two years there. I was banging my head against a brick wall: the more I talked to them, the more it seemed nobody was listening. 'We cannot have her in this school; we cannot meet her needs.' I asked why . . . it wasn't her fault they were not meeting her needs.

> There was no thinking about what could be done, just 'Well we can't meet them'. That was it. The academic results were more important than Linda's needs. That's sad, very sad.

SPECIAL SCHOOL EXPERIENCE

Special school experience also varied, with Donna commenting on a lack of structure and inconsistency in practice, poor parent liaison and low expectations. Louise was critical of the lack of sensitivity and consultation about moving her child to another special school placement and the rejecting and exclusionary feelings that arose.

> The move was supposed to be our choice, but they'd made their minds up and the move from mainstream to special school, it's a foregone conclusion. We looked at school Y [severe learning difficulties], and I was justifiably horrified: they weren't prepared for our visit, and I said, 'You're not taking him there', and we went to school Z, saw the head teacher. Although things weren't wonderful, they were better. They were putting him in the second class . . . I think Mr Davies was an excellent headmaster; he really put his body and soul into it – it was his life. He was very sincere.

SCHOOL IDENTITY AND EXPECTATIONS

The extent to which a school identified with or saw meeting the needs of a pupil with autism as an acceptable part of its aims, practice and feelings of security was a crucial factor in pupil success and parent satisfaction. The overarching whole school tolerance and willingness to meet needs is the most significant factor for inclusion. Wall (2004) stresses the need for 'all staff who come in contact with the child [need] to understand that he has an inherent developmental difference, which causes him to behave and respond in different ways to other pupils' (p. 139).

Carol summed up this school ethos debate:

> It's the [whole] school, teachers and support assistants . . . people make the difference, a school is a building . . . support comes from the people, who are with or against her. If

they are not with you, it's just a losing battle, you may as well give in. It was far too big, far too many children and far too much activity going on . . . school B [where Linda now attends] is a village school.

PARTNERSHIP, PROFESSIONAL VARIABILITY, THOUGHTFULNESS AND BOUNDARIES

PARTNERSHIP AND PARENT PROFESSIONAL RELATIONSHIPS

Dale (1996) saw the limitations of partnership as needing to be openly acknowledged, so that dissent is seen as part of a negotiating approach bringing together diverse and discrepant viewpoints and reconciling them for joint decision-making. The background to dissent can lie in illusions and defences as they relate to beliefs about self and identity. The background of parent dissent, frustration and bewilderment can link to different disciplines and agencies, conflicting advice, duplication of services, confusing input to the family, as well as rivalry between colleagues. Again, competitive working, mutual blame and lack of knowledge about the values and priorities of other services can lie beneath the rhetoric of professional partnership with major negative impacts on parent–professional partnerships.

For Barton (1997), an inclusive professional would listen to unfamiliar voices, be open, empower all members and celebrate so-called difference in dignified ways.

Similarly, the moral values that partnership aspires to would include truth, respect, care and compassion, and these values would be expected to apply equally between professionals, as well as between parents and professionals. Such professional values would involve negotiation (Dale, 1996) and human thoughtfulness (Nixon, Walker and Clough, 2003). Not all professional practice described has demonstrated these values. Thoughtfulness was shown when parents were informed of important issues through evening telephone calls, or where a mother was taken aside at the busy clinic and given comforting, reassuring and honest words after a diagnosis shock. Many other examples of Nixon's effective professionals reaching out to their public have been described.

Nixon also highlights professional judgement, where common-sense guidelines were unclear and multiple interpretations possible. Such practice was exemplified in instances where educational psychologists supported parents in challenging schools regarding good inclusive practice and perhaps later also helping them to see that circumstances require a change of placement, perhaps helping Carol to recognize the situation 'where you may as well give in'.

PROFESSIONAL BOUNDARIES

Professionals varied in the extent to which they were able to help, and this was related to where boundaries were drawn. On occasions professional competence was linked to degree of specialization in autism and recognition of the parent as expert, with Donna pointing out:

> James doesn't see his doctor, but again they should understand that autistic children don't like going to the doctors and even the ones who go don't like being kept waiting for long, which is usually the case. But, the more specialized people, for example Dr Wilson, yourself and M [teacher in charge of unit at school] are great. They've been really helpful and supportive and listened – that's the main thing – listened and taken on board what I've said. Not just nodded and made the right noises and let it go in one ear and out of the other. They've listened and that's important, because I know James better than anybody, I know what's right for him. Sometimes, somebody on the outside can suggest things and you'll think, well I haven't tried that and I will give it a try. But, at the end of the day, I know what will work with James, what fits with James and what doesn't.

Sheila, Carol and Mary described how the mainstream support teacher had provided the most consistent support and on occasions would challenge schools. Sheila was supported at meetings by these staff: 'She's really been very good if there's problems at school . . . she lets me know.' Carol was glowing in her appreciation of the head of this service: 'he has been an absolute tower of strength'.

Mary described school coping issues, as well as consistent support from the mainstream support teacher:

> She'll ring at nine o'clock at night . . . if there's problems at school . . . she rings me . . . We've had ups and downs with school . . . This year, it's been excellent . . . His class teacher's been very good . . . She's got a good understanding. She's looked at ways of unlocking Terry, ways of integrating him into the class and she really has achieved a lot . . . Terry's done very well and enjoyed attending. The year before was a shocker, a disaster. Basically, Terry was the first child with autism in that school and they just didn't know how to handle or approach him. We had various meetings, at one we asked several times if they wanted him . . . eventually they said no. It was bad.

The variability of professionals and the meshing with parents' own preferred style was highlighted by Louise:

> Maybe it's different for everyone . . . Some people aren't suitable for us and might not be suitable for some of the jobs that they are doing. When Simon moved from School Y, they said he was going and it was underhand . . . but they need to be more sympathetic to others, to think what parents are going through – how they feel. Some people are sympathetic and helpful and it's the same with the special schools: they vary.

OTHER THOUGHTFUL PROFESSIONALS

Many other professionals received positive comments from parents. Speech and language therapists were often a major source of help, at around the time of diagnosis. Louise, in particular, found this, while experiencing distant reactions from the consultant involved and found the approachable community nurse cheered her up ('if nowt else') and she saw the specialist consultant as compassionate and more down to earth. Steph was particularly positive about this consultant:

> Dr Wilson has always been in contact and at the end of the phone for parents. She'll always ring you back about things that you contact her about . . . she always tries to attend reviews to get the right support, which is not easy. She seems to understand so well . . . and made me feel as though she is the only other person except myself who understands Kelly's needs.

Steph noted how the educational psychologist acted as a change agent for her daughter by encouraging a change of school. Several parents mentioned the helpfulness of one particular member of the parent partnership service (especially in provision conflict situations) who had also assisted with setting up a parent autism support group.

SERVICE TRUST AND IMPROVEMENT

Trust in services seemed to relate to particular individuals, though general ethos was described for schools. Some mothers recognized progress and developments, such as the Early Bird programme and the parent information and support base. Yet there were concerns about the child development clinic's impersonal diagnosis process and lack of parent preparation and professional awareness. Such a formal process seems to provide an experience that parents need to defend against, though for professionals it is seen as removing illusions so that the parents acquire certainty, adopt the label and hopefully begin the reconstruction process. Professionals as the messengers become the bearers of bad news (Dale, 1996) and can experience parental negativity. Nevertheless, there is a need to listen to parents' views, which can run counter to conventional parent–professional power relations. Donna highlighted her feelings of intimidation at the child development clinic, the circuitous route and the need for questioning opportunities after a period of time to absorb information.

On the other hand, Sheila saw the diagnostic process and interagency links more positively, especially after receiving LA and other support for her son after the development clinic assessment. Her experience was more recent, without the complication of special school placement and additional learning difficulties, with Adrian receiving support from starting school . . . now there's a lot of links, the support teacher and the school are in contact and the psychotherapist sent in a report for the review, which was useful. It's good to have all the help and advice that you can get at review time.' This latter comment related to the 'constant battle' to maintain support levels.

Steph mentioned the need for awareness raising and described the helpful session that Kelly's older sister had given to the class. She, like many parents of pupils with autism in secondary school, was aware of alternative types of special provision in mainstream schools: 'Yes, if there had been a unit in a mainstream school, I feel Kelly would have achieved a lot more.'

She also saw a need for more befriending support, increased liaison between services and was optimistic about her role as a family support worker and encouraging service liaison: 'We have had no home support, there is no befriending service set up, but I feel this would be good for her . . . Nobody links, I wish they would . . . you have to repeat things over and over. Reviews are important, but many professionals don't know her.'

Further general themes mentioned by parents, which linked to national and local parent group discourse, included the need for improved agency meshing through shared data systems and raising professional autism awareness. Other provision issues related to a planned closure of a special school with autism provision, befriending, transition support, growth in the number of pupils with autism, focused help at transition stages, group support for older pupils and the need for resourced secondary school autism provision. Many of these issues are currently being addressed. Essentially, trust in services was seen to concern individual professionals rather than services generally.

PARENT SUPPORT GROUPS, POWER AND PARENT PROFESSIONAL RELATIONSHIPS

In the study, I initially consulted with the two parent support groups about research and interview questions and attempted to ground the research in a local context. The views and concerns expressed by these groups were taken forward to a multidisciplinary LA policy group and led to the setting up of a joint parent professional group.

PARENT GROUP IDENTIFICATION

In the individual interviews, mothers highlighted their usefulness. Donna and Mary chaired their respective groups and Steph was a family support worker for the local Autistic Society. Donna was understandably glowing in her praise of the group:

> I met lots of other parents and that's helped a lot. There's a sense of belonging; you feel a lot less isolated, as there are other parents with more gruesome horror stories than you. It's been wonderful meeting other parents . . . Hopefully, I can help to improve future support for other parents so that they don't have to go through the same. There's a place where you can come and get information. They can have a visit from a family support worker and do social and new things . . . It gets you out of feeling helpless; it is empowering for parents and helping others makes you feel better. They're beautiful children with no physical or outward signs of difficulty. You can pass on tips to others. I was depressed prior to the diagnosis, particularly in the mornings. My hopes and aspirations were smashed.

Mary found the support group most helpful, because parents understood particular issues or problems. Another parent, Louise, gave a different perspective and had seen the benefit of a group for herself, but no longer saw it as necessary. Carol said, 'It provides a constant reminder that your child is not being difficult, just to be awkward or naughty. They are doing it because they have this condition, which makes them behave in a certain way.'

Sheila also recognized the benefits of a parent group behaviour management course, which she saw as helping her marriage survive in the short term: 'the course helped our marriage ... that kind of behaviour management support group is absolutely brilliant ... just knowing you're not on your own, that you are not the only person with a child with difficulties and that you can access information.'

THE RESEARCHER AND PARENT GROUP MEETINGS

Initial meetings were held with the two LA parent support groups, and the discussion was predominantly about provision with little conversation about the personal experience side. This is in keeping with discussions about defended subjects (Hollway and Jefferson, 2000) and positive illusions (Taylor and Armor, 1996).

Following an action research approach, the provision concerns raised by the group were taken to the LA Autism Working Group, and a joint parent–professional liaison group was established with two representatives from each of the support groups and four professionals from different agencies, including the Health Services. The issues raised by the parent groups were discussed over five evening meetings and information and explanations given. The meeting notes and content were disseminated to members of the support groups. Issues discussed included education resourcing systems, social services provision, autism awareness, statutory support and secondary school provision.

The parent group element of the study assisted with gathering multiple perspectives in a broader local and critical context. Billington (2000) argues that such groups are orientated towards improving provision, which was certainly found, though the two groups differed in their emphasis in parent social support and action demanded from others. Capacity for control and change was evident so that participants explained why their conditions were frustrating and suggested alternative actions. Indeed, much of the multi-agency working together agenda from *Every Child Matters* (Department for Education and Skills, 2003) was foretold in these parent group meetings and subsequent interviews with mothers.

The purpose of meaningful parent feedback is to provide professionals with an understanding of child and family needs, by gaining multiple perspectives through consumer views. For critical approaches, action planning is also involved arising from understanding and interpretation. The groups also emphasized the need for the LA to listen more to parents, as well as the variability in professional awareness and the need for more health visitor training.

Armstrong (2003) describes resistance forming behind the backs of dominant groups and how such parent resistance to professional power was demonstrated in the study. For example, there was heated debate about the aims and outcomes of the group and local authority practice framed resistance, so that parent voices were constructed by the existing local structures of power. The professionals established themes from concerns raised and invited speakers for future meetings so as to provide structure and no doubt control, or perhaps professional resistance. When funding was discussed, parent impotence and uncertainty were illustrated by the following: 'I think there is a lot of misunderstanding. The Local Authority thinks school should be doing it and vice versa . . . you're fighting between both.'

The language of power maintained a distance between parents and professionals, who continued to sit on separate sides of the table.

CONCLUSION

This chapter will draw to a close by highlighting the following implications: making a difference, conceptualizing the essence of experience, developing awareness, parent support, training and child management, *Every Child Matters* and multi-agency working, and service improvement and parent feedback.

MAKING A DIFFERENCE

As a researcher in a local authority setting, there is a need to address real issues and give initial planning attention to the organization of subsequent action. Cycles of planning, acting, observing and reflecting are central to any action research approach. The LA's policy body needs to give further consideration to findings from the interpretative account and related discussion. The missed opportunity of continuing the parent–professional group should be revisited so that a periodic focus on parental concerns can be maintained. The study has attempted to provide a balance between interpretative and critical approaches, so that it is descriptive and interpretative, yet there has been a degree of critical interest, with some desire to make a difference. Agreed, longer-term, national and local action plans are required, such as parent-friendly assessment and diagnostic procedures, where a Health Authority commitment to consider change will be required.

CONCEPTUALIZING THE ESSENCE OF EXPERIENCE

The study helps us to see that reconstructed cognitive functioning or perceptions of phenomena can depend on illusion and help to provide a positive, detached view, while seeing things clearly can be associated with depression and inactivity. Illusion, rather than being maladaptive, may be essential for adequate coping. For Taylor *et al.* (2001), psychological beliefs such as optimism, personal control and sense of meaning can protect both mental and physical health from the negative effects of traumatic events. Also, we are helped to understand self-aggrandizement, perhaps shown by Carol, and unrealistic optimism (Mary). Similarly, exaggerated perceptions of control seemed present within the parent groups, and they also seemed to see professionals as having exaggerated control, so much so that professionals spent time explaining their limitations or boundaries within the liaison group. All these processes seem to be associated with psychological adjustment and managing anxiety so that when beliefs are challenged active efforts are made to restore or enhance them. This can result in professional discomfort, and parent political resistance can be understood in these terms.

DEVELOPING AWARENESS

Professionals need to understand the feelings aroused in parents by discovering they have a child with autism and the emotional and practical problems that ensue. First-time parents are often thought to be more at risk of not recognizing the early developmental signs of autism, and may be harder to reach.

Beliefs and attitudes may be ideological illusions that help to preserve a social order, which is alien to collective experience and needs. Such illusions could concern categorization and diagnosis, where the professional and parent cultures and resource allocation procedures encourage an overfocus on the child within the family, with possible child management implications. All these factors affect the position of fathers, the achievement of consistent approaches and harmonious marital relationships. Such considerations relate to the defended subject, attribution, locus of control and positive illusion discussions. Essentially, ways need to be found to consider the findings with professionals, parents and children.

PARENT SUPPORT, TRAINING AND CHILD MANAGEMENT

The key themes from the interpretative research were unfulfilled wishes, the child as the central focus, control and self-reliance and the listening professional. There is a particular need for appropriately trained listening professionals to support and assist parents to deal with difficulties, particularly non-compliance and such training can draw on these research findings. A balance of child understanding and change strategies is required, which is shared by the family and all agencies through a key worker or lead professional.

We need to be mindful of the gradually unfolding symptoms of autism, which dictate that professionals tread a delicate path when working with parents to provide help in keeping with their needs and conceptualizations at different stages. Furthermore, following Taylor (1983), professional awareness requires recognition that reconstructed cognitive functioning and behaviour can depend on illusion and provide a positive but defended view. Practitioners should be prepared for parental resistance to acceptance, for reasons that have been discussed.

A detailed professional understanding of the parent readjustment process, stemming from unfulfilled wishes, is necessary to develop the listening professional. A graded, flexible, joined-up and patient support programme is implied, so that parents can adopt a more relaxed approach, where control is shared. Parent support groups should be encouraged and helped to develop realistic aims, as should parent representation on LA groups. Knowledge and understanding can be disseminated about parent experience and needs, as well as professional support procedures, limitations and priorities. Parents and parent groups require honest discussion of roles to help with recognizing the differing power and position of parties, which might help to redress the potentially disempowering effects of partnership.

EVERY CHILD MATTERS AND MULTI-AGENCY WORKING

Such an approach would assume an individualized support plan, using a holistic view of the family with individual professionals, operating within a coordinated multi-agency framework of service delivery. Multiprofessional teams are being developed to overcome professional rivalry and the random service contact, which was dependent upon the knowledge or goodwill of individual professionals in making appropriate referrals (Brimblecombe and Russell, 1988). Local ways need to be established for smaller, more specialized, perhaps centrally based autism services to mesh into a local or neighbourhood delivery model. Disability, special educational needs, inclusion, Common Assessment Framework (CAF) and lead professional procedures need to be brought together for the benefit of all children, including those with autism. Hopefully, professional understanding of parent experience will underlie such developments.

Such teams need to develop a negotiating climate, and Bion (1961) suggests that members have some personal authority to hold an opinion and perhaps change it. Following Dale (1996), partnership between professionals seems to require the same type of negotiating model, as does partnership with parents.

Services need to realign themselves within such developing contexts and teams, with changing priorities, so that they work to create the future, involve and help others to learn and provide an emphasis on continuous improvement for the benefit of children. Work in local children's centres is required, with regular panel discussion and consultation opportunities that emphasize outcomes for the child. All professionals need to bring an awareness of the dangers of categorizing, pathologizing and the deficit model, particularly where mental health and social emotional needs are concerned, including autism, in the context of developing CAF procedures. Professionals need to function from an interpretative base, as scientific practitioners, collaboratively assisting with action research.

SERVICE IMPROVEMENT AND PARENT FEEDBACK

In considering parent feedback and service improvement, as with many government initiatives, there are dangers of an overemphasis on centrally determined targets and control, which can cause us to miss important elements. This tendency was evidenced in recent Home Office difficulties concerning immigration policy, where an overemphasis on failed asylum seeker targets has led to a de-emphasis on immigration-related public safety risks. We need to listen to and understand parent voice and the interpreted meaning so that a balance between harder indicators and targets and more qualitative interpretative and critical approaches is achieved. We should remember that marginalized and 'hard to reach' parents will always exist as a challenge for engagement in partnership work with professionals. The listening professional, in reaching out to the 'hard to reach', needs to be mindful that the respondent's story represents part of their identity and psychological world (Smith, 1995), which requires recognition and understanding. An understanding of the essence of experience is required by professionals and, indeed, by parents – and this should be developed from research studies such as this.

REFERENCES

Armstrong, D. (2003) *Experiences of Special Education*. RoutledgeFalmer, London.
Barnard, J., Prior, A. and Potter, D. (2000) *Inclusion and Autism: Is it working?* National Autistic Society, London.
Barton, L. (1997) Inclusive education: romantic, subversive or realistic? *International Journal of Inclusive Education* **1** (3), 231–242.
Billig, M., Condor, S. and Edwards, D. *et al.* (1988) *Ideological Dilemmas*. Sage, London.
Billington, T. (1996) Pathologising children: psychology in education and acts of government. In: E. Burman, G. Aitken, E. Alldred *et al.* (eds). *Psychology Discourse Practice: From Regulation to Resistance*. Taylor and Francis, London.
Billington, T. (2000) *ASD Specialist Educational Psychologist Project Interim Report*. Wirral Metropolitan Borough Council.
Bion, W. (1961) *Experiences in Groups*. Tavistock Publications, London.
Brimblecombe, F. and Russell, P. (1988) *Honeylands: Developing a Service for Families with Handicapped Children*. National Children's Bureau, London.
Burman, E., Aitken, G. and Alldred, E. *et al.* (1996) *Psychology Discourse Practice: From Regulation to Resistance*. Taylor and Francis, London.
Carr, W. and Kemmis, S. (1986) *Becoming Critical: Education, Knowledge and Action Research*. Falmer Press, London and Philadelphia.
Dale, N. (1996) *Working with Families of Children with Special Needs*. Routledge, London.
Department for Education and Skills (2003) *Every Child Matters*. The Stationery Office, London.
Department for Education and Skills (2004) *Removing Barriers to Achievement: The Government's Strategy for SEN*. The Stationery Office, London.
Geshe, K.G. (2003) *New Meditation Handbook*, 4th edn, Ulverston, Tharma Publications.
Hollway, W. and Jefferson, T. (2000) *Doing Qualitative Research Differently*. Sage, London.
Law, I. (1997) Attention deficit disorder: therapy with a shoddily built construct. In: C. Smith and D. Nyland (eds). *Narrative Therapies with Children and Adolescents*. Guilford Press, New York.
Nixon, J., Walker, M. and Clough, P. (2003) Research as thoughtful practice. In: P. Sikes, J. Nixon and W. Carr (eds). *The Moral Foundations of Educational Research: Knowledge, Inquiry and Values*. Open University Press/McGraw-Hill Education, Maidenhead and Philadelphia.
Oakley, S. (2004) Narratives of parents whose children are diagnosed with ADHD: Implications for practice, University of Sheffield MSc. Special Study.
Reid, K., Flowers, P. and Larkin, M. (2005) Exploring lived experience. *The Psychologist* **18** (1), 20–23.
Rowe, D. (1991) *Wanting Everything*. HarperCollins, Glasgow.

Selfe, L. (2002) Discussion paper: Concerns about the identification and diagnosis of autistic spectrum disorders. *Educational Psychology in Practice* **18** (7), 335–341.

Smith, J.A. (1995) Semi-structured interviewing and qualitative analysis In: J.A. Smith, R. Harre L. and Van Langenhove (eds). *Rethinking Psychology*. Sage, London.

Smith, J.A. (1999) Identity development during the transition to motherhood: an interpretative phenomenological analysis. *Journal of Reproductive and Infant Psychology* **17** (3), 281–289.

Taylor, S. (1983) Adjustment to threatening events; a theory of cognitive adaptation. *American Psychologist* **38**, 1161–1173.

Taylor, S. and Armor, D. (1996) Positive illusions and coping with adversity. *Journal of Personality* **64** (4), 873–898.

Taylor, S., Kemeny, M., Reed, G. *et al.* (2001) Psychological resources, positive illusions and health. *Advances in Mind–Body Medicine* **17** (1), 1470–3556.

Wall, K. (2004) *Autism and Early Years Practice: A Guide for Early Years Professionals, Teachers and Parents*. Paul Chapman Publishing, London.

Wolfendale, S. (1999) Parents as partners in research and evaluation: methodological and ethical issues and solutions. *British Journal of Special Education* **26** (3), 164–169.

8 Exploring Joined-up Solutions for a Child with Complex Needs

HEATHER NORTHCOTE

INTRODUCTION

In light of the many changes to the ways in which agencies are likely to be working with children in the future, this is an appropriate time to explore some of the problems and potential solutions to joined-up, multi-agency working. This chapter particularly aims to identify the strengths and weaknesses of the Common Assessment Framework (CAF) as a procedure for promoting and supporting effective multi-agency working through the early identification of need, and to explore how this framework might interlink with some of the more specialized assessment protocols currently employed by different agencies. In order to do this, the development and aims of the CAF and '*lead professional*' role will be explored within legislative and professional contexts. A case study will also be used to illustrate some of the strengths and weaknesses in this way of working, and identify ways in which agencies and individual practitioners can be more effective. In introducing the case study, the issue of what makes a 'complex case' and a child or family 'hard to reach' will also be considered, in addition to the exploration of how the new protocols may generate better outcomes for all young people.

CONTEXT

The introduction of a CAF is one of the key initiatives in driving forward joined-up, multi-agency working practices through enabling agencies to communicate more effectively and promote earlier identification of a child's needs (Department for Education and Skills, 2003). The CAF is a core component of the *Every Child Matters: Change for Children* programme (Department for Education and Skills, 2004), the aims of which are:

- to ensure that parents and carers have the information that they may need at an early stage to support their children;
- to ensure that children and young people have a clear voice;
- to encourage children and young people to take responsibility for their own development.

How to Reach 'Hard to Reach' Children: Improving access, participation and outcomes. Edited by K. Pomerantz, M. Hughes and D. Thompson.   Copyright © 2007 by John Wiley & Sons, Ltd.

In order to locate the CAF within the current context of working with children, it is useful to reflect on the legislation and guidance that provide the foundation for the development of alternative working practices.

Although no single piece of legislation covers issues of child law, the current child protection system in the United Kingdom is based on the *Children Act 1989*, which was intended to reform and clarify the laws affecting children (Bennett, 1992). Although this was hailed by the then Lord Chancellor as 'the most comprehensive and far-reaching reform of child law which has come before parliament in living memory' (Walters, 2005, p. 1), subsequent legislation from both statutory and case law has amended the legislation of the Children Act 1989. Examples of such statutory legislation include the *United Nations Convention on the Rights of the Child 1989*, the *Human Rights Act 1998*, the *Education Act 2002* (Section 175), the *Adoption and Children Act 2002* (Section 120) and the *Children Act 2004*. However, although the United Nations Convention on the Rights of the Child 1989 was ratified in 1991, it should be noted that it has not become part of UK law, although the Government has said that it regards itself bound by the demands of the convention (Lyon *et al.*, 2003, cited in Walters, 2005), and it is widely held that the *Children Act 1989* was based on this guidance (Bennett, 1992). As such, *Every Child Matters: Change for Children* (Department for Education and Skills, 2004) sets the context for the development of new ways of working stating that 'the government's aim is for every child, whatever their background or their circumstances, to have the support they need to reach these five outcomes: be healthy; stay safe; enjoy and achieve; make a positive contribution; and achieve economic well-being. This means that the organisations involved in providing services to children (from hospitals to schools, police to voluntary groups) will be teaming up in new ways, sharing information and working together, to protect children and young people from harm and help them achieve what they want in life' (http://www.everychildmatters.gov.uk/aims/). However, while education and social services departments are combining in LAs, many services remain outside Children's Services. It should be noted that the Children Act 2004 does not replace or amend the Children Act 1989; instead, it sets out the process for integrating services to children as recommended by Lord Laming (2003), so that every child can achieve the five outcomes outlined in the *Every Child Matters* Green Paper (Walters, 2005).

Thus, the CAF can be seen to be a key contributor to the most recent legislative amendments to child law and government guidance, in that it is designed to standardize the approach to assessment of additional need and support the process of agencies working together. However, another key component of such changes in working practice is the development of information sharing protocols to support effective communication between agencies (http://www.ecm.gov.uk/deliveringservices/informationsharing). The issue of effective communication reaches further than the development of an embedded common language, as individual agencies each have their own regulations regarding confidentiality along with a requirement to comply with legislation, such as the *Data Protection Act 1998*. There have been far-reaching discussions about the interpretation of the data protection legislation, and guidance has been tightened up as a result of serious incidents involving children (particularly following the Bichard Inquiry (Bichard, 2004), but it is interesting to note the solicitor Georgina Nunney's observation that 'No enquiry into a child's death or serious injury has ever questioned why information was shared. It has always asked the opposite' (Department for Education and Skills, 2006b, p. 3). However, confidentiality and communication between services remain contentious issues and, although the development of Children's Services comprising education, social services, health services, police and voluntary agencies was introduced through the Children Act 2004 to support the process of multi-agency working, issues of confidentiality and communication seem to be unclear and largely unresolved at this time.

A starting point in this process is the development of a national index, which will be available throughout England by 2008. The Information Sharing Index (IS Index) will enable practitioners to access information about an individual child they are working with. It will facilitate the sharing of information by allowing practitioners to find out whether a common assessment has been carried out and enable them to identify and contact other people working with the child (Department for Education and Skills, 2006b, p. 11). However, as there will not be any case notes on this system, guidance on the information that can or should be shared between professionals will still be critical to its success. In the Western Isles abuse case in Scotland (2003–2004) although information sharing protocols ensured that data was logged and shared, 'Nobody sat down and did the analysis of the social care and health records' (Ruth Stark, professional officer (Scotland) at the British Association of Social Workers, quoted in Smith, 2005, p. 11). At present in England, guidance on information sharing that can be universally applied remains elusive. In addition, regional pilots are currently being developed to explore the processes and procedures, but as there have not been any guidelines regarding the format or structure of these systems, there are likely to be significant differences between each of the information sharing databases piloted, and a subsequent lack of consistency when these are combined to form the national database.

The CAF forms part of a process for the early identification of needs. In many cases the assessment framework will identify the need for integrated support from a range of services and at that stage a lead professional will be designated who will coordinate the involvement of professionals and services identified by the CAF. The assessment may also be completed for a child where a single practitioner or service is identified as being able to address the needs of the child and family; in such a case a lead professional would not be needed. There are high expectations that the CAF will be a holistic, child- and family-centred, empowering process which supports early identification of need and improves joint working, communication and the sharing of information, in addition to rationalizing assessments and supporting better referrals (Department for Education and Skills, 2006a). In order to achieve these goals, children and young people are assessed across three domains: development of the child (be healthy; enjoy and achieve), parents and carers (stay safe) and family and environmental (achieve economic well-being; make a positive contribution) reflecting the five outcomes of *Every Child Matters* (ECM; Department for Education and Skills, 2003).

The CAF is not intended to replace the assessment protocols of other agencies when more specialized involvement is required, except in the case of Connexions' Assessment, Planning, Implementation and Review (APIR) system (Department for Education and Skills, 2006a). However, there is a clear intention that it will be adopted by all agencies working with children and young people. As there is clearly a large amount of overlap between the data collected using the CAF and that required for the completion of other assessment pro formas, such as ASSET used by the Youth Offending Team (www.youthjusticeboard.gov.uk), there will inevitably be an impact on these assessment frameworks. As such, careful consideration will need to be given to developing systems to incorporate information and inter-relate the various assessments to ensure that the CAF can inform and add to these specialist assessments without merely reproducing data in another form: adding another layer of bureaucracy rather than simplifying the whole assessment process.

A third factor in the effectiveness of the changes in working practices outlined in the Children Act 2004 and *Every Child Matters: Change for Children* (Department for Education and Skills, 2004) is the development of the integrated approach. Such multi-agency working is described in three ways: a multi-agency panel, a multi-agency team or an integrated service (Department for Education and Skills, 2006b, p. 9). Positive factors in multi-agency working include an increase in the influence and impact of the work through avoiding duplication of effort, opportunities to learn about other agencies' perspectives, roles and processes, and the development of shared values (Webb and Vulliamy, 2001). Teamworking can also provide a more holistic approach to client need (Cook, Gerrish and Clarke, 2001) and ensure practitioners are positioned in such a way as to address complex needs, which would be beyond the remit and expertise of any single profession (Freeth, 2001). Although these benefits are equally relevant to each of the three multi-agency work structures outlined above, the multi-agency team is clearly the best structure to provide a holistic service required from the CAF, as barriers between services are minimized and a multi-agency team will have shared objectives. Teamworking also supports the development of better communication between professionals thus reducing the likelihood of clients falling between the services (Northcote, 2003). Multi-agency panel and integrated service structures are probably the easiest to introduce although they retain some of the barriers between the agencies despite improved liaison or co-location of services. Both could offer some opportunities to extend the awareness of individual practitioners, particularly through a multi-agency panel – although there are often issues of resources and funding attached to this way of working.

At this stage, it will be helpful to consider how the procedures set out in the Children Act 2004, including the CAF and related legislative and cultural changes, might influence an individual child through the introduction of a case study. This will allow many of the issues and processes of multi-agency working, early identification and assessment of need and information sharing to be reviewed in terms of real children's experiences. Chelsea (not her real name) is described below in terms of the five outcomes of *Every Child Matters: Change for Children Outcomes Framework* version 2.0 (http://www.everychildmatters.gov.uk/publications/?asset=document&id=16682).

Following the description of Chelsea's needs, the factors that identify her as a complex case and 'hard to reach' will be evaluated.

CHELSEA: A CASE STUDY

BE HEALTHY: PHYSICAL AND MENTAL HEALTH

Chelsea is eight years old. Her mother consumed alcohol and heroin during pregnancy. Alcohol and heroin are teratogens (substances that interfere with the normal development of the foetus). Heroin increases the danger of premature birth and accompanying problems, such as low birth weight, hypoglycaemia (low blood sugar), intracranial haemorrhage (bleeding within the head) and breathing difficulties (American Council for Drug Education, 1999). Alcohol is known as a neurobehavioural teratogen as it causes damage to the brain and subsequently changes behaviour. Neurobehavioural teratogens can cause central nervous system damage at a lower dose than is necessary to cause physical malformation of the foetus (Saskatchewan Institute on Prevention of Handicaps 2003). The term Foetal Alcohol Spectrum Disorder (FASD) is used to refer to the three alcohol-related disorders: alcohol-related neurodevelopmental disorders (ARND), alcohol-related birth defects (ARBD) and Foetal Alcohol Syndrome (FAS). ARND occur when there is a lower dose of alcohol resulting in a change in brain function with a pattern of behavioural and learning problems. ARBD occur with a higher dose, often typified by deformed facial features, microcephaly (small head size) and pre- and post-natal growth abnormalities (BBC, 2004). FAS is characterized by three groups of symptoms (Saskatchewan Institute on Prevention of Handicaps, 2003):

- growth deficiency: smaller physical size into adulthood;
- central nervous system dysfunction: intellectual and developmental disabilities, short attention span, learning disabilities, hyperactivity, poor muscle tone and poor coordination. The brain also fails to grow, staying smaller than others of the same age;
- facial abnormalities: the face does not form in the usual manner often having small eye openings, drooping eyelids, flat wide nose bridge, thin upper lip or flattened philtrum (groove between nose and lip).

Chelsea has FAS and was placed in the Special Care Baby Unit at birth to address feeding difficulties and withdrawal symptoms. At two and a half years, the paediatrician reported that Chelsea had sparse hair and a thin upper lip, flattened philtrum and long slender fingers. She was very petite with her height at the lower end of the average range. Her weight was much lower, and her head size much smaller than would be expected for a child of her age. Chelsea had an alternating convergent squint and other visual difficulties.

FAS is a lifelong condition caused by maternal alcohol consumption during pregnancy, and is thought to be the leading known cause of mental retardation in the

Western World (Abel and Sokol 1987, cited by Ryan and Chionnaith, 2006). It is estimated that 12% of births worldwide are affected by alcohol in some way (US National Institute on Drug Abuse 1992, cited by BBC, 2004) with 1% of children born each year having either ARND, ARBD or FAS – some $1\frac{1}{4}$... million births each year (Sampson *et al.*, 1997).

Although the primary disability is the impairment of brain function (organic brain damage) including memory, judgement and learning, additional secondary disabilities often develop after birth, such as mental health problems, disrupted school experience, involvement in criminal activity, confinement, inappropriate sexual behaviour, alcohol and drug problems. However, protective factors, particularly a safe, stable and structured living environment, can prevent or reduce the impact of these secondary disabilities (Saskatchewan Institute on Prevention of Handicaps, 2003).

Chelsea has a history of sleep difficulties and night terrors and assessments indicate that Chelsea's ability to regulate her emotions is poor, particularly at home. Additional attachment-related difficulties were reported by the clinical psychologist and social worker, who became involved through the Health Service because of concerns about sleeplessness, eating, extreme tantrums, running away and attention difficulties. The paediatrician reported that Chelsea seemed shy at two years old during the consultation, and became frightened and distressed by the medical examination. When Chelsea was five years old, she killed her brother's hamster by squeezing it. When the teacher asked her about what had happened, Chelsea said that she knew that the hamster would die. Chelsea is also reported to masturbate regularly at home and at school and she was also reported to be self-harming in school when she was six years old.

STAY SAFE: FAMILY SITUATION

Chelsea lived at home with her mother and older half-brother Tom for the first year of her life. Chelsea and Tom have the same mother, but different fathers. At this time there were concerns about neglect, about the numbers of adults in the house and about the prevalence of alcohol and drugs. Chelsea is not reported to have bonded with her mother during this time, and it is believed the children had largely to fend for themselves. Chelsea and Tom were removed from the care of their mother and taken into foster care on an Interim Care Order when Chelsea was 14 months old; this followed an incident where Chelsea had been given vodka in her bottle.

Almost one year later, both children went to live with Tom's paternal grandmother on a Residence Order in their mother's home town, almost 200 miles from where they had been living; their mother did not return with them. The children had regular contact with their mother for just over a year, until she became pregnant with her third child. At that time contact stopped for two and a half years, although there were occasional telephone conversations during their weekly visits to their maternal grandfather's home. Chelsea and Tom's mother also suffered a stroke around the time of the baby's birth, and has limited use of her right arm and leg as a result.

At present, the children have regular weekly contact with their maternal grandfather and his partner, irregular contact with their mother's sister and her family and infrequent, irregular contact with their mother (Christmas, birthdays, etc.). Chelsea does not have any contact with her father, who is believed to be a Schedule 1 offender. It is uncertain whether he presents a risk to children. Tom's father committed suicide before Chelsea was born.

ENJOY AND ACHIEVE: LEARNING AND DEVELOPMENT, TALENTS AND INTERESTS

Chelsea was issued with a Statement of Special Educational Needs when she was just over four years old. Assessments throughout Chelsea's life indicate that she has general developmental delay. Her visual skills, speech and language skills and social interaction skills are particularly delayed; more recent assessments of her cognitive ability indicate that she has an uneven profile of strengths and weaknesses. Chelsea's teacher observed that Chelsea had begun to make progress academically and socially during Year 2, although concerns regarding Chelsea's distractibility and poor concentration were expressed in Year 3 as Chelsea seemed to be becoming more demanding and disruptive. This may relate to the changing curriculum demands on transfer to Key Stage 2. However, assessments indicated that Chelsea's academic attainment is in line with her overall cognitive ability.

MAKING A POSITIVE CONTRIBUTION: SOCIAL SKILLS AND BEHAVIOUR

Chelsea's teacher in Year 1 reported that she had two main friends at this time. However, her peers were becoming more aware of her masturbating and this was beginning to play a part in isolating Chelsea socially. Chelsea is quite a vulnerable child in that she finds it difficult to respond appropriately in social situations and will run away from the house even if she is undressed, or not properly dressed. Assessment by the educational psychologist indicated that Chelsea found it difficult to regulate her behaviour at home and at school. This is particularly related to Chelsea being aggressive and stubborn, but she is also described as a very loving child. Chelsea is reported to respond well to firm management at school.

ACHIEVE ECONOMIC WELL-BEING: FREE FROM LOW INCOME

Many of Chelsea's difficulties relate to the diagnosis of FAS. In addition, Chelsea has also had very negative experiences early in life, which have further affected her emotional development and access to early-learning situations. All of these factors will affect her ability to achieve economic well-being in the future as her health, learning, social development and emotional needs are likely to present Chelsea with long-term difficulties. Although her home situation during the first year of life was likely to have been a low-income household (because of the reliance on and abuse of alcohol and other illegal drugs), her life with Tom's grandmother seems to be in a more secure and caring base. However, some of Chelsea's behaviour seems to be challenging her carer's parenting skills.

WHAT MAKES THIS A COMPLEX CASE?

Chelsea's primary needs relate to the diagnosis of FAS. Evidence from medical studies of young people with FAS indicates that it is likely that an infant or young child with FAS might experience a range of difficulties, including:

- being overwhelmed by stimulation;
- having difficulty establishing a regular routine for daily living;
- experiencing sleep disturbances;
- having a poor sucking response;
- failing to thrive;
- having delays in walking, talking and toilet training;
- having difficulty following instructions;
- having difficulty obeying rules;
- showing increased distractibility and hyperactivity;
- having poor impulse control;
- showing delayed physical and cognitive development;
- using vocabulary that obscures their ability to comprehend;
- having poor memory;
- appearing capable of concrete and abstract thinking without actually having the ability;
- having increased temper tantrums;
- showing increased negative behaviour (such as lying, stealing, etc.);
- having difficulty predicting sequences of events;
- having difficulty understanding the consequences of actions;
- having difficulty separating fact from fantasy;
- experiencing difficulties in social situations, including inappropriate sexual behaviour;
- being easily influenced by others.

(Saskatchewan Institute on Prevention of Handicaps, 2003)

Chelsea clearly experiences many of the difficulties that are related to a diagnosis of FAS, and this in itself may be judged as evidence of complexity as the impact of FAS is observed in so many areas. However, while FAS can have far-reaching effects on health, learning and development, it is the additional layers of need that identify Chelsea as a complex case. These include Chelsea's early experiences, including neglect and possible abuse, her experience of changes in her living accommodation and broader family situation (including parental contact and placement stability) and her limited social and emotional development (including attachment difficulties). These factors also have an impact on the likely outcomes for Chelsea as a child with FAS, as one of the key strategies to maximize the life outcomes for children and young people with FAS is the provision of a safe, stable and structured living environment (Saskatchewan Institute on Prevention of Handicaps, 2003). The additional difficulties that Chelsea experiences clearly mark her as vulnerable when considered against the framework of resilience identified by Daniel and Wassell (2002). They identify six domains of resilience: social competencies, secure base, talents and interests, education, friendships and positive values. Although there is clearly overlap between the five outcomes of ECM and other measures of complexity and vulnerability (e.g. the Looking After Children materials, Parker *et al.*, 1991), these domains highlight the complexity of Chelsea's case through clarifying the importance of social skills and development, social understanding and the ability to make and sustain friendships as resilience factors, in addition to the other areas of need. There is clearly also an inter-relationship between the domains and contexts: *more limited resilience makes a young person more vulnerable to mental health difficulties and bullying* (Daniel and Wassell, 2002).

The pre-assessment checklist of the CAF is designed to support professionals in deciding whether assessment using the CAF is appropriate. If the pre-assessment checklist had been completed at any time during the pregnancy or the first few years of her life, Chelsea would have been identified as having needs in all five areas. The *Thomas Coram Research Unit Report* describes children with significant and complex needs as including: children who are the subject of a child-protection plan, 'looked after' children, care leavers, children for whom adoption is the plan, children with severe and complex special educational needs, young offenders involved with youth justice services (community and custodial), children diagnosed with significant mental health problems and children with complex disabilities or complex health needs (Boddy, Potts and Statham, 2006). As such, Chelsea has been a 'looked after' child, she has severe and complex special educational needs and complex health needs and it is the combination of all of these areas of need that make the recognition of Chelsea being a complex case more certain.

WHAT MAKES A CHILD 'HARD TO REACH'?

Despite the evident complexity of Chelsea's needs, these alone do not make Chelsea 'hard to reach'. Although the 'hard to reach' concept is not clearly defined, there are a range of factors, such as feeling vulnerable or threatened by the support services, that increase the difficulty in identifying and supporting families and children, many of which were highlighted in the Victoria Climbié Inquiry (Laming, 2003). 'Hard to reach' may be viewed as comprising those who are hard to see, hard to find, hard to engage, hard to retain or hard to change (see introductory chapter) and it can be a useful construct to apply to work with families as a reflective practitioner.

The factors that seem to play the greatest role in making Chelsea and her family 'hard to reach' at an early stage are the factors relating to her mother's drug misuse. Individuals are more likely to be secretive or dishonest about behaviour that society generally views negatively or that is perceived to show the person in a bad light than about behaviours that create a more positive image (Brenner, 1981). In addition to this the unequal balance of power between the interviewer and interviewee in interview situations (the most common method of obtaining information) can also affect the openness and honesty of the individual's responses (Foster and Parker, 1997), and the level of trust the individual has in the interviewer often depends on the perceived agenda of the interviewer: who they seem to be, where they have come from and their reasons for asking questions (Powney and Watts, 1987, cited in Northcote, 2003). As such, Chelsea's mother is unlikely to have been honest and open about her alcohol consumption and drug use prior to the pregnancy or birth, making it difficult for services to support her and promote a more positive outcome for Chelsea; although given the severity of the impact of alcohol consumption on the foetus, if a woman is pregnant and consuming alcohol it is clear that she needs help and support (http://www.fasalaska.com/basis.html), but Chelsea's mother's perception of this is likely to have been skewed by fears of prosecution. As a result of her fears, she may have been quite secretive about the pregnancy in order to avoid the perceived interference from Health or Social Services, or her levels of substance abuse may have resulted in her being unaware of the pregnancy for a large proportion of the term.

A further factor that makes Chelsea 'hard to reach' is the change in geographical location from her mother's house and foster care placement in one part of the country to her current residence approximately 200 miles away. Although a degree of continuity would be expected from Social Services as the case transferred from one Local Authority (LA) to another, in practice this can be very time-consuming and demanding for services that are overstretched and understaffed. The precise detail of these arrangements at the time of Chelsea's move is unclear; however, the subsequent involvement of Social Services to support the family has been quite limited, suggesting that this process was minimal in the first instance. In addition to the transfer between Social Services, Chelsea's health care also transferred to an alternative Primary Care Trust. Although it is likely that case notes were transferred between the two health authorities, the lack of continuity of staff involvement with Chelsea from her early years may have adversely affected the support she received later. Chelsea's access to education has not been disrupted by the move, however, as the Residence Order was issued prior to Chelsea reaching statutory school age. Subsequent involvement from education support agencies has been subject to staff changes, though, mirroring some of the difficulties in communication and consistency experienced by the other agencies.

The third factor in identifying Chelsea as 'hard to reach' has been her carer's capacity to identify and address Chelsea's needs and to explore ways in which agencies could support the family. Issues such as attending health appointments, being open and honest about the difficulties Chelsea poses and recognizing what Chelsea and the family need seem to have posed problems for Tom's grandmother.

Again, some of these issues relate to the likelihood of increased secrecy for an individual who feels their skills or attitudes are being judged or challenged: in this case, it may have been hard to admit that she found Tom relatively easy to care for and Chelsea much more difficult as this may be perceived as favouritism because Tom is her blood relative but Chelsea is unrelated to her. She may also have felt that she should be able to coordinate appointments and manage Chelsea's difficult behaviour more successfully, having already raised six children of her own; and a further concern may have related to Chelsea masturbating frequently as Tom's grandmother may have felt that this made her, or her family or ex-partner, vulnerable to accusations of abuse.

WILL THERE REALLY BE CHANGE FOR. . .

. . .CHELSEA?

In this case, it is unclear whether the CAF would have added any value to the process of identifying Chelsea's needs early, as there has clearly been involvement from Social Services from quite an early stage. However, it may be that completion of the assessment form early in the pregnancy may have helped the practitioner using it to ask questions that would have elicited more information regarding Chelsea's mother's alcohol and drug misuse, thus identifying her level of need and providing support at a much earlier stage. This assertion relies on two fundamental assumptions, that:

- Chelsea's mother was engaging with a professional at the time of the pregnancy;
- the practitioner did not have the skills or knowledge to explore these areas of possible need without the guidance of the CAF, or did not have the skills to provide a way of meeting the needs identified.

In such a case, the CAF may help a less-skilled practitioner explore some of these difficult issues, but would not necessarily help them to draw accurate conclusions about the level of risk these behaviours posed to the unborn child as there are no specific risk factors highlighted on the form. The Government is attempting to address the issue of practitioners having adequate skills and knowledge through ensuring there is a common core of skills and knowledge for the children's workforce (Department for Education and Skills, 2005). However, it is also valuable if the reasons behind individuals' judgements can be explained, as recognized during the Western Isles abuse case in Scotland. It was noted in the review of the case that professionals must explain why they attach importance to some issues and not others, and that the thinking behind those judgements must be explicit so that they can be challenged and debated (Smith, 2005). There is also a possibility that the CAF would need to have been completed by a practitioner in Adult rather than Children's Services (e.g. police, health, social or voluntary services) as Chelsea's mother may have been engaging with these services when she became pregnant. The common core of skills and knowledge does not apply to practitioners in Adult Services, and some of the risk factors identified by the CAF may then have been overlooked in drawing conclusions to the assessment and identifying solutions.

Where the CAF could have played a significant role in this case would be through ensuring that the background information regarding Chelsea's early history and development was not lost or diluted at the point of transfer between LAs. However, this is not a novel solution, as documents such as *Looking After Children* (Parker *et al.*, 1991) were developed 15 years ago to gather and share such data, but these documents have not been used systematically. This was also the case in the Western Isles, where it was reported that systems which were already in place were not accessed (Smith, 2005). Therefore, although any completed assessment form, with additional information added as further agencies became involved, could have provided a valuable source of data, this will only be an effective procedure if the assessments are used consistently. It is also uncertain at this time how the completeness of this form could be ensured without it being held on a central database, as each agency could end up adding the information from their involvement on to a completed form, but these would not necessarily be merged or amalgamated in any way. It is therefore possible that a paediatrician and a behaviour support teacher may both update their copy of the CAF at a similar time, but neither is adding information to the form that the other has updated. Thus, although information is shared, there may be delay or drift (Smith, 2005). It may be appropriate for the practitioner who completed the CAF initially, or the lead professional in cases requiring integrated service provision, to be responsible for maintaining a full and complete version of the CAF, but this may be disempowering to the child and their family. In addition, this person would need to be easily identifiable from the information on the IS Index, and it would also be useful if the date of the most recent updates to the CAF form were easily accessible from this database.

As Chelsea has been identified as a complex case requiring involvement from a range of services, a lead professional would have been appointed to coordinate service delivery for Chelsea as part of the assessment process. Determining the role of a lead professional could have been a beneficial way of supporting this family given some of the concerns regarding the capacity of Tom's grandmother to identify the family's needs and access to services. This role may also have identified some ways of working with agencies from Chelsea's mother's LA to support her needs from Adult Services and also address some of the issues around contact with her children. However, although it is unclear whether this coordination of multi-agency working would have added anything to the services' involvement in supporting Chelsea and her family, the lead professional should have been able to support Tom's grandmother in arranging and accessing appointments with services, thus easing the pressures on her somewhat.

...CHILDREN IN A BROADER CONTEXT?

Within a context of multi-agency working, the CAF appears to make an insubstantial contribution. In order to be accessible to a range of children's workforce practitioners with the core skills and knowledge necessary to complete the assessment form effectively, the framework seems to culminate in the expectation that fairly simplistic judgements can be made which will resolve the problem. The implication of this is that the child's needs can be met quite easily by the named services completing these actions; and the action plan in the Conclusions, Solutions and Actions section of the assessment form seems to point to short-term actions that will either add information through further assessment or put something in place which will resolve the difficulty. This may be sufficient in some less complex cases, where the CAF form will help to identify and access a coordinated response more readily than previous processes. However, in the majority of cases and particularly the more complex ones, the required actions are going to be long-term and will require constant revision in light of the changes to the child's needs.

There is a danger in such cases that the decision to make a referral and gather further information may be viewed as an action to meet the child's needs, when this is really just a further part of the process. Actions to meet a child's needs require additional services delivered by frontline staff that make a difference for the child; this may be in improving the home environment (housing or finance), extending the child's skills or experiences (provision of toys or access to Portage) or developing the parents' behaviour management skills, for example. The only way that the CAF will actually realize any changes in frontline service delivery will be through harnessing the creativity of multi-agency discussions and planning, which in turn supports practitioners in delivering their professional services effectively. However, this also depends to a great extent on the capacity of practitioners to have a degree of autonomy over their work and resources to enable them to meet needs more flexibly. Unfortunately, the lengthy timescales associated with more specialist assessments such as statutory assessment of special educational needs, which allow access to further resources, are still likely to delay the possibility of making changes for children. Thus, unless the CAF is used creatively to plan and coordinate multi-agency provision in more complex cases, and support the allocation of resources, it is likely that it will merely add another layer of bureaucracy to the current systems.

Exploring this idea of additional bureaucracy further, it seems unlikely that the CAF will succeed in reducing the amount of times parents or carers have to tell their story to different professionals. As an educational psychologist, I expect that I would want to review and explore the background information held on the CAF as part of my involvement in order to ensure that the information was complete and accurate. This also allows the family to reflect on how things have changed as part of a more dynamic approach to working with the child. The exact level of exploration of this information would clearly depend on the complexity of the case, but is also likely to reflect the skills and knowledge of the practitioner who completed the assessment form in the first instance. As such, there appears to be an issue regarding the basic requirements of the form, particularly for children and young people who have more subtle or more complex needs or where there are more sinister, hidden needs in the environment about which parents or carers may be defensive. Indeed, professionals asking similar questions at different times can also support the exploration of some child-protection or youth-offending issues. The discrepancy between reports of events can be a key factor in identifying additional needs that the parents, carers or young people might be attempting to keep hidden. However, in some cases, repetition may be overwhelming and frustrating for the family.

A further concern, relating both to defensive or reluctant engagement from the family and to attempts to conceal information, reflects the issue of individuals feeling vulnerable or threatened by the involvement of support services. To some extent, the practitioner's skill in identifying and evaluating such behaviour is addressed through the expectations for the common core of skills and knowledge in the children's workforce, but in reality such disengagement tends to be overlooked by services and agencies because the family are disengaged with the processes. This is frequently seen in the health service where families do not attend appointments and are then discharged from that service (this in itself could be a child-protection issue, but the capacity for follow-up is very limited). For families that do engage, but in a limited way, it takes quite a skilled practitioner to elicit the relevant and useful information required to make accurate and effective judgements regarding the child's needs. In such cases, the initial completion of the CAF form may not be adequate and will, therefore, need to be revisited at a later date by a professional with a wider range of skills in information gathering techniques. This in itself could increase tensions between the family and the practitioner as it may appear that the family's honesty is in doubt. However, a related issue reflects the demand made by the Children Act 1989 for the child's voice to be heard more clearly (Bennett, 1992), and ongoing exploration of the child's views and wishes will be crucial in ensuring the holistic nature of professional involvement as the child develops, although practitioners must continue to be sensitive in their exploration of traumatic events (Kate Trench, supervisor for Childline, quoted in Smith, 2005).

A related issue addresses the requirement for the CAF form to be completed with the family and for their informed consent to be obtained to support information sharing between professionals. The CAF is intended as an empowering experience for the child and family (www.ecm.gov.uk) but it may be viewed that refusal to cooperate in completing the CAF form is a child-protection issue. In such a case, the family do not have a choice about whether they wish to participate in this process or not, and as such the process cannot really be viewed as empowering at all. A similar concern arises around the issues of the family giving informed consent about who this information can be shared with. The guidance indicates that although consent should be obtained, information may still be shared without consent if this is deemed to be appropriate (http://www.ecm.gov.uk/deliveringservices/integratedworking/training/caf). Again, this process does not really empower the family and may exacerbate tensions between the family and the services that could support them.

Although it has been acknowledged that a fully completed CAF form may help to ensure that information is transferred between staff when changes occur, a further issue arises when staffing changes lead to a change in the lead professional. One of the major components of the process is the appointment of a coordinator who can liaise with the child, their parents or carers and the professional services involved and develop a positive, supportive relationship with the family. However, there are inevitably going to be changes in staffing and turnover in some agencies that could effectively discount them from being able to commit to the lead professional role, despite being well-placed otherwise to take this on. It is also likely that a family will be asked to choose who the lead professional will be at quite an early stage, thus restricting their choice. Where such an early decision results in an inappropriate choice, or the relationship breaks down, the involvement of an independent body such as Parent Partnership to mediate between parents and lead professionals may also be required. This likelihood increases with the proposals for the lead professional to be a budget holder who is able to 'buy in' additional services, as it is possible that there may be conflicting opinions about how this funding should be used. Such a responsibility also puts additional pressure on the lead professional who may not have been in such a position before. Although it is clearly not possible to legislate against staffing changes, it is an important component in supporting the CAF that agencies are proactive in recruiting and retaining staff; training and supervision to manage the novel aspects of the new roles will be particularly pertinent to this process. Staff recruitment and retention also affects the possibility of developing effective multi-agency working structures, as agencies that are understaffed will have much less capacity to participate in the creative, problem-solving multi-agency discussions which are intended to underpin the CAF process in securing improved outcomes for children.

The impact of using an embedded common language that is accessible to all services and the family appears on the surface to be a sensible idea. However, it is apparent that it often is the lazy usage of shortened terms which actually confuses communications between services (even those within the same agency). For example, in a recent conversation with an education welfare officer, it was apparent that the educational psychology assessment which had been completed in school (making recommendations on how school staff could support the young person's learning and inclusion) was believed to have been a statutory assessment of the child's special educational needs (which would result in a Statement or a Note in Lieu being issued by the LA) because the school had said he was being 'assessed'. It is clearly important therefore that any language needs to be used carefully, whether it is through using plain English to avoid unnecessary jargon or just avoiding lazy abbreviations of specific terms. This applies at all levels, from the initial completion of the CAF form to the specific language employed as more specialized assessments are undertaken. However, when working with professionals from other agencies, it is important that practitioners are aware that similar phrases may have different meanings to different agencies and that they feel confident and comfortable checking out exactly what is meant by each professional. This is a particularly important role for the lead professional in that they need to be very clear that any information they are feeding back to the family is accurate and clear.

CONCLUSION

The CAF seems to be a new version of the kind of documentation that has already been published to gather and share information, although these documents have not been used systematically by agencies or practitioners in the past. This begs the question of whether this new process will be any different or whether it is merely adding another layer of bureaucracy to current practice. Part of the ability of the CAF to deliver in this way will depend on the ability of services to work in truly multi-agency teams which can all sign up to the new process; however, even the plans for multi-agency working seem to be quite haphazard at present with very few LAs having multi-agency structures in place. The development of multi-agency teams may support the identification of more creative and helpful support packages with increased frontline delivery for some of the more complex cases. However, the reluctance of some of the key Children's Service providers to engage in a joint LA system also creates barriers to effective teamworking through increasing the difficulties in information sharing between practitioners, services, agencies and professionals working with different age ranges. Beyond a change of name, there do not seem to have been any significant changes in the way the children's workforce engages with children and their families or shares information, in spite of Lord Laming's report urging recommendations to be implemented within a two-year timescale. As such, it seems unlikely that any of the procedures relating to the CAF will actually make a difference to a child or family who are particularly 'hard to reach'. Thus, tragic events such as Victoria Climbié's death are unlikely to be prevented by the introduction of this framework, without further substantial investment of time and resources to support the multi-agency structures and information sharing protocols across services, age ranges and LAs.

Discussion Points

Do we really need a CAF or would greater awareness of how other services work, who they work with, how they can be contacted and so on be sufficient to make the changes which the CAF is designed to support?
Does the CAF fit where it is meant to or does it just add another layer of bureaucracy?
Are there enough appropriately skilled practitioners to use the CAF effectively?
Will the CAF actually facilitate more joined-up approaches?

REFERENCES

American Council for Drug Education (1999) Drugs and pregnancy, http://www.acde.org/parent/Pregnant.htm, accessed 11 July 2006.

BBC (2004) Consuming alcohol during pregnancy: the consequences, http://www.bbc.co.uk/dna/h2g2/A2788563, accessed 3 February 2007.

Bennett, P.L. (1992) An Introduction to the Children Act 1989. *Educational Psychology in Practice* **7** (4), 202–206.

Bichard, Sir Michael (2004) *The Bichard Inquiry Report*. The Stationery Office, London.

Boddy, J., Potts, P. and Statham, J. (2006) *Models of Good Practice in Joined-up Assessment: Working for Children with 'Significant and Complex Needs'*. Thomas Coram Research Unit, University of London.

Brenner, M. (1981) *Social Method and Social Life*. Academic Press, London.

Cook, G., Gerrish, K. and Clarke, C. (2001) Decision-making in teams: issues arising from two UK evaluations. *Journal of Interprofessional Care* **15** (2), 141–151.

Daniel, B. and Wassell, S. (2002) *Adolescence: Assessing and Promoting Resilience in Vulnerable Children 3*. Jessica Kingsley Publishers Ltd, London.

Department for Education and Skills (2003), *Every Child Matters*. The Stationery Office, London.

Department for Education and Skills (2004) *Every Child Matters: Change for Children*. DfES Publications, Nottingham, http://www.everychildmatters.gov.uk/aims/.

Department for Education and Skills (2005) *Common Core of Skills and Knowledge for the Children's Workforce*. DfES Publications, Nottingham.

Department for Education and Skills (2006a) *Common Assessment Framework Children and Young People: Managers' Guide. Integrated Working to Improve Outcomes for Young People*. http://www.everychildmatters.gov.uk/deliveringservices/caf/, accessed 11 August 2006.

Department for Education and Skills (2006b) *Making it Happen: Working Together for Children, Young People and Families*. London.

Foster, J.J. and Parker, I. (1997) *Carrying Out Investigations in Psychology: Methods and Statistics*. The British Psychological Society, Leicester

Freeth, D. (2001), Sustaining inter-professional collaboration. *Journal of Interprofessional Care* **15** (1), 37–46.

Laming, Lord (2003) *The Victoria Climbié Inquiry: Report of an Inquiry by Lord Laming CM 5730*. The Stationery Office, Norwich.

Northcote, H.R. (2003), Using theoretical, rhetorical and practical perspectives to evaluate the effectiveness of an inter-agency collaborative panel: a case study. Unpublished MSc thesis, University of Sheffield.

Parker, R., Ward, H., Jackson, S., Aldgate, J. and Wedge, P. (1991) *Looking After Children: Assessing Outcomes in Child Care*. The Stationery Office London.

Ryan, S. and Chionnaith, M.N. (2006) *Fetal Alcohol Spectrum Disorders: Students and Schools*. Irish Department of Education/Science and National Institute for the Study of Learning Difficulties, Trinity College Dublin, http://www.fasaware.co.uk/education_docs/FASD_studentsschoold_dublin.pdf, accessed 3 March 2007.

Sampson, P.D., Bookstein, F.L, Little, R.E. *et al.* (1997) Incidence of foetal alcohol syndrome and prevalence of alcohol-related neurodevelopmental disorder. *Teratology* **56** (5), 317–326.

Saskatchewan Institute on Prevention of Handicaps (2003) *Foetal Alcohol Spectrum Disorder: A resource for professionals, UK version 2003*. http://www.fasaware.co.uk/web/FAS%20Book.pdf, accessed 3 March 2007.

Smith, R. (2005) Information failed in Western Isles. *Children Now* 19–25 October 2005, pp. 11.

Walters, H. (2005) *An Introduction to Child Protection Legislation in the UK*. NSPCC Information Briefings. http://www.nspcc.org.uk/Inform/OnlineResources/InformationBriefings/ChildProtectionLegislation/Home_asp_ifega26036.html, accessed 5 February 2007.

Webb, R. and Vulliamy, G. (2001) Joining up the solutions: the rhetoric and practice of inter-agency cooperation. *Children and Society* **15** (5) 315–332.

9 Engaging the Hardest to Reach Parents in Parenting-Skills Programmes

NICOLA McGRATH

INTRODUCTION

Every Child Matters, the DfES Green Paper (2003a), proposes a range of measures to reform and improve children's care. The document suggests that the current Government would like to develop services which are open to all families and which could include parents' education programmes. These programmes would be targeted at the parents of 5- to 8-year-olds because research has shown that this is the group where there is the most significant impact on behaviour (DesForges, 2003). The Government proposed at least six weekly sessions where parents were to be trained in behaviour techniques.

This chapter sets out to broadly examine the current body of knowledge surrounding multi-agency working before considering parenting-skills programmes and how we can best engage 'hard to reach' parents in such programmes. The voices of parents who have taken part in parenting-skills programmes, managed by the current author, are reflected in the text. The role and dilemmas of a multi-agency team supporting such an initiative are explored throughout the chapter alongside research that could inform those working in the field of the pitfalls which lay ahead. The chapter concludes by providing suggestions for how we can best engage parents in such programmes and how as professionals working in multi-agency teams we can best support and manage such programmes.

MULTI-AGENCY WORKING

A body of research is beginning to emerge surrounding effective multidisciplinary, multi-agency and interdisciplinary working. The advent of *Every Child Matters* in 2003 has led many services to begin questioning how they can work more effectively alongside or, indeed, with other agencies in light of the Children's Trust model.

How to Reach 'Hard to Reach' Children: Improving access, participation and outcomes. Edited by K. Pomerantz, M. Hughes and D. Thompson. Copyright © 2007 by John Wiley & Sons, Ltd.

There are many problems associated with multi-agency working. For example, Maddern *et al.* (2004) suggest that:

one of the many challenges facing multi-agency working is how to avoid and overcome misunderstandings which stem from professionals' use of language which reflects different backgrounds and orientation.

(p. 152)

Maddern *et al.* (2004) further state that educational psychologists (EPs) in particular are 'uneasy with "medical language"' but insist that unless professional groups effectively communicate with one another, schools in particular may become 'ideological battle grounds for professional rivalries' (p. 152).

Wilson and Pirrie (2000), citing Clark (1993), state:

It is clear from the literature that 'putting people together in groups representing many disciplines does not necessarily guarantee the development of a shared understanding'.

(p. 2)

Furthermore, Warmington *et al.* (2004, p. 2) suggest that the 'professional boundaries between agencies, expressed in disparate goals, perspectives and priorities, have often impeded interagency working'. They go on to state that boundary crossing 'enables horizontal professional relationships to be conceived in terms of the *spaces* that they offer for renegotiation of interagency working practices and reconfiguration of professional identities' (p. 9).

Certain factors can encourage effective multidisciplinary working. For example, Wilson and Pirrie (2000) suggest those of importance to be:

- *Personal commitment (and hybrid professionals)*: committed individuals were seen as 'champions' to the success of multidisciplinary teams. It was especially fortunate if an individual in a multidisciplinary team viewed themselves as 'a bit of a hybrid' in that they do not have a particular disciplinary axe to grind. Atkinson (2002) suggests that what will emerge are 'hybrid professional types' who have personal experience and knowledge of other agencies. This will include knowledge of 'cultures, structures, discourse and priorities'.
- *A common goal*: the importance of a shared vision is stressed even though actualizing the shared vision can be laborious and time-consuming.
- *Clarity of roles and communication*: role establishment is highlighted. Equally important is the opportunity to reflect on professional practice within each role, which can be encouraged by team members sharing insights on each other's practice.
- *Institutional support*: the degree to which organizations support multidisciplinary working varies, but lack of institutional support can be a barrier to success.
- *The establishment of the 'player manager'*: the role of the 'player manager' is both to contribute and lead teams drawn from different professional groups.
- *Training*: training is needed for teams to function effectively together.

It is important to consider these factors in the construction of parenting programmes delivered by multi-agency teams.

PARENTING PROGRAMMES

BENEFITS

Researchers from within the NHS argue that much of the current knowledge on parenting programmes in mental health settings has been carried out under ideal research conditions, such as university research clinics (Scott and Stradling, 1987, Spaccarelli, Cotler and Penman, 1992; Cunningham, Bremner and Boyle, 1995). However, other research reveals that parenting programmes are being employed in the community (Gill, 1998; Miller, 2000; Zeedyk, Werritty and Riach 2002, 2003) and some key research findings have been established as indicated below:

The DfES (2003b) states:

> research has shown a clear association between behaviour and conduct problems in early childhood and parenting practice that is characterised by harsh and inconsistent discipline, low levels of positive parental involvement and poor monitoring and supervision.

(Department for Education and Skills 2003b, p. 1)

Around two-thirds of young children show improved behaviour after a parenting intervention (Fonagy *et al.*, 2002). Shorter parenting programmes of six to eight weeks are appropriate for parents dealing with mild oppositional difficulties, whereas longer programmes of between 12 and 25 weeks can be necessary when children demonstrate more entrenched behavioural problems (Fonagy *et al.*, 2002).

There appear to be particularly useful outcomes for both parents and children who join parenting groups. When parents join a parenting group, they often have certain common uniting factors. For example, Ghate and Hazel (2002) surveyed 2000 parenting programmes across Britain and discovered that there was a significant association between being in poor emotional health (measured by the Malaise Inventory and featuring factors such as depression, well-being, self-esteem and psychological distress) and having responsibility for a child who is behaviourally challenging (defined in terms of externalizing behaviours, such as bedtime refusal, rather than internalized behaviours, such as depression). Similarly, Gill (1998) in his review of two parenting programmes discovered that parents enter a parenting programme often with experiences of parenting that focus on 'powerlessness, fatalism and an inability to control leading to a downward spiral of learned helplessness' (p. 10). His experience stresses that parenting programmes have the potential to break 'such vicious circles and enabled parents to climb the slippery slope leading to greater hope and self confidence' (p. 10).

The literature reflects that the majority of parents who complete all or most of the parenting group sessions find them useful, and the success of the programmes appears to link to positive outcomes for both parents and children. For example, Taylor and Biglan (1998) cite a number of articles which indicate that both parents and children benefit from behavioural interventions primarily because the intervention itself changes parenting practices. For example, parents:

- praise their children more;
- set clearer calmer limits;
- criticize their children less often;
- smack their children less.

Parents benefit from reduced parental stress, improved communication and conflict resolution with their partners and improved marital relationships.

There is evidence to suggest that parenting groups are seen by parents to appear to be cumulatively supportive. For example, Gill (1998) discovered that the overall rating of support received from other parents in a group setting gradually rose each session and greater parental confidence in some cases led to parents almost taking on the role of therapists for others. Equally, greater confidence led to a positive parenting self-image where the parent felt in control rather than out of control and powerless. Gill summarizes this finding with the realization that 'profound changes can take place in a relatively short period of time and at relatively little expense' (p. 3).

Furthermore, Reid and Webster-Stratton (2001) add that parents go on supporting each other long after the group has ended using other parents as a resource to help them solve problems.

GETTING PARENTS INVOLVED

So how do we get parents involved? Ghate and Hazel (2002) discovered that the most frequent reason why parents did not use a parenting service was because they did not see that service as relevant to their needs. For example, parents did not see the programme or intervention as fitting with their wider life circumstances and stresses or the individuals involved were not part of their specific social networks. An additional example of why parents do not use a parenting programme include non-Caucasian families who view parenting programmes as inaccessible because of barriers, such as language differences or differences in child-rearing practices. Similarly, fathers' needs may be different from mothers' in terms of what they want from support services (Ghate, Shaw and Hazel, 2000). For these reasons Moran, Ghate and Van der Merwe (2004) argue that services offering parenting interventions need to have a clear idea of the needs of their market.

Pugh, De'Ath and Smith (1994) question which programmes worked for which parents and which strategies were appropriate for the most vulnerable families. Our understanding can be enhanced by considering the findings of Gill (1998), who states that while 'materials and methods used provide a framework and map for parents to follow' parents initially have to 'believe in that route' (p. 15) and concludes, 'the maintenance and generalisation of change over time continues to remain a challenge as does engaging those "hard to reach" families'. Gill discovered that parents who were the 'hard to reach' were those with such entrenched beliefs and attributions that they 'continually rationalised why they should do nothing ("yes-but" answers) and were resistant to cognitive restructuring', that is to say they were unable to turn negative beliefs around.

Webster-Stratton (1998b) suggests that when setting up a parenting programme in school the participation of administrators, teachers and other agencies already working in school is of vital importance as these adults are usually already committed to the programme's goals and methods. Webster-Stratton (1998b) also stresses the importance of developing a committee or 'advisory steering group' whose job it is to design recruitment strategies and training for, and evaluation of, the programme. The committee should ideally comprise teachers, those already working with families in the community and, most importantly, parents themselves. The committee initially conducts focus groups with groups of teachers, family service workers and parents to 'define and prioritise needs and goals and to develop a recruitment plan, select sites for the intervention and agree a schedule and time line' (Webster-Stratton, , p. 187). These strategies help build shared ownership and, Webster-Stratton argues, engender a commitment to the programme's eventual success.

Webster-Stratton (1998a) suggests that marketing a parenting programme needs to be carried out in messages which promote the positive outcome of the programme, for example that the programme is designed to help children succeed in school rather than a programme to reduce behavioural problems (a gain of something desired, rather than a reduction of something unwanted). The programme must also reflect the needs of the community in which it is based. For example, certain cultures may want to promote certain goals. For this reason, she insists that the programme must be culturally sensitive.

Zeedyk, Werritty and Riach (2002) report on the Parents Altogether Lending Support (PALS) programme, which was introduced in 1998 in Dundee. The aim of PALS was to give parents the opportunity to explore 'new ways of dealing with challenges that everyone faces in bringing up children' and to increase 'the life chances of young children by supporting parents in their parenting roles' (p. 319). Parents were recruited through 'open access' and the sessions were aimed at 'any parent wishing to think about and discuss their own approach to bringing up children' (p. 319).

The parents met once a week for six weeks in small groups where they worked through a programme designed to identify their strengths as parents and to create an action plan for facilitating change in their child's behaviour. Zeedyk, Werritty and Riach carried out a follow-up study that involved 21 carers who had completed the course between one and three years previously. They asked the carers what had been going on in their lives at the time when they had been thinking about joining the parenting programme.

The answers included:

- family pressures such as toilet training, children starting new levels of school, moving house or divorce;
- extreme problems such as domestic violence, rape of a daughter, return of children from foster care;
- mental or physical health problems of themselves or other family members such as depression, a child with eating disorders and a schizophrenic parent.

All of the above carers were trying to manage some degree of challenging behaviour from their children. Zeedyk, Werritty and Riach (2003) remark that the family pressures that the carers were experiencing were acute and 'resulting from a specific event or a particular constellation of events for which they had been unprepared' (p. 24). For parents experiencing either acute or chronic family situations, the parents believed that at the point of joining the PALS programme their own coping strategies were 'insufficient or ineffectual' (p. 27).

Recruitment

Parents who participated in the PALS programme hoped that the programme would give them 'new tools for managing the challenging behaviours presented by their children' (Zeedyk, Werritty and Riach, 2003, p. 24). When Zeedyk and her colleagues asked the parents why they had joined the parenting group, many of them used the words 'coping strategies' or 'solutions' to illustrate what they hoped they would gain from involvement in the PALS programme. It appeared that the most important factor in the decision the parent made to join the group was 'the degree to which the programmes purpose matched their own needs' (Zeedyk, Werritty and Riach, 2003, p. 24). On this point Webster-Stratton (1998b) argues, 'this population has been "unreachable" not because of their own characteristics, but because of the characteristics of the interventions they have been offered'.

An additional factor that encouraged parents to become involved was the encouragement of another person, with almost all of the parents joining because they had heard about the programme through word of mouth, for example from professionals they trusted, such as family centre staff or from other parents. Zeedyk, Werritty and Riach (2003) summarize this discovery by suggesting that:

> even where a) parents have already classified themselves as needing some support and b) a support programme is available in their area, the personal input of at least one other person is usually needed to facilitate the enrolment process.
>
> (Zeedyk, Werritty and Riach, 2003, p. 25)

Zeedyk and her colleagues also found that – and this was perhaps more important than providing information about the content of the forthcoming course – parents stressed the importance of 'guarding against people being put off enrolling' (Zeedyk, Werritty and Riach, 2003, p. 29). Recruiting strategies should therefore focus on parents' possible concerns as well as publicity materials. However, parents should be involved in all stages of the group and programme design including the design of publicity materials, carrying out the publicity, informing local professionals and facilitating groups. This echoes the findings of Webster-Stratton (1998b).

We also need to consider how to keep parents involved. What appear to be the most important factors in determining continued involvement? One factor may be to consider group interventions as opposed to programmes targeted at individuals or individual families.

BENEFITS OF PARENTING GROUPS

Cunningham, Bremner and Boyle (1995) and Lawes (1992) found that while individual parent training is effective (when compared to a control group) no individual parent training achieved the level of change produced by group-based programmes. Evans (1976) compared a clinic-based programme, which worked with individual parents, with a community-based group programme and a waiting-list control group. Parents reported significant changes in the community-based group, which was not only more cost-effective but parents were also more likely to use this group than individual clinic-based groups. Smith (1996) suggests that groups:

- help socially isolated families meet others;
- build a sense of cohesiveness;
- provide opportunities to share views and learn from each other;
- provide appropriate role models;
- provide support;
- can be powerful in developing confidence and self-esteem.

Many of these views are echoed by Pugh De'Ath and Smith (1994), who suggest that group discussion is particularly valuable for the opportunity it presents for drawing on the personal experiences of members of the group and relating any educational input directly to those experiences.

One word of caution is raised by Scott (2006), who suggests that the group format may not work for everyone as 'the most crisis-ridden, suspicious families' may need to be seen in their own homes so that immediate concerns such as heating and finances can be addressed before parenting can be tackled.

Also of importance appears to be the choice of parenting group packages and the type of group model used. Moran Ghate and Van der Merwe (2004) judge programme effectiveness by categorizing 2000 examples of parenting programmes in terms of their score on the Scientific Maryland Scale (SMS) and their own judgement based on the qualitative data gathered for each programme. They list over 20 US and non-UK parenting programmes and 19 UK parenting programmes, which they state, 'vary tremendously in terms of scale, format, popularity, government backing and effectiveness'. More recently, sophisticated tools have begun to emerge that help facilitators select the most appropriate package. An example of such a tool is the Commissioners Toolkit (Parenting UK, 2007).

Probably the most well-established parenting programme in both the United States and the United Kingdom is the Webster-Stratton (1992) parent training programme an example of which is *The Incredible Years* training package. This programme is delivered to groups of parents through a trained therapist or mentor.

An important component of the Webster-Stratton parent training programme is the employment of the *collaborative model*. The collaborative model is cited by a number of researchers, including Webster-Stratton and Herbert (1994) and Gill (1998). The collaborative model is 'a set of methods which enable practitioners to engage and get alongside families and communities' (Gill 1998). The model's strengths are that it identifies parental strengths and values their unique experiences of their own children. There is, therefore, no expert and no client as such. Collaboration literally means 'to work together', thus implying a reciprocal relationship that is 'based on utilising equally the trainers' and the parents' knowledge, strengths and perspectives' (Webster-Stratton, , p. 189). Gill (1998) adds, 'you can use a range of methods and have a different starting point and still achieve impressive results as long as you listen to parents and respond to their need for collaborative support' (p. 7).

KEEPING PARENTS ON BOARD

But families do drop out. Taylor and Biglan (1998) state that while families with a high number of problems (multi-problem families) have an increased likelihood of failure, behaviour interventions can still be effective with many of these families. They argue that when planning services for these families, in addition to the group intervention, it is important to consider the additional services that might be offered as well as considering how, when and where to offer such services.

Webster-Stratton (1998a) suggests that even highly motivated parents may not be able to continue participation because of work commitments, illness or other life events. She stresses that it is the group leader's role to remove as many physical or psychological barriers as possible for parents.

Buchanan (2000) highlights the importance of trust, stating:

> the parents with whom we work may have experienced more than their fair share of life's adversities, which will have further bruised their fragile self confidence. If we as helpers are to work effectively with such parents we need to tread carefully to gain their trust. Without this trust, no matter what approach we use, our efforts will fall on stony ground and may actually cause harm.

(Buchanan, 2000, p. 27)

Barlow (1998), in reviewing 255 studies on parenting training, found that the average drop-out rate was 28%, although in one study it was as high as 41%. Parents most likely to drop out were those whose children had more presenting problems, mothers under great stress, ethnic minorities and families at greatest socio-economic disadvantage. However, in Gill's (1998) study there were a number of reasons why parents did less well. These included:

- time pressures (which led to poor attendance or homework tasks not being completed, which made participants feel left behind);
- poor organization;
- forgetting to carry out agreed tasks;
- negative self-belief or doubt ('I've tried this before and it doesn't work');
- being locked into a downward cycle of reinforcing behavioural patterns (unable to stand back and analyse);
- externalizing problems and lack of closeness to child or ability to relate positively;
- overwhelming need for personal support.

Webster-Stratton (1998a) suggests that certain organizational factors help alleviate difficulties which parents face. She discovered that night-time groups were the most successful for attracting both mothers and fathers who would otherwise be working during the day. Other families preferred groups that took place in the day when the children were in school. In certain groups night-time dinners, babysitting and transport have also been offered.

Webster-Stratton (1998a) states that some parenting groups offer incentives, such as course credits, which are provided for those that may use the experience to contribute to an academic course. Lotteries may also be held and all parents (and children) receive certificates and a celebration party at the end. Webster-Stratton (1998a) adds that although such incentives originally attracted parents to the programme, after attending for a while parents stated that they would have continued coming anyway regardless of whether there were lotteries or bonuses. This suggests far greater dynamics at work that keep the parents attending, such as group cohesion and support and collaboration between the group leader and the parents.

Gill (1998), reporting on the *Fun and Families Programme*, suggests that a number of factors motivated parents to continue to attend. The first of these was the commitment to completing homework. As progress was discussed weekly during the group, parents did not want to let themselves down, be seen to be not fully contributing or to be viewed as failures. The homework tasks also facilitated generalization to the home and reinforced the emphasis on learning and practising. Homework also was linked with increases in parental motivation, confidence and commitment. Other factors that were rated highly by parents were handouts to reinforce the main points. Parents also found the use of video clips useful, although role play by parents and children was not highly rated by parents. In addition, Gill found that offering a crèche, which enabled parents to have a break and concentrate on content, providing refreshments, which helped encourage social interaction and friendship, and starting with a warm-up were seen by parents to be helpful and effective and encouraged continued attendance.

Interestingly, Taylor and Biglan (1998) state that it is important for parents to experience some degree of struggle when they enter a parenting group. For example, parents who state that they have tried the strategies and believe that none of them works display a natural resistance which, providing they remain attending, will increase and then decrease during therapy. Such parents make more lasting gains than parents who maintain high levels of resistance or who float through the intervention without experiencing any struggle.

THE NORTH OF ENGLAND PILOT PROJECT

What follows shortly are the voices of parents who took part in a series of parenting courses that were run by a Child and Family Mental Health (CAFMH) worker, a teacher from the Behaviour Support Service (BSS) and, in a supportive role, myself, an educational psychologist (EP) throughout 2003/2004. This was the second strand of a pilot project involving both small group work for children (the first strand) and parenting courses aimed at developing behaviour management and parenting skills for those parents whose children had been targeted for the small group work. This model was based on research which suggested that when social skills training with children is carried out at the same time as parenting programmes, parents are able to reinforce children's learning within such groups (Department for Education and Skills, 2003b). Throughout the current text, the multidisciplinary pilot project will be known as the NEPP (North of England Pilot Project). The following key messages from research into parental training programmes at that time influenced the launch of the NEPP:

- Parenting programmes are hard work but they do work. They need to be set up carefully, made as interesting as possible and delivered in a convenient location.
- Group programmes that incorporate video modelling seem to be just as effective, and cheaper, than individual parenting programmes and are more attractive than those using written materials.
- Programmes should be entered into on a voluntary basis where possible.
- The skills of the individual therapist have an impact on retention rates.

(Department for Education and Skills, 2003b, p. 2)

The initial NEPP model was based on the DfES (2003b) pilot project outline, which involved staff in schools targeting children who were experiencing social and/or emotional difficulties in school or children who potentially could benefit from extra social and emotional skills training in small groups (small group work). The parenting course was offered to the parents of the children identified for the small group work in school. The parents involved were amongst the 'hard to reach' in light of the fact that they were often not contactable by telephone and that they faced a number of major life stresses not directly relating to, but affecting, their parenting styles (e.g. domestic violence, financial hardship and a combination of such factors). In the first cycle, places were offered to parents and members of the child's extended family. Seventeen parents and carers were contacted by letter and invited to attend a subsequent parents' meeting. Those whom staff at school most wanted to involve were visited at home by the CAFMH worker. This process was carried out in a relatively short space of time, approximately six weeks.

Two parenting courses that had identical content were offered at different times of the day in order to, it was hoped, minimize the impact of childcare commitments.

All parents were contacted by phone and given relevant information about the course. Three parents did not attend the course because of work commitments, four because their partner was attending and two because of lack of interest. Eight out of the originally targeted 17 parents and carers attended the initial session of the parenting course.

At the time the main parent group leader (CAFMH worker) selected a formal package entitled *The Noughts to Sixes Parenting Programme* (Quinn and Quinn, 1995) to be delivered during the parenting course. This programme adopts a behavioural approach over six to eight sessions. It takes the form of:

- structured sessions;
- practical exercises and tasks;
- opportunity to observe and practise skills;

- agreed homework tasks with structured weekly feedback;
- practical application of social learning theory;
- incremental focused change;
- continued opportunities for collaborative and group problem-solving.

The parenting course was supported with short video clips and parents received a book (manual).

The drop-out rate from the initial cycle of running the parenting groups was high (62.5%). This drop-out rate was higher than the highest found by Barlow (1998), who reviewed 255 studies on parenting training (the highest drop-out being 41%). Just three of the original eight parents completed all of the sessions. Of those that dropped out, one dropped out after the first session without giving a reason, one parent attended two sessions then cited work commitments for the drop-out, one parent attended four sessions but then felt that the content was not useful and two parents (a couple) attended six sessions but then dropped out because of domestic violence.

THE VOICES OF PARENTS

The voices of parents are heard in the following section. It is important to point out that this study was small scale in its nature and therefore whether or not the findings could be generalized to larger-scale studies must be considered.

At the end of the first cycle of the parenting course, parents were asked a series of questions to provide qualitative data. Information was obtained from two separate written questionnaires, from two different perspectives. First, parents were asked questions by the behaviour support teacher who had led the group work aimed at the children of the parents involved in the parenting course. Five parents responded. This included the three parents who had completed the parenting course and two who had completed the first part of the parenting course but had then dropped out. Question 3 below refers more especially to the changes observed (by the parent) in the child but is included here because of the obvious inter-relationship between what the parents had learned in the parenting group and the skills that the children had learned in the small group work.

Question 1: *What have you found helpful?*
Four of the five parents made a statement in this section. One parent stated that she had found the strategies (learned from the parenting course) useful. The other three remaining parents mentioned the importance of talking with their child and sharing experiences. For example, one parent stated, 'Knowing about the things K has been doing meant we have been able to talk about his feelings more.'

Question 2: *Is there anything you would like to change?*
Four parents stated that there wasn't anything that they would like to change.
One parent stated that she was very pleased with what had changed.

A further parent commented, 'I would have liked it if we could all have got together, parents and children, and done an activity together.'

Question 3: *Have you noticed any changes in your child?*
All of the parents stated at least one change in their child or children. Two comments concerned feelings:
'S is opening up more, expressing her feelings instead of hurting herself.'
'C can recognize my feelings and talk about them.'
Three comments concerned behaviour/relationships and/or confidence:
'M is more confident in himself and takes more pride in what he does, more sociable with friends.'
'Big improvement in J's behaviour, better relationships.'
'B has tried harder to calm down when getting irate. She is more aware of my needs.'
One parent commented on how their child was trying to understand their parent's behaviour:
'C now asks, "Why are you shouting at me?" He would never have done this before.'
One very happy parent stated:
'The changes have been brilliant in all three of my children. Just bit by bit but when it all comes together there's a big smile on all our faces.'

Question 4: *Have you used any strategies at home which would help in school?*
One parent stated:
'No, it's the other way round. What is going on in school should be carried out at home.'
Three further comments included:
'Sticking to the boundaries.'
'"I" messages work brilliantly (e.g. "I don't like it when . . .").'
'Respect is a big thing and the tone of our voices.'
The three parents who completed the course were also asked a number of questions.

Question A: *What did you want to achieve and what did you hope to gain by attending the parenting course?*
All three of the parents replied to this question and they all gave multiple answers. Unravelling their answers revealed that two of the parents wanted to attend the group to gain some new ideas about parenting. For example, one parent stated:
'Try new ideas – see what was on offer.'
One parent stated that she was seeking a better relationship and understanding with her children:
'I wanted a better relationship with my children. I wanted to understand why they do what they do.'
One parent stated that she wanted to meet other people and share ideas, while another reflected on the level of responsibility she felt in working with her child and the amount of continued effort it took:
'I know my daughter has problems – she was going to the children's group. I know what I should be doing, but it is difficult to keep it going.'

Question B: *Did the course give you what you wanted?*
All three parents gave positive responses to this question. One stated:
'It has reinforced my parenting skills and helped me keep a perspective.'
The other two parents also expressed answers that reflected how they had changed their own behaviour and approach to their child. Parent two said:
'Yes, I have changed. I am not as aggressive. I do not shout as much, I stop and think, I have more tolerance.'
Parent three said:
'I find my son much happier. I can help him put the smile back on his face. I used to see it as a sulk, but now I know he needs support to know that I am there for him.'

Question C: *What has been useful?*
Again, all three parents gave positive and multiple responses. They all stated strategies that they had tried, as a result of being part of the parenting course, that had worked for them. For example, parent two stated:
'I liked the "I messages", it was the best thing about the course, saying; "I don't like it when you fight" instead of "stop fighting", it really works.'
Parent two also emphasised a more collaborative relationship which had developed with her children stating:
'I like to give the children options instead of telling them what to do. I like encouraging and praising them, they thrive on praise and started doing things for themselves.'
Parent three reflected how she had learned the importance of sometimes not intervening by:
'Stepping back and letting them sort out squabbles.'
Parent one again reflected on her own behaviour changes stating:
'I read to her every night regardless of her behaviour. I don't make threats; I used to do that a lot. I shout less.'

Question D: *What was not useful?*
Here Parent one gave the most negative answer stating, 'Some of it got on my nerves a bit, but I think that was to do with timing. I haven't been able to put as much in as the others.'
Parents two and three had had difficulty trying out particular strategies when they were first introduced.

Question E: *Have you seen an improvement in your child's behaviour?*
Two parents responded to this question by reflecting on changes in the relationship between their child and themselves. For example, Parent one said:
'My daughter seems more aware of my needs. I don't know if that's a good thing; is it too much responsibility?'
Parent two reflected on the difference in both her child and herself:
'A big improvement: he looks at me and listens to me – our relationship has improved.'
'I feel better in myself. I am not as angry-head. I'm not as stressed out. I sought help for myself. I learned that I don't have to be a parent all of the time, I don't have to be

at home all of the time. I can have things for me. I went off to get a job. It has opened my eyes a lot.'

Question F: *What was good about the course?*
Two parents mentioned the manual that came with the course as being useful. Parent two mentioned the ethos of 'no blame':
'It's about give and take, no pushiness and no reprimands.'
She later added:
'I have done five [parenting courses] before and it has been this one that worked.'
Parent three liked the fact that it covered a variety of age groups and she liked the video. Parent one enjoyed sharing experiences and making friends, adding:
'I know it is not just me or my child that finds it hard work.'

Question G: *What could have been better about the course?*
All three parents wished there had been more parents interested in attending the course. Parent one stated that four or five people would have been better. Two parents wanted a place to smoke.

Question H: *Knowing what you know now, would you do the course again?*
One parent said yes. Parent one stated that 'you need to put into it to get out'. Parent three stated:
'If you are offered help, you should go and see if it can help.'

Question I: *Any other comments?*
The answers from this question indicated that the three parents who had completed the course had become friends and had taken all of their children out to tea. Parent three stated:
'Thank you. The kids still fight, because they are brothers, but our relationship is better and I feel better about my skills.'
On the whole parents had joined the course to gain new ideas and better relationships and understanding with their children.
These answers indicated that for those parents who completed some or all of the course there had been very positive changes in the relationships they had with their children, their level of understanding of their child's behaviour and the types of strategies, behaviours and skills they now used when faced with confrontational situations at home. Some parents also found that the experience of being part of a group of parents helped them to 'normalize' their experiences with their children. Gill (1998) had found similar results in his study of two parenting programmes with parents feeling able to 'share difficulties and realise that they are not alone!' (p. 2). For one parent, the parent who was most ready to take on this type of intervention, the parenting course had even been a life-changing experience as she had, for the first time, sought employment.
The second cycle of parenting groups were run in a school serving a similar socio-economic area as the first cycle. Teachers, senior staff and administration staff worked with the NEPP staff to identify children, and their parents and carers were approached. The behaviour support teacher and CAFMH worker spent a considerable amount of

time visiting homes and selling the programme to the parents at an individual level. In this cycle the role of the EP widened. Agencies outside the project who knew the families well were approached to obtain contact details and to help build a family profile of each of the families involved. For example, on one occasion the EP linked with the education welfare office to obtain such details.

The groups were run in an on-site children's centre, which it was hoped would encourage parents to feel more relaxed. Parents were also able to smoke outside. Five parents completed this round of parenting courses. At the beginning of the course the parents were asked:

What do you think you as parents might gain from taking part in this project?

In answering this question, four parents referred to the fact that they were hoping to learn different approaches. For example, Parent B stated, 'I am hoping I will learn how to cope and control behaviour and learn that I'm not the only one going through the same problems.'

At the end of the sessions the parents were asked eight follow-up questions.

Question 1: *What benefit did you get from doing this course?*

All of the parents could think of at least one benefit. Three parents mentioned being more calm and/or patient. For example, Parent A stated:

'It helped a lot, how to calm down, walk away instead of shouting.'

Parent D stated:

'Calmer, more respectful; if I give respect, then they give it to me.'

Question 2: *Have you or has anyone else noticed any changes in you as a parent?*

Again three parents mentioned being more calm and/or patient. Parent D said:

'People have noticed I'm more patient: not shouting or screaming as much.'

Question 3: *How much did you enjoy the course (score out of 10)?*

The average score was 7.4. With the range being five to 10.

Question 4: *What did you like? (Prompts were given if the parents gave no response, e.g. the group, the room, the presentation.)*

Four parents reported positively on the location of the programme, three parents liked the group leader and three parents liked the room itself. Two parents liked the other people in the group. Other responses (suggested by one parent in each case) included the way the materials were presented, being able to talk freely and finding it easy to listen. Comments concerning the group leader included 'approachable', 'down to earth' and 'brilliant'.

Question 5: *What did you dislike?*

There were five categories of response here. Three parents did not like the video, one parent commented that they did not like the behaviour support teacher and a further parent commented that they did not like the manual. Another parent stated that they felt intimidated by someone else in the group.

Question 6: *What was useful about the course (e.g. any specific skills you have learned)?*

One parent focused her response on the delivery, stating that the group was 'warm and friendly', and the video was 'funny'. Three other parents talked about specific techniques that they had found useful. Parent E said:

'I learned some different techniques. It was a good break.'

Question 7: *What could be improved when we run the next one?*

Responses were varied and included reminding other parents of the rules, the video and the course being too short. The need to demonstrate the strategies in a variety of settings such as on holiday or going to the shops, what to do when they get bored, was also mentioned. One parent stated:

'Parents need to be told that their children's behaviour isn't as bad as the children on the video. I thought "My child's not as bad as that. Do you think my child is that bad?"'

Question 8: *What should happen now the course has finished? Are there things you would like to keep going or develop further?*

Two parents stated they would like a more advanced version of the course. One parent thought the course was too short and wanted to keep going. One parent wanted to have a role in further courses. Finally, one parent stated how she planned to spend more time with her children.

It appeared that most of the parents entered this cycle of the parenting course hoping to learn new approaches to parenting.

In summary, all of the parents found the experience to be beneficial and enjoyable. An interesting outcome was that the majority of parents felt calmer or more patient as a result of taking part. All of the parents could name aspects of the course or course delivery or location that they liked, the room and the group leader being the most often quoted answers. Aspects that were disliked were related to clashes of personality, and there was some criticism of both the video and the manual. As in the first cycle, parents believed that they had learned some useful strategies. On the whole, the group situation was felt to be positive, in fact so positive that some parents did not want it to end!

Overall, the majority of parents found the course useful, and for one parent in particular being a member of the parenting course was a life-changing experience.

These findings are reflected in the wider literature. For example, Zeedyk, Werritty and Riach (2002) discovered that parents who had been involved in the PALS programme stated that the group had enhanced their self-confidence. In some cases, this had generalized to other aspects of their lives. For example, some parents had sought out new jobs or educational opportunities. This is a similar finding to Gill (1998), who found that, following training, parents were ready to sort out their own lives beyond parenthood.

In both cycles, parents had found the interactions with other group members to be beneficial. Again, this finding is reflected in the wider literature, with Gill (1998), for example, discovering that parents preferred being supported through a group rather than individually because of mutual support and learning from others. Zeedyk,

Werritty and Riach (2003, pp. 27–28) suggests that personal exchanges between participants had an impact in three different domains:

- The first was the acquisition of parenting skills. While the PALS course had given the participants the tools that they sought and the ability to implement the skills, the forum had provided an opportunity to discuss the ideas with other parents enabling the parents to become confident and motivated to apply them.
- Parents realized that they were not alone, and hearing other people's experiences gave parents a new context for making sense of the challenges they faced.
- Thirdly, speaking to other participants helped parents get to know other people in the area. This created new opportunities for support and friendship and 'a new context within which to make sense of the job of parenting'.

(Zeedyk, Werritty and Riach, 2003, p. 28).

Some parents who took part in the NEPP reported that they now felt more patient and were calmer as a result of taking part in the parenting course. These outcomes are reflected by Taylor and Biglan (1998, p. 47) who amongst other benefits report that parents often set calmer limits and experience reduced parental stress after being involved in a parenting intervention. Zeedyk, Werritty and Riach (2002) found that parents reported being more patient and that they shouted less often.

Parents throughout both cycles of the current programme reported that they found certain strategies to be useful, for example a number of parents mentioned the use of 'I messages'. Gill (1998) discovered that the teaching of strategies helped parents understand their children's behaviours and provided building blocks to change. Similarly, Zeedyk, Werritty and Riach (2003) note that 43% of their parents reported that they had learned new parenting skills and strategies as a result of being part of the PALS programme.

Group size was an issue, especially for the first group of parents, and appears to be one of the crucial aspects that can contribute to the success or failure of a parenting course.

Zeedyk, Werritty and Riach (2003) found that, while small groups on the whole were favoured by the parents (so that parents could make exchanges), groups which are too small have 'insufficient participants to keep the conversations active and dynamic' (p. 28). The optimum group size is seen to be around six.

Without doubt the success of both cycles of parenting course had a great deal to do with the group leader, who was able to talk to parents in a collaborative and supportive manner. The role of the leader has been explored in many parenting programmes. Webster-Stratton and Herbert (1994) suggest that the group leader has five distinct roles. These are to:

- build a supportive, collaborative relationship with the parents (achieved through self-disclosure, humour, optimism and acting as an advocate for parents, e.g. in the child's school);
- empower parents through reinforcing and validating parents' insights, helping them modify powerless thoughts and building family and group supports;

- teach through role play, explaining, suggesting, giving assignments, reviewing, using videotape examples and ensuring generalization;
- translate cognitive, behavioural and developmental concepts into words that parents can understand and apply. This includes the reframing of childhood experiences;
- lead and challenge, set limits, pace the sessions and deal with resistance.

Taylor and Biglan (1998) state that empathy and effective teaching are important aspects of group leadership. In addition, they report on a two-dimensional skill base needed by a group leader, which encompasses a relationship dimension characterized by warmth and humour and, secondly, a structuring dimension characterized by directiveness and self-confidence. They suggest that 'each of these dimensions predicted successful outcomes when added to each other' (p. 45).

Gill (1998) suggests that fun and humour, the ability to sell and believe in the programme's effectiveness and the sharing of professional and parenting experiences with anecdotal stories were all key components in the dynamic process which 'enabled group leaders to get alongside parents' (p. 4).

HOW CAN WE ENGAGE THE 'HARDEST TO REACH' PARENTS IN PARENTING PROGRAMMES? HOW CAN PROFESSIONALS WORKING IN MULTI-AGENCY TEAMS ACHIEVE SUCCESS?

Certainly, throughout the body of accumulated research and the findings reported here we have learned that to engage 'hard to reach' parents we have to consider how we set up such programmes and how we maintain them. Buchanan (2000) states that 'we have a duty to ensure that the interventions we use are those with the best chance of helping. Ethically we have no right to be involved unless we have done our homework' (p. 27).

There are certain factors that appear to encourage participation. As professionals we need to consider such factors when setting up parenting programmes aimed at 'hard to reach' parents. These factors include:

- Knowing your marketplace and target audience well. Offer a programme that parents believe matches their needs at the time and which involves professionals that they know and trust from their own community. Consider the readiness of each individual parent to become involved.
- Considering the language and cultural sensitivity of the participants.
- Involving professionals in community settings that are already committed to the aims of the programme.
- Setting up a committee to steer the programme that involves members of the parenting community you intend to involve. The aim of this is to build shared ownership. Also word of mouth from other parents is your most powerful tool in facilitating recruitment.

- Marketing the programme positively. Promote the positive outcomes. Advertise the use of the collaborative model that values the parents' own experiences of their children.
- Offering group programmes rather than interventions aimed at individuals. A group size of around six is favoured.
- Considering offering additional incentives such as a crèche, meals, transport and group times that fit with the needs of the parents.
- Involving parents from the first round of parenting programme with the next round.

EPs are well-placed to facilitate parenting programmes and in supporting multi-agency work in this area. The DfEE (2000) report on the role of educational psychology services suggests that EPs should 'develop multi-agency approaches to support schools and parents'. In light of the Children's Services model, parenting programmes and multi-agency working are set to continue to be a high priority in the near future. Moran, Ghate and Van der Merwe (2004) state:

> it might almost be said that the term 'Multi-agency working' was invented for parenting support: certainly there can be few areas of health and social care in which the imperative for multi-agency working is quite so strong.

(Moran, Ghate and Van der Merwe, 2004, p. 20)

CONCLUSION

Many of the factors that require addressing in the set up and maintenance of parenting programmes are not glamorous and, as the DfES (2003b) suggests, require a great deal of hard work. For multi-agency teams to be successful in supporting parenting programmes it may be important to consider the following factors:

- Multi-agency teams require time together to establish shared goals, vision and commitment if such a programme is to be successful. Pugh, De'Ath and Smith (1994, p. 220) suggest that while a great range of professionals are involved in parent education and support 'few see it as an integral part of their work load'.
- The role of each of the professionals in the team needs to be defined.
- The inclusion of hybrid professional types who are able to see beyond their own professional boundaries will be of benefit. Such individuals often have the capacity to build up experience and knowledge of other agencies.
- Support from all of the institutions that provide a professional to the team is of benefit especially in the areas of steerage and supervision.
- The appointment of a player manager who will be able to both guide and have first-hand experience of the project.
- Secure a group leader who is skilled at developing collaborative relationships with parents.
- Be realistic. Give yourselves time to establish the team and a steerage group in the community. Undergo joint training.

There appears to be a wealth of research and resources on parenting programmes that help to identify features of the many parenting programmes and interventions which look promising. However, it is only now that we are beginning to learn and understand how we can best recruit and retain those parents who are 'hard to reach'. Most recent thinking suggests that maybe it is time to adopt a more radical approach to recruitment. Scott, O'Connor and Futh (2006) suggest that it may be useful to screen a whole population, wherever feasible, in order to correctly identify those most in need so that service delivery can be altered to try and engage these parents. In addition, Scott, O'Connor and Futh (2006) tentatively suggest that it may now be time to change the culture of the workplace so that training opportunities could include attendance at such courses. This is the case in some areas of Australia where parenting programmes are delivered in the workplace. They cite Sanders and Turner (2005), who suggest that this can lead to a happier and more productive workplace.

To echo Hutchings and Lane (2006), those delivering parenting programmes and interventions to 'hard to reach' parents:

> need to take responsibility for making them accessible and relevant: only then can they be effective even with the high risk, disadvantaged children, who in the past often had poor outcomes

(Hutchings and Lane, 2006, p. 483)

This will remain both a challenge and an opportunity for professionals working in this field.

REFERENCES

Atkinson, M., Wilkin, A., Stott, A., Doherty, P. and Kinder, K. (2002) Multi-agency working: a detailed study. *LGA Research Report* **17**, NFER.

Barlow, J. (1998) Parent training programmes: Findings from a systemic review. In: A. Buchanan and B.L. Hudson (eds). *Parenting, Schooling and Children's Behaviour*. Ashgate, Aldershot.

Buchanan, A. (2000) You're walking on eggs: findings from research into parenting. In: A. Wheal (ed.). *Working with Parents: Learning from Other People's Experience*. Russell House Publishing Limited, Dorset.

Clark, P.G. (1993) A typology of multidisciplinary education in gerontology and geriatrics: Are we really doing what we say we are? *Journal of interprofessional Care* **7** (3), 217–227.

Cunningham, C.E., Bremner, R. and Boyle, M. (1995) Large Group Community Based Parenting Programmes for Families of Preschoolers at Risk for Disruptive Behaviour Disorder; Utilization, Cost Effectiveness and Outcome, in NHS National Electronic Library for Health, http://www.nelmh.org/page_view.asp?c+15&fc=005003&did=1207

Department for Education and Employment (2000) *Educational Psychology Services (England) Current Role, Good Practice and Future Directions*. The Stationery Office, London.

Department for Education and Skills (2003a) *Every Child Matters*. The Stationery Office, London.

Department for Education and Skills (2003b) Appendix 1 'Group Based Interventions for Children 4–8 Years.' Behaviour and Attendance Pilot Project notes. Unpublished.

DesForges, C. (2003) *The Impact of Parental Involvement, Parental Support and Family Education on Pupil Achievement and Adjustment.* DfES London.

Evans, E.G. (1976) Behaviour Problems in Children. *Child Care and Health Development* **2** (1), 35–43. In NHS National Electronic Library for Health.

Fonagy, P., Target, M. and Cottrell, D. *et al.* (2002) *What Works for Whom? A Critical Review of Treatments for Children and Adolescents.* Guilford Press, New York.

Ghate, D. and Hazel, N. (2002) *Parenting in Poor Environments: Stress Support and Coping.* Jessica Kingsley Publishers Ltd, London.

Ghate, D., Shaw, C. and Hazel, N. (2000) *Fathers and Family Centres: Engaging Fathers in Preventative Services.* Joseph Rowntree Foundation/York Publishing Services, York.

Gill, A. (1998) Extract from Group work results. What makes parent training groups effective? Promoting positive parenting through collaboration. Unpublished PhD, University of Leicester, http://www.freenetpages.co.uk/hp/AndyGill/results.

Hutchings, J. and Lane, E. (2006) Reaching those who need it most. *The Psychologist* **18** (3), 480–483.

Lawes, G. (1992) Individual parent-training implemented by nursery nurses: evaluation of a program for mothers of pre-school children. *Behavioural Psychotherapy* **20** (3), 239–256, In NHS National Electronic Library for Health http://www.nelmh.org/page_view. asp?c+15&fc=005003&did=1207

Maddern, L., Franey, J., McLaughlin, V. and Cox, S. (2004) An evaluation of the impact of an inter-agency intervention programme to promote social skills in primary school children. *Educational Psychology in Practice* **20** (2), 135–155.

Miller, I. (2000) Kirklees Metropolitan Council Psychological Service Summary of Progress, April to November 2000: The Butterfly Project. Unpublished.

Moran, P., Ghate, D. and Van der Merwe, A. (2004) *What Works in Parenting Support? A Review of the International Evidence.* DfES, London, http://www.prb.org.uk/wwiparenting/ RR574.pdf, accessed 4 February 2007.

Parenting UK (2007) Commissioners Toolkit, www.toolkit.parentinguk.org/, accessed 4 February 2007.

Pugh, G., De'Ath, E. and Smith, C. (1994) *Confident Parents, Confident Children.* National Children's Bureau. London.

Quinn, M. and Quinn, T. (1995) *The Noughts to Sixes Parenting Programme.* Family Caring Trust, County Down.

Reid, M.J. and Webster-Stratton, C. (2001) The incredible years parent, teacher and child intervention: targeting multiple areas of risk for a young child with pervasive conduct problems using a flexible manulised treatment program. *Cognitive and Behaviour Practice* **8**, 377–386.

Sanders, M.R. and Turner, K.M. (2005) Reflections on the challenges of effective dissemination of behavioural family intervention: our experience with the triple p: positive parenting program, *Child and Adolescent Mental Health* **10** (4), 158–169.

Scott, M.J. and Stradling, S.G. (1987) The evaluation of a group parent training program. *Behavioural Psychotherapy* **15** (3), 224–239. In: NHS National Electronic Library for Health http://www.nelmh.org/page_view.asp?c+15&fc=005003&did=1207.

Scott, S. (2006) Where next? Improving children's lives, preventing criminality. *The Psychologist* **19** (8), 484–487.

Scott, S., O'Connor, T. and Futh, A. (2006) *What makes Parenting Programmes work in Disadvantaged Areas?: The PALS Trials.* Joseph Rowntree Foundation, York.

Smith, C. (1996) *Developing Parenting Programmes.* National Children's, Bureau, London.

Smith, C. and Pugh, G. (1996) *Learning to be a Parent.* Family Policy Studies Centre, London.

Spaccarelli, S., Cotler, S. and Penman, D. (1992) Problem solving skills training as a supplement to behavioural parent training. *Cognitive Therapy and Research* **16** (1) 1–18. In: NHS National Electronic Library for Health, http://www.nelmh.org/page_view. asp?c+15&fc=005003&did=1207.

Taylor, T.K. and Biglan, A. (1998) Behavioral family interventions for improving child-rearing: a review of the literature for clinicians and policy makers. *Clinical Child and Family Psychology Review* **1** (1), 41–60.

Warmington, P., Daniels, H., Edwards, A. *et al.* (2004) *Learning in and for interagency working: conceptual tensions in 'joined up' practice.* Paper presented at Teaching and Learning Research Programme Annual Conference Papers. 5th Annual conference 22–24 November 2004.

Webster-Stratton, C. (1992) *The Incredible Years Package.* Webster-Stratton, Seattle.

Webster-Stratton, C. (1998a) Adopting and implementing empirically supported interventions: a recipe for success. In: A Buchanan (ed.). *Parenting, Schooling and Children's Behaviour-Interdisciplinary Approaches.* Ashgate, Hampshire.

Webster-Stratton, C. (1998b) Parent training with low income families. In: J. Lutzer (ed.). *Handbook of Child Abuse Research and Treatment.* Plenum Press, New York.

Webster-Stratton, C. and Herbert, M. (1994) *Troubled Families Problem Children: Working with Parents: A Collaborative Process.* John Wiley & Sons, Ltd, New York.

Wilson, V. and Pirrie, A. (2000) Multidisciplinary teamworking indicators of good practice. *Spotlight 77*, The Scottish Council for Research in Education, 1–4.

Zeedyk, M.S., Werritty, I. and Riach, C. (2002) The PALS Parenting Support Programme: Lessons Learned from the Evaluation of Process and Outcome. *Children and Society* **16**, 318–333.

Zeedyk, M.S., Werritty, I. and Riach, C. (2003) Promoting emotional health through parenting support programme: What motivates parents to enrol? *International Journal of Mental Health Promotion* **5** (4), 21–31.

10   Whose Voice is it Anyway?

MARY CHILOKOA AND JANE McKIE

INTRODUCTION

Children in our society occupy marginalized positions. Research with children is often difficult because of this marginalization – they are 'hard to reach'. Focus groups are one of the research techniques that academic researchers use, engaging a group of young people in discussion, recording their views and presenting them to the wider community. This is a set of research practices with historical, cultural and political aspects, producing knowledge in a certain way with the hope that this enables the child's voice to be heard. However, research is not in and of itself an innocent activity. In this chapter, we look at the possibility that research practices are mistaken for the child's voice, and the child actually remains beyond reach.

We attempt to explore this hypothesis and how we came to it, by describing the context from which our original and subsequent thinking came. Then the theoretical assumptions which informed that work are looked at, highlighting the specific challenges which exist when doing research with children. We suggest that how far research is able to acknowledge and work with these challenges becomes significant to being better able to capture the full account of children's views and perspectives. In so doing, we have endeavoured to create a space to consider and reconsider issues which we feel have a great bearing on working with and researching children and, specifically, how far they are subsequently constructed as, and become, 'hard to reach'.

The origins of this chapter come from parallel interpretivist studies by the authors involved in educational psychology research. The first study involved an evaluation of a peer mediation system in a primary school. Focus groups were used as an evaluative tool with children randomly selected from Year 1 through to Year 6, with the children from Years 5 and 6 who were peer mediators, and with lunchtime supervisors. The second study was a critical exploration of the processes and interactions at play within the focus groups of the first study. Here, the video and audio recordings of the groups, questionnaires and semi-structured interviews were used to build up a picture of what happens in focus groups.

To illustrate the difficulties that can occur, this chapter includes examples of the authors' experiences with focus groups. However, while drawing on these studies, this chapter is more than a reworking of the research results. It is a collaborative venture by the authors, in which the specific issues of 'hard to reach' children and

How to Reach 'Hard to Reach' Children: Improving access, participation and outcomes.   Edited by K. Pomerantz,
M. Hughes and D. Thompson.   Copyright © 2007 by John Wiley & Sons, Ltd.

focus group methodology are considered in the wider context of research in general. In particular, the chapter represents a reflective journey jointly undertaken by the authors themselves, whereby ideas and assumptions held during our original research endeavours were scrutinized and re-evaluated.

As such, then, what this chapter is not about is an attempt merely to say how focus groups could be 'done better'. Rather, it is an honest exploration of the idea that no matter how 'well' one attempts to do research with children in order to give them a voice, it is vital to recognize that the way that research itself is set up will invariably affect and influence what is gathered, and consequently the 'voice' that is heard.

RESEARCH AND CHILDREN

Power relations are intrinsic features of human relationships; as O'Kane says:

> Working within a historical and cultural context in which children's voices have been marginalized, researchers face great challenges in finding ways to break down the power imbalance between adults and children, and in creating space which enables children to speak up and be heard.
>
> (O'Kane, 2000, p. 137)

The inherent power relations between children and adults, which come from historical, cultural and political discourses, can make children 'hard to reach' when it comes to research. In research with children, the hope is that the child will provide knowledge and the adult will learn from this. This reversal of fortunes for the child is, of course, not of their making. Research is still an adult agenda, and it is adults who will decide any consequences. We need, therefore, to uncover how research produces children's voices, and within this notions of power and control. The purpose is to endeavour to reveal the ways in which social reality is produced, by an exploration of how the researcher has structured the way it is defined in the first place.

In order to do this, we look first at the history of focus groups. This means of researching did not just suddenly appear, but has developed into a particular way of finding out what people are thinking.

FOCUS GROUPS

Focus groups have been used as market research techniques since the 1920s. Focus groups, then termed 'focused interviews', were introduced to the social sciences by Merton, Fiske and Kendall (1956). Most of the procedures that have come to be accepted as common practice in focus group interviews are laid out in this seminal work.

No real interest in this type of approach was shown within the social sciences until the 1980s. In fact, several distinct approaches to focus groups have evolved, including the market research tradition, academic and scientific research and participatory research. It is the academic and scientific research approach that will, on the whole, be explored in this chapter, although input from the market research tradition has been influential.

Focus groups as a research method collect information through group interaction on a topic determined by the researcher. Typically, a focus group involves six to 12 participants. The group have a commonality, that is they are similar to each other in a way important to the research, for example in terms of age, gender or particular experiences. The group is run by a facilitator (typically the researcher), who asks pre-prepared questions and encourages participants to respond and interact in a comfortable, permissive environment. The fundamental data that focus groups produce are transcripts of the group discussion.

The role of the facilitator is seen as central to the focus group by many researchers (e.g. Morgan, 1993; Barbour and Kitzinger, 1999). A permissive and non-critical climate is viewed as important, as this encourages people to feel free to give their sincere thoughts, feelings and attitudes. Interaction is crucial, and the facilitator helps this by ensuring that the discussion is productive (all relevant issues are covered and in sufficient depth) but control over the content is minimal: only the issues to be focused on are determined in advance. Listening and questioning skills are also viewed as important as they help to establish productive interaction.

There is much agreement amongst researchers that it is the occurrence of group interactions which makes focus groups different and valuable as a method. According to Morgan (1988, p. 12):

> The hallmark of focus groups is the explicit use of the group interactions to produce data and insights that would be less accessible without the interaction found in a group.

Krueger and Casey (2000) argue that the focus group presents a more natural environment than that of an individual interview because participants are influencing and influenced by others, just as they are in life. The aim of focus groups is to get closer to participants' understandings of, and perspectives on, certain issues and the freer and more dynamic situation of a focus group may actually access better data than a more subdued and formal encounter.

The basic assumptions underpinning focus groups as a method suggest that:

- people can be enabled to say what they want to, and have freedom to do this;
- group interaction creates a dynamic situation that can enhance information received from individuals alone;
- any problems of being in a group can be overcome by the facilitator, or are seen as adding to the ecological validity of the data.

USING FOCUS GROUPS

Focus groups are a means of finding out about people's perspectives. However, once put into action they are a methodology; the way in which the researcher views human behaviour and how knowledge is created fundamentally affect how the research is actually done and the outcomes. This methodology is, of course, also shaped by the social, cultural, historical and political limitations within which the researcher works.

Research in the social sciences can come from two main positions, positivist and interpretivist. The important separation between these two paradigms rests on approaches to reality. Using the positivist approach, the researcher acts as an observer of social reality. Interpretivist researchers (and some would use the term qualitative in the same way) see themselves as central to the research and the sense that is made of it. Although it is mainly the interpretivist perspective of focus groups that will be addressed in this chapter, positivist use will be mentioned very briefly below, simply because this approach is used quite often by researchers.

POSITIVIST RESEARCH

Traditionally, focus groups used by market researchers operate within a clear positivist paradigm. That is to say, participants are viewed as passive subjects who hold a range of opinions and preferences on a range of matters. These opinions and preferences are 'discovered' within the focus group. These opinions are then disembedded from the context in which they arose and reported as individual views.

Some academic researchers also use the methodology in this way. The participants are treated as an aggregate of individuals who represent specific social groups. In this way, the aim becomes how to get the most information possible about the topic the researchers are interested in.

Inside a positivist framework, fundamental issues of power and control are either explained away in simplistic ways or are ignored. Within focus group literature, for example, there is the view that focus groups inevitably reduce the researcher's power and control. This is thought to happen simply because the researcher is outnumbered by participants, and so the balance of power shifts (Morgan, 1988), but ignores the fact that the researcher sets the agenda.

Given the already marginalized position of children, there is a real fear that:

> If the rhetoric of listening to lay voices or consumers is adopted unreflectively, rather than critically challenged, the resulting knowledge will reinforce the dominant position of those with power.
>
> Cunningham-Burley, Kerr and Pavis, 1999, p. 191)

We would question the potential that focus group methodology has to provide a challenge to existing power structures in the hands of a researcher who does not see the differing power structures between children and adults in the first place.

There is the fear that focus groups used in this way may appear to offer the voices of the children on the surface, but in fact the children remain in much the same position as before. No fresh understanding is obtained, but there is the double blow of an apparent veneer of democracy to support the systems that exist.

An extreme, but real-life, example of this was a head teacher of a secondary school who wished to find out what the young people thought about bullying in the school.

He set up a series of focus groups, with himself as facilitator. What the young people felt freely able to say in this situation is obviously up for question, but none the less the head teacher was able to say he had asked their opinions and used these to support the existing anti-bullying policy.

INTERPRETIVIST RESEARCH

The use of focus group methodology with children in an interpretivist paradigm is assumed to be very different from positivist research as described above. There follows a brief explanation of the interpretivist perspective, followed by an account of some difficulties that we experienced in implementing the outcomes of our research.

Within the interpretivist perspective, reality is assumed to be socially constructed and so findings are dependent on the social context of focus groups. Particularly relevant is the primacy given to lay accounts as appropriate topics of research, and the diverse and multiple realities that they generate. The emphasis is on active involvement of, and dialogue among, participants. There is an awareness of the issues that affect the researcher and the participants, such as power relations and context. This approach then uses the responses from focus groups in quite a different way, interpretations of which are interwoven into an understanding of what is happening. Interpretivist research does not claim to be objective in the sense used from the positivist paradigm. Instead, the hope is to create a different representation of the phenomenon at issue by interpreting constructions of social reality.

However, research from any perspective can become vulnerable to supporting traditional power structures. It becomes crucial, therefore, to pay attention to the power relations between those funding research and researchers, and the social context within which research is commissioned, funded and conducted. These matters affect the outcomes of research, in this particular case, what happens to the children's perspectives.

> The dangers in research of exploitation arise where qualitative research is treated as (only) a method divorced from wider structures of power.
>
> Burman, 1997, p. 797)

Research, therefore, should not be seen as separate from the context within which it exists. Being mindful of this requires a corresponding awareness of practices that can serve to reinforce the status quo and, as such, existing inequalities. This notion is echoed by Hughes (introductory chapter), where he talks about the 'institutional processes' that can lead to children and families being marginalized. In addition, he refers to the idea that agencies are often set up around the needs and agendas of organizations rather than 'shaped to meet the needs' of children and families. This resonates with the notion that research practice too can work to reflect its own agenda, and in so doing fail to capture all the elements that are pertinent to an understanding of the children being researched, whose perspectives are supposedly being sought.

Within our studies, we felt that it was important to draw out the many possibilities affecting the responses given within the focus groups. For example, the children may have been given particular perspectives on peer mediation during the original introduction of the scheme and were simply repeating these because they felt they ought to, whether they truly believed these perspectives or not.

Regarding the children in focus groups, there is no way of knowing how their responses, in such a novel context for them, were influenced by the fact that they had not really been given a real choice in participating but had been informed by class teachers that they were to be involved, as was the case. This is not only an issue regarding how much informed consent children in such situations are able to give but also a question of whether this places added pressure on those taking part in the focus group. Similarly, although with adults one is normally able to presume consent, it is equally possible that the lunchtime supervisors felt under some pressure to take part because the school had agreed to pay them for their time. The outcomes of the studies interpreted these constructions of social reality, hoping to create representations of what was happening with regard to peer mediation in the school without leaving out the complexity of power relations and social context.

However, the outcomes of the research were fed back to the school in a summarized form. This shortened version effectively meant that the interpretivist approach taken became much more similar to a positivist approach. That is, the children's and adult's perspectives were presented as if they were static opinions and the interplay of power relations and context, as illustrated above, were lost. We now realize that we dipped into this setting – and then dipped out again. This really became a veneer of democracy, and it was obvious that the research did not challenge the way systems already are for children.

This is worth bearing in mind as interpretivist research is looked at in more detail. All research is a part of a wider social setting, and research that is not seen to be factual can sit very uneasily with the discourses of management and politics.

MANAGING POWER RELATIONS?

Focus group methodology can produce children's voices in ways that are not anticipated. Research practices can be mistaken for the child's voice. The intention now is to look at how this may happen, turning first to how group interactions and power relations are treated within this type of research.

The trademark of focus groups is the explicit use of group interactions. Research on people in groups talks of roles, norms, interactions and conformity. The emotional aspect is also much spoken of in terms of compliance, resistance, hostility and anxiety. It would seem then that focus groups are complex places for children, and certainly may be as complex as the child's normal peer groups.

These issues of control, context and interactions are all inter-related. As Paradice (1999, p. 204) says:

> Human interaction is complex, and underpinned by many layers of meaning that are influenced strongly by culture and the power relationships that exist within that culture.

It seems important, therefore, to note that the power relations and context within which communication takes place will have a fundamental effect on what happens in the focus groups and consequently the outcome of the research. Alderson (1995, cited by Christensen and James, 2000, p. 6) argues that the inherent power relations between researcher and researched in childhood studies must be seen as reinforced by more general cultural notions of the power relations which exist between children and adults.

From an interpretivist stance, groups are complex places to be and, from the point of view of focus group method, this is seen as advantageous. This is because the focus group situation is seen as more like real life, an informal setting in which all of the issues mentioned above will play their part. However, the argument becomes untenable for 'hard to reach' children who will be represented in focus groups just as they are in real life – as 'hard to reach'. This view of power relations as manageable through the interpretations of the researcher seems limited, as the voice of the child can be overcome and structured by the situation in which they find themselves.

TAKING PART IN FOCUS GROUPS: BEING THERE OR SAYING SOMETHING?

Within focus group literature there seems to be little or no interest in the levels of verbal participation. In focus groups, it's what people say that is significant, even if this is interpreted to gain an understanding of meanings. There was a great deal of variation in verbal participation in the observed focus groups with children. In every group there was at least one child who did not speak at all, and in the majority of groups there was at least one, and more often two or three children, who made a very minimal contribution verbally.

The non-contribution or minimal contribution from some children highlights some important difficulties for focus groups. The meanings behind a child not saying any-thing, or very little, need to be explored. Issues of participation are explored elsewhere in this book. Pomerantz (Chapter 3) describes a pupil whose verbal contribution is minimal but none the less significant. As part of her research she has noted it and, despite the silence, is aware of some of the issues that may underlie it. She asks also how well pupils (the most vulnerable in particular) are engaged in decision-making and thus able to make a positive contribution. She argues that the most vulnerable, hard to reach and marginalized young people remain 'largely silent'. As such, there could be said to be some link between how far young people feel genuinely listened to, with their contributions making a difference to outcomes in their own lives, and their subsequent willingness to participate.

DOES SILENCE SPEAK VOLUMES?

In these particular studies, the researcher looking at peer mediation only became aware of the huge variation in participation because of the parallel study on interactions. Those who did not contribute verbally were of no interest and were not commented upon (this was not seen as meaning anything important for the research).

So, clearly power is exercised to include or exclude certain types of knowledge. One of the aims of focus groups is to uncover the voices of the marginalized and 'hard to reach', but it seems there is a problem. When the knowledge produced challenges conventional wisdom about what constitutes proper research, it is suppressed as knowledge. In other words, there is no space for silence in research results; so it remains unacknowledged as having a meaning. This demonstrates the way that the conceptualization of credible knowledge is discursively shaped, and conversely what is not to be accepted as knowledge.

You may argue that no research covers all aspects of human life, and focus group methodology really does have to limit itself to certain parameters.

Besides, there may be perfectly ordinary reasons why a child does not participate. For example, these may relate to personality, mood or simply not having anything to say. In order to explore this, let us return to the scene of focus groups.

SETTING THE SCENE

Within focus group methodology, as already mentioned, a facilitator runs the focus groups. Often, the facilitator is also the researcher, and this was the case in our studies. Within our focus groups, the facilitator provided juice and biscuits for the young people and started the groups off in a relaxed manner. It was apparent, though, that the facilitator was a central person in the focus groups, who had considerable control over who spoke and when. For the vast majority of the time, then, turns were taken in speaking. In fact, the facilitator suggests this at the start of the session. However, another suggestion was ignored: that of 'talking to one another'. It is interesting to note that interaction between the children on a verbal level very rarely took place, but on a non-verbal level there were many exchanges of glances. As mentioned above, power relations between children and adults are important, and it would seem that the children in this study occupy a marginal position. This is probably reinforced by the fact that the facilitator had been introduced to the children in an assembly, and, although no longer one, quite possibly still acted like a teacher and was obviously part of the establishment in some way. All of this was probably apparent to the children.

It is not suggested that a formal setting is better or worse than a more informal setting, just different. What we are suggesting is that any setting has a great deal to do with producing people. This is a different way of looking at individuals. Rather than suggesting that there is a separation between the self and the social world, so that the social context might ' "impinge" upon or "influence" the self rather like a snooker or billiard ball might collide with another ball, changing their direction momentarily, but this influence is seen as occurring between two already constituted and contained entities' (Wetherell and Maybin, 1996, p. 221), we are suggesting a different view of individuals, in which they are viewed as 'always dynamic and multiple, always positioned in relation to particular discourses and practices and produced by these – the condition of being subject' (Henriques et al., 1998, p. 3).

It is timely, then, to return to our studies and look at what the children's perspectives were on focus groups, and further insight was given by the follow-up questionnaires that the young people completed. The majority of respondents viewed being in the focus groups as a positive experience and felt that they could say what they wanted to. This is perhaps re-emphasized by responses to a question about how interviewees viewed being in a focus group compared to being in an interview. Only two children (out of six) did not choose the focus group outright, and they were neutral about which was preferred. In this case, it can be inferred that some children do indeed find the focus group easier, and some extracts from the interviews are used to illustrate this.

YEAR 5 CHILD: BOY

Researcher: OK, so which way do you prefer, talking here now with me or in the focus group?
Child: It's quite a good way talking individually as well, but it's a bit better in the group.
Researcher: So, why is it better in the group?
Child: Because you've got more people that you know around you – more comfortable.

YEAR 2 CHILD: BOY

Researcher: Right, right. So what's, so me and you sat here, what's difficult about that?
Child: Erm. I'm always ... er ... talking.

What is important is the insight this gives us into the complexity of research situations. If focus groups are preferred because they are 'easier' in that the process is not so intense, this begs the question of what *type* of perspective is being accessed and makes clear that the situations in which young people find themselves can make a difference to what they do and say. Of course, the same is true of the authors of this research, and it should not be forgotten that our view of focus groups as complex places to be can sometimes overshadow more simplistic explanations:

Researcher: What did you like? [about being in the focus group]
Pupil: The biscuits.
Researcher: I had one of them, they were nice, weren't they?

ARE FOCUS GROUPS HOMOGENEOUS?

To return to those young people who do not participate in focus groups, we need to be interested in them as the suggestion is that they may be produced by the social setting, becoming 'hard to reach' and unable to contribute.

It would be foolish indeed to attribute this solely to the research situation in which children find themselves. The particular discourses that surround children in focus groups are much wider and more diffuse than this. Yet focus group methodology often treats the groups as homogeneous: the group is chosen for some common feature as far as the researcher is concerned. There is no acknowledgment of the positions held by children, which are themselves composed by issues of class, gender, relationships, power, history and culture.

We ignore who knows whom, who bullied whom, who is not friends, who is being abused: the complexity of human life. This may seem like a return to individualization, but in fact it is more a view of people as being forever produced from the discourses that surround them. By ignoring this and instead making a claim for some form of commonality that suits us, we may place children in a position in which they are produced as unable to speak.

TOM

As an illustration of this, we want to talk about Tom. Tom's body language indicated that he did not want to be in the group at first, and he made no contribution. Although his questionnaire cannot be identified individually, none of the children in his group made any indication that they had not enjoyed being in the group or had not wanted to contribute.

Tom had been selected prior to the focus group as a child to be interviewed. He refused. He then told us that he had not wanted to take part in the focus group either but had been told by his teacher that he had to.

For us, this was a clear indication that the children had very little choice but to accept their 'invitation' to join the focus group. To refuse may have seemed impossible or to entail such a cost that remaining was the only option. His refusal of the invitation to be interviewed was possible, we think, because this was given verbally as a true invitation and therefore could be declined.

This discourse is about roles, both of the child's and the researchers'. Differential status and power relationships have influenced this situation, and it seems:

> Even from the outset, the extent to which we are prepared to involve children . . . depends on theories or assumptions we make about them.
>
> (Moore and Sixsmith, 2000, p. 151)

Tom was produced as 'hard to reach', and his silence spoke volumes, but this did not form part of the outcome of the focus group research.

CONCLUSION

At the beginning of this chapter, we introduced the idea that research practices can be mistaken for the child's voice; in other words that research as a set of historical, social and cultural practices produces a particular set of actions for researchers. Although these sets of actions may vary from one research position to another, underlying all positions are assumptions about the way to do things, and these assumptions are rarely noticed or questioned. Looked at critically, our contention is that these assumptions shape research practices in ways that may overcome the child's voice in favour of research, or indeed the wider discourses of management and politics.

The notion that these assumptions are rarely explicitly brought out as significant, not only to the way that we perform research with children but also to the understandings of the perspectives that are obtained from this research, formed the basis of our own journey of inquiry. The journey for us in exploring our own work with children opened up a space for considering what we thought we knew, allowing us to look at research in a different way. Within the children's workforce, attempts are being made to change what is done to meet the needs of children and families and find new ways of generating solutions. Research with children that are 'hard to reach' should form a supporting branch for this attempt and to be truly effective will need to look critically at the processes of research.

REFERENCES

Barbour, R.S. and Kitzinger, J. (eds) (1999) *Developing Focus Group Research: Politics, Theory and Practice*. Sage, London.

Burman, E. (1997) Minding the gap: positivism, psychology, and the politics of qualitative methods. *Journal of Social Issues* **53** (4), 785–801.

Christensen, P. and James, A. (2000) *Research with Children: Perspectives and Practices*. Falmer Press, London and New York.

Cunningham-Burley, S., Kerr, A. and Pavis, S. (1999) Theorizing subjects and subject matter. In: R.S. Barbour and J. Kitzinger (eds). *Developing Focus Group Research: Politics, Theory and Practice*. Sage, London.

Henriques, J., Hollway, W. and Urwin, C. *et al.* (1998) *Changing the Subject: Psychology, Social Regulation and Subjectivity*. Routledge, London and New York.

Krueger, R.A. and Casey, M.A. (2000) *Focus Groups: A Practical Guide for Applied Research*. Sage, London.

Merton, R.K., Fiske, M. and Kendall, P.L. (1956) *The Focused Interview*. Free Press, Glencoe, IL.

Morgan, D.L. (1988) *Focus Groups as Qualitative Research*. Sage, Newbury Park, CA.

Morgan, D.L. (1993) *Successful Focus Groups: Advancing the State of the Art*. Sage, London.

O'Kane, C. (2000) The development of participatory techniques: facilitating children's views about decisions which affect them. In: P. Christensen and A. James (eds). *Research With Children: Perspectives and Practices*. Falmer Press, London.

Paradice, R. (1999) Deconstructing development: a challenge for educational psychology. *Educational Psychology in Practice* **15** (3), 201–206.

Moore, M. and Sixsmith, J. (2000) Accessing children's insider perspectives. In: M. Moore (ed.) *Insider Perspectives on Inclusion: Raising Voices, Raising Issues*. Philip Armstrong Publications, Sheffield.

Wetherell, M. and Maybin, J. (1996) The distributed self: A social constructionist perspective. In: R. Stevens (ed.). *Understanding the Self*. Sage, London.

Concluding Chapter
Validating and Using Children's Views: Professional Dilemmas about Working Inside Agencies

DAVID THOMPSON AND JO HOLT

WHO ARE THE 'HARD TO REACH'?

The phrase 'hard to reach' has crept into discussions about the education and welfare of children and young people from a variety of sources, from government agencies, academic commentators and professionals working with the young people and their families in the educational and social service sectors. Hughes (introductory chapter) gives a range of definitions of what the phrase might mean from the different workers in the field. However, implicit in these definitions designed to make clear which groups of young people are being talked about is a recognition that they do represent a particular challenge to the professionals and other adults concerned. Those concerned adults are admitting to themselves and to others that these young people are in danger of drifting away from the best intentions and services being offered, are drifting to a place where they are out of range of social influences and of learning and training opportunities. They are avoiding the usual socialization processes whereby a community looks after its young, to teach them what they need to know for effective operation in the adult world as they mature. They are approaching the point of dropping out of the usual routes to responsible adulthood, to the detriment of themselves, their families and the wider community. The usual mechanisms of involvement and communication between the young people and the adults concerned are breaking down. The best efforts of the adults around them and of the young people themselves are in danger of failing to keep them involved with important parts of their community. It is this looming sense of failure and waste that heightens adults' concerns about the young people's learning, behaviour and welfare, and no one likes to see their efforts and time being wasted or the young people in their care drifting away into a private limbo, into real and imagined dangers.

Which groups can be seen as being 'hard to reach?' In the end, the term could be applied to members of practically any group where the adult responses and services are not matching the people's needs. The various chapters in this book give examples

How to Reach 'Hard to Reach' Children: Improving access, participation and outcomes. Edited by K. Pomerantz, M. Hughes and D. Thompson. Copyright © 2007 by John Wiley & Sons, Ltd.

of how some concerned professionals in some services at this time in the United Kingdom are responding. The problem is recognized at a political level also, as Hughes (introductory chapter) points out. However, the 'hard to reach' young people and groups may appear at any time to any professional or parent; the parent who becomes aware that their child has stopped communicating with them, is spending a lot of time with a group of friends and seems to be taking school less and less seriously faces similar dilemmas to those members of the caring agencies who realize that they have very little idea how the young person for whom they have some responsibility spends their day, or judges what is appropriate behaviour. Young people being 'hard to reach' is not a new phenomenon. In any changing material and cultural world they have to try to grow up in that culture in flux, and in doing so they will evolve standards of behaviour and expectations that are different from what their parents and carers expect in some respects. The adults have to see they need to exert themselves to stay in contact with the young people, and recognizing the young people are currently 'hard to reach' in the first place is the first step towards re-establishing contacts. In these attempts to re-establish contact, listening to what the young people have to say is one of the first steps, and this is one of the reasons why children's voices have such a prominence in this volume.

It is not only young people who may become 'hard to reach'. Pomerantz, (Chapter 6) discusses occasions when professionals themselves are 'hard to reach', either by the young people or by colleagues, and suggests a more open-ended format for the typical case conference to address this. Willis (Chapter 7) gives an account of officers of a Local Authority (LA) recognizing that parents of a group of children with particular special needs have high expectations of the services the LA could provide, to help structure the LA services to the best effect and to learn how to give support to this group of parents to stay in touch with their children. Essentially, being 'hard to reach' is a statement about communication processes, the importance given to them and the abilities all concerned have to communicate meaningfully as young people approach adulthood.

MULTI-AGENCY INVOLVEMENT

In practice, when young people are thought to be at risk of failure of some sort by their parents, teachers or other responsible adults, the adults tend to involve some kind of specialized agency from the welfare professions. These may be support staff in school or external agencies from health, education or social services departments of the LA. If events do not go well, more professionals tend to get involved in support of the young person and family, and the issue of effective communication between the outside agencies and the young person and their family becomes important. Effective multi-agency coordination has been an issue for a number of years in the United Kingdom (Cameron and Lart, 2003; Craig, Huber and Lownsbrough, 2004) and successive governments have made it a higher and higher priority until the current legislation for integrated Children's Services was passed. This administrative background is discussed in detail by Hughes (introductory chapter) in this volume. One of the practical aspects of the new administrative arrangements supported by Government has been the idea of establishing a Common Assessment Framework, whereby the first external professional to become involved with a young person and their family carries out an initial assessment of the situation that can then provide the basis for work by other professionals. Northcote (Chapter 8) gives a detailed description of how all the different agencies involved with one young person did in fact work together, and asks how the Common Assessment Framework would have helped.

The general problem in this situation of many different professionals being involved, of course, is that they each tend to have specific roles and tasks prescribed by their agencies, their training and often by statute, and have limited time and skills available in their work with the young person. If the needs of the young person actually are needs that do fit into the role definition and time availability of one of the professionals, then the multi-agency system works well. If the particular needs are not matched by the role of one of the professionals, then the young person tends to be referred on to another agency, in hope. Unfortunately, because young people are different, their needs tend not to be predictable (Lown, Chapter 4). Working with other people to help support the young person is an inescapable aspect of trying to reach young people drifting away, but it does introduce a complicating set of local circumstances for those involved, which do have to be managed well for success (Hughes, introductory chapter). Otherwise, the young person and their family are likely to describe the professional involvement as a waste of time, consisting of lots of promises but no help of the type necessary. This is a clear failure of local management of the services. Managing for success is discussed further below, after considering the reasons why young people become 'hard to reach'.

DIFFERENT REASONS FOR BECOMING 'HARD TO REACH'

At first sight, it is tempting to see the main reasons for a young person seeming 'hard to reach' as characteristics of the young person themselves. When parents are faced with teenagers in difficulty who are never around to talk to (and if they do talk, talk in emotionally toned monosyllables), it appears easy to find who is to blame for the situation. However, after asking the question 'How did things get this way?' much more complex reasons appear. Various chapters give detailed pictures of the processes leading to becoming 'hard to reach', some relating to the reactions of the adult institutions to the young person, which tend to increase their marginalization (Lown, Chapter 4; Pomerantz, Chapter 3), some to the problems of the effective matching of services to needs (Willis, Chapter 7; Northcote, Chapter 8), and Turner (Chapter 1) looks at the relationships between the young people and the staff they meet, taking the young people's views as one of the sources of information about the strengths and difficulties in that area. One contributor (James, Chapter 2) focuses on the internal self-presentational processes of the young person, providing a picture of the developing identity of the 'hard to reach' young person.

QUESTIONS OF IDENTITY

One of the major themes emerging from the chapters addressing the internal emotional processes of those young people drifting away is the theme of their emerging identity, reminding us that becoming 'hard to reach' as far as the adults are concerned may be an important part of the way the young person establishes their own identity among the friendship groups, activities and adult-dominated organizations they come into contact with. Lown (Chapter 4) discusses the importance of the friendship group supporting return to school after a period away, and James (Chapter 2) discusses the importance of self-presentation, or 'putting on the style'. Self-presentation occurs through behaviour, dress and values (those activities valued) and through aspirations. Some of the values of the adult world are expressed through engineering the involvement of the young people in activities valued by the adults, such as education and vocational training, and one of the implicit aims of most adult-led institutions is that eventually the young people will learn to share this value system and accept aspirations for this kind of success.

However, one of the important elements for the young person in this process is that they do in fact succeed in meeting these aspirations, often expressed as changes in status, and amended group membership as well as meeting the particular targets relating to the progress made in the adult-sponsored activities. If they anticipate failure, then they protect themselves from the likely loss of self-esteem or failure by opting out of the activities and the targets. Their anticipation of failure may be arising from anxiety as they approach new situations, or it may be based on a fairly realistic assessment of their own existing skills. By the time a young person reaches adolescence, they may have been failing to progress academically as well as the average child of their age group for five years or even more, and this will have become a part of the young person's assessment of their own current skills and of their expectations of success when facing future challenges. From the point of view of the adults, seeing young people reject activities and targets valued by adults for little obvious reason contributes to seeing the young people as becoming 'hard to reach' and drifting away from the adult-dominated world. For these young people, the tension comes from finding it difficult to continue to develop a sense of identity and competence under the particular conditions set up for them by the adult world.

A sense of identity is also gained through group membership, and becoming involved with a friendship or acquaintance group with values and expectations different from the adult world is also another way in which young people can become 'hard to reach'. This is particularly true if the young people find themselves in association with a number of other young people with similar relationships to the adult world and under similar pressures. In these circumstances, the gradually increasing alienation from the adult world itself becomes a defining part of the new identities of the young people, and creates resistance to adult attempts to reach them and build up new communication patterns. The work reported by Pomerantz (Chapter 3) illustrates well the way in which schools with behaviour policies based on a loose form of behaviour modification theory can end up failing to recognize the underlying need of the young people for emotionally based communication with adults. If this occurs, procedurally structured adult expectations and school management processes can appear from the pupils' perspective to be confirming their view that looking for meaningful emotional communications with adults is a waste of time, and that a much more satisfying sense of identity is achieved by building a new set of values and expectations of each other's behaviour with others of their own age. Turner (Chapter 1) describes how some underachieving young people in underachieving schools are themselves aware of their own needs for support from adults, and think they are not receiving it. The group of pupils that Turner worked with also perceived help and support from teachers and other adults as being dependent on successful learning: teachers give help to 'the ones that are already on the second book in class' (Chapter 1, p. 36). Teachers may well want to challenge this perception, but because the dynamic we are dealing with in this piece of research is the pupil's emerging sense of identity as an unsuccessful learner, the pupil's perception of this particular reality is the one that matters.

CREATING INCLUSIVE LEARNING SPACE FOR YOUNG PEOPLE

Describing a young person as 'hard to reach' implies that someone is doing the reaching, to make sure that this young person grows up included in the adult world rather than becoming increasingly distanced or marginalized. Schools are undoubtedly the main adult-led institution that all children have experience of and spend much time in, and in recent years the idea of an inclusive school has received much attention across the educational world. This development has received the support of central government as well as much of the educational community. Many of the ideas, teaching strategies and aspects of school organization relevant to making schools more inclusive are also relevant to reaching those seen as 'hard to reach'.

The crucial assumption behind the inclusion movement is not that young people should be helped to fit into schools' requirements and expectations of behaviour and attitudes but that the schools should adapt their requirements and procedures to take account of the needs of the young people. Doing this is much easier said than done, as schools also have other aims to achieve and pressures to deal with: to maximize examination results and SAT results, to use resources efficiently and control their financial situations and to satisfy parents and Ofsted that they are achieving these aims. Doing this in ways that are flexible enough to meet the needs of young people when they show signs of becoming less involved in the whole process and less interested in communicating with adults is not easy. However, it is a beginning for the adults to realize that the pupils themselves are not enjoying losing contact and losing the feeling of being supported by the staff in their learning. They would rather remain easy to reach if the adult system could gear itself to recognize their increasing maturity and capacity to make choices.

Many documents and training materials illustrate what might be done (see, for example, Department for Education and Employment, 1999). Pomerantz (2004) provides a very good example of the ways that pupils can participate in the school processes when they have been given permission and help to do so, and also demonstrates that able underachievers can also be seen as one of the groups of 'hard to reach' young people. Schools working towards inclusion as an aim do rely on an adequate level of resourcing and effective management. To successfully re-involve the 'hard to reach' young person also does require a high level of sophistication and competence from local services, including schools, as the dynamics of child development, particularly at adolescence, are complex, intense and often unpredictable.

WORKING WITH PARENTS

In many ways, the adults most involved and most concerned about the progress of the young people who are 'hard to reach' are their parents. These, of course, are not always around, and the lack of effective parent figures is one of the great difficulties faced by some young people. The other professionals working with them also recognize the enormous stresses produced on the young people by the lack of effective parent figures, providing a major challenge to Children's Services to rectify the situation through greater development of fostering, adoption and befriending schemes.

Supporting parents has been a consistently approved but often poorly developed strand of professional work, probably because it is preventative work, with successes hidden, rather than crisis-driven. Three chapters in this volume give examples of working with parents who are still trying to maintain contact with their 'hard to reach' children and document the parents' voices describing their struggle. McGrath (Chapter 9) gives an evaluation of a formal course run to help parents deal with some of the emotional pressures they feel during parenting, Willis (Chapter 7) gives a picture of how service managers can work with concerned parents, involving them with LA services by listening to their views on ways to improve local services, and Northcote (Chapter 8) looks at the patterns of interaction of professionals with one family and assesses the extent to which they really made useful contact with the parents. Through these collections of parents' voices, the emotional reality, resourcefulness and commitment of the parents is exposed, wanting an equivalent response from the professionals.

Lloyd Bennett and Reid (Chapter 5) also remind us that families, and particularly parents, are a crucial source of support for migrant children settling into local schools after moving from stressful situations elsewhere.

AIMS, RESOURCING AND COMPETENCE OF LOCAL CHILDREN'S SERVICES

Since 2005, education and Social Services at a local level in the United Kingdom have been administratively linked, at a level of strategic management and sometimes at a level of service delivery by the individual professionals, as reviewed by Hughes (introductory chapter). This is the current attempt by central government to reform public services to make them more responsive to need and to provide a better use of resources. Whether this particular reform succeeds is a matter for historians of the future rather than this volume. It does, however, give a local management context to thinking about providing help to young people becoming 'hard to reach', as for professionals employed by the LA or the Health Service the local management goes much of the way to defining their staffing, management structures and accountability structures for the service. It also goes a long way to defining their professional tasks, especially where the services are statutory. Even though in theory Children's Services departments are one administrative entity at a strategic management level, involving schools and other children's support systems together, at a service delivery level they still need to coordinate different service delivery systems together. To some extent they represent the 'management of public services by creating one huge department to encourage coordination' school of administrative thinking, as opposed to the 'management of public services by creating different agencies, each with a specific brief and separate accountability systems, to encourage a focus on deliverable services' approach. At the time of writing, the Education Services and Social Services appear to be moving one way, towards integration of administrative structures, and the Health Services moving in the opposite direction, with increasing delegation of tasks to semi-independent bodies. Whichever approach is current, twenty-first-century public services involve many specialized professionals and sections, which will always require management of different professional groups and services to secure the best outcomes for young people. One process that will define the effectiveness of Children's Services will be how effective they are at contacting and remaining in emotional touch with the children who are drifting away from the usual routes through schools and families into a productive adulthood, to be able to still act to support and guide young people as they find their own feet. This is, in fact, another way of claiming that the welfare of children is their main aim, working with parents and school staffs as primary carers.

COMMENTARY ON SUCCESSFUL WORKING TOGETHER

Holt (2004) gives a detailed picture of the views of different professionals on successful and unsuccessful management strategies where professionals work together. We have heard from other contributors of the parents' perceptions of successful professional practice in helping their young people, and Holt's research details the views of the professionals themselves on those aspects of their organizations that helped and that hindered collaborative working with those from other professional groups or agencies. Holt interviewed workers from two different professional groups in two different LAs, and reached a number of conclusions about important factors.

STRUCTURAL AND PROCEDURAL FACTORS

Sometimes agencies adopted defensive mechanisms and procedures at higher management levels, especially relating to funding, or to casework initiatives which might relate to funding. This defensiveness also extended to approve procedures for contacting other professional groups. Frontline workers described situations whereby they sometimes chose to work outside the formal mechanisms in order to work collaboratively. The ability to autonomously create informal links that act as catalytic bridges between professional groups was valued by the workers, even if this was contrary to the positions adopted by agency managers, as this could be the quickest way to achieve effective collaboration. The workers also perceived some of the targets put forward by agency managers as irrelevant or distracting. For example, educational professionals saw some educational targets for inclusion operating in schools as working against those for raising standards of achievement, particularly for vulnerable children or those 'looked after' by the LA. They also saw instances where the needs of some children were not able to be met by the provision available, particularly if the families moved round a local area. They also felt that even when these problems were identified, agencies were slow at addressing them.

The professionals interviewed were aware of their agencies trying to adapt the changing administrative contexts, but often their attempts to change were frustrated. Such developments as attempting to provide further training were frustrated by high workload made worse by high staff turnover; collaboration between professional groups was complicated by their working with different quality-assurance mechanisms; and where casework decisions were taken by managers rather than by the professionals themselves the decisions were taken too slowly or, indeed, too quickly if other factors intervened for the manager. Different professional groups and agencies often had different decision-making routes and styles, which might have been difficult to understand outside the group concerned.

Information collection and updating of records and uncertainty about protocols for sharing information with colleagues were seen as further sources of frustration. They also felt frustrated that there were few channels to pass information upwards. This meant that it was difficult to inform managers of new needs perceived first by professionals, which in turn meant the new needs could not be addressed proactively or cooperatively by agencies as a whole.

Differences between professional groups and their contexts of work can lead to the gap being perceived as a boundary by the workers involved, and this boundary can be reinforced by the difficulties of making contact due to working practices and time availability. Where such boundaries between and within different agencies and schools are strongly demarcated at the client contact level of the organizations, collaborative practice is compromised. Such practice is also compromised where the desired outcome is not shared between the workers in the different agencies. For example, a school may be proposing to exclude a 'looked after' child, but other professionals' perceptions of the difficulties in school include other factors originating outside the school, and they may feel that exclusion is not in the best interests of the child.

Similarly, where funding implications of clinical decisions are not worked out on the basis of openly stated and agreed protocols, professionals from different agencies may withdraw from cooperative or coordinated activity in order to protect resources.

When such boundaries are effectively overcome, the bridging points are often established by individual action designed specifically to make or maintain contact. This process, driven by individual initiatives, is a crucial part of setting up and maintaining collaborative activity between professionals. The personal characteristics of individuals skilled at creating these catalytic bridges are identified by the workers involved as self-confidence and self-belief, flexibility, tenacity, empathy, resilience, a high level of conflict-resolution skills and a commitment to problem-solving often using solution-focused methods. Workers identified a need to feel supported in their working across boundaries by trust from colleagues and managers, shared knowledge and values and opportunities for reflection within their own working environment. They felt these organizational characteristics were particularly desirable when workers were expected to build cooperative teams across agency boundaries.

In times of rapid internal and external change, the capacity of the organization and professional groups to respond to change is clearly of considerable importance. When the professional groups in this study were asked to consider whether their organizations could be termed 'learning organizations', they expressed considerable reservations. They felt that learning and organizational change often took place on the hoof, and as a consequence of mistakes or immediate need rather than from a managed assessment and agreed process of change amongst staff used to adapting their working practices to changing circumstances. The response to the possibility of formal evaluation and monitoring of the effectiveness of the services was typically felt to be, 'Yes, that may be a good idea, but who is going to be expected to do it?' This assumption that evaluations are to be carried out by someone else and may have little relevance to the day-to-day practice is an important aspect of organizational climate, and organizational climate has been demonstrated to be a powerful factor affecting individual workers in terms of facilitating the development of the personal characteristics in the workers that underpin collaboration (Glisson and Hemmelgarn, 1998). Frequent reorganizations, and climate where change is perceived to be constant, are unhelpful to effective collaboration, a finding supported by Easen, Atkins and Dyson (2000), who suggest that this is because changing personnel and structures make it difficult to establish personal contacts and mutual trust across boundaries. It seems clear from studies such as this that effective working across boundaries depends on organizational conditions encouraged and regulated by middle and senior managers in the agencies, and goes a lot further than an agreement by senior administrators that collaborative working would be a good idea.

LISTENING TO CHILDREN'S VOICES

Why has listening to children's views about their situations suddenly become talked about and valued? Hughes (introductory chapter), Lown (Chapter 4) and many other contributors comment on the importance of this process for effective welfare services. Many of the studies reported here are based on listening to children's views about themselves, their own situation and the adults and Adult Services that they are in touch with. There are a number of reasons for this:

- Listening to children's opinions on their own situations has been increasingly mentioned and approved of in government guidance, as discussed by Hughes (introductory chapter).
- In clinical situations where changes might be made in the care or education programme to better meet the needs of the children, their involvement in the decision

and acceptance of the relevance of the change is a major factor in the success of the new arrangements, whatever they may be.

- If young people and their families are seen as consumers in an overall market-orientated management vision, their views on the adequacy of the services they receive are an important source of feedback to the providers of those services.

- From the point of view of researchers, children's views give a perspective on the ways in which services and institutions operate, which is complementary to but distinctly different from the perspectives of management and staff.

- The voice of the child comes from the interaction between the child's personality, their family and social background and the adult-dominated institutions of the school and the community. This perspective is especially important, because to understand the dynamic changes occurring to the identity of the young person, the researcher and other professionals must understand this interaction between a child's personality and the social context in which they live.

In addition, in the current situation, where accountability is a constant refrain for public services, listening to children (by using a variety of research methods) gives a very useful and generally applicable research strategy for learning about the impact of services for young people and their families on their welfare and progress.

This process of listening to children is not without quicksand, however, as Chilokoa and McKie (Chapter 10) point out. Even when researchers are aiming to present children's views clearly and unambiguously, the process of interpretation and presentation itself through its selectivity and focus on certain issues can distort the actual meanings of the young people unless great care is taken to preserve the independence of their voices. If this can happen in research presentations, it is probably more likely to happen in presentations of children's views by adults in clinical situations, as the expectations of adults and staff of adult-dominated organizations about what activities and procedures are appropriate in the situation will be that much stronger than in a research context. In some situations, the final safeguard may be to have the young people themselves present in decision-making meetings, providing they have been properly briefed beforehand and the chairperson of the meeting is aware of their need for structure, space and support. In others, it may be better to have an adult advocate present, with the single role of helping the young person present their views and carrying no accountability to other agencies or services with responsibilities for service delivery. Ultimately, the safeguard is the awareness by the caring adults that the eventual success of those changes is seriously in question and everyone's efforts may be in vain unless the young person is involved in taking the decisions and becomes committed to change.

DEVELOPING AND USING SMALL-SCALE RESEARCH PROJECTS TO MONITOR SERVICE EFFECTIVENESS

Local managers and their staff have a key role in the successful use of research in developing services, and the role of the managers in particular is often overlooked. They need to be confident enough to accept the involvement of researchers in the evaluation of the services they are managing, and to indicate to their staff the acceptability of the research. It is helpful if they also have some ideas about what kinds of questions research can answer, certainly enough to take part in a discussion with the researcher, and some ideas of how the results of the research might be used to help the organization develop. Many of the ideas behind the concept of the learning organization as mentioned above are relevant, but it is very likely, particularly under the conditions of near-constant top-down change, that few of the characteristics of learning organizations will be present in most sections of Children's Services. The goal for the manager will be to gain some feedback on the processes occurring in particular sections of the organization and to involve staff sufficiently in the research aims to make some change possible as a result of the feedback from the research.

Some Children's Services, like some of the social services departments and education departments which preceded them, might have employed research officers to make some contribution to the management processes. If such individuals exist, they can provide some help to managers on how to use other research projects, which may have been proposed by managers themselves, by staff in pursuit of higher degrees and other qualifications or by researchers from higher education interested in exploring some specific aspects of service delivery.

Probably the commonest form of research project proposed by managers and undertaken for purposes of evaluation is the survey, almost always questionnaire-based, which can sometimes give useful information. However, small-scale survey research very frequently suffers from poor conceptualization of the research questions and confused data collection and interpretation. Under these conditions, the survey results will be of very little value and the opportunity for change and development from the feedback from the survey is wasted. This situation usually arises because the original brief for the survey has been framed to exclude questions being asked that may call into question standard procedures and assumptions used by the organization and its management, or because management wants the results at best yesterday or at worst tomorrow, giving insufficient time for development of the research methods. Other reasons for the survey being compromised may be the assumption that no additional staff time is needed to do it, or that respondent confidentiality has to be limited due to management desire to identify specific locations for remedial action.

Other forms of research using children's views include individual and group interview designs, focus group designs, case studies of particular institutions using mixed research data-gathering methods and studies using structured data-gathering methods designed for use with children and young people, such as the Repertory Grid (Cohen, Manion, and Morrison, 2000). The outcomes can cover the full range of applicability and sophistication, beginning with very specific and limited-in-scale evaluations of a series of meetings with the direct aim of improving future service delivery (such as McGrath, Chapter 9) when the project or service being evaluated is in a pilot phase in that particular locality. More complex and broad evaluations can lead to more extensive and theoretically interpreted research projects embedded in a complex pattern of service delivery. This type of study is aiming to make more transparent the processes of interaction over a longer period of time (such as the studies in this volume by Turner, Chapter 1 and Pomerantz, Chapter 3). It is probably true to say that the more complex study is unlikely to be achieved without the direct help of researchers from academic institutions or agency staff undertaking research degrees in such institutions. One type of study often overlooked but potentially very useful to organizations is the purely bibliographic study, where the researcher looks for and interprets existing research reports from elsewhere relevant to the questions being asked by the local managers.

LASTING DILEMMAS FOR THOSE WORKING WITH 'HARD TO REACH' YOUNG PEOPLE

Readers will have realized by now that re-establishing links with young people who are seen as 'hard to reach' is more of an art than a science, and that while we can describe principles which other workers have demonstrated to be valid and effective, each situation for each young person is unique, requiring unique solutions. Certain dilemmas keep appearing, however, when the basic principles appear to contradict each other. This is usually because the professionals and the young people and their families have to use both principles some of the time, and have to learn to switch from one to the other at some point. In the following section, we will explore some of these dilemmas.

IDENTIFY AND LABEL OR INCLUDE?

This is usually the initial dilemma. When do those involved with a young person becoming 'hard to reach' formally recognize that there is a problem and prepare to pay special attention to them? Some social criteria for recognition of problems are easy to see. These would include drug taking, getting into trouble with the police and using violence as a part of any social relationships. At these points formal recognition of the issue at that time becomes inevitable. How long, however, should such recognition and the special attention resulting last for? Should the equivalent recognition be given when other young people commit the same transgressions but manage to avoid being noticed and don't get caught? They presumably are equally in need. What about the other numerous ways in which young people can become 'hard to reach', but without crossing one of these social boundaries? Many negative issues influencing young people's mental health, or their progress through the normal stages of adolescent development, do not involve social transgressions serious enough to be formally identified and given a diagnosis, or a label. Even if there is no diagnosis or label, however, various aspects of a young person's situation can be described in a way which implies that the description and its implications are somehow permanent. Such negative descriptions can even reach the national media – hoodies and single parents being two recent examples in the United Kingdom. If young people dealing with stressful issues are not formally identified, however, should their difficulties be ignored by the adults around them?

The disadvantage of accepting such a permanent description, of course, is that the label may well mean that both the adults and the young person at the centre of concern see the young person as deviant, or at least on the borders of most social groups. They become a young person who is not expected to meet the usual standards of behaviour for any particular group and so could reasonably be seen as not belonging to that group. Parents, and many professionals, resist such an acceptance, as they fear reasonably enough that if the permanent description is accepted the problem becomes worse as the deviance becomes accepted into the sense of identity of the young people. The chapters in this book describe the experiences of young people, using their own words, how they have to deal with failure and rejection when they are seen as underachieving, or are excluded from school, or are not cared for. They feel that their experiences must reflect objective reality, and so they come to terms with the experiences by accepting that they are different from other students, with all the implications. They base their future behaviour on the assumption they are on the margins of their groups.

The alternative, of course, is to refuse to make the formal recognition (which often is defined as a public recognition of some sort) but at the same time try to change the way the adults relate to the young person concerned, to stay in touch with them. The hope is that in this way the situation can be improved without running the risk of the permanent description becoming embedded in the identity of the child and the way adults relate to them. The inclusion movement in education is a good example of how procedures and attitudes can be changed to give as much opportunity as possible for young people to stay in contact with their school community even though they may have some difficulties in doing so.

As in the example above, this particular dilemma is solved by the adults and the young person realizing that a permanent description does not have to be permanent. Words can be used descriptively at one time without implying that the description can never change, or that the description implies a label that should then govern how the young person is dealt with in the future, or that the description implies a membership of a category of people with similar characteristics. Giving a description can be temporary, given only to enable people to talk about the issue without any assumptions of category membership or permanence. In this way, children's difficulties can be formally recognized, but handled as temporary.

This is not difficult to say, but in practice everyone using temporary descriptions is well used to having to explain to new contacts that, although the young person at present may be going through difficult circumstances of some sort, they are not permanently different. Our usual use of language does not easily recognize temporary descriptions.

EXTRA SUPPORTS FOR THE YOUNG PEOPLE OR LET THEM LEARN FOR THEMSELVES?

When young people in difficulty are supported to help them overcome problems, how soon should such help cease? When should they be expected to fend for themselves?

Should such questions be settled by administrative procedures: when they reach a particular age, or when the time or money available for the support runs out? When reaching them seems most difficult to the people around them, should the adults' response be that they will have to fend for themselves? Is this properly recognizing the independence of the young person, or abdicating responsibility? In practice, parents and professionals and other young people decide as best they can, feeling very much on their own.

SHOULD WE IGNORE CHILDREN'S BELIEFS AS NAIVE OR ACT ON THEM AND SO CHANGE ADULT PRACTICES?

One of the benefits of listening to children's voices is meant to be the additional involvement with their future, and the people in it, that being heard gives them. As long as they say roughly what the adults expect, their voices are welcome. Problems appear, however, when their wishes and comments run against the received adult wisdom, especially if their wishes are for changes in the procedures they are a part of or other ways of working that the organization has adopted. Whom do the adults side with when conflicting desires emerge, the young person or their own organization?

These tensions become particularly important when disagreement is over outcome decisions influencing the young person's life. When a case conference concludes that a young person should leave their current school and move to a special school across the city but the young person wishes to stay at their current school, how is the disagreement to be resolved? Should a child in difficulties be sent to a new school of a different type when they see the move as an unjust rejection and begin by resisting the best attempts at bridge building by the staff of their new school? How might the situation be resolved more consensually?

TARGETS OR CREATIVE FREEDOM FOR THE PROFESSIONALS?

The last dilemma leads on to the next, already mentioned in the discussion of effective multi-agency working above and highlighted by the research carried out by Holt (2004). When they are faced by unusual circumstances or unpredictable tensions in supporting young people, professionals from different agencies may need to solve these problems by negotiating with each other, or with the parents and families, or even with the young person themselves. However, for the negotiations to be effective, the professionals may need some flexibility themselves, to change how much time or money is spent in a particular situation, to change the procedures they are operating with or to change the other people or the other agencies they are operating in partnership with. These flexibilities may well run against established practice in their own agency, or against their own role description or task description, or be seen to be against their manager's 'right to manage' by taking decisions at the individual professional level rather than at the managerial level. The worker has a straight choice: 'Do I do what I see as in the best interests of the client by being creative in approaches to solutions or do I follow my agencies' or my profession's usual procedures?' In examples where the procedure itself has become part of the management's targets for achievement or part of the accountability system for the individual professional, the dilemma is even greater. However, if we avoid seeking novel solutions because they may challenge existing agency practices, we are unlikely to get very far in improving access, participation or outcomes for the young person.

RELATIONSHIPS OR OUTCOMES FOR THE AGENCY AS PRIORITY TARGETS?

This dilemma nestles inside the one above. Public services are organized as bureaucratic structures, with pre-specified budgets, organizational aims and procedures, and targets for accountability of the agency – which workers are expected to focus on. However, at the point where it matters, at the point where the adults in all roles are actually reaching out to the young people in need of support, the essential structure and guiding principle for the adult and the young person is the developing relationship between the two people. Their contact is seen by both as a personal one, and the young people in particular tell us in the preceding chapters that relationships with their teachers and supportive adults are what they are looking for. The relationships occur inside the social structures determined by the public service statutes, but the essential quality of the contact is that of a relationship between two people. All five outcome areas of the *Every Child Matters* agenda (Department for Education and Skills, 2003) supported by the Government involve contacts between supportive adults and young people, and the capacity to develop relationships with adults is even more essential for the minority of those young people who might be seen as 'hard to reach'. How can the agencies employing the professionals best support them to assist the young people to develop that network of relationships which will link them to the community for the next 50 years?

THE CENTRAL IMPERATIVES OF STAYING IN TOUCH

All the contributors to this volume, from their experiences with various groups of young people, their parents and professional staff, would claim that the central imperative for reaching out to young people drifting away from the adult world is to be prepared to spend time and energy in communicating with them. Both are often in short supply in our busy public services, which are often underfunded with staff having workloads set at a level where their maximum efforts are required every day. Young people are always growing up and constructing new worlds away from their parents' generation, but they do really appreciate their elders finding the time and place to share some of their concerns and provide learning opportunities for them. If every child really is to matter, then every child has a right to learn from their elders in a time and a place where that learning can be effective, and everyone recognizes the need for time spent together.

REFERENCES

Cameron, A. and Lart, R. (2003) Factors promoting and obstacles hindering joint working: a systematic review of the research evidence. *Journal of Integrated Care* **11** (2), 9–17.

Cohen, L., Manion, L. and Morrison, K. (2000) *Research Methods in Education*, 5th edn. RoutledgeFalmer, London.

Craig, J., Huber, J. and Lownsbrough, H. (2004) *School's Out: Can Teachers, Social Workers, and Health Staff learn to live together?* Demos/Hay Group Education, London.

Department for Education and Employment (1999) *Social Inclusion: Pupil Support*. DfEE Publications, London. Circular 10/99.

Department for Education and Science (2003) *Every Child Matters*. The Stationery Office, London.

Easen, P., Atkins, M. and Dyson, A. (2000) Interprofessional collaboration and conceptualisations of practice. *Children and Society* **14** (5), 355–367.

Glisson, C. and Hemmelgarn, A. (1998) The effects of organisational climate and interorganisational co-ordination on the quality and outcomes of Children's Service systems. *Child Abuse and Neglect* **22** (5), 401–421.

Holt, J. (2004) Corporate parenting – a joined up solution?: A study of communication between professionals supporting the education of children in public care. Unpublished MSc thesis, Education Department, University of Sheffield.

Pomerantz, M. (2004) Belper school able underachievers group 2002–2003. In: T. Billington and M. Pomerantz (eds). *Children at the Margins*. Trentham Press, Stoke.

Glossary

In recognition of issues relating to common language as one of the barriers to effective joint working, this glossary aims to promote and facilitate communication and understanding. It has been developed by initially merging other existing glossaries. Some of the terms have been taken from the DfES's ECM web site (Common Core), from Dartington Social Research Unit's site and from a Sheffield social work glossary.

This has required us to exercise some caution, as, for instance, the glossary on the ECM web site (which can be accessed at http://www.everychildmatters. gov.uk/_files/33FD9CD0A57DD27CBBA559ACCE40235D.pdf) is 117 pages long! We have tried to retain core concepts and definitions that are often confused or misunderstood by practitioners working in multi-agency settings, as they relate to some of the ideas in this book concerning the 'hard to reach', although not all of the terms are used in the book. It is not a comprehensive glossary including *all* terms used in Children's Services, or terms that are frequently used in multi-agency settings but which are well understood. Instead, we try to bring together and explain overlap between different words that are used by different agencies to explain similar things. We try to indicate where some terms have become less fashionable and where other terms are preferred, together with the reasons for this.

Abuse	A deliberate act of ill-treatment that can harm or is likely to cause harm to a child's safety, well-being and development. Also used with reference to adult use of alcohol and substance.
Accommodated	A child in need who is looked after in residential care, foster care or accommodation that is not their own home, with the agreement of the parent or person with parental responsibility.
Adoption support	The range of services that may be provided to support the various parties affected through the adoption process and beyond. The term encompasses a wide spectrum of services such as advice, counselling, help with accessing other public services, practical help and financial support. Some of this could be education-related. The LA's responsibilities in this regard have recently been enhanced by the Adoption and Children Act 2002.

How to Reach 'Hard to Reach' Children: Improving access, participation and outcomes. Edited by K. Pomerantz, M. Hughes and D. Thompson.   Copyright © 2007 by John Wiley & Sons, Ltd.

Agency	An organization in the statutory or voluntary sector where staff, paid and unpaid, work with or have access to children and/or families.
Allocated cases	Means that a case is under active supervision, generally by a social worker within a social work team. Allocation of children on the Child Protection Register is a social services performance indicator.
BEST	Behaviour and education support team.
BIP	Behaviour improvement programme.
BME	Black and minority ethnic.
CAMHS	Child and Adolescent Mental Health Service.
Care order	A court order in which the LA assumes parental responsibility (shared with the parents) and becomes responsible for looking after the child.
Carer	Often used as an alternative term to 'parent'. In relation to children with a disability, a carer is a parent, relative or guardian who supports the child. Parent carers may be entitled to an assessment and services under the Carers and Disabled Children Act 2000.
Chain of effects	The accumulation and sequence of risk factors that leaves individuals vulnerable to long-term problems.
Child in need (CIN)	The Children Act 1989 defines a *child in need* as a child who 'is unlikely to achieve or maintain, or to have the opportunity of achieving or maintaining, a reasonable standard of health or development without the provision for him/her of services by a local authority'. All disabled children come under this definition.
Child or young person	Someone up to the age of 19 (up to the day before their nineteenth birthday), care leavers up to the age of 21 (up to the day before their twenty-first birthday or beyond if they are continuing to be helped with education or training by their LA) or up to 25 (up to the day before their twenty-fifth birthday) if they have learning difficulties or disabilities.
Child-protection case conference	A joint meeting for all organizations that are involved with a child, such as children's social services, police, health, education and probation. Where the child's name is placed on the Child Protection Register, the meeting would agree a Child Protection Plan outlining action and responsibilities.
Child-protection liaison teacher (CPLT)	A nominated teacher who is responsible for liaison with Social Services in relation to children who give rise to

child-protection concerns. In primary schools, this will often be the head teacher.

Child Protection Register (CPR)
A list of all children in a local area about whom there is a serious concern of abuse or neglect. They will go on the register after a child-protection conference decides it is necessary. The information on the register is kept confidential. It is available only to people working in or with Social Services to help the child and family. A child-protection plan is then implemented to address the issues of concern, and is monitored by a core group of professionals involved with the family.

Child and young person's development
How babies, children and young people grow and develop (physically, intellectually, linguistically, socially and emotionally).

Children at risk
Children are placed on the Child Protection Register, held by LAs, when it is agreed that they are at continuing risk of being abused or neglected and require a child-protection plan.

Children's Services
A series of activities organized (but not necessarily provided) by health, education, social and police services as well as voluntary agencies on behalf of children with the intention of addressing an identified social need.

Code of practice
A framework for effective school-based support, encouraging a staged approach through partnership in order to address special educational needs.

Common Assessment Framework for Children and Young People (CAF)
The CAF is a nationally standardized approach to help practitioners in any agency assess and decide how to meet the unmet needs of a child. As part of a wider programme of work to provide more integrated services to families, the CAF aims to support earlier intervention, improve multi-agency working and reduce bureaucracy for families, reducing the number of inappropriate interagency referrals, separate assessments and different agencies working with the child. Where the child has urgent or complex needs, requiring specialist assessment and intervention, the common assessment information will feed into the specialist assessment process.

Communication
The exchange of thoughts, messages or information; using spoken language, body language, tone of voice and gestures that demonstrate listening and understanding.

Concern
A suspicion or a belief that a child may be in need of help or protection.

Context	The circumstances that are relevant to a situation.
Control group study	An evaluation of an intervention that compares the progress of children or young people who receive the intervention with that of a similar group of children who do not; the control group may be arrived at by randomly allocating candidates who meet the target group criteria 'on' and 'off' the intervention (randomized controlled trial), or by identifying a comparable group of children in receipt of another service (quasi-experimental design).
Coping	The process of actively seeking to deal with specified difficulties in one's life.
CPD	Continuing professional development.
Deficit	A weakness, the lack of a skill normally found in many children (or adults) of a similar age.
Designated teacher ('looked after' children)	A nominated teacher who is responsible for liaison with Social Services in relation to 'looked after' children in a school. This person is jointly responsible, with the child's social worker, for producing the personal education plan (PEP).
Developmental delay	Developmental delay refers to a lag in development rather than to a specific condition causing that lag. It represents a slower rate of development, in which a child exhibits a functional level below the norm for his or her age. A child may have an across-the-board developmental delay or a delay in specific areas.
DfEE	Department for Education and Employment, which became the . . .
DfES	Department for Education and Skills (used currently).
Early intervention	Aimed at stopping those children and young people at highest risk of developing social or psychological problems, or those who show the first signs of difficulty, from displaying unnecessarily long or serious symptoms.
EBD	Emotional and behavioural difficulties.
Effectiveness	The extent to which the actual outcome (measured in terms of a child's health and development) approximates to the desired outcome *and* can be attributed to the intervention under scrutiny.
Empathy	Able to understand and identify with another person's feelings.

Engagement	Involving the customer (namely children, young people and their families) in the design and delivery of services and decisions that affect them.
EP	Educational psychologist.
EPS	Educational Psychology Service.
Ethics	A code of behaviour agreed to be correct, especially that of a particular group, profession or individual.
Evaluation	The task of working out whether a course of action is effective. In the context of Children's Services it might refer to the use of research procedures to investigate systematically the effectiveness of interventions in terms of improving children's health education and development.
EWO	Education welfare officer.
False-positive	Used to describe a child or young person who is predicted to develop a specified problem but who does not.
False-negative	Used to describe a child or young person who is not predicted to develop a specified problem but who does.
Fieldwork	Generally refers to the work of social workers who visit children and families in their homes, and whose teams have a responsibility for a particular area.
Foster carer	A person who provides a home for a 'looked after' child, on either a long-term or short-term basis. Foster carers work either with the LA or with an independent fostering agency (IFA). They are paid an allowance, but are not usually employees of the LA or the IFA.
ICT	Information and communications technology, sometimes referred to as . . .
IT	Information technology, for example the Internet and e-mail.
IEP	Individual educational plan. An overview of objectives and broad methods for addressing a young person's special educational needs under the code of practice.
Inclusion	Identifying, understanding and breaking down barriers to participation and involvement.
Information sharing	Passing on relevant information to other agencies, organizations and individuals that need it in order to deliver better services to children and young people.
Knowledge	Awareness or understanding gained through learning or experience.

LA	Local Authority. This is generally becoming a preferred term as in many areas the Local Education Authority (LEA) has ceased to exist, now that Education departments and Social Service departments have merged.
Longitudinal studies	Research that measures the subjects at two or more points in time, usually months or even years apart.
'Looked after' children	A child who is in the care of the LA because of a court order or one who is accommodated by the LA on a voluntary basis.
LSU	Learning support unit.
Multi-agency working	Agencies, organizations and individuals working together.
Need	Refers to the requirements for healthy development. The *basic* needs of all human beings are physical health and autonomy, which in turn require that *intermediate* needs for shelter, nutrition, significant primary relationships, basic education and so on are met. When basic needs are not met, they result in *harm* to the individual. Needs can be met by a range of *satisfiers*: just as nutritional needs can be met by various types of food, so social needs can be met by different types of service. With these points in mind, a child can be defined as *in need* if his or her health or development is actually impaired or likely to become so without some kind of specialist remedial intervention. This definition is enshrined in the England and Wales Children Act 1989, where it is advanced as the concept that should drive Children's Services provision (the idea of needs-led as opposed to supply-led services).
Neglect	Failing to provide for, or secure for, a child the basic needs of physical safety and well-being.
NQT	Newly qualified teacher.
Ofsted	Office for Standards in Education.
Out of city/authority	An out of city or authority placement is where a 'looked after' child is placed in a residential unit, or with a foster carer outside of the administrative area in which they live. There may be many reasons for this, such as that it is not safe for the child to remain in the LA, or that there is no suitable placement in the LA.
Outcome	The effect of a process (such as a service) on a child's health, education and development.
Output	The effect of a process (such as a service) on an administrative indicator, for example the rate of children in care, the

number of arrests or convictions and whether or not a child received special educational help.

Parents
Includes those who have parental rights as defined in law and those who have care of a child, for example foster carers and co-habitees.

Parental responsibility (PR)
Defined in the Children Act 1989 as, 'All the rights, duties, powers, responsibilities and authority which by law a parent of a child has in relation to a child and his property.' In all cases, the mother has PR, and the father will have as well if he is married to the mother, or if he has acquired it through a court order or by jointly registering the birth of the baby with the mother. PR lasts until the child has reached 18.

Partnership
Refers either to agencies working together to address children's needs or to agencies working with children and families where the focus is on establishing joint understanding of needs and the services required to address those needs.

PCT
Primary Care Trust.

Performance indicator
A measure of how well an agency is performing against set criteria, usually with a focus on outputs rather than outcomes.

Personal education plan (PEP)
Every 'looked after' child must have, within 28 days of coming into care, a PEP, which details the steps that will be taken to ensure that the child will be educated to his or her maximum potential. The social worker and designated teacher are responsible for producing the PEP.

Practitioners
Staff who work directly or indirectly with children, young people and/or families and can include (but is not exclusive to) police officers, doctors, nurses, teachers, nursery staff, social workers, therapists, dentists, youth leaders, leisure and recreational workers, housing staff and staff who work in criminal justice, mental health or drug and alcohol services. It can also refer to volunteers who come into contact with children.

Prediction
A reasoned, advance statement or declaration about some event or outcome. Used in the Children's Services context in the sense of a medical prognosis (a prediction of the course or outcome of a disease or disorder).

Prevention
Activity to stop a social or psychological problem happening in the first place (see also *Early intervention*, *Treatment* and *Social prevention*).

Protective factor
An attribute or circumstance that works in certain contexts to reduce or modify an individual's response to particular

combinations of risk and thereby reduces their susceptibility to a range of social or psychological problems.

PRU — Pupil referral unit.

PSHE — Personal, social and health education.

PSP — Pastoral support programme: a school-based intervention to help individual pupils who are at risk of fixed- or long-term exclusion to manage their own behaviour.

Psychopathology — Behaviour that is atypical, that leads to significant impairment in functioning, that causes psychological dysfunction/distress, and the diagnosis of which is reliable (e.g. eating disorders, ADHD, autism). Also used to mean the study of the causes and nature of mental disease or abnormal behaviour.

Psychosocial problems — Used to describe difficulties in the lives of children and young people the roots and manifestations of which are social and/or psychological in nature (e.g. crime, depression, misuse of drugs).

Qualitative measurement — Tries to capture reality as it is seen and experienced by respondents and attempts to present the information gathered in a detailed and complete form (e.g. notes from observations and responses to unstructured interviews) rather than using numbers or formulae. Attaches strong value to intimate knowledge and acquaintance with research subjects and context.

Quality of life — An umbrella term to capture both an individual's objective circumstances (e.g. poor living standards, ill-health, fractious relationships, little enrichment) and their subjective appraisal of those circumstances (e.g. inferred from evidence of distress, anxiety or unhappiness).

Quantitative measurement — Concentrates on observations that lend themselves to numerical representations, for example answers to structured questionnaires, police arrest data, school attendance records.

Quasi-experimental design (QED) — An evaluation method whereby children referred to the programme in question are compared with a group of matched children referred to another programme or to one in another geographical area.

Reliability — Refers to the ability of a data-collection instrument to produce consistent results. A method is judged to be reliable when it consistently produces the same results, particularly when applied by different researchers or to the same subjects at different points in time (when there is no other evidence of change).

Residence order	A court order that decides where the child is to live and with whom. The granting of a residence order to someone automatically gives him or her parental responsibility for the child if they do not already have it. Parental responsibility obtained as a result of a residence order will continue until the order ceases (usually at age 16). LAs often pay an allowance to support these arrangements.
Residential unit	Otherwise known as a 'children's home'. A place where older 'looked after' children live, with residential social workers. The practice in some areas is to develop small, family style units with 3–4 children, rather than large, old-style homes, which sometimes had 10–15 children.
Respite care	Any service, such as a holiday club or a week in a residential home, that looks after the child in order to give their carer a break from caring. Respite care should also be beneficial and enjoyable to the child.
Reviews	There are various requirements for social work cases to be reviewed, particularly child-protection and 'looked after' child cases. Reviews are carried out by a reviewing officer, who checks that basic standards relating to the frequency of visits by the social worker, education, health and so on are met. The process is not dissimilar to special educational needs reviews, which are held for children with statements at least once each year (annual reviews) and for non-statemented children as and when deemed necessary.
Risk	An aspect of the individual or their environment that predisposes some children to specific social or psychological problems.
Safeguarding children	Taken to mean that all agencies working with children, young people and their families take all reasonable measures to ensure that the risks of harm to children's welfare are minimized; and where there are concerns about children and young people's welfare all agencies and individuals take all appropriate actions to address those concerns.
SALT	Speech and language therapist.
SATs	Standard Assessment Tasks: National Curriculum tests that are taken at the end of the Key Stages (at ages seven, 11 and 14).
SEAL	Social and emotional aspects of learning.
SEBD	Social, emotional and behavioural difficulties.
SEBS	Social, emotional and behavioural skills.

Sensitivity	The extent to which a service is adaptive to the context, for example not alienating a child or family when addressing a high-risk situation or complex need.
Service	A technology or mechanism for alleviating people's problems; in the present context, the activity intended to meet a child's educational, welfare, developmental or health needs and so achieve desired outcomes.
Significant harm	Under the Children Act 1989 this is the threshold for compulsory intervention into family life. A court may only make a care or supervision order if it is satisfied the child is suffering or likely to suffer significant harm and that this is due to lack of parental care or control.
Skill	The ability to do something, usually developed through practice, training or experience.
Social exclusion	Involuntary detachment from mainstream society, usually as a result of the long-term accumulation of multidimensional disadvantage.
Social prevention	Seeks to reduce the damage that those who have developed a disorder can inflict on others in a community and/or on themselves. Not to be confused with the prevention of social problems.
Special educational needs (SEN)	A child has special educational needs if he or she has a learning difficulty that calls for special educational provision to be made for him or her. A child has a learning difficulty if he or she:

- has a significantly greater difficulty in learning than the majority of children of the same age;
- has a disability that either prevents or hinders the child from making use of educational facilities of a kind provided for children of the same age in schools within the area of the LA;
- is under five and falls within either definition above or would do if special educational provision was not made for the child.

A child must not be regarded as having a learning difficulty solely because the language or form of language of the home is different from the language in which he or she is or will be taught.

SpLD	Specific learning difficulties.
Standardized scales	A discrete series of self-report questions, ratings or items used to measure a concept. The response categories tend to

	be in the same format (yes/no or 1 = very good to 5 = very poor). Usually, such scales have been tested substantially and been found capable of achieving acceptable levels of reliability and validity. They are quick to administer, suitable for statistical calculations using summed or weighted scores and generate results that require little interpretation by the investigator. They can be a useful way of obtaining subjective assessments of experience or for broaching delicate topics sensitively.
Statement (of Special Educational Need)	A formal document following a time-limited period of assessment that details a young person's educational needs and how these are to be met.
Transition	A change of passage from one stage of a process to another. For example, moving from infant education (Key Stage 1) to junior education (Key Stage 2).
Treatment	Seeks to stabilize or achieve realistic outcomes among those who develop serious manifestations of a social or psychological problem. Also used as a generic term to refer to the service provided, particularly in a health context.
Validity	Refers to the ability of an instrument to produce findings that are in agreement with the conceptual idea. A measure is valid if it measures what it is supposed to measure.
Within child	Used to refer to problems that are considered to be deficits – 'within the child'. This contrasts with understandings of problems which children experience, which are based more on an interactionist perspective (how environmental features, such as parents, teachers, other pupils, affect a child with some difficulties or difference).
YOT	Youth offending team.

Appendix 1
Bibliography of Key Documents

In this section, some of the key documents are described, using summaries frequently obtained from the documents themselves. The *Every Child Matters* web site (accessed at: http://www.everychildmatters.gov.uk/) has been a main source. Many are available via this web site – especially at http://www.everychildmatters.gov.uk/publications/ – but see comments below. Also useful was the Children Services Network (accessed at: http://www.csn.info/index.jsp).

The Children Act 1989 required that supporting children and families should be a major LA responsibility, with Social Services being able to call upon assistance from health and education, in order to discharge these duties.

Part III of the **1993 Education Act** (Section 166) placed a duty on social work services and health authorities to assist education in responding to children with special needs.

Excellence for all Children, Meeting Special Educational Needs was published by the DfEE in October 1997. It pledges that by 2002 'there will be improved cooperation and coordination between local education authorities, Social Services departments and health authorities, with the focus on meeting children's special needs more effectively'. Chapter 7 includes a section entitled 'Cooperation between local agencies' and states that, 'Effective collaboration between LEAs, social services departments and health authorities is essential. Too often the fragmentation of services between different statutory agencies, competition and tight budgets has left parents to take responsibility for coordinating provision for their child.' And further states, 'The need for closer cooperation starts in Government. The National Advisory Group on SEN includes people with expertise in education, health and social services. We will work towards effective coordination of policy for young children in these areas by strengthening links between the DfEE and the Department of Health' (Chapter 7, Paragraphs 4 and 5, p. 71).

A public inquiry was set up after the tragic death of Victoria Climbié in February 2000. The *Victoria Climbié Inquiry: Report of an Inquiry by Lord Laming* was published in January 2003 by the Stationery Office and set out recommendations to address the root causes of the failure to keep her safe. A number of references to multi-agency practice were made. For instance, the report states that effective support for children and families cannot be achieved by a single agency acting alone but depends on a number of agencies working well together. It also refers to the

How to Reach 'Hard to Reach' Children: Improving access, participation and outcomes. Edited by K. Pomerantz, M. Hughes and D. Thompson. Copyright © 2007 by John Wiley & Sons, Ltd.

need for a structure, reinforced by statute, 'which has at its centre a clear process for both decision making and monitoring of performance; for example, it should not be possible for multi-agency plans to safeguard children to be drawn up and then left solely for social services to implement' (p. 361).

Six months before the report of Lord Laming's inquiry was published, *Serving Children Well: A New Vision for Children's Services* was published by the Local Government Association (2002, LGA Publications, London). This proposes the comprehensive mapping of need and services to enable appropriate targeting. 'It promotes the coordination of services whilst avoiding the dangers inherent in structural change. It facilitates preventive measures by locating services at a local level in the framework of a national performance management system which pulls agencies together in a model of cooperation and partnership' (p. 1). Existing structures, rather than structural change, are developed into a model for delivery of outcomes, which is local and community-based and relies on the concept of a service hub: a universal service which has contact with all children in the locality. In some local areas, the hub is based on the population of a secondary school and a cluster of primary and special schools. The boundary of the hubs is described as needing to be clear to the communities and all the agencies providing services. Based within this hub would be a multidisciplinary team of local professionals who would deliver or commission services for individual children and their families. The team envisaged would resemble the model of community mental health teams and would be crucial in closing the gaps in services and ensuring a cohesive approach where intervention is needed. Interestingly, this document notes that 'establishing this team would require additional funding' (p. 16).

Every Child Matters (ECM) was published in September 2003 by the Stationery Office and was the Green Paper for the Children Act 2004. This is regarded as a core document that sets out a national, long-term programme of change and contains **five key outcomes** for children and young people: being healthy, staying safe, enjoying and achieving, making a positive contribution and achieving economic well-being. Common expectations are given for all those who work with children and young people. ECM explains how the Government will support local change and sets out a timeline of future developments.

On 11 February 2004, the Government launched *Removing Barriers to Achievement: The Government's Strategy for SEN* (Department for Education and Skills, London), which included 'delivering improvements in partnership' as a key area. The vision referred closely to ECM and included: 'schools working together to support the inclusion of all children from their local community, backed up by good quality specialist advice from the local authority and health services, working in multi-disciplinary teams' (p. 26) and the 'greater integration of education, health and social care to meet the needs of children and families' (p. 72).

Every Child Matters: Next Steps was published on 4 March 2004 (Department for Education and Skills, London), the same day as the **Children Bill** was introduced to Parliament, and it sets out the purposes of the Bill and the next steps for bringing about change in Children's Services. It emphasizes organizing multidisciplinary services around the child, young person or family and the need to ensure clear accountability and better integration between all such services.

The Children Bill received Royal Assent on 15 November and became the **Children Act 2004**, which laid a firm foundation for a number of linked concepts. Under Section 10 of the Act, there is a duty for each Children's Services Authority (CSA) in England to cooperate to improve children's well-being. This emphasizes clearly that part of a professional's responsibility is to communicate with other professionals. (Interestingly, while CSAs have a statutory duty to *lead* this agenda, schools do not have a statutory duty to *follow*.)

Child and Adolescent Mental Health: National Service Framework for Children, Young People and Maternity Services (2004, Department of Health, London) is seen as integral to the programme outlined by ECM and was described as a '10 year programme intended to stimulate long-term and sustained improvement in children's health' (p. 8). It aims to ensure fair, high-quality and integrated health and social care from pregnancy, right through to adulthood. The framework states that experience before birth and in early life has a significant impact on the life chances of each individual and that improving the health and welfare of parents and children is the surest way to a healthier nation. At the heart of the Children's National Service Framework (NSF) is a fundamental change in thinking about health and social care services. It is intended to lead to a cultural shift, resulting in services that are designed and delivered around the needs of children and families using those services, not around the needs of organizations. This NSF is aimed at everyone who comes into contact with, or delivers services to, children and young people.

The NSF is described as a 'developmental standard' within the NHS Standards Framework set out in *National Standards Local Action: Health and Social Care Standards and Planning Framework 2005/06–2007/08* (2004, Department of Health, London) the key planning document for the 2005–2008 period. The NSF embodies the ECM commitment to change services for children and young people so that they are designed and delivered around the needs of children and families using those services. Successful delivery will depend on the LA and other partners as well as on health organizations. Children's trusts will, therefore, need to ensure that the delivery of the NSF is fully reflected in their work.

The standards require services to improve access to services for all children according to their needs, particularly by co-locating services and developing managed Local Children's Clinical Networks for children who are ill or injured.

Every Child Matters: Change for Children was published late in 2004 by the Department for Education and Skills. This set out the action to be taken by local areas to ensure that services meet the needs of children, young people and families and government actions to support local areas. *The Outcomes Framework* (was published with ECM and can be found at http://www.everychildmatters.gov.uk/publications/) supports the Five Outcomes with underpinning aims. It also links Public Service Agreement targets and other key indicators with inspection judgements and criteria, including how annual performance assessments contribute to LAs' Comprehensive Performance Assessments. The *Framework for Inspection of Children's Services*

(2005, Ofsted, London) and inspection criteria for joint area reviews, prepared by Ofsted in consultation with other relevant inspectorates, define how the contributions to the outcomes made by settings and services will be assessed. Together these documents provide the framework for the outcome-led approach and the context for local areas to develop their child-centred, outcome-led vision. This was accompanied by *Every Child Matters: Change for Children in Schools* (2004, Department for Education and Skills, London).

In December 2004, the DfES began consulting on the statutory guidance relating to *Interagency Cooperation to Improve the Wellbeing of Children: Children's Trusts* (which had been published by that department earlier that same year). The guidance deals with what it terms the five essential building blocks of a Children's Trust:

- A child-centred, outcome-led vision, concerned both with the delivery of universal services to all children and the more specialized services that only some will need.
- Integrated frontline delivery organized around the child, young person or family rather than the professional boundaries of existing agencies. The vision includes multidisciplinary teams that are co-located in easily accessible places, have continuous professional development, appropriate clinical and professional supervision, management and governance, with clear lines of accountability.
- Integrated processes, where effective joint working is sustained by a common language and shared processes. This includes a Common Assessment Framework used across agencies, effective information sharing arrangements and the re-engineering of other local processes and procedures to support, rather than inadvertently distort, joint working.
- Integrated strategy (joint planning and commissioning), shared resources and pooled budgets.
- Interagency governance, where the cornerstone is the creation of a strong integrated governing board or structure representing all key delivery partners at senior level.

The multi-agency practice envisaged is seen as ensuring that children, young people and their families are able to benefit from a wide range of people working together, and also from the application of specialist skills and knowledge when required. The availability of sufficient suitably trained staff is described as a key area for attention, nationally and locally, and the *Common Core of Skills and Knowledge for the Children's Workforce* (2005, Department for Education and Skills, London) sets out the key skills and knowledge for the children's workforce. It sets out six key areas of expertise that everyone working with children, young people and families, depending on the nature of that work, should be able to demonstrate. A key focus of the Government's workforce development proposals is to support effective collaboration among all practitioners and professionals.

The Children's Workforce Strategy was published on 1 April 2005 by the Department for Education and Skills as a consultation document, along with two linked documents: the *Common Core of Skills and Knowledge for the Children's Workforce* and the ***Common Assessment Framework for Children and Young People (CAF)***. *The Children's Workforce Strategy* sets out the Government's vision for the children's workforce and a number of national and local actions to realize this vision for the workforce as a whole and for those sectors that face the most urgent issues. Like most of the other documents, it links to other key areas, including the remodelling agenda, identifying extended schools as, 'where the school system needs to go to deliver the five outcomes set out in Every Child Matters' (p. 7). 'Co-locating services in schools, bringing together different services, including health and social care, provides a basis for service integration and new ways of working across services' (p. 60). A number of references are made to multi-agency working, expressing the desire to 'develop a workforce that is confident in operating across professional and institutional boundaries, using common assessment processes to identify needs, and developing new ways of delivering services to improve children's outcomes' (p. 10).

The common core of skills and knowledge identifies multi-agency working as one of six areas of expertise, and the Children's Workforce Network (England) will aim to support the development of a coherent, skilled and effective workforce and improve the quality of inter-agency working.

In 2005, a web-based multi-agency working toolkit (now entitled **Setting up multi-agency services**; http://www.everychildmatters.gov.uk/deliveringservices/multiagencyworking/) was released in order to provide support to middle managers and practitioners in developing multi-agency working at strategic and operational levels. It aims to highlight examples of good practice and provide guidance on: vision and purpose, recruitment, developing policies, development and training, management and supervision, case management systems, monitoring and evaluation, and working in mainstream settings.

Published in July 2005 by the Department for Education and Skills, ***Youth Matters*** (the Green Paper for youth) argues that many local teenagers are effectively excluded from provision and that too many youth services offer a poor service. The document starts from an understanding that while existing services – Youth Services, Connexions, mainstream services and a wide range of targeted support programmes – have made a crucial contribution, they do not amount to a coherent, modern system of support. It states that in the current system in England:

- services do not always meet the needs of individual young people;
- the various organizations providing services and help for young people do not work together as effectively or imaginatively as they should, with the result that money and effort are wasted;
- not enough is being done to prevent young people from drifting into a life of poverty or crime;
- services are failing to exploit the full potential of the Internet, mobile phones and other new technologies;
- teenagers and their parents do not have enough say in what is provided.

(Paragraph 72, p. 18)

The approach to reform outlined in *Youth Matters* is based on six underpinning principles:

- making services more responsive to what young people and their parents want;
- balancing greater opportunities and support with promoting young people's responsibilities;
- making services for young people more integrated, efficient and effective;
- improving outcomes for all young people, while narrowing the gap between those who do well and those who do not;
- involving a wide range of organizations from the voluntary, community and private sectors in order to increase choice and secure the best outcomes;
- building on the best of what is currently provided.

In September 2005, the first phase report of the **national evaluation of Children's Trusts** was published. The interdisciplinary team, based at the University of East Anglia (UEA) in Norwich in partnership with the National Children's Bureau, reported on the first of a three-year evaluation and included multidisciplinary working in practice.

In December 2005 the Government announced new arrangements for the **integrated inspection of children's services**, which was prompted by the proposals set out in the *Every Child Matters* Green Paper.

Annual performance assessment and joint area reviews (JARs) will monitor the delivery of local change programmes. The assessments will look at the ways services are working together locally to improve outcomes. They are intended to:

- target inspection activity explicitly around clear outcomes for children, and be focused on the user, unconstrained by service boundaries;
- guide inspection and assessment of all universal, targeted and specialist services in so far as they relate to children;
- make arrangements for the effective coordination of inspection activity to prevent duplication and to reduce burdens and pressures on those inspected.

JARs started to take place from September 2005, assessing the quality of services and making judgements about how well services work together to improve the well-being of children and young people.

JARs will provide the means to analyse the effectiveness of local cooperation and integration. As part of the strategy to give young people a direct voice in the provision of services that affect them, the inspectorates will seek their views when conducting JARs.

Reviews will take the place of separate inspections of council education and children's social care services and will cover other services provided in the local area. Evidence from other inspections, such as in schools and residential settings, will contribute to the coverage.

Normally, reviews will take place at the same time as corporate assessments of councils for the comprehensive performance assessment (CPA), with documentation, judgements and methodology aligned to make the processes complementary.

Making it Happen: Working Together for Children, Young People and Families was published in June 2006 by the Department for Education and Skills and focused on information-sharing, the CAF and the role of the lead professional.

Twelve local areas formally trialled the **Common Assessment Framework** and the role of the lead professional during 2005–2006. Trials were evaluated by the UEA. Over two-thirds of LAs chose to use the CAF during the trial year, and materials were issued in April 2005 to support implementation. Evaluation reports can be downloaded from the DfES research web site. Alongside the UEA evaluation, the DfES worked with the trialling groups to identify any early lessons, enabling them to share good practice and inform further development of the CAF materials. Following wide consultation, revised CAF materials were issued, including a practitioners' guide, managers' guide, CAF form, pre-assessment checklist and supporting tools, all of which can be downloaded (http://www.everychildmatters.gov.uk/deliveringservices/caf/).

The lead professional is described as a key element of the integrated support that the Every Child Matters: Change for Children programme is aiming to provide for children and young people who have additional needs, so as to secure better outcomes. They take the lead to coordinate provision and act as a single point of contact for a child and their family when a range of services are involved and an integrated response is required. Appointing a lead professional is seen as central to the effective frontline delivery of services for children with a range of additional needs. When the role is delivered in the context of multi-agency assessment and planning, underpinned by the *Common Assessment Framework* or relevant specialist assessments, it ensures that professional involvement is rationalized, coordinated and achieves the intended outcomes. Two guidance documents were issued in April 2006 for managers and practitioners to help them implement and carry out lead professional work. These documents updated and replaced the guidance issued in July 2005 and, again, can be downloaded (http://www.everychildmatters.gov.uk/deliveringservices/leadprofessional/).

Pathfinders for **Targeted Youth Support Teams** were set up following *Youth Matters* in order to explore how ECM might be implemented. Aims of the integrated team are to:

- provide wrap-around support, via a lead professional, for individual children, young people and their families who have multiple needs;
- deliver effective preventive work for groups of vulnerable children, young people and their families;
- provide an outreach, support and training role for practitioners within the mainstream and more specialized services.

Starting with pilots in 11 authorities, it has been extended nationally to 50 more LAs since October 2006. The ECM web site gives details and a toolkit, which outlines the mobilize, discover, deepen, develop and deliver (M4D) process.

In September 2006, the Cabinet Office published ***Reaching Out: An Action Plan on Social Exclusion***. Research in practice (http://www.rip.org.uk/index.asp) explains that the action plan sets out the Government's renewed plans for tackling social exclusion, the 'persistent and deep seated exclusion of a small minority' (p. 8). It adopts a lifetime approach but, in respect of adult years in particular, it targets adults described as living 'chaotic lives' (p. 10). It details five guiding principles that inform the Government's approach: better identification and earlier intervention, systematic identification of what works, stronger multi-agency working, more personalized services for those at risk and encouragement of 'compacts' with at risk families and individuals, and better management of underperforming LAs, while giving effective service providers more room to innovate. The plan focuses on key groups, including children in care and children born into vulnerable circumstances. Specific measures include:

- a series of pilots to test different approaches to tackling conduct disorders in childhood, including intensive home-based interventions such as multi-systemic therapy;
- 10 health-led parenting support demonstration projects from pre-birth to age two, to include evaluation of targeted support;
- improving the skills of midwives and health visitors to promote and support early intervention during the early years;
- trials to begin, by April 2007, of a new evidence-based assessment tool for use by community midwives and health visitors to improve targeting and support;
- the Government considering the potential role of a new Centre of Excellence for Children's and Family Services, which would identify, evaluate and disseminate best practice for working with socially excluded groups.

The Social Exclusion Task Force was tasked with completing a scoping study and pilot projects for which £6 million over three years was to be allocated. These pilots were to test the effectiveness of alternative approaches to improving outcomes for those with chaotic lives and multiple needs.

On the 26 October 2006, the Local Government White Paper *Strong and Prosperous Communities* was published. It promotes community and neighbourhood engagement (by aiming to empower citizens and communities), it strengthens leadership and proposes a new framework for LAs and partners to work together. It is in two volumes. The second contains thematic chapters on community safety, health and well-being, vulnerable people, children, young people and families, economic development, housing and planning, climate change, and the third sector. This volume also contains three specific references to 'hard to reach'.

Appendix 2
Searching for Explanations and Responsibilities as to Why Some Clients May be 'Hard to Reach'

(with acknowledgement and thanks to Michael Pomerantz)

Within-client and within-home factors	Within-agency factors
Clients come from a wide range of social classes and groups	Agency staff project a middle-class and professional image
Perception that the professional doesn't care	Bureaucracy, lack of staff, staff stress, staff illness, temporary staff, frequent changes of staff, cases closed prematurely, lack of follow-up
Perception that the professional is prejudiced	Institutional or cultural racism, ethnocentrism, discrimination
Perception of a threat to one's own identity and defensive posture	Stigma associated with agency; lack of cultural awareness
Lack of confidence and trust in the professional	Staff incompetence, abuse, neglect
Lack of a feeling of safety coupled with fears and frustration and no faith in the agency (beyond help)	Negative host culture and poor local image of the agency; lack of investment
Need and a desire to find one's own solutions (Rogerian ideal)	Agency fosters dependency, patronizing staff attitudes
Reluctance to leave home and keep appointments; feeling intruded upon and a need to protect personal space	Agency prioritizes staff needs over client needs, unwelcoming environment, intrusion of personal space
Client needs acceptance, warmth, empathy with a familiar context	Agency cannot provide acceptance, warmth and empathy; it needs to be efficient; the context is unfamiliar
Limited linguistic and literacy competence; need to be heard while possibly feeling inarticulate	Inappropriate interactional style and language/literacy demands of the professional; agency may not actually be listening
Naivety and arrested role development	Lack of appropriate role models in the community
Experience of loss	Inability to identify and address loss

(Continued)

How to Reach 'Hard to Reach' Children: Improving access, participation and outcomes. Edited by K. Pomerantz, M. Hughes and D. Thompson.   Copyright © 2007 by John Wiley & Sons, Ltd.

Within-client and within-home factors	Within-agency factors
Lack of investment and motivation and a passive position	Lack of ability to promote the agency and what it offers
Lack of positive family identity	Inability to compensate for what the family fails to provide
Need to address own agenda	Need to address the agency's agenda
Pessimism and scepticism	History of failure to address pessimism and scepticism
Mental health and criminality issues within child and family	Inability to address mental heath and criminality issues
Vulnerability	Minimal or absent screening for vulnerability
Resilience factors underdeveloped	Resilience within the child is underestimated and neglected; lost opportunity
Client and family are playing games like avoidance and defaulting; desire to be left alone; DNA (did not attend)	Agency fails to understand the games and intervene appropriately; systemic strategies underutilized; minimal multi-agency teamwork visible; agency seen to be interfering rather than intervening
Client is overwhelmed with negativity	Agency fails to challenge the negativity with alternatives
Family moves too frequently (e.g. Travellers), records go missing	Agency is unable to reduce unnecessary moves like evictions
Client looks for outside explanations and interventions	Agency attributes all or most responsibility to the client
Client feels needy and neglected and seeks inclusion	Agency feels the client is selfish and distances itself; agency colludes in some exclusion processes
Client holds strong values	Agency misunderstands or devalues client values
Client disengages and quits	Agency closes the case and blames the client or family
Client needs choices	Agency does not provide extensive choices
Client is not mobile and needs a local resource that operates in the evenings and weekends	Agency is located at a distant venue with a normal day pattern of appointments
Client needs accessible, understandable and effective tools	Agency tools are inaccessible, confusing and possibly alien
Client focus is on immediate and personal needs	Agency focus is upon systems, generalizations, risks, patterns, trends, data, compliance, meeting targets, passing audits, self-maintenance and protecting the zone of comfort
Client is unfamiliar with ECM agenda and revolution	Staff are overdosed with government policy, organizational changes and lengthy publications
Client still has to work with too many uncoordinated professionals and agencies	Staff assume the client is aware of and approving of all that is changing within agencies

Within-client and within-home factors	Within-agency factors
Clients live with problems constantly	Staff can switch off and go home
Client may feel isolated and in a minority with less personal power and control	Staff are surrounded by like-minded colleagues and traditions that maintain power and control
Client rarely uses written records	Staff are overly dependent upon written records and IT that does not support easy communication between agencies
Client may have been abused or damaged by people helpers in the past	Staff may be unaware of client's previous history with people helpers
Client may feel personally marginalized	Staff may stereotype the client as marginalized
Client may have extensive and complex needs	Staff may stereotype client as overly needy and dependent
Client may project a dangerous image	Staff may be frightened of the client
Client may have complicated needs	Staff may only see the problem from one perspective
Confidentiality is a right	Confidentiality is a problem and may create a barrier to help
Client needs help now	Agency has a lengthy waiting list or suggests a referral elsewhere
Client has been silenced by parents and been manipulated to present themselves and family in a positive light	Agency fails to get beneath the tip of the iceberg and see the real problems

Appendix 3
Developing Good Practice with 'Hard to Reach' Children and Families

This document is an attempt to develop some thoughts about good practice principles for 'hard to reach' children, young people and families. The principles are drawn from a longer draft document developed by a group set up during the development of the Ecclesfield and Parson Cross Service District in Sheffield. The group was called 'Hard to reach children, young people and parents'.

The aims of the group included:

- Identify better ways of working with vulnerable groups.
- Consider the barriers that are preventing services from being more effective (and understand and work to overcome these at individual, agency and systemic levels).
- Identify the organizational features that would make children and families easier to reach.
- Develop and promote a good practice guide.

PRINCIPLES FOR GOOD PRACTICE IN REACHING VULNERABLE GROUPS

A. We are children- and young-people-centred. (We advocate and support the interests and views of children and young people and have high expectations of them. We make a visible commitment to involving children and young people, underpinned by appropriate resources, to build a capacity to implement policies of participation. We value children and young people's involvement. Children and young people have equal opportunity to get involved. Policies and standards for the participation of children and young people are provided, evaluated and continually improved.)

B. We do things *with* young people, rather than *to* them, that they have chosen.

C. We operate with trust, integrity and mutual respect, both internal and external to our organization.

D. We are responsible and accountable. We encourage risk-taking within a framework of individual ownership and accountability.

E. We genuinely value equality and diversity, celebrating individuality, social and cultural differences.

F. We work collaboratively, with partners listening to each other, breaking down barriers and working towards a common goal.

G. Our multi-agency links facilitate the asking of critical questions about professional practice and enable professional and agency experience and practice to be shared.
H. We are a reflective learning organization, open to feedback and criticism while constantly striving to improve.
I. We seek to understand children and young people's stories.
J. We aim to remain neutral without stigmatizing children and young people further.
K. We spend time on cultivating relationships with children, young people and families.
L. We consider and challenge language that excludes and alienates.
M. We look for small steps to change and progress.
N. When we evaluate change, we consider the speed of the client.
O. Our service and our practitioners declare and communicate clearly our principles and standards.
P. We understand what active referral and advocacy means.
Q. We consider the effects of our actions on children, young people and families.
R. We engage with the person first, then the problem.
S. We challenge structures that might get in the way.
T. We avoid the seven deadly sins (see Scott, 2006).
U. We have the ability to identify and respond to vulnerable children.
V. We know how to engage with children and allow them to express their concerns.
W. A child or young person is not an adult and their overall welfare is of paramount importance.
X. We understand and respect parental responsibility.
Y. We know when to seek the advice of others (and make an appropriate referral).

WHAT NEEDS TO HAPPEN FOR:

- there to be a good shared understanding of the role of the lead professional?
- workers to have received adequate training so as to function in the role of the lead professional, so as to complete the CAF, to keep multi-agency data sharing systems updated?
- there to be full multi-agency representation at meetings about 'hard to reach' children, young people and families?
- workers to be able to identify the most vulnerable children, young people and families?
- effective multi-agency practice to effect positive outcomes for children, young people and families?

FINALLY...

In relation to the 'hard to reach', which of the five ECM outcomes are you particularly contributing to at present?
Which of the outcomes are you currently less successful with?
What are some of the obstacles or barriers to your establishment reaching children, young people and families more effectively?
How might you and your agency work at removing some of these?

Some Key Questions

How might you and your agency develop and adopt the principles above?
How might you and your agency use this book?
Do you, your agency or your LA have a way of identifying the most vulnerable children, young people and families (and is it important to do this)?
Is your school, establishment and LA clear about the key aspects of integrating practice CAF, multi-agency data collection, lead professionals?
Does your establishment have multi-agency planning meetings where concerns relating to health, education and social care can be discussed with a range of agencies?
What other approaches and processes do you use to facilitate multi-agency working?
Which agencies are under-represented in your attempts to work at a multi-agency level with the 'hard to reach'?
How might you address this and encourage some agencies to engage with your establishment more effectively?
Are the ideas in this book relevant to you and, if so, how might you discuss them at a wider level, across different agencies?

REFERENCE

Scott, S. (2006) Improving children's lives, preventing criminality. Where next? *The Psychologist* **19** (8), 484–487.

Index